THEN CAME THE RAILROADS

The Century from Steam to Diesel in the Southwest

THEN CAME

The Century from Steam

THE RAILROADS

to Diesel in the Southwest

by Ira G. Clark

NORMAN : UNIVERSITY OF OKLAHOMA PRESS

The publication of this work has been aided by a grant from
THE FORD FOUNDATION

Library of Congress Catalog Card Number: 58–6849

Copyright 1958 by the University of Oklahoma Press, Publishing Division of the University. Composed and printed at Norman, Oklahoma, U.S.A., by the University of Oklahoma Press. First edition.

To my Father and Mother

Preface

THE PENETRATION of railroads into unsettled or partially settled areas brought together two factors of fundamental importance in shaping the course of American development. In the trans-Mississippi West, the railroad, precursor and handmaiden of industrialization, touched the agrarian frontier and the two matured together. Too often, however, the effect of railroads on specific regions has been lost in the stirring tale of railroad building. Then, too, the significance of connecting lines and those leading to the Gulf has been overshadowed by spectacular projects designed to reach the Pacific. The story of the railroads merely begins with the account of the engineers who stretched thousands of miles of shining rail into the wilderness, overcoming the tremendous obstacles which blocked their paths. The purpose of the present work is to trace railroad influence on the development of economic, social, and political patterns and on the establishment of farms, trading centers, industries, and cities in the region primarily tributary to the Gulf of Mexico.

The geographic limits of this region have been arbitrarily fixed at the Mississippi River (except for the cities of New Orleans and Baton Rouge) to the east; the Missouri, the Kansas, and the Smoky Hill rivers to the north; and the western borders of Kansas and Texas to the west. It is obviously impossible to treat thoroughly the influence of railroads in so wide an area in a single volume; the intent of this work, then, is to be suggestive. The choice of topics, therefore, has necessarily been selective.

Chapters 4, 8–9, 16–18, 28–30, and 34 describe the growth of an expanding rail network as it opened new areas to settlement. They are included in order to provide an adequate background of the railroad construction which paralleled other developments in point of time. Slight attention has been given to details of construction, operation, or financing except insofar as they directly influenced the economic or political development of the Gulf Southwest.

In mentioning various cities in the Gulf Southwest, I have used the original spellings of their names until the time when the modern spelling was adopted. A few of the old names have remained the same, but many of them have subsequently been changed. In cases where there were several spellings. I have chosen the one most commonly used.

It is impossible to express adequately my gratitude to the dozens of people who have helped to make this work possible. The interest I have in railroad history and my desire to contribute in some small way to its understanding are due to the inspirational instruction and guidance of many former teachers, particularly Professor Edward Everett Dale of the University of Oklahoma and the late Professor Frederic L. Paxson of the University of California. To the American Philosophical Society, whose generous financial assistance from the Penrose Fund made the research possible, and to the administration of New Mexico College of Agriculture and Mechanical Arts, who released me from many duties in order that I might pursue the writing, I am particularly grateful.

I am indebted to Mr. Thomas Winthrop Streeter of Morristown, New Jersey, for materials he furnished from his own library, and to Mr. L. P. East, recent president of the American Railway Development Association; J. M. Prickett, vice-president of the Kansas City Southern; J. B. Shores, director of public relations of the Texas and Pacific; W. H. Hobbs, director of research for the Missouri Pacific; and the late Lee Lyles, assistant to the president, Atchison, Topeka and Santa Fe Railway Company, for making much important information available. Messrs. Arthur W. Large, until recently general agricultural agent for the Chicago, Rock Island and Pacific, C. B. Michelson, director of agricultural development for the St. Louis–San Francisco, and the late Harry M. Bainer, general agricultural agent for the Santa Fe System, supplied me with a wealth of detail drawn from their many years of experience. The staffs of many libraries have been unfailingly co-operative and helpful.

Two of my colleagues, Professor Sigurd Johansen and Assistant

Preface

Professor Simon F. Kropp, and Assistant Professor Lowell L. Blaisdell of Texas Technological College have contributed to the progress of this work in numerous ways which have made the writing less laborious. Professors Blaisdell and Kropp read the entire manuscript and made many suggestions which have reduced the number of errors which inevitably appear. Finally, to my wife, Jennalee McFall Clark, I am deeply grateful, not only for her reading and appraisal of the manuscript, but even more for her unlimited forbearance during the long course of its preparation.

IRA G. CLARK

Mesilla Park, New Mexico
January 24, 1958

Contents

	Preface	vii
1.	1850	3
2.	The Quickening	12
3.	Pacific Projects and Sectional Rivalries	18
4.	The Birth of Southwestern Railways	25
5.	Attractions and Rewards	33
6.	Rumblings in the Territories	42
7.	The War Years—and After	46
8.	Down to the Gulf	58
9.	The Boom and Reckoning	65
10.	The Granger Fringe	73
11.	The Westward Impulse	84
12.	The Town-Dwellers	91
13.	Buffalo Hunters, Cowmen, and Farmers	101
14.	The Lusty Country	108
15.	The Waters Cease Running	119
16.	Jay Gould Invades the Southwest	131
17.	Jay Gould's Rivals	145
18.	Interlude in the Nineties	160
19.	The Passing of Aids	163
20.	Indian Territory Succumbs	168
21.	The Restricted Wild West	175
22.	Peopling the Plains	182
23.	Stillborn Towns and Growing Cities	192

24. A Changing Economy	205
25. Grievances	216
26. The Temper of the Times	222
27. The Course of State Legislation	227
28. B. F. Yoakum, Entrepreneur	235
29. Approaching Maturity	244
30. The Newcomers	251
31. Further Population Shifts	258
32. Farming in the Dust	263
33. Growing Industries	275
34. Between Two Wars	281
35. Agricultural Education Renewed	290
36. From Strawstack to Smokestack	300
37. A Century in Retrospect	312
Bibliography	318
Index	325

Illustrations

Arthur E. Stilwell	*facing page*	96
Samuel W. Fordyce		96
William Edenborn		96
Cyrus K. Holliday		96
The first Rock Island *Rocket*		97
Early-day diner		97
Wood-burning Katy locomotive		112
Locomotive of the eighties		112
Wood-burning Texas & St. Louis locomotive		113
St. Louis, Arkansas & Texas locomotive		113
Freight train at Painted Cave, Texas		208
Shooting buffalo		208
Passenger train about 1900		209
Locomotive of the early 1900's		209
Laying track		224
Driving bridge piles		224
Early-day freight train at Butler's Bluff		225
The *Southern Belle* at Butler's Bluff		225
Texas Spring Palace		256
Fort Worth in 1849		256
Frisco steam locomotive		257
The Santa Fe *Chief*		257
Santa Fe Pleasure Dome Lounge Car		272

Then Came the Railroads

Winding through West Texas	272
Southern Pacific's *Sunset Limited*	273
Diesel-powered freight train	273

Maps

Railroads of the Gulf Southwest in 1860	52
Railroads of the Gulf Southwest in 1870	86
Railroads of the Gulf Southwest in 1880	148
Railroads of the Gulf Southwest in 1890	186
Gulf Southwest Railroads, 1950	302
Gulf Southwest Railroads, 1950	304

THEN CAME THE RAILROADS

The Century from Steam to Diesel in the Southwest

CHAPTER 1

1850

St. Louis bustled with activity, sincere in its belief that it was, and would remain, the great interior city of the United States. The migration to California and Oregon stimulated trade and effectively advertised this natural gateway to the trans-Mississippi West. Pierre Laclede's old trading post had now reached 80,000 in population, three-quarters of whom were recent arrivals. On the streets the twang of the upper Mississippi blended with the soft inflection of the South, the guttural of Germany with the brogue of Ireland, as the people went about the serious business of making a living and, incidentally, building an even greater city. Neither the disastrous fire which swept the business district in 1849 nor the cholera epidemic which followed almost immediately could retard the growth more than temporarily.

Fur trade remained a prime factor in the economy of St. Louis, but the streams of raw materials flowing down the Mississippi, the Missouri, and the Illinois had given the city a flourishing milling industry, breweries and distilleries, tanneries and saddleries, carriage and wagon works, and soap, candle, rope, and bagging factories. In turn, the interior demanded sod plows; the river, steamboat engines; and the cane plantations far to the south, refining machinery.

Eastern Missouri was no longer a part of the frontier. A number of settlements near the river dated from the preceding century and, since 1789, had been served by a trail which linked St. Louis with New Madrid. Venerable old Ste Genevieve was enjoying a rejuvenation as the result of newly opened iron deposits at near-by Pilot

Knob and Iron Mountain; Herculaneum served as a concentration point for lead from the French settlement at Old Mines and from Potosi and Caledonia.

St. Louis claimed the Missouri and its tributaries as the city's particular domain. Hardy pioneers had pushed up the sluggish river, which was the chief artery of commerce. Wagon roads replaced the ancient trails along both banks. Travelers might follow the old Market Street Road, now extended to Jefferson City and prosaically renamed the State Road. Or, if they wished, they could travel the historic course of westward migration along the north bank into the Boon's Lick country, from which the road derived its name. Small towns were strewn along these roads to supply migrants into western Missouri with trading centers and markets.

Many roads of local importance diverged from the river routes, while a few, such as the Salt River Road from St. Charles to the Des Moines River, the Springfield Road dropping south from Jefferson City, and the State Road from Boonville to southwestern Missouri, became major paths of commerce.

An overland trail from the Missouri River brought Santa Fé into the orbit of St. Louis. Old Franklin, as the western terminus of the St. Louis stage, was the original point of departure for Santa Fé traders until the capricious river swept the town away. The restless westward movement then bestowed this favor on the villages clustered near the great bend of the Missouri. From there wagon trains began their long, slow journey to what had been, until 1846, the remote northernmost outpost of Mexico, crossing en route a region inhabited by roving Plains Indians.

A wagon trail, later to be called the Old Wire Road, bisected the angle formed by the courses of the Mississippi and the Missouri and fed St. Louis from the southwestern part of the state. Passing over rolling hills and into the northern Ozarks, it served a progressively sparser population as it wound across the Big Prairie and into a timbered area which would await post bellum development. The trail extended to Springfield, situated at the end of the road whose name it bore.

Native and German farmers established agricultural communities in the eastern third of the triangle formed by the Missouri River and the Old Wire Road, and population spilled southward almost to Arkansas. Other settlers were diverted west to settle along the Osage and its tributaries. Even along the western border of the state, isolated communities were springing up.

The bulky raw materials not absorbed by local processors moved down the rivers to New Orleans. The majestic Mississippi was the central cable from which strands twisted away to serve all parts of its great valley. The tremendous export trade, second only to that of New York, had pushed New Orleans into fourth place among American cities.

Pre-eminently a commercial city, New Orleans lacked the diversity of St. Louis. The highly stratified society, which reflected the preponderance of planters and professional people, was acutely accentuated by the institution of slavery. New Orleans was a city of profusion and extravagance, contrasting strangely with the vast interior frontier of which it was both master and servant.

The bulk of Louisiana's half-million population was concentrated on the Mississippi south of Baton Rouge, but a number of established towns were strung along the river bank as far north as Lake Providence, near the Arkansas line. The Red River, wandering diagonally across the state from southwestern Arkansas after twisting from the west and forming part of the northern boundary of recently annexed Texas, was second only to the Mississippi in attracting settlers. Alexandria, the southern terminus of the road from Little Rock, historic old Natchitoches, and youthful Shreveport were its major shipping points.

The valleys of the Black, the most important of the Red's many tributaries, and of the Ouachita, which fed the Black, had attracted settlers. The old Ouachita River post of Fuerte Miro, renamed Monroe, served cotton planters to the east and farmer-stockmen of the hill country to the north and west. The Ouachita wound out of the north from Arkansas, where Champagnolle Landing, Camden, and Arkadelphia were within the economic orbit of Louisiana. Plantations lined the wide, slow rivers, while the forests from which the lands were reclaimed stretched far into the interior.

"Cajun country," home of the God-fearing but lighthearted descendants of the French who were forcibly removed from Acadia by their new English masters in colonial days, stretched west from below New Orleans across Bayou Lafourche, Bayou Teche, and the Vermilion River. New Iberia to the south and Opelousas to the north were its more prosperous communities.

Then Came the Railroads

Overland transportation was confined to a few major routes. One road from Texas, the Old Spanish Trail, passed by Lake Charles to sweep southeast below Grand Lake and terminate at New Orleans; another, the San Antonio Trace, reached Natchitoches, from which point three roads diverged, one northeast to Monroe, the second to the Mississippi at Vidalia, the third southeast to Opelousas. Nolan's Trace cut diagonally from the southwest part of the state, by way of Alexandria, to the general vicinity of Vidalia.

Arkansas, lying between Missouri and Louisiana, represented the raw frontier. With a sparse population and no city worthy of the name, fourteen-year-old Arkansas was hindered in its development by its most obvious natural resource—timber. There were few markets for lumber that were not already served by more strategically located sawmills, and the slow, back-breaking task of clearing land discouraged agriculture. The rugged Ozarks and Ouachitas limited settlement in the western half of the state to the river valleys. Man also had contributed to the natural barriers to advancement. The ruinously speculative and corrupt activities of the short-lived State Bank and the Real Estate Bank had robbed the state of what credit it possessed.

What settlement there was followed the usual course, pushing up river valley paths worn by Indians long before the coming of the white man. On occasion, physiographic features dictated the blazing of trails which cut across this pattern. Crowley's Ridge, rising above the swamps of the Mississippi and the St. Francis, was a natural thoroughfare from southeastern Missouri to Helena, near the confluence of these rivers. The Southwest Trail cut diagonally across the state from the northeast, avoided swamps to the east and mountains to the west, and branched below the Arkansas to serve both the Red and the Ouachita. A state road ran north from Van Buren to join the Old Wire Road in southwestern Missouri. The federal government added another overland route in 1824 when it marked a military road through the swamps and forests which separated Memphis from Little Rock.

Settlement had spread from historic old Arkansas Post across Grand Prairie, where settlers were served by Pine Bluff. Cotton growers on the western margin of the alluvial plain turned to Little Rock, the capital, which was classified as a city by virtue of its corporate charter. A few villages, former missions or trading posts, were strung along the Arkansas and its major tributaries west of Little Rock. On the

1850

extreme western boundary, Fort Smith and Van Buren enjoyed booms as points of departure for expeditions into the Indian country, Texas, and the gold fields of California.

Another line of settlement followed the course of the White River and its tributaries. Rock Roe was the transfer point from the Little Rock stages to White River packets, while Jacksonport, at the confluence of the Black and the White, was the commercial and social center of northeast Arkansas.

A few inland towns in Arkansas achieved prominence by virtue of their locations along the overland trails. In the extreme northwest the State Road served Bentonville and Fayetteville. Deep in the southwest, politically important Washington was on the Southwest Trail (which followed a route almost parallel with present-day U. S. Highway 67), which terminated at Fulton, the extreme outpost of white settlement prior to the annexation of Texas.

Texas, incorporated into the United States only five years before, excited the imagination by its size and stirring history. The bulk of its two hundred thousand people, however, was confined to the bottomlands of the Colorado, Brazos, Trinity, Neches, and Sabine rivers.

The island town of Galveston had the choice location commercially. The leading city in Texas, it boasted a population barely over four thousand, with industry as negligible as that in the remainder of the state. Connected with Galveston Bay by Buffalo Bayou, Houston was a rival of Galveston for the Brazos River trade, a prize worthy of capture because of its cotton and cane plantations, which antedated the republic.

Another line of settlement which attracted the Galveston Bay rivals followed the Trinity. Scattered towns dotted the west bank. Located at the forks of the Trinity in the fertile blacklands, four-year-old Dallas boasted a wagon works and a brick factory, a lumber mill and a ferry. A few miles west, Camp Worth housed a garrison which guarded the frontier. Cotton farms lay south of Dallas, while to the north and west, the Peters colony functioned as part of a Kentucky promotional scheme.

Most of the area between the Trinity and the Louisiana line had a semblance of settlement. Trappers and traders operated in the forested swamplands surrounding Sabine Lake. Beaumont had grown up on the Neches, and settlement cautiously edged around the tangled jungle known as the Big Thicket. A community at the head of navigation of the Sabine had existed for many years and under many names until it was stabilized as Orange. Violently lawless villages in the so-called Neutral Ground dated from the Mexican period; Nacogdoches, historically the eastern outpost of Spain, lay on the western border of that troubled strip. To the north, between the Neches and the Sabine, cotton plantations nourished a few new marketing towns. Above the great bend of the Sabine, immigrants from the north had established several settlements. Jefferson, near Caddo Lake on Big Cypress Bayou, overshadowed neighboring Marshall.

The Red River served as a means of entering lands lying south of the Indian Territory. Half a dozen small towns served the cotton planters. Farther west the Republic of Texas had founded Fort Preston at the site of Colonel Holland Coffee's trading post; Gainesville, established as a way station on one route to California, represented the deepest penetration of Texas along the Red.

The older Texas settlements were, with few exceptions, west of the Brazos. Some of Austin's followers established themselves as ranchers and cotton planters on the Colorado River. Well up the Colorado, the village of Waterloo, now called Austin, had been designated as the capital, but its growth was slow. The coastal area south of Matagorda Bay could boast a pair of older towns and the thriving new port of Indian Point. Irish settlements lined Aransas Bay and extended inland beyond Beeville, and the smugglers' base on Corpus Christi Bay assumed an air of respectability as an assembly point for emigrants to California.

San Antonio was beginning to have a few non-Spanish residents by 1850, and in the triangle formed by San Antonio, Austin, and Fredericksburg the German influence was strong. Brownsville, on the Río Grande, was a concentration point for California-bound travelers following the river to Eagle Pass and across northern Mexico. Completely removed from the remainder of Texas both geographically and culturally, a chain of Spanish towns lay along the Río Grande at the western extremity of the state. Magoffinsville, across the river from the Mexican city of El Paso del Norte, was as Mexican as its neighbors in all but name.

The line of westernmost settlement ran from Gainesville through Dallas and Waco to Austin, west to Fredericksburg, then southeast to Corpus Christi, with a spur up the Río Grande to Eagle Pass. The lands beyond were uninhabited except for the distant El Paso settlements and were accepted as being a part of the "Great American Desert," over which Indians would always roam at will.

1850

Overland travel in Texas was primitive. Only by the loosest construction of the term could the trails dating from the Mexican period be classified as roads—marked trees directing travelers across treacherous sands and through morasses of mud, swamps, or tangled thickets. The roads of Spanish origin centered at San Antonio. The major thoroughfares were those to Louisiana, but others led to Goliad, to Monclova, Coahuila, and to the Río Grande crossing at Presidio del Norte. A trail branching from the San Antonio Trace served Laredo. Austin's Anglo-American colonists also had connected their settlements by trails.

Other roads dated from the period of the Republic. One military highway was constructed from Austin to the Red River while another was surveyed from San Antonio to the mouth of the Kiamichi. A stage road, opened between Houston and Austin in 1841, was extended to San Antonio in 1850. Emigrants from beyond the Red River blazed new trails from the termini of the Southwest Trail and the Texas Road.

North of the Red and west of the states abutting on the Mississippi, a great plain broken only by the western sweep of the Ozark and Ouachita mountains, was Indian country. It was the easternmost part of the vast geographic barrier to the Pacific land of promise, occupied by wild nomads who added to the hazards of the arduous overland journey. It was a land of little apparent value, its only productivity a small amount of agricultural surplus grown by reservation Indians along the eastern fringe.

The region immediately west of Arkansas had been dedicated to the Civilized Tribes, uprooted from their ancestral homes during the Jackson administration and removed to that area, then the southwestern extremity of the United States, which was considered a part of the "Great American Desert." These Indians were concentrated east of the Cross Timbers. A few of the more enterprising, notably mixed-bloods, had carved from the communal land systems of their tribes a ranching and plantation society based in part upon Negro slavery. These lived in comfort on their holdings on the Red, the Canadian, and the Arkansas, but the bulk of their fellow tribesmen enjoyed only meager returns from small patches of corn or cotton and a few head of scrub stock, supplemented by hunting, fishing, and trapping. To the north the indigenous Osages occupied the Neosho Valley, while the United States government had established reservations along the Missouri boundary and the Kansas River for various smaller northern tribes.

Then Came the Railroads

Bitter internecine conflict, arising from the removal treaties and the antagonism of native and immigrant tribes, gave the country a tradition of violence. The legend of geographic inhospitableness and the existence of desirable lands elsewhere did, however, save it from the avarice of white intruders. In isolated areas along the Missouri line, a few impatient landseekers were beginning to eye the Indian lands covetously, but to the general public, if it thought of the question at all, the removals had solved permanently a vexatious problem.

The neighbors to the west of the removed Indians were Plains tribes who depended on the great buffalo herds to furnish them most of the necessities of their simple existence.

The only whites legally resident in the Indian country were the soldiers stationed at scattered frontier garrisons, licensed traders operating at remote posts, and missionaries carrying on their work at lonely stations. A string of forts along the eastern border of the Indian country constituted part of the strand of frontier defense which, at the time of its creation, was considered of relatively permanent nature. The church kept pace with the military as various sects founded missions. Traders built their stations where they could depend for profits upon Indians, military establishments, and emigrant trains bound for Texas or California. The only other permanent settlements were of Indian origin.

The great bulk of the Indian country trade was overland. Besides the Santa Fé Trail and the military roads connecting various forts, two trails were of prime significance—the Texas Road and the route to California by way of the valley of the Canadian. The Texas Road was an extension of the trails leading down into southwestern Missouri and northwestern Arkansas, proceeding south by the Creek Agency at Three Forks and by the trading post at Boggy Depot to Red River, opposite Preston, Texas. Another trail of some importance was the one which travelers from southern Arkansas had marked across the Choctaw Nation to Fort Towson Landing on the Red.

Only in the deep southeast did river traffic play a major role. There steamboats served Fort Towson and near-by Doaksville from the Red, and Fort Gibson and the trading post at Webbers Falls from the Arkansas. A few smaller vessels ascended these rivers farther and even plied the waters of the Neosho.

The Gulf Southwest of 1850 was a land of some promise along its eastern edge. It had two great cities of which it could be justly proud and a certain maturity of settlement along the banks of its major streams. The remainder of the country was, at best, a rude frontier apparently incapable of any considerable development. As for the lands beyond the navigable waters, they were a part of the "Great American Desert," by general agreement unfit for civilized habitation.

CHAPTER 2

The Quickening

THERE WAS LITTLE to suggest in 1850 that the region south and west of St. Louis could be productive of railroad agitation. The value of rail transportation had been proved in the East, but except for a short line operating west from Chicago after 1848, railroads had scarcely invaded the West. True, a wild-eyed visionary named Asa Whitney gained a number of converts to his scheme for linking the Oregon country to the Great Lakes, and the flurry of excitement thus created would not die. But not until 1853 would a railroad reach Rock Island, Illinois, to give the Mississippi its first connection with the Atlantic seaboard, and another four years would elapse before East St. Louis and Memphis could boast that distinction.

In spite of the remoteness of the Gulf Southwest, however, its people actually had been discussing the advisability of building railroads for more than fifteen years. The immediate need was for lines to reach the raw materials of the back country rather than for lines to connect cities.

Louisiana had the distinction of pioneering railroads in the Mississippi Valley. Three short lines, actually horse-drawn street railways, were operating in the early thirties, but these projects, lying in or very near New Orleans, had no connection with the west bank of the river.

The pioneer effort west of the Mississippi was the Red River Railroad, incorporated in 1833 as the Alexandria and Cheneyville, which served Bayou Boeuf from Alexandria. It passed into the hands of a young planter, Ralph Smith, who continued to operate it until the

The Quickening

Civil War, when it was dismantled. Horses furnished the power to draw the carloads of cotton and cane over wooden rails to the Alexandria terminus.[1] Other projects designed to reach from points opposite New Orleans to Opelousas and Alexandria were discouraged by the panic of 1837. Louisiana had offered to advance its credit and subscribe to stock in railroad enterprises, but the panic so disrupted state finances that a clause in the new constitution forbade both of these practices.[2]

Although Louisiana led in achievement, Missouri surpassed it in discussion and debate. As early as 1833, aggressively ambitious New Franklin secured a charter for a lottery, the profits to be used to build a railroad to the Missouri River, one mile away. The lottery operated for years, but the profits went to speculators rather than to railroad builders.

The St. Louis Internal Improvement Convention of April 30, 1836, was the first significant step in arousing general interest in railroad construction. Eleven counties sent sixty enthusiastic delegates to endorse a general internal improvement program which included railroads. Governor Lilburn W. Boggs, St. Louis banker and businessman, staunchly supported attempts to develop transportation facilities. He envisioned St. Louis as a great commercial city, with railroads as the handmaidens of the metropolis. Under the spell of the convention and the state administration, the legislature authorized the building of eighteen local railroads with an aggregate capital of seven million dollars.[3] The panic, which struck almost as the legislature was acting, dissipated all hopes for immediate construction.

At its next session the legislature considered a drastically reduced number of applications for charters, but none weathered the storm of legislative hostility. An act creating a Board of Internal Improvements did provide for surveying a railroad route from St. Louis to supposedly rich mineral deposits at Iron Mountain.

The railroad issue, together with the closely related questions of a general incorporation law and corporate liability, was one of several state problems undermining the political domination of able, imperious Thomas Hart Benton, spokesman for Jacksonian Democracy.

---

[1] Walter Prichard, ed., "A Forgotten Louisiana Engineer," *LHQ,* Vol. XXX, 1127–28; AGS, *Louisiana,* 241, 665; Balthasar H. Meyer, *History of Transportation in the United States before 1860,* 480.

[2] Alcée Fortier, *A History of Louisiana,* III, 230, 232, 237.

[3] Lewis H. Haney, *A Congressional History of Railways in the United States,* I, 367; Robert E. Riegel, "The Missouri Pacific Railroad to 1879," *MHR,* Vol. XVIII, 3–4.

The Benton, or "hard," faction of the Democratic party brought to the legislature an agrarian fear of "monied monopoly" and a demand for rigid restriction on all corporations. St. Louis and other growing cities demanded more liberal treatment of investors in order to attract new capital.

The number of successful applications for railroad and other transportation company charters was limited to eight during the period of "hard" Democratic supremacy from 1840 to 1846. The Iron Mountain was among these. It received no state aid, and its supporters had to beat down amendments which would have permitted the legislature to repeal the charter at any future time and make stockholders liable for corporate debts in proportion to the amount of stock each held. During this period a convention was called to revise the antiquated state constitution. In spite of a substantial adjustment of representation in favor of the cities, St. Louis overwhelmingly rejected the new constitution because the "hard" majority secured the inclusion of articles providing as general restrictions those which they were unable to impose on the Iron Mountain. Critics of the "anti-monopoly" provisions insisted that they would effectively bar all railroad projects because sane investors would never risk their capital under such conditions.

The attitude towards corporations was decidedly friendlier as the power of the "hard" faction waned. This was reflected in the large number of railroad charters favorably acted upon after 1846.[4]

Meanwhile Missouri had secured its first railroad. It stretched from James R. Allen's mill to a point on the Missouri River opposite the town of Lexington, a distance of five miles. Mules drew carts over sawed-oak rails laid by Negro slaves belonging to Allen.[5]

Texas was another hotbed of railroad agitation. Scarcely had the last shot been fired at San Jacinto before enterprising Texans turned to the pressing need for improved transportation. In its initial session, the Congress of Texas acted favorably on a petition bearing the signatures of Stephen F. Austin and other leaders requesting a charter for the Texas Railroad, Navigation and Banking Company. This corporation proposed to construct and operate a comprehensive system of rail- and waterways along the coast and also to engage in banking operations.

[4] Simon F. Kropp, "The Struggle for Limited Liability and General Incorporation Laws in Missouri" (M. A. Thesis, University of Missouri, 1939), 9, 19–26, 48–78, 98–100.

[5] "The First Railroad in Missouri," *Western Journal & Civilian*, Vol. VIII, 308–10; R. B. Oliver, "Missouri's First Road," *MHR*, Vol. XXVI, 12–17.

The Quickening

Violent opposition towards the company developed immediately. Although most of the criticism was directed against the banking provisions, Dr. Anson Jones, later president of the republic, attacked the entire project. His arguments were in essence those with which the Missouri General Assembly was preoccupied—the betrayal of the people into the hands of a monopoly. Dr. Jones was elected to Congress on a good Jacksonian platform which attacked the company and demanded concellation of its charter. He carried the fight to the floor. The contending factions never pushed the issue to its conclusion, for, although apparently a substantial amount of stock was subscribed, the widespread distress accompanying the panic of 1837 dried up all outside sources of capital, and the Texas Railroad, Navigation and Banking Company withered away.[6]

The Republic of Texas granted three other railroad charters. The first was that of the Brazos and Galveston Company, promoted by Galvestonians in a move to gain ascendancy over Houston. A. C. Allen fathered the idea of the Houston and Brazos Valley Railroad to offset any advantage which might accrue to Galveston by reason of its projected road. Intense town rivalry likewise inspired the third charter. Andrew Briscoe, one of the promoters of Harrisburg, secured a charter for the Harrisburg Railroad and Trading Company to construct a line to the Brazos. Although none of these projects materialized, the Harrisburg company was the forerunner of the Buffalo Bayou, Brazos and Colorado Railroad.[7]

Meanwhile, sentiment developed in favor of Texas' constructing its own railroad system. Advocates of the plan actually convened at Houston in 1842, but enthusiastic endorsement was of little avail in the absence of any means of financing so ambitious a scheme; nonetheless, the idea persisted through the days of the republic and into the period of statehood. State Senator John W. Dancy revived the project in 1850 after Texas received $10,000,000 from the United States for relinquishing its claim to disputed lands. Dancy proposed that the state use part of this money and some of the public lands to finance a railroad from Galveston and Matagorda bays into the interior, with extensions east and north to New Orleans, Memphis, and St. Louis. The state would build it with slave labor, then lease it to private individuals for operation.[8]

[6] S. G. Reed, *A History of the Texas Railroads* (hereafter referred to as *Texas Railroads*), 10–21; Andrew F. Muir; "Railroad Enterprises in Texas, 1836–1841," *SHQ*, Vol. XLVII, 339–48.

[7] Reed, *Texas Railroads*, 30–38; Muir, "Railroad . . . 1836–1841," *SHQ*, Vol. XLVII, 345–70.

Then Came the Railroads

From the date of annexation until 1850, years of relative quiet as far as the public-ownership project was concerned, the legislature had granted charters to nine private companies. Eight permitted their charters to lapse, but one, the Galveston and Red River, did in the course of time construct and operate a railroad line.

Arkansas, more in a spirit of hope than anticipation, granted charters in 1837 for construction between Little Rock and Helena, Little Rock and Napoleon, and Columbia and Bayou Bartholomew.[9] All eventually lapsed.

Of the railroad projects conceived in the trans-Mississippi area prior to 1850, the boldest was the product of the fertile imagination of General Edmund P. Gaines, military commander in the West. Responding to a Senate resolution of 1837 requesting proposals for an adequate means of frontier defense, General Gaines departed from tradition to insist that the heart of any plan must lie in the rapid transportation of troops. He recommended the continued maintenance of all existing western forts, with the addition of eight others to form a chain from the mouth of the Sabine to the west end of Lake Superior. All would be linked by rail and tied to the Atlantic seaboard by four to six trunk lines.

The network of western military railroads would center about a main line from Memphis to the upper Sabine River, with branches up both the Red and the Canadian to their outermost military posts, and another down Sabine Ridge to the mouth of the river. A second railroad would run from St. Louis to Fort Gibson, with a branch up a fork of the Merrimac and across to a proposed fort on the Osage. Other lines would serve the posts north of the Missouri.

The strange series of documents[10] which Gaines presented, first to the House Committee on Military Affairs, then to various state governors, and finally to individual members of the Senate, combined personal pique and crusading zeal. Despite his persistent refusal to admit defeat, Gaines' plan was given only the briefest consideration. Undoubtedly his lack of personal popularity had something to do with the summary dismissal of the project. His unre-

---

[8] S. S. McKay, "Texas and the Southern Pacific Railroad," *SHQ*, Vol. XXXV, 7; Reed, *Texas Railroads*, 40–53.

[9] *Acts of Arkansas, 1837–1838*, 50, 65, 86.

[10] *Communication from Major-General Gaines, U. S. Army, relative to a System of Railroads; Memorial of Edmund Pendleton Gaines to the Senate and House of Representatives . . .; Letter of Major-General Gaines to the Governor of Mississippi;* 26 Cong., 2 sess., H. Ex. Doc. 256.

The Quickening

strained criticism of the War Department and some of his superior officers, his long-time feud with General Winfield Scott, and his open charges of political influence in high military places did not endear him to his professional associates. Even without this personal factor, however, the constitutional and financial problems involved would have defeated a more popular advocate.

There were many weaknesses in General Gaines' thinking and planning. He had no technical knowledge upon which to base probable building costs, and his insistence that revenue traffic would pay construction costs in a few years was fanciful. He failed to grasp the many engineering problems inherent in the construction and operation of railroads.

Despite its obvious weaknesses, Gaines' plan embodied some essentially sound principles. He was far ahead of many of his contemporaries in foreseeing the revolution that was occurring in transportation. He anticipated the soundest constitutional arguments to be employed later by friends of the Pacific railroad. While falling into the same errors as they in estimating the earnings of a railroad operating through uninhabited country, he expressed just as clearly the necessity for rapid transportation in binding the Union together. Finally, he saw the frontier as dynamic, continuously pushing westward and requiring a mobile defense rather than isolated military posts. Eleven years later, Lieutenant Matthew F. Maury presented the same arguments, both military and financial, with the warning that since all the world coveted California, the United States could hold it only by building a railroad to the Pacific.[11]

[11] 31 Cong., 1 sess., *H. Rep. 439*.

CHAPTER 3

Pacific Projects and Sectional Rivalries

WHEN ASA WHITNEY first proposed the construction of a railroad to the Pacific, all routes south of the forty-second parallel were automatically eliminated since they would traverse and terminate on Mexican soil. The picture changed completely after the United States annexed Texas and acquired the Mexican Cession in 1848, because every Mississippi Valley town with political influence became a potential terminus. The only serious contenders south of the Missouri, however, were St. Louis, Memphis, Vicksburg, and New Orleans.

In the early discussions of the Pacific railroad there was less sectional bias. When none but northern routes were available, even some Southerners grudgingly supported the Whitney plan until it appeared to have some chance of success. The proposals of the late forties remained nationalistic in tone, modified primarily by the desires of localities to benefit themselves. After the stormy Congressional session of 1850, however, grave constitutional issues for which slavery became the symbol were closely associated with the railroad debates. The acrimony which marked consideration of Pacific railroad bills contributed in no small degree to the rising tension which was to split the Union as the next decade opened.

To whip up the necessary local enthusiasm, rival cities turned during the late forties to that time-honored western institution—the convention. Memphis held one in 1845 which discussed the Pacific project incidentally. At that time Colonel James Gadsden recommended a southern route, even though it would run through Mexican lands to reach the Pacific.[1] The same year, Lieutenant Maury advocated an international railroad from Memphis to Monterey, via El Paso.[2] Rival cities failed to criticize these proposals as vigorously as one might have suspected, because the possibility of their fulfillment was remote; besides, the river towns from St. Louis south had not yet embraced railroads enthusiastically. They were content to rest their future prosperity on the lucrative water traffic which had built them. With the accession of lands from Mexico, however, fierce competition developed among the rivals.

Thomas Hart Benton switched from his defense of an all-water route to advocacy of an isthmian railroad, and then, jealously guarding the interests of Missouri, championed a central route from St. Louis to the Pacific via the upper Arkansas and the Humboldt. New Orleans, fearing the diversion of its trade if the West Coast connection were up the river, supported a railroad through the Isthmus of Tehuantepec. Jefferson Davis favored a southern route, preferably originating opposite Vicksburg, while Memphis interests pressed for a railroad from the vicinity of neighboring Hopefield, Arkansas, either by way of the Canadian River and Albuquerque, or southwest through El Paso. The violent rivalry extending from towns on Lake Superior to the mouth of the Mississippi worked to the benefit of Stephen A. Douglas, whose proposed terminus at Council Bluffs, Iowa, eventually took on the appearance of a compromise.

Arkansas set a series of railroad conventions in motion when, in January, 1849, Little Rock citizens requested Memphis to sponsor one. Memphis agreed and, despite changed plans, postponements, and a temporary loss of interest because of the disastrous cholera epidemic, finally called a meeting for late October. St. Louis immediately arranged a "national" railroad convention for an earlier day in the same month.

Approximately one thousand delegates representing thirteen states assembled at St. Louis. The convention resolved itself into a battle between the antagonistic ambitions of St. Louis and Chicago and a bitter factional struggle for control of the Democratic party in Missouri. The Illinois delegation, headed by Douglas and enriched by the experience of its own convention in 1847, was bound by instructions to support a "compromise route" from Council Bluffs to the Pacific, with privately built branches from the eastern terminus to

---

[1] LeRoy R. Hafen and Carl C. Rister, *Western America*, 539–42.
[2] Robert S. Cotterill, "Early Agitation for a Pacific Railroad," *MVHR*, Vol. V, 398.

Chicago, St. Louis, and Memphis. Newspapers of the host city attacked Douglas and forced his resignation as chairman of the convention—not, however, before he named Henry S. Geyer, a Missouri Whig with anti-Benton support, as his successor. The passing of the old order in Missouri was apparent when, after rejecting an ambiguous resolution calling on Congress to act in regard to a Pacific railroad, the convention repudiated Benton by adopting a proposal in line with the Illinois instructions. The action followed a bitter debate which almost forced premature adjournment.[3]

Benton and Douglas were notably absent from the group who went on to Memphis. Lieutenant Maury, who had fathered and advertised the Memphis route, served as the presiding officer of the convention. He threw it into an uproar, however, when he opened the first session by proposing the immediate construction of a railroad across the Isthmus of Tehuantepec. The feelings of Arkansas and Tennessee delegates were further ruffled when an official committee from the St. Louis meeting suggested that the resolutions adopted at St. Louis demonstrated a desire for co-operation and harmony. Later, when James B. Bowlin of Missouri, in an ill-chosen phrase, berated Memphis for selfishly rejecting the "olive branch" proffered from St. Louis, he was informed that all that convention tendered was a "railroad branch." Meanwhile, various delegates introduced resolutions representing the aspirations of their respective sections.

The convention's committee on resolutions was faced with the unenviable but unavoidable task of naming a specific route. Memphis, supported by the Tennessee, Arkansas, and Texas delegations, secured the passage of a resolution recommending a railroad from a point on the Mississippi between the mouths of the Red and the Ohio, preferably Memphis, across Arkansas and Texas to El Paso, thence to San Diego. There was bitter opposition to the resolution and, although it was finally adopted, one account of the proceedings stated that its acceptance was due to an error in the reading.[4] The resulting memorial to Congress was ignored because of more pressing problems.

The Pacific railroad issue became increasingly confused after 1850. Inseparable from other sectional controversies, complicated by constitutional difficulties, and subjected to constant pressures from competing cities, it was one of a number of measures which led to nothing

[3] Robert S. Cotterill, "The National Railroad Convention in St. Louis, 1849," *MVHR*, Vol. XII, 205–15; *Cong. Globe*, 33 Cong., 1 sess., App., 964.

[4] Robert S. Cotterill, "The Memphis Railroad Convention, 1849," *THM*, Vol. IV, 83–94; 31 Cong., 1 sess., *H. Rep. 439*, 7–12.

but wrangling each time it came before either house of Congress. The Whitney and Douglas routes faced opposition from a number of quarters. Benton's pet Missouri project, Senator Thomas J. Rusk's proposed route from Memphis through Arkansas and northern Texas, and the House Public Land Committee's bill for a railroad from Vicksburg to San Diego with a branch from El Paso to Fort Smith, each had its adherents.

Both houses of Congress considered Pacific railroad measures during the spring of 1853. Opponents of all such projects, fortified by many constitutional arguments, rallied to the support of the Broadhead amendment, which provided for a preliminary survey to determine the most practicable route. The amendment was defeated, but sectional disagreements split the ranks of the railroad's proponents to defeat specific bills. Friends of the project did salvage the provision authorizing a reconnaissance of the various routes. They secured an amendment to the military appropriation bill authorizing the expenditure of $150,000 for preliminary surveys in spite of opposition from the very group which conceived the Broadhead amendment in order to defeat more specific legislation.[5]

Army engineers surveyed the major routes and made elaborate reports on their findings. Secretary of War Jefferson Davis prepared an analysis which, from his point of view, eliminated all but the thirty-second-parallel, or extreme southern, route. The thirty-fifth-parallel route by way of Fort Smith and Albuquerque was the only possible rival of the more southerly course; all routes farther north were rejected on the grounds of ruggedness of the terrain, severity of the weather, and the generally inhospitable character of the country.[6]

A storm of criticism greeted the report. Davis was accused of serving the South rather than the nation. Critics charged that the War Department's interest in developing artesian wells in the area, experimenting with camels for use in the desert, and engineering the Gadsden Purchase were all a part of a conspiracy to force the adoption of the southern route. The federal subsidy granted in 1858 to the overland mail operating along this line seemed to verify these suspicions.

Meanwhile, the Pacific railroad project became inextricably bound up in the debates over the highly explosive issue of slavery in Kansas

[5] *Cong. Globe,* 32 Cong., 2 sess., 125–27, 280–86, 315–21, 341–43, 350–55, 421–23, 469–74, 489, 502–509, 660–62, 671, 675–81, 696–715, 740–56, 765–75, 798–99, 815–23, 837–41; App. 178–81, 186–87, 212–17, 221–29.
[6] "Report of the Secretary of War," *Pacific Railroad Surveys,* I, Part 1, 10–30.

and constitutional limitations on the power of the central government. In 1855, the year following the passage of the Kansas-Nebraska Act, Stephen A. Douglas introduced a bill for three Pacific railroads, one each for the northern, central, and southern sections of the nation. It weathered a deluge of proposed amendments and finally passed the Senate, only to die in the House.[7]

The sectional battle over railroads continued through successive Congresses until the Civil War. While a South Carolina convention was dissolving the ties which bound that state to the Union, Samuel R. Curtis of Iowa was energetically pushing through the House of Representatives a bill for two Pacific railroads; while the Gulf states were seceding, the Senate was debating the measure and amending it so drastically that it was acceptable to no one.[8]

Secession automatically ended consideration of all southern routes. It removed from Congress the southern bloc which had opposed the Pacific railroad on constitutional grounds. It was now possible to agree that the road must be built and to select a route. A decade of bitter debate had preceded the action which authorized the building of the Union Pacific. No other question revealed more starkly the widening breach between constitutional philosophies which no longer had common ground upon which to compromise. It dramatized the changing temper of sectional interests as the controversy broadened from disagreement over the best route to veiled references to sinister influences at work, finally emerging as an issue which some southern members insisted could be resolved only by withdrawal from the Union in the event a northern route prevailed.

An Indian problem of particular concern to the Southwest was inherently tied to the Pacific railroad issue. The creation of a "permanent" Indian frontier by removal of many eastern tribes beyond the line of white settlement had only temporarily eased a perennial source of friction. The policy was doomed from its inception, enjoying its brief period of success only because the lands occupied by the resettled Indians were slightly in advance of the restless agricultural frontier and were still considered a part of the "Great American Desert." Pacific railroad projects simply hastened its collapse.

Indian removals also played a small part in determining the route which the Pacific railroad would follow. The Indians north of the

[7] *Cong. Globe,* 33 Cong., 2 sess., 316–19, 330–41, 353–57, 747–51, 805–14.
[8] 38 Cong., 1 sess., *H. Rep. 428; Cong. Globe,* 38 Cong., 1 sess., 2410–11, 2444–46; *ibid.,* 38 Cong., 2 sess., 162–71, 250–63, 290–94, 381–89, 409–10, 426–33, 521–26, 543–46, 609–18, 638–39.

thirty-seventh parallel were weakened remnants of once great tribes or were nomads who could plead only occupancy of the land. South of that line, however, the powerful Civilized Tribes had salvaged from their removal treaties the promise that they would remain undisturbed by white intruders in their new homes. President Andrew Jackson advised the nation that "the pledge of the United States has been given by Congress that the country destined for this people shall be forever 'secured and guaranteed them,' "[9] and his successor granted them letters patent to their lands. Indian policy would require reexamination should a Pacific railroad be projected westward through the lands of the Civilized Tribes.

A few enthusiasts, none of whom could boast the political influence of a Stephen A. Douglas or a Jefferson Davis, argued the virtues of the thirty-fifth-parallel route by way of the Canadian River and Albuquerque. The most vocal was Representative John S. Phelps. A fellow Missourian, James Craig, accurately summarized the attitude of the general public and those favoring more northerly routes:

He [Phelps] knows, and every member knows, that the emigration to the Pacific, amounting to sixty thousand people a year—men, women, and children—take the route [by South Pass] which the majority of the committee desire to have the railroad take. My colleague knows, and every member knows, that an emigrant does not find himself winding his way to the gold fields of California, or to the Pacific, on the thirty-fifth parallel route, unless he has lost his way. You cannot find a stagecoach dragging its slow length along on that route, unless you go back and find a $600,000 subsidy to send it there.[10]

In short, the traditional routes to Oregon and California and the desires of the most powerful proponents of the Pacific railroad dictated that it was the central and northern Indian frontier which must succumb first.

The breaking of the Indian frontier was directly attributable to railroad influence, and it brought with it the end of the uneasy sectional truce of 1850. The extent to which Stephen A. Douglas championed the Kansas-Nebraska bill in the interest of his candidacy for the presidency might be debatable, but certainly a prime motive for

[9] James D. Richardson, *A Compilation of the Messages and Papers of the Presidents,* III, 171.
[10] *Cong. Globe,* 36 Cong., 1 sess., 2410.

Then Came the Railroads

his action was his desire to open to settlement Indian-occupied lands through which the Pacific railroad of his choice would run.[11]

The Pacific railroad debates stimulated nationwide interest in possible routes. Members of Congress became painfully aware of names which a short time before were entirely outside their field of knowledge. True, the potential eastern termini were well-known cities, but the intermediate points would determine the course to be followed. Whether a Missouri railroad should run by the mouth of the Kaw or by Springfield; whether a line originating at Memphis should go by Fort Smith, thence west along the Canadian River or by El Paso; whether a road from Vicksburg through Shreveport would be better than one crossing Louisiana by Opelousas—these were questions which Congress did not answer, but in pondering them turned the attention of promoters to their possibilities for development.

[11] This interpretation has been presented most convincingly by Frank H. Hodder in two articles: "The Genesis of the Kansas-Nebraska Act," SHSW *Proc. for 1912*, 69–86; "The Railroad Background of the Kansas-Nebraska Act," *MVHR*, Vol. XII, 3–22.

CHAPTER 4

The Birth of Southwestern Railways

THE MOST important result of the Pacific railroad agitation was its stimulation of local building, an activity cut short by the panic of 1857. Many of the proposed roads were promoted in the hope that they would eventually become segments or branches of a transcontinental route. Others were of local nature and were designed to tap areas of potential production for the benefit of specific towns. The normal procedure was for the promoters to secure a charter from the state legislature, organize the company, and then request a grant of public lands to aid in the construction.

Public-spirited citizens of St. Louis, spurred to action by the enthusiasm generated at the railroad convention of 1849, pushed incorporation of the Pacific Railroad of Missouri. Its route lay from St. Louis to the confluence of the Missouri and Kansas rivers on the western border of the state. It was anticipated that the city would soon be served by railroads from the East, and with a railroad already in operation across Missouri, St. Louis would be the logical terminus for the Pacific railroad. Thomas Allen, Colonel John O'Fallon, and Daniel D. Page were the prime movers and the first officers of the Pacific of Missouri. It was Allen who rode across the state and used his oratorical gifts to sell the railroad to hostile farmers. He also directed the drive for private and public subscriptions.

Construction began at St. Louis on Independence Day, 1851, and on December 23, 1852, the *Pacific,* first steam locomotive west of the Mississippi, made its initial run to Cheltenham, five miles away. Late in 1855, the celebration of the linking of St. Louis with the state capital was halted by tragedy when the Gasconade River bridge collapsed under the weight of the train, killing twenty-eight passengers. The Pacific of Missouri reached Syracuse before the outbreak of the Civil War, but it was not to enter Kansas City until October 3, 1865.[1] Meanwhile the Hannibal and St. Joseph, following a route considerably north of the Missouri River, spanned the state early in 1859.

St. Louis favored a Pacific railroad by way of the Kansas River, but a number of Missourians, led by Representative John S. Phelps, joined with Arkansans and western Tennesseans in promoting the Canadian River route. Since there was a possibility that this course might be selected, the legislature authorized the Pacific Railroad to construct a branch running southwest from Franklin, thirty-eight miles from St. Louis, to a point on the state line below the Osage River. The Southwest Branch reached Rolla before the Civil War stopped construction.[2]

Although railroads to the western border held the interest of most Missourians, many St. Louis businessmen were more concerned with reaching the mineral deposits at Iron Mountain. The St. Louis and Iron Mountain secured a new charter in 1851; after it had worked out a compromise with the War Department on crossing lands occupied by the arsenal and Jefferson Barracks, it built rapidly to Pilot Knob.[3]

Missouri and Arkansas jointly sponsored the Cairo and Fulton Railroad. Its promoters, many of them associated with the Iron Mountain, planned to build from the Illinois Central at Cairo, Illinois, to the Red River town of Fulton, Arkansas, which had attracted considerable support as eastern terminus of a southern Pacific railroad. Originally an Arkansas project, the Cairo and Fulton secured a Missouri charter early in 1854 and within two years extended a line from Birds Point, opposite Cairo, west to Buffington.[4]

A new transportation era had arrived. Railroads released St. Louis from complete dependence on waterways, particularly after the bridging of the Mississippi and the arrival of railroads from the East. The city, however, considered the Mississippi the life line of its commerce until well after the Civil War.

[1] 31 Cong., 1 sess., *S. Misc. Doc. 59;* Riegel, "The Missouri . . . 1879," *MHR,* Vol. XVIII, 11–14; Edward J. White, *Past and Future Influence of Railroads on the Development of Missouri,* 3–5.

[2] ICC, *Val. Rep.,* XLI, 498–99.

[3] *Cong. Globe,* 32 Cong., 2 sess., 477–78; App., 369; *ibid.,* 34 Cong., 1 sess., 1107–1108, 1317–21, 1334, 1518, 1539; App., 48; W. J. Thornton, "Early History of Railroads in Missouri," MSHS *Proc., 1902,* 6–7.

[4] ICC, *Val. Rep.,* XL, 408–409, 601–603.

The Birth of Southwestern Railways

The enthusiastic new member of the Union—Texas—stridently demanded a comprehensive transportation system in the fifties. Its citizens were certain that this was the key to prosperity, but there was some opposition. Certain inland towns, fearful of losing their lucrative trade from overland freighting, supported the resistance of stage and freight lines to rail intrusion. Texas itself had plans for developing its waterways, and a number of private companies operated on the network of rivers. These rivals, however, were unable to stem the rising agitation for railroads.

Dancy's proposed state-owned railroad remained a live issue until 1856. E. M. Pease defeated Dancy for the governorship on this issue in 1853, but two years later Pease was re-elected on a platform endorsing Dancy's basic proposal. His highly controversial recommendation for a state-owned co-ordinated system of rail and water transportation failed to be adopted in the state legislature.[5]

Railroads did not develop in proportion to the ambitious plans of their promoters; nevertheless, there were eleven short lines operating in Texas before the Civil War. The objective in practically every case was to reach deep water directly or to provide tap roads to form connections with Gulf ports.

The Buffalo Bayou, Brazos and Colorado, or the "Harrisburg Railroad," was the first to operate in Texas. It was the lineal descendant of Andrew Briscoe's Harrisburg Railroad and Trading Company. In 1847, General Sidney Sherman, an early railroad enthusiast, acquired a large share of Briscoe's property, obtained financial backing in Boston, and secured a charter for a railroad to originate at Harrisburg, serve the Brazos country, and terminate on the Colorado.

Construction began late in 1852, and the road officially opened semiweekly mixed train service between Harrisburg and Stafford's Point (twenty miles) on September 7, 1853. Its locomotive, the *General Sherman*, was the second to operate west of the Mississippi River. A little more than two years later, the rails reached the east bank of the Brazos, opposite Richmond, then crossed the river on a makeshift low-water bridge. On the eve of the Civil War, the line was operating to Alleytown, on the Colorado. The outlook was promising, for there were steamship connections at the one end and a stage line through the wilderness to San Antonio at the other.[6]

[5] McKay, "Texas . . . Railroad," *SHQ*, Vol. XXXV, 7–11; Reed, *Texas Railroads*, 50–52.
[6] P. Briscoe, "The First Texas Railroad," TSHA *Quar.*, Vol. VII, 279–85; ICC, *Val. Rep.*, XXXVI, 428.

Then Came the Railroads

When the Harrisburg Railroad reached Richmond, it began to divert traffic from Houston to Galveston. Houston businessmen were aroused and secured legislative authorization for the city to bond itself up to $100,000 to build the Houston Tap. Within eight months it was operating to its connection at Peirce Junction. A separate enterprise with a similar name, the Houston Tap and Brazoria, drew its support from planters of Brazoria County and the promoters of the Houston and Texas Central. By 1859 it had constructed a line from Peirce Junction to East Columbia over a roadbed built largely by slave labor, with ties and bridge materials furnished by planters in payment for their stock. This railroad did not start operating immediately.[7]

On March 11, 1848, the Galveston and Red River obtained a charter to build from Galveston Bay to some point on the Red River boundary of Texas east of Coffee's Station. Galveston merchants ridiculed promoter Ebenezer Allen as an impractical visionary; Galveston had a water connection with Harrisburg, terminus of the more recently chartered Buffalo Bayou, Brazos and Colorado, which was already penetrating the major agricultural area of the state. Assistance came to Allen from an unexpected quarter when, early in the summer of 1853, farmers from Chappel Hill, sixty-one miles north of Houston, called on Houstonians to talk over with them the problem of how they could best move their crops. A preliminary discussion at Houston resulted in a split between advocates of railroads and of plank roads. The pro-railroad faction, led by Paul Bremond, named the delegates, and the Chappel Hill convention recommended the building of the Galveston and Red River Railroad, with Houston the starting point.

By September, 1856, construction had progressed so far that a mixed train was chugging over the first twenty-five miles between Houston and Cypress. Slowly the road pushed north to Hockley, then to Hempstead, and to Millican, which remained the terminus through the war; meanwhile the name of the railroad was changed to the Houston and Texas Central.[8]

An amendment to the Galveston and Red River charter, providing that it could construct no branches until after its main line had reached the Red, led to the building of the Washington County Railroad. The farmers of Washington County had subscribed to stock in

[7] ICC, *Rep.*, CXLIX, 645; Reed, *Texas Railroads*, 82–83.
[8] ICC, *Val. Rep.*, XXXVI, 578–80, 617.

The Birth of Southwestern Railways

the older corporation on the assumption that the railroad would cross the Brazos twice in order to serve them. The cost of bridging the river was so great that the Galveston and Red River offered to build a branch from Hempstead through Washington County to Austin instead. Since the amended charter postponed all but main-line construction, the Washington County subscribers determined to build a railroad of their own from Hempstead to Brenham. This they did in much the same manner as that used by the builders of the Houston Tap and Brazoria. Short-lived operations between Hempstead and Chappel Hill began early in 1860.[9]

The Galveston, Houston and Henderson was the first attempt of Galvestonians to overcome the initial advantage that their own lackadaisical attitude had permitted to slip away to Houston and Harrisburg. Chartered early in 1853, this road was to penetrate the East Texas timber belt. Though a Galveston enterprise, it was conceived neither as a purely competitive endeavor nor as an instrument for cutting into the territory of existing roads. Before any work began, Houston became interested and subscribed to the stock equally with Galveston. Grading commenced in 1856 at Virginia Point, on the mainland opposite Galveston, and before the Civil War this railroad was operating into Houston. Ferry service into Galveston was unsatisfactory, and the city built a bridge, which was put into service in 1860. The Galveston, Houston and Henderson has remained practically unchanged to the present.[10]

The other ante bellum Texas roads which were of permanent importance were the Southern Pacific (in no way connected with the present Southern Pacific Lines), the Memphis, El Paso and Pacific, the San Antonio and Mexican Gulf, and the Texas and New Orleans.

The Southern Pacific Railroad was a highly speculative venture involving one New York and three Texas charters. Its first Texas charter empowered the Texas Western Railroad, an abortive promotional scheme, to construct a railroad across the state from east to west. In July, 1852, some five months later, a group of promoters including former Secretary of the Treasury Robert J. Walker, former Congressman T. B. King, and Dr. Anson Jones, last president of the Republic of Texas, secured a New York charter for the Atlantic and Pacific Railroad.

Since no positive steps were taken toward building across Texas,

[9] *Ibid.*, 579, 621; Reed, *Texas Railroads*, 73–74.
[10] ICC, *Val. Rep.*, XXXVII, 24–25; Reed, *Texas Railroads*, 76–78.

the state legislature created the Mississippi and Pacific Railroad late in 1853. The charter, together with a large land grant, was to be awarded to the company which could offer the best terms for building the Texas section of a Pacific railroad and which could also post a $300,000 bond to guarantee fulfillment. The Atlantic and Pacific bought the Texas Western charter and was the only bidder for the Mississippi and Pacific. Over a gubernatorial veto, it prevailed on the legislature to renew the Texas Western charter, even though it never posted bond and was guilty of unethical practices which prompted the withdrawal of Dr. Jones. This was done under the new corporate name of Southern Pacific Railroad. The company actually did lay some twenty-three miles of rail between Marshall and Swanson's Landing on Caddo Lake.

The Memphis, El Paso and Pacific was closely associated with the Southern Pacific and, with it, was a parent of the present Texas and Pacific. It was chartered in 1853 as the Texas section of a proposed railroad from Memphis to San Diego. The legislature anticipated that it would serve North Texas and the middle Mississippi area, while the Southern Pacific would serve Central Texas and the South. Since an overflow on the Red made it impossible for the company to bring rails up the river above Jefferson, that city became the temporary eastern terminus. By 1860, five miles of track had been laid, and considerable grading had been done in the direction of Clarksville.[11]

Another railroad which came into being before the war and survived to become a major factor in modern Texas transportation began its corporate life as the Galveston Bay Railroad and Lumber Company, which proposed to tap the timber resources of the Sabine. It was renamed the Texas and New Orleans Railroad Company in 1859. Meanwhile, construction had started from both ends of the road. A line building east from Houston reached Liberty in 1860; one building west from Orange arrived the next year.[12]

The San Antonio and Mexican Gulf dated from 1850. Its promoters hoped to give San Antonio an outlet on Matagorda Bay. Financial difficulties delayed construction until 1856, when a timid beginning was made from Port Lavaca. The road was within two miles of Victoria when, in 1859, it was reorganized because of mismanagement and questionable financing. After Texas seceded from the Union, it

[11] ICC, *Val. Rep.*, XXIX, 579–82; McKay, "Texas . . . Railroad," *SHQ*, Vol. XXXV, 24–26.
[12] ICC, *Val. Rep.*, XXXVI, 510.

did finally reach Victoria, only to be almost completely destroyed during the course of the war.[13]

Of the prewar railroads, the Eastern Texas was the only one which did not survive the conflict. Conceived in 1852 as the Henderson and Burkville, the route, the name, and the ownership changed many times until a group of Beaumont businessmen secured possession, adopted the name Eastern Texas Railroad, and decided to connect Henderson with Sabine Pass. In 1861 the road was placed in operation from its Gulf terminus to Beaumont, with thirty miles graded beyond.[14]

Railroad fever did not burn as brightly in other parts of the Southwest as it did around St. Louis and the Texas Gulf Coast. Louisiana was still wedded to its superb system of waterways. Consequently, most Louisiana schemes were associated with the Pacific railroad, with Vicksburg and New Orleans the potential termini.

Of four rival Louisiana corporations, two were abortive and two were partially completed and in operation at the beginning of the war. The New Orleans, Opelousas and Great Western, chartered in 1852, stretched from Algiers to Lafourche Crossing, fifty-two miles, by November, 1854. Three years later another thirty miles had been completed to Brashear City, on Berwick's Bay, where goods could be transferred to ships bound for Texas ports. Although the grading had reached almost to Opelousas before the war, all attempts to extend the line to the Sabine were futile, despite the efforts of New Orleans to secure an all-rail connection with Texas before Memphis or St. Louis could do so.[15]

The Vicksburg, Shreveport and Texas was a transcontinental project dating from 1853. Before the beginning of the Civil War one segment had been completed from Delta Point, opposite Vicksburg, to Monroe, and another had been started from Shreveport toward the Texas line.[16]

The decade of the fifties was a period of comparative prosperity in Arkansas, which participated in the wave of railroad excitement. Tangible results were far behind enthusiasm, however, since the term "prosperity" was purely relative, applicable to the state only in comparison with its badly impaired credit of earlier years. The first Arkansas projects were conceived as a part of the Pacific railroad, with

[13] *Ibid.*, 399, 436; Reed, *Texas Railroads,* 89–93.
[14] Reed, *Texas Railroads,* 87–89.
[15] ICC, *Val. Rep.*, XXXVI, 670–71, 694.
[16] *Ibid.*, XXVI, 517, 546.

Then Came the Railroads

Cairo, Illinois, Memphis, Tennessee, and Gaines's Landing the most likely eastern termini. In 1851, Arkansas granted a charter to the Mississippi, Ouachita and Red River, projected to run from Gaines's Landing to Fulton. Two years later the Memphis and Little Rock, the Cairo and Fulton, the Arkansas Midland, and the Little Rock and Fort Smith secured charters.

Arkansas placed its chief reliance on the Memphis and Little Rock, which would connect the Arkansas capital with Hopefield, across the river from Memphis. Prospects were bright as the railroad slowly stretched towards the St. Francis River, finally reaching it at Madison early in 1858, just as the railroad ran out of funds. This thirty-eight-mile strip, operated almost entirely over pile trestle bridges through treacherous swamplands, represented the effective mileage of Arkansas at the outbreak of the war. After Arkansas seceded, a road was completed and, according to published advertisements, opened on February 20, 1862, between Little Rock and De Valls Bluff, on White River, with stage and packet service from that point to Madison, where travelers could entrain for Hopefield.[17]

The only other ante bellum construction was the sketchy, unused track of the Mississippi, Ouachita and Red River running from Eunice across overflow lands in the general direction of Bayou Bartholomew.[18]

The depression of 1857 stopped western railroad building short. Some desultory construction continued until the war, but activity was to lag generally until the hectic days of the early seventies. In 1860 Missouri led the southwest with approximately 800 miles of operating roads, followed by Louisiana with 335 (most of which lay east of the Mississippi), and Texas with 307. Arkansas had only 38.

[17] Dallas Herndon, "History of the Little Rock & Memphis Railroad Co.," *RIM*, Vol. XVII, No. 10, 87; F. J. Nevins, "Seventy Years of Service," *RIM*, Vol. XVII, No. 10, 26–27.
[18] Charles E. Brough, "The Industrial History of Arkansas," AHA *Pub.*, Vol. I, 207.

CHAPTER 5

Attractions and Rewards

THE MEAGER railroad mileage of 1860 had been created only by the greatest effort. Enthusiasm alone did not lay track; that required capital. Since the agricultural West was notoriously lacking in present material wealth, cash had to be coaxed from its places of security in the East. Shrewd bankers were not overly impressed with the soundness of transportation enterprises which were designed to penetrate sparsely settled areas and which depended on revenues from anticipated future growth. Additional incentives were needed.

Individualist though he might be, the western pioneer was not averse to securing governmental assistance—national, state, and local—and, incidentally, saddling any or all with a considerable debt. He operated on the assumption that increased productivity, population, and land values would quite rapidly take care of the obligations incurred in attracting capital. Consequently, the western politician was busily engaged in promoting various aid projects, whether his stage was a "mass" meeting in a sparsely settled western township or the halls of Congress. The railroads must be wooed.

It was to the central government that the West first turned for aid. The idea of using federal subsidies to promote railroad building was of recent origin, but the principle was based on precedent dating back to turnpike days. As a matter of fact, the earliest of the internal improvement programs offered limited possibilities to railroads. This was the policy of paying 5 per cent of the net proceeds from the sale of public lands within each state to the state. Three-fifths, the so-called "3 per cent fund," was to be applied to internal improvements within the state; the remainder, the "2 per cent fund," was to be used in promoting transportation to its borders. Congress modified the policy in 1836 by permitting payment of the entire sum to the state.

Most of Missouri's 2 per cent fund had been spent much earlier, but Thomas Hart Benton tried unsuccessfully in the forties to secure payment of the entire amount, contending that his state had received no benefits from the earlier expenditures. His successors did recover what little remained of Missouri's share shortly before the Civil War. It had already been pledged to railroad corporations. At almost the same time, the Arkansas legislature voted to lend $100,000 from its 3 per cent fund to the Memphis and Little Rock Railroad, but had to secure this sum from state revenues when it became known that there was no federal money remaining.[1]

The Pre-emption Act of 1841 provided that nine western states (including Missouri, Arkansas, and Louisiana) and all others admitted into the Union in the future would receive an additional 10 per cent of the net proceeds from the sale of public lands within their respective bounds, and each would be entitled to 500,000 acres to be dedicated specifically to internal development. The federal government also donated large acreages of swamplands. First recommended by Senator Solon Borland of Arkansas in 1848, Louisiana was the first state to secure swamplands. Arkansas and Missouri followed shortly thereafter. The three received about twenty million acres in all, much of which was used to encourage railroad construction.[2]

The movement to secure federal grants of land along the courses of proposed railroads was more direct and of greater importance than the earlier aid programs. The apparently inexhaustible supply of public land appeared to be the best possible substitute for liquid capital. Proponents of this policy could justify their stand on the grounds that the government could double the price of reserved sections and suffer no financial loss; also railroads would increase the value of an area manyfold by encouraging new settlement. The opposition insisted that the constitution acted as a bar to such activity; furthermore, the grants would result in wholesale speculation in public lands. Some eastern congressmen favored what they considered a more

---

[1] Matthias P. Orfield, *Federal Land Grants to the States*, 77-80, 84-85, 90-97; Haney, *A Congressional History of Railways in the United States*, I, 349-53; *Cong. Globe*, 31 Cong., 2 sess., App., 138-41, 173-77.

[2] Orfield, *Federal Land Grants to the States*, 100-102, 112-19; Haney, *A Congressional History of Railways in the United States*, I, 361.

Attractions and Rewards

equitable distribution in which all the states would share; some from the west resisted specific grants which would favor rival areas.

Illinois was the first to achieve success when, in 1850, Congress granted lands to that state to aid in the construction of the Illinois Central. Two years later Missouri secured similar assistance for the Hannibal and St. Joseph, the Pacific of Missouri, and the Southwest Branch. The Pacific and the Branch received an estimated 1,161,255 acres. Within a year Missouri acquired another 200,000 acres for the Cairo and Fulton, while Arkansas was granted well over 1,000,000 acres for the Cairo and Fulton, the Memphis and Little Rock, and the Little Rock and Fort Smith. A period of relative inactivity followed; then Louisiana, among other states, received over 1,500,000 acres, which it dedicated to the building of the Vicksburg, Shreveport and Texas and the New Orleans, Opelousas and Great Western. There were no grants during the Buchanan administration because the President firmly opposed the policy and blocked by veto those bills which did fight their way through Congress.[3]

All the first grants were uniform in pattern: alternate sections extending six miles back on each side of the proposed route, with an additional fifteen-mile strip reserved as indemnity lands in the event the railroad sections were already occupied. The General Land Office would withdraw the lands as the railroads filed their location maps, and title was to pass as each twenty-mile section was completed.

The only other federal aid in the prewar period was a general act of August 4, 1852, which granted railroads hundred-foot rights of way through the public domain, with the privilege of taking earth, stone, and wood from adjacent lands. The act was first limited to ten years but was extended from time to time until it was made permanent in 1875.[4]

The Free Soil platform of 1852, condemning grants to corporations and demanding free lands in limited quantity for bona fide homesteaders, was only a faint harbinger of things to come, drowned in the clamor of the West for more effective transportation.

Railroad enthusiasts did not limit their appeals to the central government alone. State legislatures had much to offer; indeed, they were in many respects a richer field than Congress. Although they had less

---

[3] John B. Sanborn, *Congressional Grants of Land in Aid of Railroads*, 115–17; *Cong. Globe*, 41 Cong., 2 sess., 1902–1904; *Cong. Rec.*, 50 Cong., 1 sess., 5917.
[4] Haney, *A Congressional History of Railways in the United States*, II, 20.

to tender, they usually gave of it more freely. State assemblymen were usually sympathetic listeners, even though they might be interested in rival projects. There was always a good chance that by co-operative effort the sponsors of various railroads could all benefit.

Missouri was the first state to embark on a program of really large proportions. Thomas Allen, state senator and president of the Pacific of Missouri, introduced a bill in 1851 to aid his road and the Hannibal and St. Joseph by means of state loans secured by first mortgages on the properties. The state would issue bonds only after the companies had expended sums equal to the loans. Under the terms of this and similar measures, Missouri issued bonds in excess of $23,000,000, all of which sold somewhat below par. The Hannibal and St. Joseph and the Pacific Railroad were the first to benefit; subsequently, the Southwest Branch, the St. Louis and Iron Mountain, the Cairo and Fulton, and several roads north of the Missouri River received aid.[5]

Gradually Missouri relaxed its safeguards, and aid bills became increasingly speculative. It was difficult for assemblymen to resist pleas such as that of Benjamin W. Grover, who, from the Senate floor, exhorted:

They [the railroad promoters] come as an association of individuals and corporate bodies, who have invested their means, and incurred liabilities to the aggregate amount of over *seven millions* of dollars, in works, the direct effect of which will be to create a value to the State of forty millions of dollars, in lands alone; to make an annual saving in transportation to the farmers of Missouri of over two and a half millions of dollars; to bring to light the immense *mineral wealth of the State;* to bring in emigrants from the older States by hundreds and thousands; to stimulate the industry and exertions of every man in the State, and to cause Missouri to assume her proper position among the members of the Confederacy.[6]

Missouri abandoned its program to all except partially completed lines in 1857. The last aid bill to receive serious consideration passed in the legislature in 1860, only to be vetoed by the governor. The final legislation designed to assist a railroad was an emergency war measure of 1864 which permitted the Pacific of Missouri to issue first mortgage bonds and subordinate the state claims to the position

---

[5] ICC, *Val. Rep.*, XL, 435; *Tenth Census*, VII, 634–39; John W. Million's *State Aid to Railroads in Missouri* is the exhaustive study of this phase of Missouri history.

[6] *Speech of Hon. Benjamin W. Grover, of Johnson County, Delivered in the Senate, Feb. 16, 1855,* 4.

of a second mortgage. Meanwhile, all of the railroads except the Hannibal and St. Joseph defaulted in their interest payments.[7]

After its unfortunate experiences with state aid in the thirties, Louisiana was somewhat more cautious than Missouri. A constitutional revision in 1852, however, did modify the strict prohibition adopted in 1845 against public assistance to railroads. The new provision permitted the state to subscribe up to one-fifth the paid-up stock held privately. Shortly thereafter the legislature declared this to be mandatory. As a result, Louisiana subscribed a total of $1,100,000 to the New Orleans, Opelousas and Great Western, the Baton Rouge, Grosse Tete and Opelousas, and the Vicksburg, Shreveport and Texas, and also generously assisted the roads east of the Mississippi. In 1857, the legislature provided for an internal improvement tax to meet interest payments on the railroad bonds. Before the Civil War, however, reaction against state aid had already set in.[8]

Arkansas was in positive need of railroads but had no means of attracting them. In the late fifties the legislature finally did pass an act directing the governor to subscribe to stock in the Mississippi, Ouachita and Red River and to appoint a state representative on its board.[9]

The state assembly was the key to another important source of credit. Local governments could be only as open handed in their donations as the state dictated. Fortunately for railroad builders, legislators adopted a most generous attitude in allowing political subdivisions to obligate themselves. In 1853, Missouri granted permission to county courts and city councils to subscribe to railroad stock, with the power of raising the necessary funds by bond issue or special taxation. Under this act, the city of St. Louis and St. Louis County jointly subscribed $2,400,000 to railroads entering the city. Less wealthy communities also participated, but to a lesser degree. The city of New Orleans, acting under legislative sanction, took stock in the New Orleans, Opelousas and Great Western to the amount of $1,500,000. Arkansas joined the movement mildly when, in 1858, the legislature granted to Pulaski County and the city of Little Rock the privilege of subscribing to railroad stock.[10]

[7] Meyer, *History of Transportation in the United States before 1860*, 550; Robert E. Riegel, *The Story of the Western Railroads*, 52.

[8] Meyer, *History of Transportation in the United States before 1860*, 476–79; Frederick A. Cleveland and Fred W. Powell, *Railroad Promotion and Capitalization in the United States*, 214–15.

[9] *Acts of Arkansas, 1858–59*, 57.

[10] Missouri General Assembly, *Report of the Joint Committee to Investigate Books*

Then Came the Railroads

Texas pursued an aid policy which was unique, because the state had retained its public lands when it gave up its status as an independent republic. Prior to 1852, Texas granted nine railroad charters with no mention of lands, but in February of that year the legislature provided for a donation to the Henderson and Burkville of eight sections for every mile of railroad it would put in operation within two years. All the earlier charters were then amended to give the same assistance, but with some variation in the time limits.

On June 30, 1854, the Texas legislature enacted a general railroad land-grant law. It provided that every railroad would be entitled to sixteen square miles of unappropriated land for every mile of line constructed, the land to be alternate sections taken from square blocks of not less than thirty-six sections and to be surveyed at railroad expense. Patents would be issued only after twenty-five miles of road had been completed. Each railroad was required to dispose of at least one-quarter of its grant within five years and an additional quarter in consecutive two-year periods thereafter. An amendment to the Memphis, El Paso and Pacific charter of 1856, in terms of general application to all roads, relaxed the conditions and permitted the issuance of land certificates as soon as the grading was finished. Further modifications before the Civil War made it possible for a railroad to receive ten sections for each mile of grading. The ten operating railroads and the one which had completed its initial grading at the time of secession received almost 5,500,000 acres of land, but as late as 1868 only 1,313,504 had actually been patented.

The importance of the Texas land grants in promoting railroad construction before the Civil War was perhaps questionable. To be of value, the land had to be readily marketable, and railroad lands represented only a small fraction of the 116,000,000 acres which the state owned. Loans from the Special School Fund were certainly of more immediate significance. This $2,000,000 fund was set aside from the $10,000,000 the United States paid Texas for relinquishing its claim to western lands. In 1856, the state legislature provided for loans of $6,000 per mile to railroads which had already constructed at least twenty-five miles and were grading beyond that. More than nine-tenths of the fund had been lent to six railroads before the Civil War. This policy was not revived after the war, even though it had

---

and Accounts of the Pacific Railroad Company, 12–13; Riegel, "The Missouri . . . 1879," *MHR,* Vol. XVIII, 8–10; *Acts of Arkansas, 1858–59,* 125; Henry Rightor, *A Standard History of New Orleans, Louisiana,* 302–303.

been reasonably satisfactory both financially and as an incentive to building.

Texas also embarked on a cautious local aid policy. It considered the requests of each railroad individually. The San Antonio and Mexican Gulf charter authorized stock subscriptions by any counties and towns along the line (except those on the coast) to a maximum of $50,000 each. Bexar and Victoria counties and the cities of San Antonio and Victoria subscribed the maximum. Both Victoria County and the city of Victoria protected themselves by specifying that the bonds would be issued only if the railroad crossed the Guadalupe River, which it never did. San Antonio and Bexar County were not so fortunate; they failed to guard their interests, and even though the railroad did not reach them, they were held legally liable for their obligations.

The Buffalo Bayou, Brazos and Colorado received donations from a number of counties it served. In 1856 the city of Houston secured legislative approval for a $100,000 bond issue in favor of the Houston Tap. A few years later Brazoria and Wharton counties each received legislative sanction for bonds to promote the Houston Tap and Brazoria, but in this case the railroad did not fulfill the conditions precedent to payment.[11]

Texas deviated from the normal in one other important respect. Although there was little demand for regulation of railroads in a region pleading for more effective transportation, Texas enacted such legislation. As early as 1850 the state established maximum freight rates and passenger fares in the charter of the Buffalo Bayou, Brazos and Colorado. This remained a standard practice as long as Texas retained the legislative charter system.

The same year the *General Sherman* made its initial run out of Harrisburg, the Texas legislature adopted a comprehensive railroad law, unique in that the law preceded the opening of this first line in point of time. This legislation established certain regulations governing the issuance of securities and prescribed minimum standards of construction, including a minimum gauge of six feet. The state reserved the right to reduce rates if net profits exceeded 12 per cent of the capital stock, and it also reserved the right to purchase any railroad charter after a specified period of time.

Because of the activities of the San Antonio and Mexican Gulf, the

[11] Reed, *Texas Railroads*, 52, 68–83, 91, 98–100, 131–39, 143–49, 183–85; McKay, "Texas . . . Railroad," *SHQ*, Vol. XXXV, 5–8, 11.

Then Came the Railroads

Texas legislature enacted a law in 1857 which was designed to eliminate fraud on the part of railroad officials. It required the officers and a majority of the directors of every company to live in the state, held them personally liable for all corporate debts if they declared a dividend during insolvency, and assessed severe penalties for false reporting of any material facts. This law was also an attempt to protect the rights of creditors and stockholders in case of forced sales.

Supplementary acts of 1860 anticipated many of the problems which were to plague western communities during the postwar period. Carriers were held liable for damages resulting from their refusal to accept goods and for favoritism in the handling of shipments. Railroad officials were prohibited from having a financial interest in the construction companies which were doing the building and from issuing stock other than at par. These laws protected the carriers by permitting the establishment of rates based on minimum weight and authorizing the sale of perishables not removed within a reasonable time. This legislation was substantially embodied in the constitution of 1875.[12]

The only other major regulatory legislation in the Southwest came out of the bitter contest in Missouri over general incorporation. Rural assemblymen insisted to the very end that only through separately enacted charters could the state exercise sufficient supervision and hold "monopolistic" business organization in check. Inevitably their arguments had to fail, and the struggle terminated in 1853 with the passage of a general incorporation law.[13]

The immediate effect of the earliest railroads on population growth was frequently disappointing. There was, however, a tremendous variation in the impact on specific areas. Mature Missouri counties did not benefit appreciably from their new railroads. On the other hand, where the Pacific of Missouri veered away from the river west of Jefferson City, the rate of growth was much greater, and near the western terminus it was far in excess of the state average. Phelps, an interior county served by the Southwest Branch, doubled its population within a few years.

As in the case of Missouri, the older counties of Texas did not show a great proportionate increase in population with the coming of railroads; also, newly opened sections with adequate water trans-

---

[12] Reed, *Texas Railroads,* 52–53, 56, 118–22; McKay, "Texas . . . Railroad," *SHQ,* Vol. XXXV, 5–6.
[13] Kropp, "The Struggle . . . in Missouri," 98–106.

Attractions and Rewards

portation were attractive. There was no striking difference in the rate of growth of interior counties with railroads and those with rivers. In Louisiana, with its fine system of waterways, there was only a slight correlation between population shifts and railroad building. Some increase apparently traceable to railroads could be found in Lafourche and Terre Bonne parishes in the south and possibly in Madison Parish, opposite Vicksburg, Mississippi.[14]

Neither was there the lively activity in town building which many had predicted would follow along the courses of railroads. Kirkwood, a suburban development, and Eureka were platted in the St. Louis area; then, after the Pacific of Missouri swerved to cross the prairie, towns sprang up at the end of track. Tipton enjoyed its brief triumph as terminus of both the railroad and the Butterfield Overland Mail, and was followed by Syracuse before Sedalia replaced them both as a city of permanent importance. The rise of Sedalia illustrated one effect railroads could have on older communities when prosperous Georgetown all but disappeared as the railroad town took its place. Along the Southwest Branch, Pacific, Sullivan, Cuba, and Rolla each boomed briefly as a railroad terminus.

As for town growth in Texas, none of importance can be traced to the prewar railroads. Hockley, Hempstead, and Millican were temporarily important as railheads for the Houston and Texas Central as it pushed north, but they were of brief and local significance. Brashear City, later to be called Morgan City, on the New Orleans, Opelousas and Great Western, and Tallullah, on the Vicksburg, Shreveport and Texas, were the railroad contributions to town building in Louisiana.[15]

The Southwest was to wait until railroads penetrated deeply into areas which had no navigable streams, or which had been condemned to classification as part of the "Great American Desert," before it would witness the magic of transportation in uncovering the wealth which could not be exploited otherwise.

[14] "Statistics on Population," *Tenth Census*, I, 63–64, 68–69, 78–81.
[15] AGS, *Missouri*, 399, 408–12; AGS, *Louisiana*, 392, 480; Reed, *Texas Railroads*, 71.

CHAPTER 6

Rumblings in the Territories

TURBULENT KANSAS was settled under unique conditions. Since the residents themselves would determine whether it would be slave or free under the terms of the Kansas-Nebraska Act. adherents from each of the warring camps flocked into the territory. Lawrence was the parent settlement of the abolitionist New England Emigrant Aid Society, with Topeka, Manhattan, and Emporia the principal offshoots. Pro-slave Missourians, from Platte County for the most part, established themselves at Atchison, Leavenworth, Tecumseh, Lecompton, and Franklin. A number of more or less neutral villages grew up near the eastern end of the California Trail. The population of Kansas swelled from fifteen hundred white inhabitants, including soldiers, to twelve thousand in a period of eighteen months.

The sanguinary events of the next few years, which appropriately earned for the territory the soubriquet "bleeding Kansas," did not obscure the necessity for immediate agitation for railroads. J. W. Whitfield, the proslavery Congressional delegate, demanded public lands to aid possible railroad builders. The territorial legislature granted five railroad charters in 1855 and sixteen more in 1857. It acted favorably on another batch in 1859. Only one railroad, however, was to be in operation at the time of the Civil War. That was a short-lived five-mile line connecting Elwood with Wathena. A number of corporations, notably the Leavenworth, Pawnee and Western and the Atchison and Topeka, eventually built under their ante bellum charters.

Kansas railroad aspirations were intimately tied to the confused, misunderstood, and embittered issue of admission to statehood under the proslavery Lecompton constitution. Admittedly questionable on legal and ethical grounds, but strongly supported by southern advisers close to President Buchanan, the constitution was accepted by the Senate. The House of Representatives voted to resubmit it to the residents of the territory. The solution to the deadlock had to turn on an issue which cut across the explosive slavery problem. A conference committee therefore drafted the English Compromise, which both houses subsequently adopted by narrow margins.

This controversial measure has, until recent years, been interpreted as a bribe in the form of public lands to induce Kansas to accept the constitution. Actually its operation would have been far different. The delegates at Lecompton not only doubled the normal land grant for school purposes, but also generously endowed Kansas with public lands to aid in the building of two railroads, one from the Missouri River to the western line, the other from a point on the northern border down to the Indian Territory. No other state had ever made such a demand in its constitution, and the grant was double the amount which Congress had appropriated to aid in the construction of railroads elsewhere.

The English Compromise struck out the appropriation for railroads and reduced the one for public education to conform with those of other states. The constitution, with this single separate provision, was referred to the voters of Kansas, with the provision that if Kansas rejected the constitution and proposition, it would be denied admission to statehood until it attained a population of 92,243, the average number of constituents in a Congressional district. The most rabid partisan could scarcely interpret the drastic reduction in the demands of Kansas as a bribe in the form of public lands. The final irony in the situation lies in the fact that William H. English, the much maligned author of the "conspiracy," was an anti-Lecompton Democrat who apparently anticipated the decisive rejection of the constitution which followed when it was submitted to the people of the territory.[1]

By 1860, Kansas had a population of over 100,000, most of whom were concentrated on the eastern side of the territory. Interest in railroad promotion had intensified. Edmund G. Ross, at the time a Topeka newspaper editor, suggested a convention to arouse even

[1] Frank H. Hodder, "Some Aspects of the English Bill for the Admission of Kansas," AHA *Ann. Rep., 1906,* 201–10; Ralph Roy Price, "The Lecompton Movement," *Kansas and Kansans,* II, 925–35.

Then Came the Railroads

greater public enthusiasm and to discuss means of securing financial assistance. Here was an issue upon which Missouri slaveholders and New England free-soilers could agree. The convention, meeting at Topeka on October 17, unanimously adopted a resolution requesting Congress to appropriate public lands to aid in the construction of five railroads.[2] The next year, with statehood an accomplished fact, Kansas sent two ardent railroad promoters, James H. Lane and Samuel C. Pomeroy, to the Senate. They pressed vigorously for federal aid, but the Civil War postponed construction in Kansas, as it did in the other southwestern states.

A local railroad, modestly called the Atchison and Topeka, but which was to expand eventually to become a major factor in southwestern history, was conceived in the pre-war period. It was the dream of Cyrus K. Holliday, legislator, townsite promoter, and inveterate railroad builder, who had transferred his promotional talents from Pennsylvania to Kansas. Holliday drafted a charter authorizing the proposed corporation to build a line between the two towns whose name it bore, with the added authority to extend it completely across the state. The legislature accepted the terms without debate and granted the charter on February 11, 1859.

In mid-September, thirteen men gathered at Atchison to organize the company. This original group of incorporators demonstrated the catholicity of interest in the project. Holliday was joined by ardent free-soilers, including Samuel C. Pomeroy and Edmund G. Ross, both later to represent Kansas in the United States Senate, and equally ardent proslavery advocates, including Luther C. Challis, in whose office the company was organized, and J. H. Stringfellow, editor of *Squatter Sovereignty*. Unsettled local conditions, followed by a great civil conflict, discouraged building, and it was to be almost a full decade before an engineer would start laying track for the successor company, the Atchison, Topeka and Santa Fe.[3]

The creation of Kansas established the thirty-seventh parallel as the northern boundary of a greatly reduced Indian Territory. Residents of the bordering states soon became acutely aware of the fact that this last island of Indian-occupied land would remain a constant source of friction because of the removal treaties. White men and their

---

[2] George W. Glick, "The Railroad Convention of 1860," KSHS *Coll.*, Vol. IX, 467–80.
[3] ICC, *Rep.*, CXXVII, 358–59; Glenn D. Bradley, *The Story of the Santa Fe*, 56–58; James L. Marshall, *Santa Fe: the Railroad That Built an Empire*, 30–32, 349, 386.

railroads were barred from the country of the Five Civilized Tribes for "as long as waters run."

The first breach in this paper barrier occurred in 1855, when the Choctaws and Chickasaws agreed to a railroad right of way through their nations. The following year the Creeks and the Seminoles signed a similar agreement. Cherokee leaders stubbornly resisted; nevertheless, their agent, George Butler, expressed the optimistic belief that his charges would donate a right of way and might possibly give monetary assistance to a railroad crossing their lands to connect the Southwest Branch with the proposed Southern Pacific railroad.[4]

Butler's attitude is not understandable in light of the reaction of the Cherokees to two proposals which preceded his recommendation by a few months. In January, 1857, Governor John W. Geary of Kansas had called on the legislative assembly to consider the advisability of a railroad across the Territory of Kansas in the direction of Galveston Bay. Such a road would cut the distance to a deep-sea port in half and would drive a wedge into the Indian Territory. Geary suggested that Kansas co-operate with Nebraska Territory and Texas in promoting the scheme. Robert J. Walker, Geary's successor and a railroad promoter in his own right, was even more enthusiastic about a Gulf route. At his inaugural on May 27, 1857, he painted a glowing picture of the possibilities of a railroad through the Indian Territory to Galveston, with connections serving Arkansas and New Orleans to the east, and the Pacific Coast to the west. Of course this would violate the Indian treaties, but they would no more be permitted to stand in the way of railroads and agrarian expansion than similar treaties had in the past.

Walker's intemperate remarks, following those of Geary, were so disturbing that John Ross, the able principal chief of the Cherokees, warned the Commissioner of Indian Affairs that the speeches had aroused the apprehension of all tribes in the Indian Territory.[5]

Economic depression and war diverted attention from railroad projects in the West. Kansas vainly attempted to attract investors, while Indian Territory was not forced to fight too vigorously to bar their entrance.

---

[4] Charles J. Kappler, *Indian Affairs: Laws and Treaties*, II, 710, 762; *Rep. Comm. Ind. Aff., 1857*, 201.

[5] John G. Gihon, *Geary and Kansas*, 321–22, 336, 341; *Rep. Comm. Ind. Aff., 1857*, 218–23.

CHAPTER 7

The War Years—and After

THE CIVIL WAR had a dual effect on southwestern railroads. On the one hand, it put a strain on existing lines, demonstrating the need for a comprehensive transportation system; on the other, it led to their destruction, since they lay in the zone of combat. The distress arising from physical damage was aggravated by the unfortunate association of postwar rehabilitation with Radical Reconstruction.

Troops guarded the Missouri lines most of the time, but they could not prevent sabotage by Southern sympathizers. Judge David Davis, chairman of a committee to study conditions in Missouri, reported that all the railroads had suffered such heavy damage to rolling stock and bridges that relief must be given if they were to continue to operate. Accordingly, on March 6, 1862, Congress exempted the land-grant roads of Missouri from the "free from any tolls" clause by permitting a reasonable charge for the handling of government shipments. Four months later President Lincoln authorized the Union Army to take over the Southwest Branch. The last Confederate raid on railroads in the state took place late in 1864 when General Sterling Price's forces did extensive damage to the Pacific of Missouri as far west as Warrensburg.[1]

Except for the slow westward progress of the Pacific, wartime construction in Missouri was confined to repairs and replacements.

The other railroads of the Southwest lay in the Confederate states.

---

[1] *Cong. Globe,* 37 Cong., 2 sess., 604–605, 708–10, 805–13, 859–60, 918–25; *U.S. Stat. at L.,* XII, 422, 614; Richardson, *A Compilation of the Messages and Papers of the Presidents,* VI, 116; Thornton, "Early . . . Missouri," MSHS *Proc., 1902,* 6.

The War Years—and After

Lines along the Mississippi necessarily suffered as a result of the struggle for control of the river. Those in Arkansas were patched up after they had been almost completely wrecked. Although the Louisiana railroads were of vital importance in moving men and supplies from the trans-Mississippi South, Confederate troops were compelled to destroy the line from Delta Point to Monroe to keep it from falling into Union hands. The Confederacy was concerned with linking Texas to the Mississippi by rail. Its congress authorized a loan of $1,500,000 to the New Orleans, Opelousas and Great Western to close the gap between Berwick's Bay and Orange, but with the fall of New Orleans the project collapsed. When the area it served came under the control of the Union Army, it was taken over and operated by the United States government until January 31, 1866.[2]

Far removed from the center of conflict, Texas was not harassed except for minor operations along the Gulf. Most of the railroads continued to operate, although their service was irregular. The Texas and New Orleans was used extensively until the supply line into the Confederacy was shattered. General Magruder kept the Galveston, Houston and Henderson in particularly good repair as an essential part of the defense of Galveston, and used it, in January, 1863, to recapture Galveston after the city had passed briefly into Union hands. Texas railroads did not, however, survive the war without widespread damage at the hands of Confederates in the interest of defense. The only casualty was the Eastern Texas, which was permanently abandoned after Dick Dowling took up its rails to build a fort at Sabine Pass. The rails of the Texas and New Orleans between Orange and Beaumont suffered the same fate, while the fourteen-mile strip of the Southern Pacific between Swanson's Landing and Jonesville was torn up and relaid in the direction of Shreveport. General Magruder ordered a substantial part of the San Antonio and Mexican Gulf destroyed after Corpus Christi fell to keep it from falling into the hands of Union soldiers. The other railroads escaped planned destruction, but all came out of the war in a sad state of disrepair.[3]

The recent Confederate States suffered greatly from the aftereffects of the conflict. The lethargy which followed the ending of hostilities was as disheartening as the physical damage. Although the population

[2] ICC, *Val. Rep.*, XXVI, 517, 546; *Poor's Manual, 1869–70*, 187; Charles W. Ramsdell, "The Confederate Government and the Railroads," *AHR*, Vol. XXII, 802; Prichard, "A Forgotten ... Engineer," *LHQ*, Vol. XXX, 1128, 1162–63, 1166, 1182–83, 1186; John Gould Fletcher, *Arkansas*, 182, 199.

[3] ICC, *Val. Rep.*, XXIX, 580; *ibid.*, XXXVI, 510, 670–71; Reed, *Texas Railroads*, 86–89, 122–27, 352.

Then Came the Railroads

of the United States increased by 22 per cent, Louisiana remained static, and Arkansas developed exactly half as rapidly as the nation as a whole. Texas' population increased by 35 per cent, but that was a far cry from the growth of the fifties, especially since much of its vast area was awaiting development. Missouri, in spite of its maturity, grew more rapidly than its southern neighbors, while the new state of Kansas showed a 240 per cent increase.[4]

Proud New Orleans experienced a postwar inertia which was only partially accounted for by the numbing shock of military defeat; before that disaster new routes of commerce had already started siphoning off the grain from the northern Mississippi Valley. Soon much of the cotton from territory previously tributary to the city would be moving east over railroads. Helplessly and hopelessly the great southern port watched the number of untenanted business buildings grow as the city passed into eclipse. The railroad parishes along the river, having borne the brunt of the war and the collapse of the plantation system, declined.

The rebuilding of railroads in the war-torn South was intimately tied to Radical Reconstruction. Arkansas and Louisiana suffered from legislation developed in the interest of political soldiers of fortune. Both witnessed the spectacular growth of their state debts with relatively little to show for the lavish expenditures. Texas alone escaped the worst effects of extreme "reconstruction."

Arkansas was the first to be drawn into the current. In spite of constitutional limitations on such activities, the provisional government attempted to pledge the state's credit to aid railroads. Governor Isaac Murphy, an antisecessionist Arkansan appointed by Lincoln, advocated the restoration of state credit and blocked speculative legislation at the cost of his own political future. By 1868, however, no one could resist the assaults on the treasury.

The Arkansas constitution of 1868 permitted state and local aid, but even before its adoption the legislature passed a measure providing bonds in the amount of $10,000 and $15,000 per mile for land-grant and non-land-grant railroads respectively, to a maximum of 850 miles of railroad and $10,000,000 assistance. All loans were to be secured by a first mortgage on the property. The newly created Board of Railroad Commissioners was to designate the roads to receive loans. By May, 1870, thirty-five new companies proposed to build six thousand miles of railroad. The Little Rock and Fort Smith, the

[4] "Statistics on Population," *Tenth Census*, I, 50, 60–61, 63–64, 68–69, 78–81.

The War Years—and After

Memphis and Little Rock, the Little Rock, Pine Bluff and New Orleans, the Mississippi, Ouachita and Red River, and the Arkansas Central actually received $5,350,000. The Cairo and Fulton would accept no benefits after its unfortunate experiences with state aid in Missouri.

Despite a rapidly rising debt which was already in default, legislation in 1869 provided for payment by the state of interest on railroad bonds. Four years later an act provided that practically all forfeited railroad lands in Arkansas would revert to eleven railroads, reflecting their passage into the hands of three politically powerful syndicates—Senator Stephen W. Dorsey and friends, the Rice brothers and Joseph Brooks, and the Denckla associates.

Since the session of 1873 was the last under carpetbag control, it was also the last to adopt railroad-aid measures. The following year the legislature repealed the acts of 1869 and 1873. A new state constitution guaranteed payment of the outstanding bonds but prohibited lending state or local credit in the future.

Meanwhile, promoters had not overlooked the possibilities of local aid. Various counties contributed $100,000 each to a number of different corporations, and city contributions swelled the total. In this respect, however, Arkansas' experience was no different from that of other western states which did not secede and which were never subjected to alien control.

The railroads of Arkansas were undoubtedly in need of rehabilitation at the end of the war, but the fraudulent methods used by both legislators and builders cost them dearly. Promoters frequently took their profits and then washed their hands of both the state and the railroad, leaving both bankrupt. In some cases the rails laid to qualify for one aid program were taken up and relaid elsewhere to qualify under another. Some corporations which had no intention of building secured state assistance.

Arkansas had come out of the war with two segments of the Memphis and Little Rock Railroad. The linking of these two disconnected parts by construction between De Valls Bluff and Madison was the most important achievement of the carpetbag period. After April 11, 1871, daily train service was available from Hopefield to Huntersville, across the river from Little Rock, except for those frequent occasions when high water forced discontinuance of service east of Madison. The capital city secured its direct connection two years later with the completion of the Baring Cross bridge.

Then Came the Railroads

The Little Rock and Fort Smith revived during Reconstruction and by 1871 reached Lewisburg. It had almost reached the coal fields at Clarksville before the panic of 1873 halted construction. The Arkansas Central, a consolidation of the Arkansas Midland and the Little Rock and Helena, built a road from Helena to Clarendon between 1870 and 1873, and the Mississippi, Ouachita and Red River completed its road from Chicot to Collins. In 1870, the Arkansas Central consolidated with a new corporation—the Little Rock, Pine Bluff and New Orleans, operating from Pine Bluff to Chicot—under the name Texas, Mississippi and Northwestern.[5]

The carpetbag government of Louisiana endowed railroads very generously. It endorsed second mortgage bonds of the New Orleans, Mobile and Texas, at the rate of $12,500 per mile, to a total of $875,000. The North Louisiana and Texas received similar aid in excess of $1,000,000. The state also traded $2,500,000 worth of its bonds for second mortgage bonds of the New Orleans, Baton Rouge and Vicksburg. All this assistance was given under highly suspicious circumstances. The presiding officer of the lower house of the legislature reputedly realized financial benefits from every railroad measure passed. One witness testifying before a Congressional committee complained that he spent $80,000 getting a bill through the legislature, only to find that the governor's signature was even more expensive.

Carpetbag control in Louisiana continued until early 1877. Two years later a new state constitution denied the general assembly and local governments the power to pledge their credit or funds or to subscribe to the stock of any corporation.

The results of the extravagant expenditures in Louisiana were even more disappointing than those in Arkansas. The New Orleans, Mobile and Texas advanced only to the grading stage west of the Mississippi before passing into the hands of receivers. The receivers continued to build slowly westward and were operating from Westwego to Bayou Goula when Charles Morgan, who was just beginning to create his Louisiana and Texas system, acquired the road. This spectacular

---

[5] *Acts of Arkansas, 1873,* 459–61, 475; Const. of Arkansas (1875), Art. V, sec. 33 and Art. XII, secs. 5 and 7; 51 Cong., 1 sess., *H. Ex. Doc. 6,* Part 2, 46, 48; ICC, *Val. Rep.,* XL, 411, 449–51, 606–609, 615–17, 643–45; *Poor's Manual, 1878,* 994; Powell Clayton, *Aftermath of the Civil War in Arkansas,* 237–50; Thomas S. Staples, *Reconstruction in Arkansas,* 350–56; Charles Nordhoff, *The Cotton States in the Spring and Summer of 1875,* 30–33; Samuel W. Moore, "State Supervision of Railroad Transportation in Arkansas," AHA *Pub.,* Vol. III, 17–20; from *SBN:* Fay Hempstead, "Arkansas from 1861 to 1909," III, 323–24; Charles H. Brough, "The State Finances of Arkansas," VI, 483.

operator was not a newcomer to the Southwest. He had risen rapidly from grocery clerk to fruit importer before he began to pioneer coastal steamship lines. Morgan vessels were serving Galveston while Texas was still a part of Mexico, and at the outbreak of the Civil War he was the dominant figure in Gulf shipping. At the time of his entrance into the Gulf railroad field, he was the largest shipowner in America. He added the New Orleans, Opelousas and Great Western to his holdings and constructed a branch from Schriever to Houma.

The Vicksburg, Shreveport and Texas was foreclosed shortly after the war, with the North Louisiana and Texas as the successor corporation. The new company rebuilt the entire road and completed the segment between Shreveport and the Texas line, but the Supreme Court of the United States voided its title on the grounds of fraud, thus forcing the railroad back into receivership.

Although its avowed purpose was to construct a railroad across Louisiana to Marshall, Texas, the New Orleans, Baton Rouge and Vicksburg, commonly called the "Backbone Company," was merely a promotional scheme to acquire public lands and other favors. Its scant physical properties were secured by purchase in 1870 when it took over the Louisiana Central Stem, successor to the Baton Rouge, Grosse Tete and Opelousas. The original company had haltingly laid a few miles of rail between the Mississippi and Grosse Tete and in the vicinity of the Atchafalaya River.[6]

Louisiana and Arkansas were among the erstwhile Confederate states which eventually escaped payment of a portion of their carpetbag indebtedness. Arkansas repudiated much of its railroad debt as the corrupt creation of "alien adventurers." Louisiana eventually worked out a reasonably satisfactory compromise with railroad bondholders which resulted in the funding of the "valid debt" after it had been scaled down substantially.[7]

Reconstruction did not weigh so heavily on Texas as it did on most of the Southern states. The constitution of 1868 did change the land policy. It forbade the use of the public domain as an aid to the construction of railroads, although some adjustments were made in favor

---

[6] Const. of Louisiana (1879), Art. XLIV; William P. Kellogg, *Fourth Annual Message*, 21–25; ICC, *Val. Rep.*, XXVI, 545–46; *ibid.*, XXIX, 582–84; *ibid.*, XXXVI, 670–71, 691–92, 694; "Valuation, Taxation, and Public Indebtedness," *Tenth Census*, VII, 598–600; Prichard, "A Forgotten . . . Engineer," *LHQ*, Vol. XXX, 1120, 1170–79, 1192–1209, 1213–1325; Nordhoff, *The Cotton States in the Spring and Summer of 1875*, 58.

[7] *Poor's Manual, 1876–77*, 886; William A. Scott, *The Repudiation of State Debts*, 107–27, 215–17, 276–78.

Then Came the Railroads

Railroads of the Gulf Southwest in 1860

Based on a map from the Association of American Railroads

The War Years—and After

of existing grants. The state government, however, did not abandon railroads to their own devices; it substituted direct aid in the form of bonds, to be supplied at the discretion of the legislature. Several railroads attempted to take advantage of this provision, and the International, the Southern Pacific, and the Southern Transcontinental almost succeeded.

The legislature approved $10,000 per mile for the International, the bonds to be delivered as each twenty miles was completed. The other two companies secured the passage of an act over the governor's veto which provided that together they would receive a maximum of $6,000,000. None of this aid materialized. The state comptroller refused to recognize the legality of the International bonds, and the courts held the other act invalid after all the railroads were charged with gross fraud. Eventually the state did grant to each of these corporations twenty sections of land for each mile of construction.

The only other direct aid given to Texas railroads benefited only one. By the terms of the compromise which converted its direct subsidy to lands, the International was exempted from taxation for a period of twenty-five years. The state legislature offered tax exemption to the Missouri, Kansas and Texas for two years if it would build at least fifty miles within a three-year period and would reach Austin within six years; further, it would have the option of paying 2 per cent of its earnings in the state of Texas in lieu of taxes after the period of complete exemption had passed. Its failure to meet the terms deprived the Katy of these privileges.

A constitutional amendment of 1872 replaced direct aid with land grants and re-established the earliest Texas policy of considering each request individually. The panic of 1873 limited the number of railroads which took advantage of the amendment.

After the temporary abandonment of the land-grant policy in 1868, the pressure to legalize local aid became very strong. An act of 1871 authorized cities and counties to give financial aid to railroads serving them directly if the bonds and the tax levies to retire them were approved at the polls. During the relatively short life of this measure, Smith and Anderson counties and the cities of Sherman, Dallas, Waco, Jefferson, McKinney, Waxahachie, and Tyler donated more than one million dollars to five railroads.

The restoration of "conservative" control in Texas did not lead to a too drastic revision of state policy. In time a general law granting sixteen sections of land for each mile of construction by any railroad replaced the policy of considering each request individually. Furthermore, the brief excursion into the field of local aid ended in 1874, and the constitution of 1876 put it beyond the power of all political subdivisions of the state to grant monetary aid or to extend credit to any individual or corporation.

In Texas, more than any other Southern state, the war was merely an interlude, at the end of which builders picked up the strands of transportation where they had been dropped in 1860. Some of the roads, however, were unable to throw off the effects of the war immediately. Misfortune dogged the Galveston, Houston and Henderson for a number of years. The Texas and New Orleans floundered helplessly until its receiver, Josiah F. Crosby, rebuilt the road from Houston to West Liberty in order that it could resume operation. Attempts to rehabilitate the Buffalo Bayou, Brazos and Colorado exhausted that company financially. All these roads came under the control of a Boston syndicate headed by Thomas W. Peirce. All retained their original identity except the Buffalo Bayou, Brazos and Colorado, which was reorganized in 1870 as the Galveston, Harrisburg and San Antonio.

The San Antonio and Mexican Gulf was a physical wreck. Since many of its stockholders had been Union sympathizers, Federal troops rebuilt the line between Victoria and Port Lavaca. This merely increased the indebtedness of a road which had never proved profitable. Efforts to enlist English capital failed, and in 1870 it was sold to Charles Morgan.[8]

The Civil War was a source of unmixed evil for the Five Civilized Tribes. Drawn into a conflict in which they had no interest, they were not even given the opportunity of choosing their allies. States to the east and to the south had seceded; Kansas Territory was precariously attached to the Union until the allegiance of the border state of Missouri could be determined. The Indian superintendent hastily withdrew his headquarters to Kansas. John Ross used his influence to prevent the Cherokees from seceding, while waiting in vain for assurance from Washington that the Indians would be protected. When no word came, he reluctantly yielded to the pressures which forced the Cherokees to align themselves with the Confederacy until such

---

[8] Const. of Texas (1876), Art. III, secs. 48–51; ICC, *Rep.*, CXLIX, 641; ICC, *Val. Rep.*, XXXVI, 436–37, 510, 533; *Poor's Manual, 1871–72*, 159; Charles S. Potts, *Railroad Transportation in Texas*, 87–89; Reed, *Texas Railroads*, 132–34, 148–52, 155–60, 210, 216, 258–63, 358–64, 377; Edmund T. Miller, "The State Finances of Texas," *SBN*, VI, 519–22.

time as the Ross faction could reassert its loyalty to the Union. Only the Choctaws and Chickasaws acted with virtual unanimity in adhering to the Southern cause.

Railroad projects, revived following the Civil War, were in a more favorable position than before because the divided allegiance of the tribes furnished a legal excuse for reconsidering the terms of their treaties. A concerted effort was underway to force the establishment of a regularly organized territorial government, and Indians had to make their peace with three Iowans who had little sympathy for any Indians, and none whatever for those they considered disloyal.

Indian representatives were summoned to Fort Smith in September, 1865, for preliminary negotiations. An unofficial group of railroad speculators hovered about to see that their interests were not overlooked. The first session was with the Indians who had remained loyal to the United States or who had been allied with the Confederacy only briefly. Commissioner of Indian Affairs Dennis N. Cooley lost no time in informing the shocked Indian delegates that punishment would fall on all alike. The disloyal Indians appeared next. Colonel Elias C. Boudinot, their spokesman, was much more amenable to the suggestions of Cooley than the loyal, or Ross, faction. Most of the negotiations, therefore, were carried on with those who had favored the Confederacy.

The final terms were arranged in Washington. None but the Cherokees were in a position to bargain over the right of railroads to cross their lands, because the other tribes merely reaffirmed their concessions of 1855 and 1856. As a result, railroad interests concentrated their attention on this one treaty.

Soon after the adjournment of the Fort Smith council, Boudinot appeared in Washington as the spokesman for the pro-Southern Cherokees. Although he had no official standing, he wielded considerable influence through Senator Daniel W. Voorhees. Cooley reported that Boudinot responded very liberally to railroad promoters, even to the extent of offering them lands in the territory. The official Cherokee delegation, on the other hand, refused to accede to the request for such grants, giving as their reason the intrusion of whites which would follow. They disclaimed any authority to bargain away any lands, but finally, on July 18, 1866, they did sign a treaty granting one two-hundred-foot right of way across their nation from north to south, and another from east to west.

Some actions of Congress during the period of negotiation indicated

Then Came the Railroads

the close affiliation between the treaties and railroad promotion. The parleys in Washington were scarcely under way before Senator Lane introduced a bill anticipating the terms by providing for the Leavenworth, Lawrence and Fort Gibson to cross the Indian Territory. This measure was later consolidated with those of rival companies and, as enacted, gave one railroad a right of way across the Indian Territory from the Kansas line to Red River. The bill providing for the Atlantic and Pacific to run westwardly through Indian lands passed within a week after the Cherokees signed their treaty.[9]

It was probably inevitable that the Indians would be forced to agree to the demands of southwestern states for railroad rights of way across tribal lands. The sections of the railroad acts dealing with conditional land grants, however, cannot be justified on any grounds. Section 9 of the Kansas Railroad Act provided:

> That the same grants of land through said Indian Territory are hereby made as provided in the first section of this act, whenever the Indian title shall be extinguished by treaty or otherwise, not to exceed the ratio granted in the first section of this act; *Provided,* that said lands shall become a part of the public lands of the United States.[10]

The first section had granted the railroads lands in Kansas.

The Atlantic and Pacific measure was even more strongly worded. It not only provided for conditional land grants in the Indian Territory, but added:

> The United States shall extinguish, as rapidly as may be consistent with public policy, and the welfare of the Indians, and only by their voluntary consent, the Indian title to all lands falling under the operation of this act and acquired in the donation to the road named in the act.[11]

These provisions were wholly unwarranted and changed completely the character of all future dealings between the Indians and the railroads. At a time when it was most necessary to promote the

---

[9] *Rep. Comm. Ind. Aff., 1865,* 32–41, 254–74, 313–54; *Reply of the Delegation of the Cherokee Nation to the Commissioner of Indian Affairs,* 4–6; *Cong. Globe,* 39 Cong., 1 sess., 1100–1103, 2737–38, 2819–21, 3008–3010, 3278–80, 3334–36, 3502–3503, 4058–65, 4182–83; Kappler, *Indian Affairs,* II, 910–15, 918–37, 942–50; *U.S. Stat. at L.,* XIV, 236, 289, 292, 338; Annie H. Abel, *The American Indian under Reconstruction,* 166–68; Morris L. Wardell, *A Political History of the Cherokee Nation,* 185–86, 194–95, 200; Theodore S. Case, *History of Kansas City, Missouri,* 139–40.

[10] *U.S. Stat. at L.,* XIV, 236.

[11] *Ibid.,* 292.

friendliest possible relations between the two, the railroads were in the position of being natural enemies of the Indians. The Indians could justifiably regard with suspicion all actions by corporations which would benefit so enormously by the liquidation of tribal autonomy. As a matter of self-preservation, the Civilized Tribes had to maintain delegates in Washington to guard their interests. The net result of the railroad acts was to create a united Indian opposition to all projects looking towards the slightest change in their status, because there was always the threat that such innovations would lead to the handing over of tribal lands to railroad corporations.

CHAPTER 8

Down to the Gulf

THE FIVE-YEAR period ending in 1873 was one of feverish railroad building in the United States. Roads to the Pacific, roads to the Gulf, connecting lines, and lines into undeveloped areas were pushed ahead of settlement in the expectation that they would create their own traffic by inducing settlement. When domestic capital could not meet the demand, a ready money market was available in western Europe. The wild enthusiasm could not fail to attract speculators whose reckless financing was to be called to the attention of investors so painfully at the end of the spree.

Kansas was a perfect example of the railroad mania which seized the country. Before the panic year, two railroads reached its western boundary and three its southern boundary. One of the most cherished of Kansas aspirations was a rail connection with the Gulf. Three corporations were organized for the purpose of building such a line. Leavenworth and Kansas City in particular supported the activities of two of the rivals. Thomas Carney, war governor of Kansas, and Senator James H. Lane, of Lawrence, represented the interests of Leavenworth, while Robert T. Van Horn, editor of the Kansas City *Enterprise,* and Colonel Kersey Coates drew about them a group of public-spirited citizens to champion their city.

Leavenworth supported the Leavenworth, Lawrence and Galveston, a speculative venture dating from 1858 under a different name. As the interest of Leavenworth waned, Lawrence took up the cause of this road and in time was designated the northern terminus. Its Kansas City rival also had antecedents in the prewar period. In 1856, citizens of the village of Osawatomie organized a railroad company to build to the Gulf. The project remained dormant until the summer of 1865, when Coates and Van Horn revived it as a Kansas City civic enterprise under the name Kansas and Neosho Valley. The third of the rivals, the Union Pacific, Southern Branch, drew its support from Coffey County, Kansas, where, on September 20, 1865, articles of incorporation were drafted for a company to construct and operate a railroad from the vicinity of Fort Riley Military Reservation to the Indian Territory line.

In anticipation of the Indian treaties, proponents of the three routes introduced bills in Congress to secure rights of way through the Indian Territory for their respective lines. The location of tribal lands, however, was such that it limited to one the number of railroads which could enter from Kansas. Under the terms of acts passed on July 25 and 26, 1866, the three were literally to race across Kansas. The first to reach the southern border of the state within the limits of the Neosho Valley would be entitled to the right of way and a conditional land grant.

This legislation furnished the incentive but not the capital. Colonel Coates assumed responsibility for interesting eastern investors in the Kansas City road. He approached James F. Joy, a Detroit railroad promoter bent on creating the first great midwestern system, with the support of Boston capital. To his extensive holdings, including the Michigan Central, the Chicago, Burlington and Quincy, and the Hannibal and St. Joseph, Joy now added the Kansas and Neosho Valley. It would give him a Gulf connection and possession of Indian lands which the company owned in Kansas. On June 15, 1868, the Kansas City city council transferred its interest to Joy, who renamed the railroad the Missouri River, Fort Scott and Gulf. The Leavenworth road, which had turned to Chicago for backing, likewise attracted Joy's attention; he took possession of it as well.[1]

Indian lands in Kansas proved to be an embarrassment to Joy. Both of his railroads were involved—the Missouri River, Fort Scott and Gulf with the Cherokee Neutral Lands in southeastern Kansas, the Leavenworth, Lawrence and Galveston with the Osage Ceded Lands.

---

[1] 41 Cong., 2 sess., *H. Rep. 33;* 47 Cong., 1 sess., *S. Rep. 208;* ICC, *Val. Rep.*, XXXIV, 397; *ibid.*, XLI, 369–71; *U.S. Stat. at L.*, XIV, 236, 289, 292; M, K & T Ry. Co., *Missouri, Kansas and Texas Railway Company*, 21–33; Case, *History of Kansas City, Missouri*, 139–46; Charles P. Deatherage, *Early History of Greater Kansas City*, 487–89, 583, 598–99; Richard L. Douglas, "History of Manufactures in the Kansas District," KSHS *Coll.*, Vol. XI, 102–104.

Then Came the Railroads

The Cherokees had agreed to sell their Neutral Lands to the United States in 1866. Secretary of the Interior Harlan disposed of this tract by treaty to the American Emigrant Company, a Connecticut corporation. O. H. Browning, Harlan's successor, voided the sale, and on October 9, 1867, secured the lands for Joy. The Commissioner of Indian Affairs then made a supplementary treaty with the Cherokees which validated the sale to the emigrant company, set aside the Joy transaction, and assigned the original contract to Joy. The first arrangement provided for long-term credit, the second for cash. Apparently, the reasons for validation of the first transaction were to relieve Joy from having to raise the full purchase price immediately and to deprive some three thousand settlers who had entered the Neutral Lands between the negotiation of the original and supplementary treaties of any legal title which they might have acquired.

The Leavenworth, Lawrence and Galveston was engaged in similar activities farther west. On September 29, 1865, the Osages ceded the eastern portion of their reservation to the railroad in a treaty ratified by the Senate more than a year later. During the interim, squatters occupied much of both the ceded and unceded Osage lands. In the midst of the dispute over who held the title, the Commissioner of Indian Affairs negotiated another treaty whereby the Osages disposed of their diminished reserve and their trust lands, eight million acres in all, to the Leavenworth, Lawrence and Galveston for $1,600,000, payable in thirty-two semiannual installments. This treaty was never ratified by the Senate.

Western spokesmen in Congress immediately attacked the treaties on the grounds that the Indians had no title except the right of occupancy, and that the disposition of public lands by treaty was usurpation of a Congressional function. A spokesman for the House Committee on Indian Affairs asserted that the terms were agreed upon without the knowledge of the Osages, who were forced to accept. The committee also found that a second railroad company had offered more money and better terms, but the commission had "peremptorily dismissed" this bid.

The House of Representatives adopted a series of resolutions denying the power of the Senate to dispose of lands by treaty and condemning the Osage negotiations. The *Cincinnati Gazette* and the *New York Tribune* accused Harlan and others of corruptness in the transaction, and Representative George W. Julian of Indiana branded the Osage treaty as an outright swindle by a commission picked especially for the job.

Down to the Gulf

While the legal aspects were under consideration in Congress and in the courts, the settlers on the Osage lands, in true western fashion, organized the Settlers' Protective Association. Those on the Neutral Lands organized the Neutral Lands Home-Protecting Corps, or the Land League. The Neutral Lands group was particularly violent. On July 4, 1868, Joy visited Baxter Springs, one of the few places in southeastern Kansas which viewed him with favor. On his departure he escaped from a posse only because it lost his trail. As time passed, organized violence increased. In late April, 1869, a party of railroad engineers was attacked, its members beaten, and their wagons and instruments burned. On several occasions the settlers burned railroad ties, took by force the returns of assessors who had listed railroad lands for taxation, and intimidated railroad employees. The railroad land agent at Columbus, a town set up by the settlers as a rival to Baxter Springs, was forced to leave the community, and the agent's office at Baxter Springs was raided.

After all the violence, the conflict over the Neutral Lands title was settled in favor of Joy by the Supreme Court of the United States. The Osage settlement involved a series of separate actions. The United States was substituted for the railroad as purchaser, and each settler was permitted to buy a quarter-section of land at $1.25 per acre.[2]

Meanwhile the Joy roads were building south. Hostile Neutral Lands settlers blocked the path at every turn, and the federal government finally had to furnish military protection. Despite impediments thrown in his way, Joy was able to report on April 30, 1870, that the Missouri River, Fort Scott and Gulf had reached the Indian Territory line south of Baxter Springs, fifteen miles east of the Neosho River. His own actions, however, did what the settlers had been unable to do—disqualified him from claiming the coveted right to cross the Indian Territory. In order to build through the Neutral Lands, he had been forced to diverge from the original route. On May 21, the Secretary of the Interior notified Joy that he had failed to qualify because his southern terminus was not in the Neosho Valley; further, the government had no power to grant right of way across the Quapaw reservation, which lay immediately south of his railhead.

The Union Pacific, Southern Branch, youngest contender for the

---

[2] 40 Cong., 2 sess., *H. Ex. Docs. 59, 85,* and *310* and *H. Rep. 63;* 40 Cong., 3 sess., *H. Misc. Doc. 49* and *S. Misc. Docs. 33* and *34;* 41 Cong., 2 sess., *H. Rep. 53* and *H. Misc. Doc. 150;* 44 Cong., 1 sess., *H. Misc. Doc. 167,* 224–54; *U.S. Stat. at L.,* XVI, 55, 362; Kappler, *Indian Affairs,* II, 878, 996; Eugene Ware, "The Neutral Lands," KSHS *Coll.,* Vol. VI, 154–68.

Then Came the Railroads

Indian Territory right of way, was declared the successful claimant. Faced with the same financial difficulties as other Kansas railroads, it was only five miles south of Junction City, its northern terminus, by 1869. The Cherokees, jealous of any outside influence within their nation, considered buying enough stock in the company to be represented on its board of directors, but abandoned the idea after it appeared that the road would never reach the Indian Territory. The road's Kansas incorporators finally succeeded in attracting a group of New York investors, after which building began in earnest. In April, 1870, the name was changed to the Missouri, Kansas and Texas Railway Company, which, in time, was shortened to the familiar "Katy."

The Missouri, Kansas and Texas reached the Indian Territory line more than a month after the Joy road, but it had built to a point in the Neosho Valley south of Chetopa. A special investigating commission, headed by the governor of Kansas, reported that the Katy was the first road to comply with the Congressional requirements. Joy rightfully complained that the rival road had not qualified because the act specifically stipulated a "first-class roadbed," whereas only by the loosest use of the term did the Katy have any roadbed at all at the southern end. President Grant, however, refused to question the certification by the governor. After posting the required bond, the Katy was permitted to cross into Indian Territory. On May 24, 1871, the first passenger train entered the present state of Oklahoma, carrying English and Atlantic seaboard stockholders as far as Big Cabin Creek.[3]

The Leavenworth, Lawrence and Galveston reached the Indian Territory line south of Coffeyville in 1871. Meanwhile it leased newly built short lines which connected Olathe with Ottawa Junction and Independence with Cherryvale.[4]

Fort Smith, Arkansas, was the original objective of the Katy, but once it possessed the Indian Territory right of way, its course was redirected to Preston, Texas. Following the route of the Texas Road, the railroad crossed the lands of the Cherokees, Creeks, and Choctaws, bridged the Red, and on Christmas Day, 1872, the first through train arrived at newly platted Denison.

Junction City posed a problem as the northern terminus, since only

[3] 41 Cong., 2 sess., *S. Ex. Doc. 90;* 45 Cong., 3 sess., *S. Rep. 744,* 27–28; IAD, Cherokee Papers—Railroads, File IXa–1; M, K & T Ry. Co., *Missouri, Kansas and Texas Railway Company,* App., S, T, 89–97.

[4] ICC, *Rep.,* CXXVII, 208, 214.

Down to the Gulf

one other railroad, the Kansas Pacific, served the town. To free itself from complete dependence on another company, the Katy built from its own town of Parsons, Kansas, to Hannibal, Missouri, under the charters of three subsidiaries. At Hannibal the Katy had a direct connection with Chicago. The acquisition of two short lines and trackage rights over the Missouri Pacific between Sedalia and Holden also gave the Katy roundabout access to Kansas City.[5]

The Houston and Texas Central was the Texas link in the Kansas to Gulf line. It had resumed construction in 1867, and in July, 1872, wildly cheering citizens welcomed it to Dallas. From there it built rapidly north to the state line and laid out its own town of Red River City north of Denison. For a time the railroads did not connect, as each would pass through the other's town without stopping, unwilling to surrender the benefits which would accrue from townsite development. The Houston and Texas Central finally abandoned Red River City in return for certain rights in Denison. When the first through train to Galveston passed through Denison on March 24, 1873, the long-sought Gulf connection was a reality.[6]

The Houston and Texas Central constructed important branches at this time. One of these was the extension of the old Washington County Railroad to Austin, giving the Texas capital its first railroad; the other was a branch called the Waco and Northwestern, running from Bremond to Ross. The Houston and Texas Central, with almost half the total mileage in Texas in 1873, was by far the longest railroad in the state.[7]

St. Louis aspired to a railroad to the Gulf. Its hopes were bound up in the future of the St. Louis and Iron Mountain and the Cairo and Fulton, both of which had been taken over by Missouri after they defaulted in the payment of interest on their state bonds. On July 3, 1866, the Iron Mountain got a federal land grant; a few weeks later the Cairo and Fulton grant, which had lapsed, was revived. Amidst charges of gross fraud, the state of Missouri sold both roads to the same syndicate—Thomas Allen and associates.

The Iron Mountain reached the Arkansas-Missouri line in 1869, and in 1872 and 1873, the Cairo and Fulton, building under its Arkansas charter, pushed down along the route of the old Southwest Trail to the new town of Texarkana. Under its Missouri charter, the

---
[5] ICC, *Val. Rep.*, XXXIV, 399, 481–83, 529.
[6] *Ibid.*, XXXVI, 579; *Comm. & Fin. Chron.*, Vol. XVI, 376; *ibid.*, Vol. XVII, 19; *Poor's Manual, 1871–72*, 159.
[7] ICC, *Val. Rep.*, XXXVI, 579–80.

Cairo and Fulton extended west from its prewar terminus at Buffington to Poplar Bluff and added several branches. The Cairo and Fulton and the Iron Mountain consolidated in 1874 as the St. Louis, Iron Mountain and Southern, a merger involving almost seven hundred miles of operating line in the two states it served.[8]

The International and Great Northern, which represented a combination of several short lines, was the Texas affiliate of the St. Louis, Iron Mountain and Southern. The key road was the Houston and Great Northern, chartered shortly after the war to build from Houston to the Red River and, presumably, beyond. Its Houston promoters secured financial support in New York, but there was no construction until 1871. The next year it reached Palestine, 150 miles to the north. It acquired, but did not attempt to operate, the Houston Tap and Brazoria, whose rolling stock was reduced to a single cart pulled by a mule. It also built a forty-five-mile segment from Troup to Mineola and purchased the locally financed Huntsville Branch Railway, a spur from its main line to Huntsville.

The International Railroad Company was the other major predecessor of the International and Great Northern. The promoters of the Iron Mountain and a group of Texans organized the International for the purpose of linking Fulton, Arkansas, with Laredo, Texas, but modified their plans to build from Longview, on the Texas and Pacific, to Hearne, on the Houston and Texas Central. Construction began at both ends, and by late January, 1873, the two sections met at Palestine. Realizing the advantages to be gained by uniting with the line from Palestine to the Gulf, the International consolidated with the Houston and Great Northern under the name International and Great Northern.

The final link in the St. Louis to Gulf route was furnished by the newly built Texas and Pacific, which had completed a line from Longview to Texarkana by way of Marshall.[9]

The desire of interior states to reach Gulf ports had not only been realized by the completion of two such rail connections within eight years after the close of the war, but it had also been the incentive for building two important Kansas railroads which were unable to achieve that objective.

[8] *Ibid.*, XL, 596–604; *Cong. Globe,* 41 Cong., 2 sess., 1902–1904; Million, *State Aid to Railroads in Missouri,* 152–58; Thornton, "Early . . . Missouri," MSHS *Proc., 1902,* 6–7, 37.
[9] ICC, *Rep.*, CXLIX, 608–609, 629, 639, 642, 645–46; Reed, *Texas Railroads,* 318–19.

CHAPTER 9

The Boom and Reckoning

KANSAS ASSUMED leadership in building railroads to the west as well as to the south. The Leavenworth, Pawnee and Western, renamed the Kansas Pacific, was the first. Spasmodic building towards an uncertain western terminus accounted for forty miles of construction by 1865. Work began in earnest when the company was given permission to build to Denver. The Kansas Pacific diverged from its intended course when Kansas City replaced Leavenworth as its eastern terminus. Although usually associated with transcontinental projects, the Kansas Pacific was of great local importance, especially after Abilene became the shipping point for vast numbers of cattle driven up from the southwestern ranges.[1]

Cyrus K. Holliday's Atchison and Topeka stirred slightly during the Civil War. The four years of inaction following the company's organization terminated in two events which changed the character of the road. Holliday convinced his associates that they should build west in the direction of Santa Fé, a change of plans indicated by the adoption of the corporate title Atchison, Topeka and Santa Fe. At almost the same time Kansas granted the company three million acres of land if it would build a continuous line to the western border of the state within ten years.

Major O. B. Gunn surveyed as far west as Emporia, but the Santa Fe had no capital with which to engage contractors. Finally, New York investors supplied some money, and Thomas J. Peter, of the Cincinnati firm of Dodge, Lord and Company, assumed responsibil-

[1] ICC, *Val. Rep.*, XLIV, 158–59.

ity for building. On October 30, 1868, construction officially began at Topeka, but in the direction of the coal mines at Carbondale rather than towards Atchison. The Santa Fe pushed steadily on through Carbondale and Emporia to Newton, some 137 miles west, by July, 1871. While the road paused momentarily at this raw little cattle town, the eastern end was extended to Atchison, where four railroads were available as eastern outlets, thereby releasing the Santa Fe from sole dependence on the Kansas Pacific at Topeka.

The situation was still critical. Less than two years remained in which to reach the western border of the state, 283 miles beyond Newton, in order to claim the land grant. Even so, work did not commence again until May 1, 1872, which allowed exactly ten months for completion. The tracklayers passed through Hutchinson in late June and Great Bend in mid-July, and were driven at an even greater speed as they crossed the uninhabited plains. On December 28 the job was done. It was none too soon; the company had no remaining capital, its huge land grant was practically valueless at the time, it handled little revenue traffic west of Dodge City, and the general business depression of 1873 dried up its sources of credit. The Santa Fe gave up most of its building activity in Kansas for the next several years and avoided going into the hands of receivers only by a compromise with the bondholders.

Canny Thomas Peter, fearing a possible diversion of the cattle trade away from Newton but unable to convince the Santa Fe directors that it was a serious matter, headed a group of Kansas promoters who incorporated under the name of Wichita and Southwestern Railroad Company. The maiden run on this important feeder, which extended to Wichita, twenty-seven miles to the south, took place on May 13, 1872. The Santa Fe immediately leased this road and in the course of time absorbed it.[2]

Missouri was also in a position to expand its rail facilities following the war. The Atlantic and Pacific, whose history was closely associated with that of the Southwest Branch, was the most ambitious project in the state. Having defaulted in its interest payments, the Southwest Branch passed by sale into the hands of General John C. Frémont, who reorganized it as the Southwest Pacific Railroad Company. Popularizer of the Far West, onetime presidential aspirant, and son-in-law of Senator Benton, Frémont was not interested in a short

[2] ICC, *Rep.*, CXXVII, 207, 212–13, 217, 358–59; Marshall, *Santa Fe*, 30–32, 40–44, 56–64.

The Boom and Reckoning

Missouri line but rather in the thirty-fifth-parallel route to the Pacific. He secured the passage of an act by Congress providing for the incorporation of the Atlantic and Pacific Railroad Company to carry out the larger undertaking. It carried with it the franchise to the east-west right of way across the Cherokee Nation. The legislation provided for the construction of a railroad from Springfield, Missouri, to the Pacific Coast, with an optional branch from a point in Indian Territory to Van Buren, Arkansas. Building was to be started within two years and the entire line completed by July 4, 1878.

In order to begin work on the transcontinental railroad, the first need was to finish the Southwest Pacific to Springfield. Frémont extended it only thirteen miles beyond Rolla before he sold his interest, turning his attention to the more southerly Memphis, El Paso and Pacific. His successors defaulted in their interest payments and were dispossessed, the state taking over management of the railroad, with Clinton B. Fiske in charge. Fiske worked out an agreement whereby a syndicate representing three rival groups of St. Louis and Boston investors took possession, and on March 17, 1868, the newly organized South Pacific acquired the property and franchises of the Southwest Pacific.

The new road was in constant financial difficulty, but the end of track crept slowly towards Springfield, finally arriving there in May, 1870. Meanwhile, the Atlantic and Pacific had complied technically with the requirement that construction should begin within two years by turning a few spades of dirt on July 4, 1868. With the arrival of the South Pacific, the transcontinental road was able to make real progress. It reached the state line at Seneca, eighty-seven miles from Springfield, on the first day of April, 1871, and continued to build west through the Cherokee Nation to the Katy town of Vinita. Completely exhausted financially, the Atlantic and Pacific rested here for a time. Even an act of Congress permitting it to mortgage all its properties and franchises failed to add additional mileage. In 1872, however, it boldly leased the Pacific of Missouri, which had a combined total of almost six hundred miles of main line and branches.[3]

Several short lines developed along the major railroads in Missouri. The Osage Valley and Southern Kansas, linking Boonville and Tipton, and the Lexington and St. Louis, connecting Sedalia with Myrick,

[3] ICC, *Val. Rep.*, XLI, 304–305, 477–79, 488–89, 494–99; 41 Cong., 2 sess., *H. Ex. Doc. 195;* A & P RR. Co., *Opening of the Atlantic and Pacific Railroad and Completion of the South Pacific to Springfield, Missouri;* Million, *State Aid to Railroads in Missouri,* 168–72.

became leased lines of the Pacific of Missouri. The St. Louis, Salem and Little Rock fed the South Pacific at Cuba and stretched south to Salem, while the Memphis, Carthage and Northwestern ran from Pierce City, on the South Pacific, to Brownsville, Kansas.[4]

Down in Texas, the Southern Pacific and the Memphis, El Paso and Pacific were certainly the most highly publicized if not the most successful projects in the state. The Southern Pacific rebuilt its line and by the end of 1866 was running trains from Marshall to the Louisiana boundary, with trackage rights over the Vicksburg, Shreveport and Texas into Shreveport. Its heavy indebtedness, however, forced its sale in 1869 to a Louisville, Kentucky, syndicate which extended it a few miles west to Longview. The Memphis, El Paso and Pacific also enjoyed a postwar revival under the touch of General Frémont, who rechartered it in July, 1870, as the Southern Transcontinental Railroad Company. The next year the legislature passed an act requiring the Southern Transcontinental and the Southern Pacific to construct a common line west of Shackelford County when and if they chose to continue building toward El Paso. Frémont solved any future difficulties by taking over the rival company, but another project was on foot which was to swallow both of Frémont's roads.

On March 3, 1871, Congress provided for the chartering of the Texas Pacific Railroad Company, to build along the thirty-second-parallel route from Marshall, Texas, to San Diego, California. Fourteen months later an amendatory act modified the original terms somewhat and changed the name to the Texas and Pacific Railway Company. This road acquired the Frémont properties; then, with Thomas A. Scott of the Pennsylvania as president and Grenville M. Dodge in charge of construction, the Texas and Pacific started west from Longview. By the end of 1873 it had added about 250 miles of railroad to that which it acquired from its predecessors, building from Longview to Eagle Ford, Brookston to Sherman, and Marshall to Texarkana. The line into Texarkana was of particular importance. It not only served as a link in the St. Louis to Gulf route, but also gave Dallas a Mississippi Valley connection.

Meanwhile Scott was trying to bolster his shaky finances by securing direct financial aid from the federal government. He found himself checked at every turn by Collis P. Huntington, the California railroad giant, who was determined to control the thirty-second-parallel route to the Pacific. Scott realized he had lost even while Texas

[4] ICC, *Val. Rep.*, XL, 504–505, 658; *ibid.*, XLI, 306, 503–506.

The Boom and Reckoning

and Pacific construction was in progress, so he transferred his interest to Jay Gould, with whom he had been closely associated in this Texas venture.[5]

In the early seventies, two Texas railroads suffering from wartime lethargy passed into the hands of Charles Morgan. He consolidated the Indianola Railroad, recently completed from Victoria to Lavaca Junction, with his newly acquired San Antonio and Mexican Gulf, calling the new company the Gulf, Western Texas and Pacific. In 1873 this road was extended from Victoria to Cuero, where it had stage connections with San Antonio. Meanwhile, Thomas W. Peirce and his Boston associates secured permission to extend the Galveston, Harrisburg and San Antonio through San Antonio to a Río Grande River terminus. Once on its feet, this road expanded rapidly in spite of the depression of the mid-seventies.[6]

The Rio Grande Railroad was organized during this period. For years there had been considerable discussion of a proposed railroad to facilitate the handling of goods received at the important port of Point Isabel and destined for the interior of Mexico. It was not until 1871, however, that Simon Celaya and Brownsville businessmen built the Rio Grande Railroad from Brownsville to Point Isabel. It continued to operate for many years in spite of violent storms which periodically destroyed long segments of the roadbed.[7]

By 1873 the Gulf Southwest could boast a respectable mileage. In Louisiana, the New Orleans, Opelousas and Great Western and the Vicksburg, Shreveport and Texas stretched west from the Mississippi. St. Louis had a Gulf connection through Arkansas, a railroad down into the Indian Territory which connected with another route to the Gulf, and a line reaching to the western border of Missouri. Three Kansas railroads, including one to the Gulf, reached south from the Kansas River to Indian Territory, and two others spanned the state from east to west. No Arkansas railroad had yet reached the western border of the state, but the Little Rock and Fort Smith was nearing that goal. Branches and connecting lines in Kansas, Missouri, and Texas offered great potentialities. The Southwest was on its way towards the development of an elaborate transportation system when financial conditions called an abrupt halt to its progress.

[5] *Ibid.*, XXIX, 527–28, 545–48, 580–82; Jacob R. Perkins, *Trails, Rails and War,* 247–59; Robert E. Riegel, "The Missouri Pacific, 1879–1900," *MHR,* Vol. XVIII, 175–78.
[6] ICC, *Val. Rep.,* XXXVI, 398, 401, 420, 436–37; *Tenth Census,* VII, 370–71, 460.
[7] "Last Chapter Written for Historic Port Isabel and Rio Grande Valley," *Ry. A.,* Vol. CIX, 808.

Then Came the Railroads

The panic of 1873 was peculiarly a railroad phenomenon. The depression was world wide in scope, and there were many contributing causes, but contemporary critics held that irresponsible overbuilding of nonproductive railroads was a basic factor. The rage for railroad securities was striking in light of the fact that gross earnings had fallen steadily until fewer than one-third of all American railroads paid dividends in 1872.

Promoters extended railroads into undeveloped areas of the West in the belief that they would create enough wealth to make their operation profitable. Certainly the most optimistic railroad builder should not have anticipated revenues large enough to pay construction and operating costs beyond the frontier. *Poor's Manual* for 1877-78 estimated that for profitable operation there must be a ratio of 850 persons for each mile of railroad. In 1873 the ratio for western roads was only 427. Added to their other difficulties, western lines suffered from the marketing abroad of speculative and fraudulent issues which discredited all American securities.

By the end of 1873, 89 railroads were defaulting on their interest payments, and 24 had passed into the hands of receivers. In the next few years, more than 150 railroads were to go into receivership.

Some of the more spectacular failures were in the Southwest. The Katy's suspension of interest payments on advances from the Mercantile Warehouse Security Company was one of the main reasons for the bankruptcy of that important financial institution. At the instance of Dutch bondholders, the railroad passed into receivership. The ambitious plans of James F. Joy, already threatened by the loss of the Hannibal and St. Joseph to Gould, led to such a rapid expansion that his railroad empire collapsed, with the Kansas fragments picked up and incorporated into other railroads. The Atlantic and Pacific and its subsidiary, the Pacific of Missouri, defaulted in payments to the state of Missouri, and on April 3, 1876, they were separated on the grounds of extravagance and fraud in their operation. The controlling interests in the Atlantic and Pacific organized the St. Louis and San Francisco Railway Company, which purchased the Missouri Division of the Atlantic and Pacific, the designation given that part of the railroad between Franklin and Seneca. The portion lying in the Indian Territory retained the name Atlantic and Pacific but remained under the control of the new corporation. The Pacific of Missouri was reorganized, entirely apart from its former affiliate, as the Missouri Pacific Railway Company.[8]

The Boom and Reckoning

Some roads caught in the depression were forced to continue building in spite of rigid economies. The Santa Fe was one of these. In March, 1875, it resumed construction toward Pueblo, Colorado. At its east end the Santa Fe leased a line into Kansas City, which replaced Atchison as the principal eastern terminus, and a short road recently completed from Lawrence, Kansas, to Pleasant Hill, Missouri. The second of these was foreclosed in 1877, the Kansas section remaining a part of the Santa Fe, while the Missouri section passed to a new company—the Pleasant Hill and De Soto. Towards the end of the depression the pressure of new settlement forced the Santa Fe to extend down the Walnut Valley from Florence to El Dorado, the first of the numerous feeders with which it protected its territory. The total mileage added in Kansas by lease and construction amounted to less than one hundred miles, all of which was essential.[9]

Mileage of previously incorporated railroads remained static in Arkansas, Louisiana, and Indian Territory during the economic slump. The sole exception was the Little Rock and Fort Smith, which completed its line into Fort Smith in 1876.

Texas railroads were somewhat more active. The most notable was the Galveston, Harrisburg and San Antonio, which, building west from Columbus in 1873, reached San Antonio in February, 1877. The Texas and New Orleans displayed an amazing virility which was not reflected in increased mileage. Although it was operating from Houston to Liberty, the entire road was in a sad state of disrepair. On July 16, 1875, it was reorganized as the Texas and New Orleans Railroad Company of 1874, and immediately thereafter the new management completely rebuilt the road. Another line, the narrow-gauge East Line and Red River, painfully and haltingly extended from Jefferson to Greenville by 1876. It had been created by the citizens of Jefferson, who were fighting vainly to save the extensive trade which once was theirs. The International and Great Northern was able to build from Hearne to Austin.[10] The only new enterprise of real importance was the Gulf, Colorado and Santa Fe, and most of its development came after the business revival.

There had been a marked slackening in construction in the West before the actual crash, which stopped almost all building. Between

---

[8] ICC, *Val. Rep.*, XXXIV, 325; *ibid.*, XL, 302, 478; *ibid.*, XLI, 404; *Cong. Rec.*, 47 Cong., 1 sess., 4000; Steven Frederik Van Oss, *American Railroads as Investments*, 606–607; Katherine Coman, *Industrial History of the United States*, 288.

[9] ICC, *Rep.*, CXXVII, 214–16, 406–408, 459–60, 465, 497.

[10] *Ibid.*, CXLIX, 610; ICC, *Val. Rep.*, XXXIV, 625–30; *ibid.*, XL, 618–20.

Then Came the Railroads

1872 and 1875 new mileage amounted to only one-fourth that of the preceding four years. All industries connected with railroad construction suffered, spreading the effects of the depression. The debtor West—which for all practical purposes was the entire agricultural West—placed the blame on railroads and other "monopolies." Its earlier enthusiastic support of railroad aid projects cooled, and the antirailroad sentiment which was to become so strong in the next decade was already sweeping the north central states.

CHAPTER 10

The Granger Fringe

FRONTIER PSYCHOLOGY and frontier economic conditions shaped the course of frontier action. The buoyant optimism of a youthful area, aggressive confidence in its way of life, and confirmed belief in the efficacy of law even while flouting that which acted as a restraint—characteristics captured by the pen of Mark Twain and analyzed by Frederick Jackson Turner—were the bone and sinew of western politics and economics. Few went west with the expectation of accepting a meager subsistence wrested from the soil by a lifetime of drudgery. The westerner was a promoter, living in a land of opportunity where a man could establish himself and enjoy the increment as the rest of the nation caught up with him. His claim was not a few acres of lonely prairie sod, but the foundation for a prosperous farm, surrounded by equally prosperous farms which would add value to his own. Or it might be the site of a future city, awaiting only the platting and the influx of residents.

The key to this prosperity was transportation, the perennial problem of the frontier. No other problem was ever closer or more constant; other problems could be resolved with the development of adequate, certain means of moving the produce of the West. State-constructed canals of the thirties were simply an earlier manifestation of the same demands on government which spread railroads across the trans-Mississippi states in the postwar period. It was only after each area had achieved a reasonably complete transportation system that it could question the prodigality of the government in bestowing favors.

Then Came the Railroads

The Lincoln administration ushered in the period of the most extravagant donation of the public lands, a phase of history which ended during Grant's first term. To the prevailing method of giving tracts to the states for the benefit of railroads building within their borders, Congress added direct grants to the corporations.

Kansas was the only southwestern state to participate in the wartime distribution of lands. Missouri, as a Border State, was protecting its existing lines from destruction, and the others had seceded. Having failed in the attempt to endow itself lavishly in the rejected Lecompton constitution, Kansas waited until 1863, when a measure, purportedly written by Cyrus K. Holliday, was enacted without debate. It provided for a grant to Kansas to aid in the construction of two railroads, one from Leavenworth to the Indian Territory line, the other from Atchison, via Topeka, to the western boundary of the state. The Santa Fe and the Leavenworth, Lawrence and Galveston were the recipients. The next year Kansas received lands to encourage the building of a railroad from Emporia to Fort Riley. These grants differed from those of the fifties in giving alternate sections ten miles deep on each side of the right of way, with the indemnity limits extended to twenty miles.

Public land grants to railroads of the Gulf Southwest reached their peak in 1866. On July 25 and 26, President Johnson signed bills giving lands to the Kansas and Neosho Valley for a proposed line from Kansas City southward through the eastern tier of counties, and to the Union Pacific, Southern Branch from the vicinity of Fort Riley down the Neosho Valley to the Indian Territory line. On July 27, the Atlantic and Pacific secured a grant for a railroad west from Springfield, with the usual number of sections through Missouri, but twice as many through Indian Territory. A few days earlier the Iron Mountain had gained additional lands in Missouri and Arkansas. Other actions during this session of Congress revived the Memphis and Little Rock, the Little Rock and Fort Smith, and the Cairo and Fulton, with each receiving lands in addition to the original grant after it was satisfactorily determined that there was no Confederate influence in their respective boards of directors.

The rising tide of opposition to the land-grant policy led to its abandonment after the passage of the Texas and Pacific Act of 1871. After adjustment of their various claims, the Kansas railroads received more than 4,600,000 acres, those of Missouri 1,800,000 acres, and those of Louisiana approximately 372,000 acres. The New Or-

The Granger Fringe

leans and Pacific received slightly over 1,000,000 acres in Louisiana by direct grant. Kansas realized 1,485 miles of railroad, Missouri 625 miles, Arkansas 602 miles, and Louisiana 530 miles.[1]

The federal land-grant policy has often been analyzed as being "good" or "bad." Assuming the possibility of reducing it to moral terms, the evaluation merely represents, as in all legislation, the weighing of merits and defects in the light of results. First, the West got its railroads. The liberal donations undoubtedly furnished a type of aid which encouraged investment and sped the railroad network towards completion. This, in turn, led to the more rapid settlement of the West and an almost unbelievably rapid development of the resources of the plains.

On the other hand, the grants were frequently tainted with fraud and self-interest, acting as a further drain on a standard of political morality which was already low. Little effort was made to safeguard the public interest, and, undoubtedly, donations to railroads did encourage an upsurge of speculation which led to the further depletion of the public domain. Fortunately, the fears of those who prophesied vast unbroken landed estates were never realized, even though on occasion railroads did sell to land companies.

One of the most serious defects in the policy was an inconsistency which was not appreciated at the time. The great majority of western congressmen supported both the principle of using the public lands to encourage railroad building and that of giving them away to actual settlers. The lands of greatest value were those that lay within reach of transportation facilities. The alternate sections reserved by the government could be occupied under the Homestead Law (although the homestead in such cases was reduced to eighty acres) or the Preemption Act. Obviously the railroads held their sections for sale at whatever price they could command. When these two basic concepts came into conflict, the railroads were naturally accused of becoming great landed monopolies.

Texas had its own land problem. Following Reconstruction, it had definitely committed itself to a policy of using the unappropriated parts of its domain to encourage railroad construction. Building resumed at such a furious pace that, by 1882, Texas had granted eight million acres more than the total unoccupied lands, exclusive of

---

[1] *U. S. Stat. at L.*, XII, 772; *ibid.*, XIII, 339; *ibid.*, XIV, 236, 289, 292, 338; *Cong. Globe*, 41 Cong., 2 sess., 1902–1904; *Cong. Rec.*, 50 Cong., 1 sess., 5917; Dept. Int., *GLO Report, 1928*, 20–21; Bradley, *The Story of the Santa Fe*, 63–65, 229–31.

Then Came the Railroads

those reserved for schools. Since there was no other alternative, on April 22, 1882, the legislature voted unanimously to repeal all land aid acts. Many railroads did not receive any of their expected grants. Of those which were more fortunate, the majority were unable to locate lands along their rights of way, and, although nine-tenths of their mileage was in East Texas, 84 per cent of their lands lay in uninhabited West Texas. In all, forty-three railroads received about thirty million acres.

Later students of the Texas land policy have stressed ill-advised aid, corruptness, and depletion of the state domain. Whether these criticisms have merit or not, the policy boiled down to one of protecting the public lands or using them to hasten development of an internal improvement program. While censuring specific features, even the critics seem to agree that the benefits outweighed the loss of lands and that the results were creditable.[2]

The other states, since they were more dependent upon the federal government, followed a uniform policy. Most of the general land donations to the older states had been pledged before the Civil War. The new state of Kansas, however, still held its grant intact. In the stormy session of 1866, the state legislature divided the entire 500,000 acres equally between four railroads over the protests of those who wished them set apart for the support of public schools.[3]

Except in the areas under carpetbag rule, aid programs at the state level were not popular after the war. Once the Southern states regained control of their own destinies, they adopted constitutions prohibiting the use of state credit to encourage any corporate activities. Missouri's unfortunate experiences in the fifties led to the adoption of similar limitations in 1865. Kansas alone managed to avoid this particular type of entanglement entirely. It was only in the late Confederate states, however, that the prohibition applied at the local level; cities, counties, and townships in Kansas could pledge their credit without restriction, while those of Missouri could do so only if two-thirds of the qualified voters approved it at a bond election. No attention was given to protecting political subdivisions from their reckless expenditures or insuring them any benefits from their prodigality.

The laxness of state control over local aid has been criticized gen-

---

[2] Reed, *Texas Railroads*, 130–31, 152–57, 161–63, 185–87.
[3] Edwin C. Manning, "The Kansas State Senate of 1865 and 1866," KSHS *Coll.*, Vol. XI, 359–75.

The Granger Fringe

erally. It encouraged an optimism which was already excessive, and the frontier land boomer estimated the future of his sparsely settled community by the number of railroads it could attract. Why should he not be permitted to tax his community in order to make it a rail center? Time would justify the expenditure and return the investment many times over.

The situation did lend itself to any amount of fraud. Glib promoters projected railroads for no other purpose than to secure local bonds. Sometimes an unfortunate community would fail to secure specific guarantees in return for its obligations. It might find itself the possessor of nothing more than location maps, while its bonds were in the hands of innocent purchasers.

Communities were also at the mercy of legitimate enterprises. As a matter of course, towns furnished rights of way, sites for depots and yards, and other parcels of land. In addition, the extravagant employment of local aid to attract lines encouraged corporations to survey alternate routes and have the towns along one bid against those along the other. The results were quite often unfortunate. As conservative a chronicler as James Ford Rhodes protested that western towns, townships, and counties "were recklessly employing their credit to further the railroad projects of energetic and unscrupulous men."[4]

Local aid was granted in two ways. Sometimes it was in the form of an outright donation, but usually it was an exchange of city or county bonds for those of the company. Local bonds were heavily discounted in most cases, but even so, they had far more value than all but valueless railroad securities.

Minor political units in Kansas were particularly generous. The three roads projected to the Gulf were among the first to benefit. The Leavenworth, Lawrence and Galveston exchanged a total of $1,275,000 worth of securities with the city of Independence and five counties; the Missouri, Kansas and Texas traded $365,000 in company stock for Lyon and Morris county bonds in addition to a donation of $25,000 from Fort Scott; the Missouri River, Fort Scott and Gulf transferred $550,000 of its issues to three counties and the city of Baxter Springs in return for theirs. Earlier railroads benefiting from such transactions included the Santa Fe and the Memphis, Carthage and Northwestern.

Missouri cities and counties also made contributions. Kansas City

[4] *History of the United States*, VII, 77.

did not match the earlier prodigality of St. Louis, but it did subscribe $200,000 to the Kansas and Neosho Valley, $100,000 to the Santa Fe, and $75,000 to the Kansas City, Independence and Lexington. Sedalia and Jefferson City made substantial gifts to the Pacific of Missouri, as did most of the counties along the line. Future Frisco properties received local assistance, particularly from Greene and Dade counties, which jointly pledged $600,000. The total in Missouri was in excess of $28,000,000; of this about $3,000,000 went to railroads which did not build. In a number of instances the local grants were tainted with fraud. In one celebrated case, known locally as the Gunn City Massacre, three persons, including the judge and the attorney for Cass County, were killed by irate citizens because of their participation in a fraudulent transaction.

In spite of the constitutional prohibition of the practice, several cities and counties in Texas voted bonds for aid to railroads. Galveston's $500,000 contribution to the Gulf, Colorado and Santa Fe was the largest, but this obligation was later taken over by private individuals. The remainder of the extralegal assistance was the subject of much litigation before it was finally compromised.

In its constitution of 1875, Missouri prohibited political subdivisions from giving aid, rigidly restricted the creation of debts for any purposes, and established debt limits. A year later Kansas limited local bond issues to those requested by 40 per cent of the qualified voters and approved by a majority of the votes cast in the next general election.[5]

Attacks on governmental aid terminated the honeymoon period between railroads and the West. The first defection appeared in the North Central States, where the transportation systems were fairly well developed, and railroad and local interests were already becoming antagonistic. This region became the stronghold of the Grangers.

In 1870, Illinois incorporated into its constitution the principle that the state had the right to regulate railroads within its borders; neighboring states adopted similar provisions. Soon the legislatures and the railroads were locked in a struggle which the nation watched with interest, without realizing its full import. This was the preliminary battle over whether or not the railroads would be subject to state

---

[5] ICC, *Rep.*, CXXVII, 277, 319, 437; ICC, *Val. Rep.*, XXXIV, 434–35; *ibid.*, XLI, 391, 434, 504; Const. of Texas (1876), Art. IV, secs. 45–46; General Statutes of Kansas, ch. 107; Edwin O. Stene, *Railroad Commission to Corporation Commission,* 95–97; Edwin L. Lopata, *Local Aid to Railroads in Missouri,* 105–107, 135–44; Potts, *Railroad Transportation in Texas,* 87–89.

The Granger Fringe

control. The high tide of the Granger movement was reached in 1876 when the United States Supreme Court upheld the power of the state to regulate businesses "affected with public interest" within their borders, even when the business partook of an interstate nature, if the federal government had not acted.

Railroads did not wait for later Supreme Court decisions which drastically limited this regulatory power of the state and which, in effect, made the federal courts final arbiters of the reasonableness of rates. The railroads actively campaigned for repeal of the Granger laws, and in this they were aided by the laws themselves. These pioneer efforts were not well drawn and in many cases were unworkable. As prosperity followed depression years, most of the legislation was repealed, leaving only a trace of the attempted drastic regulation.[6]

Meanwhile, the railroad land grant policy was being re-examined. The Congressional session of 1867 combined discussion of additional grants with a growing movement for forfeiture of those which were unearned. The debates of 1869 and 1870 over the Northern Pacific grant indicated the gathering opposition to federal aid. George W. Julian and William S. Holman, two Indianans, led a movement resulting in the adoption of a House resolution denouncing the land-grant policy in general. Both political parties could now safely protest the sacrificing of settlers' rights to monopolies, and after 1871 there were no railroad land grants.

Meanwhile, the movement for forfeiture gained momentum. The New Orleans, Opelousas and Great Western was the first to suffer actual loss of part of its grant when an act of July 14, 1870, declared all lands coterminous with unfinished portions of the road restored to the public domain. Agitation for additional forfeitures began in 1874 after the Supreme Court held that failure of a railroad to fulfill the conditions prescribed by the terms of the grant did not work an automatic loss of the grant; that could be accomplished only by positive legislation or judicial prescription. It was to be a number of years, however, before enough strength could be mustered to cancel any additional grants.[7]

The early reaction against railroads drew little support from the

---

[6] Solon J. Buck, *The Agrarian Crusade*, 45–49; John Moody, *The Railroad Builders*, 225–29.

[7] *Cong. Globe*, 40 Cong., 1 sess., 615–17, 797; *ibid.*, App., 113–15; *ibid.*, 40 Cong., 3 sess., 424; *ibid.*, 41 Cong., 2 sess., App., 304–10; *ibid.*, 42 Cong., 2 sess., 2095; *ibid.*, 43 Cong., 2 sess., 78–79; Richardson, *A Compilation of the Messages and Papers of the Presidents*, VI, 453; Sanborn, *Congressional Grants of Land in Aid of Railroads*, 23–24.

Then Came the Railroads

Southwest. Embryonic transportation systems, serving undeveloped states clamoring for additional railroad facilities, deserved care and protection, not harassment at the hands of an unfriendly Congress. Kansas and Arkansas, in general, did not recognize the change which was taking place in the national sentiment, and it was a poor congressman from either of these two states who could not introduce several land-grant bills. C. C. Hutchinson, in his *Resources of Kansas*, insisted that Congress should give more land than ever in order to encourage railroad building on the treeless plains.[8] Missouri was the only southwestern state which even mildly joined the attack on land grant aid to railroads.

There was one limited sphere in which the Southwest was willing to support Congressional action detrimental to the interests of railroads. That was when the land titles of corporations threatened those of the settlers or impeded the advance of homesteaders into unoccupied tracts. Kansans not only supported such legislation but assumed the leadership. James F. Joy's speculation in Indian lands created a tremendous amount of opposition to his railroads. The situation became so tense that in 1877, the Kansas City, Fort Scott and Gulf secured the passage of a law permitting it to surrender its grant without compensation because of the antagonism of local people to this segment of the old Joy lines. A few years later the Santa Fe, as successor in interest to the Leavenworth, Lawrence and Galveston, and the Katy, which had never been attached to Joy's holdings, supported legislation requesting the Attorney General of the United States to cancel patents issued to them in excess of the amount of land to which they were entitled.[9]

The Settlers' Protective Association spread from the Osage Ceded Lands to other sections of the state as cases arose in which squatters held titles adverse to those of railroad companies. The movement went underground and evolved into a secret organization after it was learned that the settlers' plans were being divulged to the opposition almost as soon as they were made.

Most of the problems involving conflicting titles were the result of ineffective administration. Once the location maps were filed, all the lands within a grant were withdrawn from public entry. The railroad then had to complete its line and perfect its title to those

---
[8] Pp. 212–13.
[9] *Cong. Rec.*, 44 Cong., 2 sess., 1509; *ibid.*, 46 Cong., 2 sess., 3894; *ibid.*, 47 Cong., 2 sess., 1759; *ibid.*, 49 Cong., 1 sess., 1415, 4109–12, 4235, 4575; Haney, *A Congressional History of Railroads in the United States*, II, 24.

The Granger Fringe

sections to which it was entitled or from indemnity lands in cases requiring adjustment. This situation, bad under any circumstances, was doubly so if the railroad were slow in building. Lands frequently remained closed to entry for many years. The western settler, never renowned for his ready acceptance of legal niceties in squatting on unoccupied ground, frequently acted first and then defended his title when the occasion arose. Obviously this course of action placed him at a decided disadvantage before the law in the event his improvements fell to the railroad.

In June, 1874, an act of Congress permitted any railroad to relinquish its claim to lands in the possession of actual pre-emptors or homesteaders, and select a corresponding amount anywhere within the limits of its grant. Immediately thereafter, Senator James M. Harvey of Kansas began pushing a measure to confirm the titles of all who had settled in good faith, in full compliance with the law, and prior to the time the local land office received notice of withdrawal. This proposed legislation would reverse a General Land Office ruling which held that title passed as soon as the directors of the company chose the route, even though the General Land Office itself would be unaware of the exact location for a time. The Senate defeated Harvey's bill on the grounds that the title had already vested in the railroads and this measure would force the General Land Office to issue patents that were clearly illegal.

Early in the next Congress, Senator John J. Ingalls, also of Kansas, reintroduced this proposal, pointing out that in the case of the Leavenworth, Lawrence and Galveston, the land was not withdrawn until five months after the board had selected a definite route, and in the case of the Missouri River, Fort Scott and Gulf, a period of sixteen months elapsed. During these extended intervals the public lands in question were apparently legally open to any settler who might care to occupy and improve them, yet he was subject to dispossession. Opponents of the measure narrowed their arguments to the dangers inherent in disturbing vested rights in the interest of settlers, many of whom were land speculators who did not represent the *"beau ideal* of human perfection." Ingalls' bill finally passed in April, 1876. It confirmed the titles of settlers whenever their entries had preceded the railroad's notification to the local land office that the lands were withdrawn on the legal proposition that a general law prevails over special laws not yet made specific.[10]

[10] *Cong. Rec.*, 43 Cong., 1 sess., 3596; *ibid.*, 43 Cong., 2 sess., 262–66, 834; *ibid.*, 44

Then Came the Railroads

The tenor of state politics followed that in Washington. Missouri, on the fringe of the Granger movement, showed some concern over railroad regulation, which was reflected in the constitution of 1875. It provided for the creation of a three-member Railroad and Warehouse Commission having the power to administer all laws governing common carriers and public warehouses.[11]

The Reconstruction government of Arkansas superficially provided some control of the railroads by establishing the post of Commissioner of Public Works and Internal Improvements, whose duty was to inspect all public works, including railroads, in which the state had an interest. The legislature of 1871 created the Board of County Clerks as a special agency for appraising railroads for tax purposes. During the panic year Arkansas established maximum rates and fares, but they were considerably higher than those in force. Actual regulation in Arkansas was made possible by the constitution of 1874, which denied to railroads the right to discriminate unreasonably between individuals, to grant rebates, to distribute passes to state officials, or to secure control of parallel or competing lines. Other provisions attempted to control speculative activities in railroad securities, a reaction to the corruptness of the Reconstruction regime. It was not until 1887 that the legislature enacted a comprehensive regulatory code to carry out the constitutional limitations imposed on railroad activities.[12]

Kansas wanted railroads so badly that most of its legislation prior to the eighties was designed to encourage construction. The only early regulatory provision was a maximum passenger fare of six cents a mile, which was adopted in 1868. The only lapse in its amicable policy occurred as the result of the depression of 1873. A few farmers' gatherings agitated mildly for regulation, and somewhat more vigorously for rate fixing, but there were no organized efforts to press the issue.[13]

By and large, Illinois, Iowa, Indiana, and Wisconsin could take

---

Cong., 1 sess., 48, 605–14, 641–50, 687–92; Elizabeth N. Barr, "The Populist Uprising," *Kansas and Kansans*, I, 1140; Haney, *A Congressional History of Railways in the United States*, II, 31.

[11] Art. XII, secs. 12–24. In 1837 the Missouri General Assembly created the Board of Internal Improvements, which was to oversee all railroads, but it was terminated before there were any railroads for it to oversee.

[12] Const. of Arkansas (1874), Art. XVII; *Acts of Arkansas, 1868*, 198, 292; *ibid., 1871*, 135; *ibid., 1873*, 425; *ibid., 1887*, 113–16; Moore, "State . . . in Arkansas," AHA *Pub.*, Vol. III, 28–29.

[13] Stene, *Railroad Commission to Corporation Commission*, 11, 17, 95–97.

the lead in attacking railroads during the seventies; it was not until the next decade that antirailroad planks were to become an integral part of the platform of any successful political candidate in the Southwest.

CHAPTER 11

The Westward Impulse

RAILROADS HASTENED the occupation of the trans-Mississippi West. Running ahead of settlement, they drew after them hordes of restless land-hungry pioneers and land speculators who eagerly seized upon lands formerly valueless because of the absence of transportation facilities. The real importance of railroads became apparent as they penetrated areas not blessed with navigable streams.

This influence was apparent even in the Confederate states during Reconstruction. Although older river communities declined, interior railroad counties continued to grow. It was particularly evident in Louisiana, where the lines running from Shreveport and Monroe showed marked increases, and along the Memphis and Little Rock in Arkansas, where the railroad did not parallel the water courses.

The same situation existed in the two loyal states. The population along the Pacific of Missouri between Syracuse and Kansas City doubled; and the Southwest Branch counties with arable land were filling rapidly. The growth in eastern Kansas was amazing. The three counties served by the Santa Fe experienced a fivefold increase throughout the sixties. Here the conditions were ideal for a railroad to determine the course of settlement—a fertile, virgin area without adequate transportation, with the railroad cutting across the scant waterways which nature had provided.

Ten years later Missouri's rate of growth was below the national average, but the thinly populated western and southern counties continued to absorb new population, with railroad counties maintaining a rate of growth approximately double that of their neighbors. Arkansas was still a frontier area lying between more mature regions. The western half of the state grew rapidly, with the bulk of the new population concentrated either along navigable streams or the newly constructed Iron Mountain, which cut across the courses of navigable streams once it had bridged the White River.

Kansas continued its rapid growth. By 1880 its population had swelled to almost one million. Settlement had advanced two-thirds of the way across the state, and a thin line followed the Santa Fe and the Arkansas River into Colorado. The middle third of Kansas was almost wholly occupied during the seventies. Settlement had followed the two prongs of the Santa Fe, one along the Arkansas, the other, built in the last years of the decade, paralleling the southern boundary of the state as far west as Harper.

Texas almost doubled its population in the seventies. The older settlements along the Gulf coast grew at less than half the speed of those in the remainder of the state, but the sparsely settled timbered counties between Houston and the Louisiana line doubled as they secured their first railroads. Far to the south, along the Texas-Mexican Railroad, a product of the post-depression years, the population increased fivefold, a rate twice that of adjoining counties. The same general pattern of growth was evident in the great triangle bounded by Fort Worth, Texarkana, and Houston as in other partially occupied areas. Where settlement had preceded railroads up river valleys, the influence of new railroads was not great; in sections with arable lands and no navigable streams, the growth was tremendous.[1]

Who were these people who followed the rails west from the Mississippi, and what were their origins? Many were restless adventurers, constantly pushing forward, leaving one partially developed frontier to move on to fresher fields. Others were landless homeseekers, intent on carving out places for themselves in a virgin country. Still others were speculators, in land, in timber, in townsites, and in minerals. By far the greater number were American born, hailing from near-by states or more completely settled areas within the same state. There was always a trickle, and occasionally a wave, of foreign born.[2]

The influx of settlers into the West was due in large part to a carefully organized campaign involving the railroads and many co-operating agencies. Promoters of transcontinental projects who built on the assumption that through traffic would return a sufficient revenue

[1] "Statistics on Population," *Tenth Census*, I, 50, 60, 63, 68, 78.
[2] *Ibid.*, 517–18; "Population," *Twelfth Census*, I, 509–11, 765–67.

Then Came the Railroads

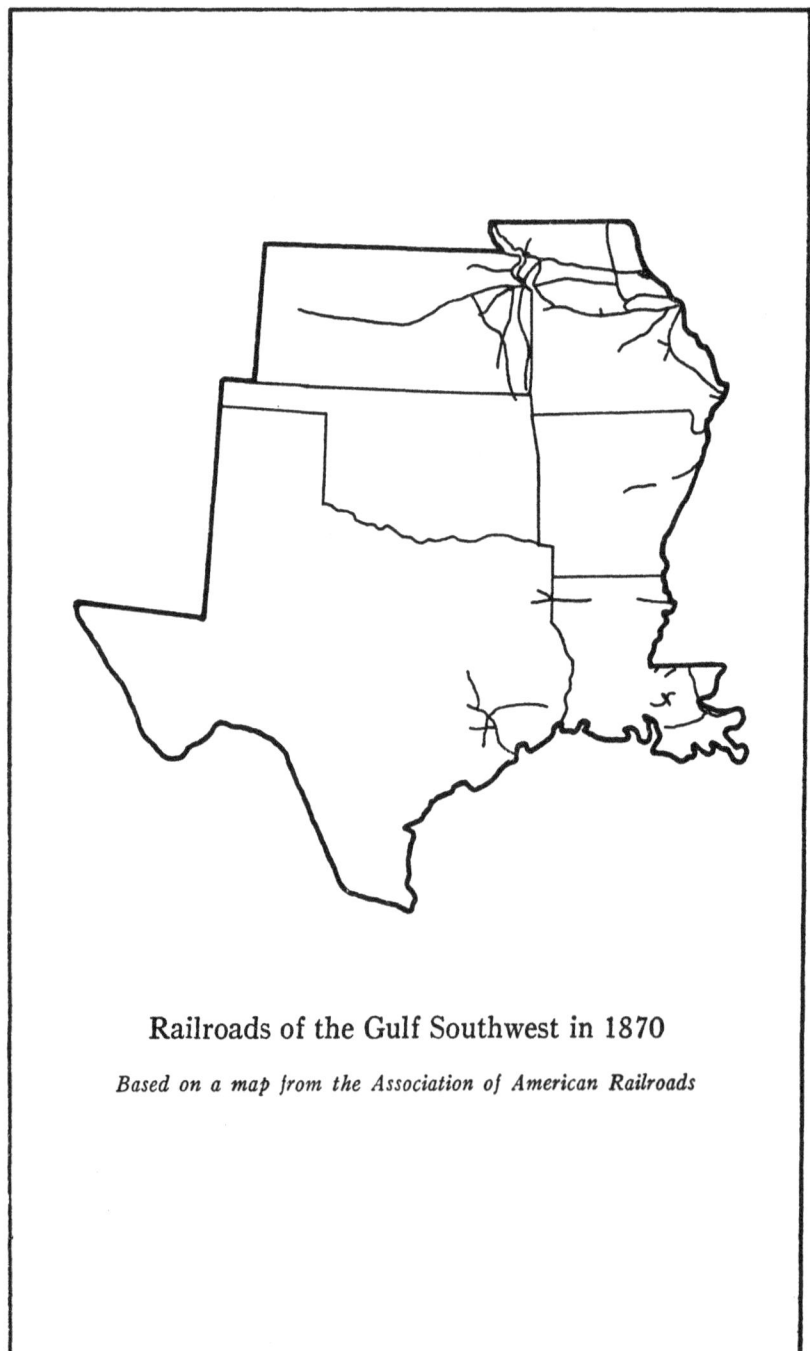

Railroads of the Gulf Southwest in 1870

Based on a map from the Association of American Railroads

The Westward Impulse

were soon disillusioned. Roads of a local character realized from the beginning that they must encourage settlement along their respective lines.

The Illinois Central was the first railroad to organize a colonization department to speed the process of settlement. The idea spread until immigration and colonization departments became an accepted part of railroad activity. The South Pacific pioneered the movement in the Southwest when, in 1868, it issued maps showing the location of agricultural and mineral lands in its territory. The Santa Fe, the Katy, and others became actively engaged in promoting settlement during the seventies.

There was considerable cost involved in the disposition of railroad lands. Surveying, appraising, and mapping required a large initial outlay. The lands then had to be put on the market and advertised extensively. Any plans to make large, quick profits from the sales were put aside as the companies realized that their most pressing need was sound, growing communities which would create revenue traffic. Only in Texas, where most of the lands did not lie along the railroads, was there any real inducement to hold them for speculative purposes, and there the state established time limits within which the sales had to take place. Railroads basically followed a policy of selling at a low price, with liberal credit terms and discounts for cash. They soon learned that it was good business to advertise lands other than their own, because the more extensively the country was settled, the greater the volume of freight. Soon settlers were occupying public lands where the army had recently had to protect railroad building crews from Indian attack.[3]

Inducing large numbers of people to stake their futures in the area west of Missouri, Arkansas, and the Gulf Coast was no little task. Many years were to pass before geography texts would discontinue spreading the fallacy of the "Great American Desert." Misinformation, accumulated for more than half a century, had to be corrected.

Railroads embarked on one of the most comprehensive advertising campaigns the nation had ever known in educating the people about the plains. The Santa Fe did not exaggerate greatly when it pointed out to the Kansas legislature in 1881 that "notwithstanding that the word KANSAS was, in the minds of the inhabitants of all the Eastern States, synonymous with grasshoppers, drouth, and starvation, yet,

---

[3] John D. Hicks, *The Populist Revolt*, 4–15; Frank Andrews, *Railroads and Farming*, 8–10, 18–19; Hafen and Rister, *Western America*, 424–25.

by the unaided efforts of these railroad corporations, an agent has been placed in every town and village in the United States and every city in Europe to correct this impression and talk and plead for Kansas."[4]

The Santa Fe educational program was scarcely under way when the drouth and grasshopper plague of 1874 gave Kansas additional unfavorable publicity. Undiscouraged, Colonel Alexander S. Johnson of the Santa Fe Land Department continued the campaign, introducing features which became standard practices for all railroads. He invited three hundred newspapermen to be his guests on an excursion through Kansas in 1875; the favorable reports which followed reached all sections of the United States and were of considerable importance in breaking down deep-seated prejudices towards Kansas. Colonel Johnson also arranged an elaborate display of the state's agricultural products at the Centennial Exposition in Philadelphia, which gave further favorable publicity.[5]

Foreign immigration offered its own special problems, and in this the competition among the railroads was particularly keen. Full-time European agents, acquainted with the language and culture of the people with whom they worked, attempted to divert immigrants to lands along their respective lines. Materials printed in many languages were broadcast throughout Europe, distributed at points of embarkation, and placed in the steerage of vessels. European newspapers, particularly German and Austrian, carried advertisements of western lands. The various railroads made contracts with steamship companies and travel agencies to encourage aliens to settle in their territories. At times railroads would employ recent arrivals as recruiting agents in the country of their birth.

The largest mass movement of foreign colonists, as well as the most highly publicized, involved the removal of some fifteen thousand pious Mennonites from southern Russia to Kansas. They were a thrifty people, with enough accumulated wealth to establish themselves, and were the finest of wheat farmers. Of German descent, they had been encouraged by Catherine the Great to settle along the Black Sea between the Dniester and the Don. Catherine extended many concessions—freedom of worship, immunity from military service, and local self-government—all guaranteed for one hundred years. Neither their aloofness nor their prosperity endeared them to the

---

[4] *Memorial of the Atchison, Topeka and Santa Fe . . . to the Senate and the House of Representatives of the State of Kansas,* 20.

[5] *Ibid.,* 18–23; Bradley, *The Story of the Santa Fe,* 127–28, 134–36.

The Westward Impulse

Russian people, and, conditions being favorable for such action at the expiration of the hundred years, the Mennonites were given a choice of becoming Russian subjects, with the subsequent loss of their privileged position, or of migrating.

A. E. Touzalin, in charge of the Santa Fe Land Department at the time, learned of their predicament and immediately set to work to attract them to Kansas. Touzalin became friendly with some Mennonites who had recently moved to Kansas from Pennsylvania and were pleased with their new location. They encouraged their coreligionists in Russia to send a delegation to look at the Santa Fe lands. After a preliminary investigation by five of their number, the first group of six hundred arrived at Peabody in the summer of 1874, settling on railroad sections.

Carl B. Schmidt, a German-born immigration commissioner, continued the recruitment, holding meetings while dodging the Russian police. As a result of his work, four hundred Mennonite families bought sixty thousand acres from the Santa Fe. In order to stem the exodus, the Russian government entered into a new agreement with those who had not migrated, permitting them to continue to practice their religion and exempting them from military service. Meanwhile, Mennonites from other parts of Europe had joined the movement to the area between the Smoky Hill and Arkansas rivers west of Cottonwood Falls.

The Santa Fe had to be on its guard throughout the course of the Mennonite migration in order to prevent other railroads from deflecting these fine settlers to other areas. Before it succeeded in holding the bulk of them, the Santa Fe was forced to provide a special train to bring the goods of the main body from Philadelphia, reduce the price of the lands, agree to haul building materials free for one year, and secure the passage of an act by the Kansas legislature freeing them from bearing arms.[6]

Nowhere was the influence of railroad propaganda on land sales more perfectly illustrated than in Kansas. Sales by the Santa Fe rose from 472 transactions involving 45,328 acres in 1872, to 1,261 transactions embracing over 200,000 acres two years later, after which the drouth and grasshoppers temporarily discouraged newcomers. About one-fourth of the lands had gone to newly arrived Europeans, one-tenth to eastern Kansans, and the remainder to purchasers from other

---

[6] Carl B. Schmidt, "Reminiscences of Foreign Immigration Work for Kansas," KSHS *Coll.*, Vol. IX, 487–97; Bradley, *The Story of the Santa Fe*, 113–24.

states, primarily Illinois, Ohio, Indiana, and Massachusetts. Sales rose again after a good crop and reached 267,282 acres in 1878, which accounted for most of the railroad lands east of Dodge City.

Alternate sections reserved by the government were passing into the hands of individuals. Nine hundred thousand acres in Kansas were occupied by eight thousand farm families in 1877. In that year the Larned and Wichita land offices sold another 1,000,000 acres. The following year settlers occupied 1,282,046 acres of federal lands and 75,000 acres of state school lands in Santa Fe territory. Within a few short years after the arrival of railroads, Kansas had been converted from a region belonging to nomadic Plains Indians to neat, cultivated quarter-sections or, in the arid regions, grazing lands.[7]

[7] Bradley, *The Story of the Santa Fe,* 124–26, 134–36; Marshall, *Santa Fe,* 76–86.

CHAPTER 12

The Town-Dwellers

THE MIGRANTS who streamed into the Gulf Southwest tended to spread thinly over the land; there were places, however, where conditions dictated heavier concentrations of population. Some were historic points where for years pioneers had converged before pouring into virgin country beyond. The banks of the Mississippi and the shores of the Gulf were dotted with older agricultural and trading settlements, which were gateways to the West. Beyond, other towns grew along the peninsulas of colonization which followed navigable streams or, more rarely, overland trails. Born of conditions which gave them precedence, these older communities developed to various stages of growth, with a consciousness of the superiority of their locations. Then came the railroads. Their penetration released overland travel from the limitations imposed by nature until all but the most hapless settlements could conceivably outstrip their neighbors.

Only St. Louis and New Orleans attained the stature of great cities before the Civil War, or even for a number of years thereafter. In 1880, St. Louis had a population of 350,000; New Orleans, 216,000. Their nearest competitor was Kansas City, with 56,000, while San Antonio and Galveston lagged with barely 20,000 each. Of the thirty cities lying south of a line through St. Louis and Kansas City, and having over 4,000 population, half were but slightly over that figure. Of the larger ones, all but San Antonio had grown on a foundation of water traffic; Kansas City alone lacked the dignity of years.[1]

The more mature cities were the last to recognize the significance

[1] "Population," *Tenth Census*, I, 447, 449, 452, 455.

Then Came the Railroads

of the new form of transportation. St. Louis and New Orleans, the first cities in the Southwest to secure railroads, remained aloof, living in the memory of lush steamboat days when the river was the great artery of trade. Recognition of the true conditions came later. In the summer of 1877, *Railway World* carried an account of the Chicago trade originating along railroad lines in the Mississippi Valley. "The people of New Orleans and other southern cities are now complaining because their business is being diverted to the northwest, and they are urging the construction of direct lines."[2]

New Orleans was the great city of the colorful river traffic, but the attachment of St. Louis to the Mississippi was almost as great. In the twenty-year period ending in 1860, the population of St. Louis increased tenfold to exceed 160,000. Steamboats lined the river front, bringing the produce of the valley to the greatest concentration point above the Louisiana metropolis. St. Louis grew throughout the sixties, outdistancing Reconstruction-ridden New Orleans by 120,000 and taking over fourth place among the nation's cities. The city was undergoing a transition of which it was largely unaware, and even while rails were stretching west, southwest, and south, there was probably more local interest in the 190 new barges and the river-front elevators. While the city anxiously indulged the whims of the river, railroads hauled the bulk of its goods. As early as 1871, two-thirds of its total freight tonnage arrived by rail.[3]

The younger cities, however, were not wedded to the idea of the omnipotence of their water routes. Kansas City, destined for prominence by its location, had already reached five thousand at the close of the Civil War when two events speeded its growth. First, the Pacific of Missouri arrived from St. Louis; then Kansas City seized the cattle trade. The first shipments from Abilene had passed through Leavenworth en route to Chicago, but Leavenworth apparently had little desire to hold the trade and certainly no intention of spending any money to offer additional facilities. Cattlemen began to ship to Kansas City. Scant as its accommodations were, they represented some improvement. In 1869 the first railroad bridge spanned the Missouri, and more stockyard space was added, but it was still inadequate. Two years later a group of Kansas City businessmen created a corporation which built a commodious feed and transfer yard, and

[2] *Ry. W.*, Vol. III, 706.
[3] "Population," *Fifteenth Census*, I, 600; "Report on Steam Navigation," *Tenth Census*, VII, 36–37; *Rep. Int. Comm., 1887*, Part 12, 53, 58.

the city immediately became a major cattle and hay market. It was already of some consequence as a grain center, and the development of agriculture on the plains was to add to its importance as a concentration point for the processing of agricultural products and the distribution of implements.

No city was ever more interested in developing a network of railroads to secure its trade territory. Ambitious, farsighted businessmen pushed the Kansas and Neosho Valley, which extended the influence of Kansas City to the Indian Territory line. The Santa Fe made the city its principal eastern terminus; the Katy also gained access, first by dependence on the Missouri Pacific but later over its own tracks. Local organizations bludgeoned the railroads into giving the city preferred rates to increase its importance as a distributing center.

Kansas City quickly outran its earlier rivals. With 32,000 people, it was more than seven times as large in 1870 as it had been five years before. This remarkable growth led to speculative land values, followed by a collapse with the depression of the seventies. The city made little progress for five years, after which its spectacular development commenced once more. Kansas City passed 50,000 in 1878, the year it dedicated its first union station, and reached the 100,000 mark by 1884.

Living in the shadow of its Missouri twin, Kansas City, Kansas, had grown unostentatiously to a town of about 3,200 by 1880. It represented the gradual consolidation of eight separate communities, only two of which existed in the turbulent prewar period. Its development was not unlike that of Kansas City, Missouri, except that it was possibly even more dependent upon railroads, and one of its segments, Argentine, was a by-product of the Santa Fe shops and yards established there in 1880.[4]

Unbound by tradition, the twin cities at the mouth of the Kansas River were aware of the vital importance of rail transportation, and they reaped a rich reward for their foresight. The decline of river traffic had little effect on them, for their future was already linked with railroads.

San Antonio and Galveston were the intermediate cities of the Southwest in 1880. They were far below the top three, but they were

[4] *Rep. Int. Comm., 1887*, Part 2, 129; "Population," *Fifteenth Census*, I, 18–20; Joseph G. McCoy, *Historic Sketches of the Cattle Trade of the West and Southwest*, 329–30; AGS, *Kansas*, 205–11; Walter Williams, "Missouri after the War of Secession, 1865–1909," *SBN*, III, 249.

Then Came the Railroads

able to look down on all others, of which none but Houston, Topeka, and Little Rock were half their size.

Old San Antonio, lazily reflecting on its romantic past, had attained a population of a little over eight thousand at the beginning of the Civil War. Spurred on by the cattle trade, it grew fairly rapidly and, with the completion of the Galveston, Harrisburg and San Antonio linking it with the coast, was truly the cowmen's capital of Texas.[5]

The history of Galveston can scarcely be dissociated from that of its early archrival, Houston. Galveston was the pioneer deepwater port of Texas, having its first terminal company in 1854 and its first regularly scheduled steamship stops in 1865. *Logan's Directory of 1873* listed it as by far the largest and richest city in the state and the third-ranking port in the nation, with its banks and wholesale houses and its dry goods, hardware, whiskey, and grocery stores the finest in Texas. With all its wealth, Galveston had only one railroad; aggressively ambitious Houston, located fifty miles inland on narrow, tortuous Buffalo Bayou, dominated this form of transportation. Houston seized the Galveston and Red River as its own under the new name Houston and Texas Central, tapped the Buffalo Bayou, Brazos and Colorado to add to its own trade and strike a blow at rival Harrisburg, and added the Texas and New Orleans to reach timber to the east. All of these ante bellum roads fed the city, while Galveston's single line merely connected it with Houston. Cautious Houston frequently disrupted the traffic by quarantining rail shipments at every rumor of yellow fever outbreaks in Galveston, maintaining the quarantine well beyond the time fuming Galveston considered necessary.

In 1873 well over half the total railroad mileage in Texas was directed from the three railroad headquarters located at Houston. Even then the city was heavily industrialized for its size, particularly in the field of agricultural processing. Its citizens prevailed upon Charles Morgan to dredge a nine-foot channel from Galveston Bay up Buffalo Bayou; Morgan then extended his newly incorporated Texas Transportation Company to a near-by shipping point, which he called Clinton, and there built docks. This marked the beginning of the Houston Ship Channel. By 1880, eight railroads, operating over 1,500 miles of track, terminated at Houston, and, with a population of 16,513, it was the third largest city in Texas.

Meanwhile Galveston continued to grow at a pedestrian gait. Irri-

[5] "Population," *Fifteenth Census,* I, 18.

The Town-Dwellers

tated by Houston's domination of the hinterland, Galveston businessmen organized the Gulf, Colorado and Santa Fe to reach the north by going around Houston. The railroad did miss that city and in time reached far into the interior, but its first important branch was to Houston.[6]

Another Texas rivalry involving more northerly towns was to result eventually in the development of two great cities in adjoining counties. Dallas, based on a cotton economy, and Fort Worth, dependent on livestock, developed each along its own peculiar course. The statement that Dallas might just as well have been located a hundred miles distant in any direction is something of an exaggeration, but undoubtedly a combination of circumstances, the most important of which was the location of the first North Texas railroads, determined its exact location and ultimate size. A prosperous little farming community, it could proudly claim almost three thousand residents by 1872. That year Dallas wooed the railroad building north from Houston in the general direction of Coffee's trading station on the Red and won it with a bonus of $5,000, a right of way through the town, and 115 acres of land. The next year, before the east-west Texas and Pacific reached Dallas, the population had already doubled, and by 1880 it passed ten thousand.

Camp Worth languished until after the Civil War and then, dignified by the name Fort Worth, achieved a degree of prominence with the rise of the cattle drives. Knowledge of the approach of the Texas and Pacific boomed the little town, which had given the railroad more than a half section of land. It was doomed to suffer a serious setback before realizing its ambition of being a railroad center. Twenty-six miles short of Fort Worth when the depression struck in 1873, the Texas and Pacific suspended construction, and the town disintegrated, with only one-fourth of its population remaining. The interruption threatened to be more than a temporary delay because a state land grant hinged on the completion of the Texas and Pacific within a specified time. Finally, the Tarrant County Construction Company, which was practically the town of Fort Worth, built the remaining twenty-six miles with its own labor, and on July 19, 1876, the long overdue first train arrived. Meanwhile the editor of the *Democrat* had printed his famous "Tarantula Map," a graphic portrayal of the

---

[6] *Ibid.*, 18–19; *Ry. W.*, Vol. II, 783–84; *ibid.*, Vol. VI, 1138; *Logan's Directory of 1873*, 126–32, 150–58; Reed, *Texas Railroads*, 83, 205, 238–42, 283–84.

Then Came the Railroads

railroad network which Fort Worth had to develop in order to become a major city. By 1880, Fort Worth was approximately one-half the size of its rival.[7]

To the east, located in a parish adjoining the state of Texas, Shreveport dominated northwestern Louisiana. It pioneered railroad construction, having a segment of the Vicksburg, Shreveport and Texas the year following the termination of the Civil War. The rail connection with Dallas before the panic of 1873 speeded Shreveport's growth, and its eight thousand population in 1880 was almost double that of the preceding census.[8]

Far to the northwest, on the Arkansas River in south central Kansas, a railroad was responsible for the growth of a town which was to be the second largest city in the state. Wichita grew up at the site of Mead's trading post. Soon, a rival, Park City, was platted across the river. At this time Thomas Peter was looking for a terminus for his branch line from Newton; Wichita, with a population of three hundred, boldly bid $200,000. It got the railroad, Park City disappeared, and Wichita almost immediately became a wild cowtown at the head of the Chisholm Trail, pre-eminent until barbed wire and local restrictions diverted the herds to Dodge City. In time, wheat replaced the seasonal cattle drives as the basis for the town's economy.[9]

Railroads were instrumental in shaping the course of the state capitals. The states of Arkansas, Missouri, and Texas had each laid out a town, located in the interior and on the banks of a major river, specifically dedicated to controlling their political destinies. The similarity in origin was the only point the capitals had in common. Jefferson City, never favorably located for trade and never an important railroad center, grew slowly. Little Rock, on the other hand, became the commercial, financial, and industrial, as well as the political, heart of Arkansas. Its period of growth, however, was to come later, since it was plagued by the aftermath of Reconstruction during the seventies. Never as economically important to its state as Little Rock nor as completely overshadowed as Jefferson City, Austin occupied an intermediate position. It was almost their equal in size in 1860. Its greatest period of growth coincided with the completion of its first rail connection. In 1871 the long-sought road from Austin to the coast

---

[7] "Population," *Fifteenth Census*, I, 18; AGS, *Texas*, 258–61; *Fort Worth, 1849–1949*, 12–14.

[8] "Population," *Tenth Census*, I, 196; AGS, *Louisiana*, 361–67.

[9] "Population," *Fifteenth Census*, I, 20–21; information from Bliss Isely, Wichita Chamber of Commerce.

Railroad Builders in the Gulf Southwest

Courtesy Kansas City Southern Lines
Arthur E. Stilwell

Courtesy Kansas City Southern Lines
Samuel W. Fordyce

William Edenborn
Courtesy Kansas City Southern Lines

Cyrus K. Holliday
Courtesy Santa Fe Railway

Courtesy Fort Worth Chamber of Commerce

The first Rock Island *Rocket*, 1852.

An early-day Rock Island diner, the *Orient*.

Courtesy Rock Island Lines

The Town-Dwellers

became a reality. The little city of 5,000 more than doubled its population in the next nine years. While part of this growth came from the development of its trade territory and the remarkable strides taken by the entire state, no small part was traceable to its railroad.[10]

None of the state capitals were so dependent on railroads as Topeka. Incorporated in 1857 by abolitionists as a rival to proslavery Tecumseh, it was almost immediately selected as the capital by Governor Charles Robinson. Cyrus Holliday, father of Topeka as well as of the Santa Fe Railway, chose it as the headquarters for his company, and in the sixties it grew from a village of less than one thousand to almost six thousand. Blessed by other railroads, it increased more than two and one-half times in size during the next decade.[11]

The continued growth and local prominence of many cities of somewhat less importance is directly attributable to railroads. In the Missouri Ozarks, Springfield's growth was shaped by its first railroad. Located at the intersection of two important overland trails and serving as a trading center for cattle growers, Springfield was a city of five thousand when the South Pacific almost arrived in 1870. Unfortunately, a group of townsite promoters, including some of the railroad's builders, established the new community of North Springfield and outbid the older city. This precipitated a feud which ended only with the consolidation of the two communities in 1887, but with two separate and distinct business districts existing to the present. In spite of local dissension, the city grew with the coming of the railroad. Lebanon and Warrensburg, in Missouri; Emporia, Fort Scott, and Coffeyville, in Kansas; and Waco, Corsicana, Palestine, Paris, and Sherman, in Texas, became towns of real importance only after the coming of their railroads.[12]

Some endings were not happy. Railroads perversely seized the wealth of one and gave it to another. Ever jealous of their position, they showed no leniency towards those who did not bid high enough for their services, or who stood aloof from them. They took particular delight in stripping river landings of their laurels.

Cape Girardeau, a prosperous Mississippi River town since the early part of the century, was barely able to hold its own after the Iron Mountain missed it in the early seventies. Upstart Poplar Bluff,

---

[10] "Population," *Fifteenth Census*, I, 28, 1056.
[11] *Ibid.*, 401; AGS, *Kansas*, 276–82.
[12] "Population," *Fifteenth Census*, I, 123, 246, 400, 600, 1056–57; AGS, *Kansas*, 173–74, 185–87; AGS, *Missouri*, 329–33; Reed, *Texas Railroads*, 180, 316, 412; information from Louis W. Reps, Springfield, Missouri, Chamber of Commerce.

less favorably situated but smiled on by the railroad, grew rapidly.

Many of the river ports in Arkansas suffered a decline as railroads built near but not through them. Cotton-shipping Champagnolle Landing, on the Ouachita, disappeared. Pocahontas, on the Black River, and Jacksonport, long the commercial and social arbiter of the Black and White rivers area, refused to donate right of way. The Cairo and Fulton thereupon established Newport, four miles from Jacksonport. Newport became a flourishing town; Jacksonport all but disappeared; Pocahontas eventually salvaged part of its future by securing a branch line. Dover, at one time the most important town between Little Rock and Fort Smith, lost most of its population and the county seat to Russellville, while Morrilton absorbed the river port of Lewisburg.

Most of the drastic changes in Louisiana were to come later, with more extensive railroad development, but Thibodaux, once the most important city west of New Orleans, effectually blocked its own growth when it thwarted the attempts of the railroad to enter.

Probably no city suffered more complete eclipse than Jefferson, which had dominated North Texas with its water transportation and its wagon routes. The new railroads cut across the roads to the town. Jefferson tried frantically to save its trade by building lines, but it had irretrievably lost its leadership to Dallas. Waxahachie, fearing an influx of undesirable residents, refused to bid for the first railroad through that section and, as a result, has since shared its territory with the Houston and Texas Central's Ennis.

In Indian Territory the Katy destroyed or restricted the further growth of a number of older settlements. The outstanding example was Fort Gibson, which carried on the most extensive trade in the Territory, supplying the agencies and licensed traders as well as military posts far to the west. It lay in the Cherokee Nation, and many Cherokee leaders, fearful of the effect of white intrusion on their people, resisted attempts of the railroad to re-enter their lands. The Katy thereupon built Muskogee, across the river in the Creek Nation. Fort Gibson dwindled, and Muskogee became the leading city in Indian Territory. As the Katy pushed south, the residents of North Fork Town moved to Eufaula, which was located on the railroad; after the railroad crossed the Choctaw Nation, famous old Boggy Depot, on the Texas Road, was replaced by Atoka, eleven miles away.[13]

[13] "Population," *Twelfth Census*, I, 461; *ibid., Fifteenth Census*, I, 121–22, 600–627; AGS, *Missouri*, 200–202, 427; AGS, *Arkansas*, 205–208, 245, 247–48, 298–99, 377; AGS,

The Town-Dwellers

The rise of new towns was as striking as and even more colorful than the influence of railroads on older communities. In Arkansas, Forrest City and Brinkley were products of the Memphis and Little Rock, while DeValls Bluff was practically so after the railroad secured control of the townsite in an unsuccessful attempt to promote it into a city. Morrilton, Atkins, and a number of smaller settlements west of Little Rock took their places alongside the old river ports. A string of new towns marked the course of the Cairo and Fulton from Moark, a railroad community of transitory importance at the northeast corner of Arkansas, diagonally across the state to Texarkana, which had just been platted on the Texas side of the line. The two railroads proceeded to dispose of the town lots in their respective states and to lay the foundations for a city destined to become an important junction for four major railroads.

Texas was the scene of much town-building. Beyond Hearne, the Houston and Texas Central penetrated a country which was largely newly opened; the long stretch to Corsicana was dotted with towns bearing the names of company officials. Other towns grew up beyond this point. The Galveston, Harrisburg and San Antonio, building west from Eagle Lake, had to create most of its stations between Columbus and San Antonio; seven of them have survived.

Several present day cities in eastern Kansas owe their beginnings to railroad builders of the seventies. Parsons, established by the Katy, and the point from which many lines diverge, has remained predominantly a railroad city. Cherryvale originated as the eastern terminus of the Southern Kansas. In western Kansas, towns sprang up as the Santa Fe arrived, or immediately before in anticipation of its coming. Doyle Creek, renamed Florence, marked the farthest point of earlier settlement. From there the tracks extended southwest to Newton, which, after its youthful fling, settled down to become an important railroad center. The end of track moved on to Hutchinson, then followed the bend of the Arkansas, leaving Nickerson, Sterling City, Great Bend, Larned, and Kinsley strung behind. It straightened out alongside the river to reach newly platted Buffalo City, which won notoriety under the new name of Dodge City.[14]

The Katy pioneered town-building in Indian Territory. Entering

Louisiana, 577–78; AGS, *Oklahoma,* 339–44; Angie Debo, *The Road to Disappearance,* 199; Reed, *Texas Railroads,* 215, 379–80.

[14] AGS, *Arkansas,* 196–99, 203–10, 213, 225–26; AGS, *Kansas,* 178–82, 198–202, 261–62, 382–86, 425–26; Marshall, *Santa Fe,* 48–51; Bradley, *The Story of the Santa Fe,* 88–93; Reed, *Texas Railroads,* 193, 208.

Then Came the Railroads

the Cherokee Nation south of Chetopa, it established a series of termini which offered no chance for townsite speculation because of tight tribal control. Vinita grew up where the Atlantic and Pacific and the Katy crossed. The Cherokee Council legislated it into existence as Downingville, but E. C. Boudinot seized lands at the junction for his own promotional schemes. Born in the midst of controversy, Vinita survived as the first important railroad town in the present state of Oklahoma in spite of its early trials.

South of Chouteau, the Katy crossed into the Creek Nation. After bridging the Arkansas, the railroad established Muskogee as its terminus to replace the vicious little tent community of Gibson Station. Checotah and Eufaula were added to the list of Creek towns before the Katy bridged the Canadian to enter lands of the Choctaws. Bucklucky Store became the temporary terminus, and J. J. McAlester, its proprietor, renamed the settlement after himself. The Katy moved on through Kiowa, Atoka, and Durant before crossing into Texas. It did not terminate at lawless Preston, but built six miles beyond to its own town of Denison. Preston quietly moved to Denison, which also became the terminus of the Houston and Texas Central after the compromise between the railroads which led to the demise of Red River City.[15]

Only a few strands of the web of rails had been spun, but the relocation of urban population was already underway. The shifting would continue—scattering hundreds of new towns through the Southwest, building struggling villages into major cities, relegating mature communities to half-forgotten names—until the rail network was complete.

[15] Grant Foreman, *A History of Oklahoma*, 179–83; Wardell, *A Political History of the Cherokee Nation*, 259; Debo, *The Road to Disappearance*, 231; AGS, *Oklahoma*, 148–55; Paul Nesbitt, "J. J. McAlester," *Chron. Okla.*, Vol. XI, 761–64; Reed, *Texas Railroads*, 210.

CHAPTER 13

Buffalo Hunters, Cowmen, and Farmers

THE SOUTHWESTERN railroads of the seventies served a diverse area, ranging from the two great cities of the Mississippi to the virtually uninhabited plains. Occupational pursuits were equally varied.

Far out on the plains, one of the most dramatic of frontier enterprises grew directly out of railroad penetration. An ephemeral occupation which never contributed greatly to the whole of the national economy, buffalo hunting was, nevertheless, of prime significance to the West because it wiped out the herds upon which the wild Plains Indians were almost wholly dependent. The destruction of the buffalo was the most important step in forcing the nomadic tribes to accept a sedentary life.

Before the great slaughter, an estimated fifteen million buffalo, divided into northern and southern herds, roamed the treeless plains. Cases were reported of trains being delayed for hours after engineers learned that it was impossible to run through the closely packed animals without derailing. For ten dollars a "sportsman" could ride a Kansas Pacific excursion train from Leavenworth to the buffalo grounds.

Railroads initiated the destruction of the buffalo by hiring skilled hunters to furnish their construction gangs with meat. In the East a craze for buffalo robes soon furnished a ready market for hides. With the collapse of railroad building in the Southwest, many tracklayers joined the ever growing ranks of the buffalo hunters, and for a time two-thirds of the population in the vicinity of Dodge City followed that calling. In 1877, the last year of the great slaughter, more than 1,500 hunters were in West Texas. Stations along the new railroad lines served as their outfitting bases and also as shipping points for the hides.

An experienced buffalo hunter could make as much as one hundred dollars a day. Equipped with a buffalo gun, ammunition, a light wagon, and the necessary equipment, and usually accompanied by a cook and a couple of skinners to "peel" the animals and stake out the hides, he would establish his camp. He hunted on foot, creeping through the grass to approach the herd as closely as possible without alarming it. He first shot the leader, and as the animals milled uncertainly, he killed them at the rate of one or two a minute, choosing as his targets those which attempted to lead the others in flight or who broke from the others. The slaughter continued until the befuddled buffalo finally broke or until the gun became too hot to fire. One grizzled hunter, Tom Nixon, killed 120 in a forty-minute "stand" during a thirty-five-day period in which he dropped 2,173 buffalo.

After the great herds were gone, thousands of tons of bleaching bones covered the plains. The bones were commercially important for use in sugar refining and in fertilizers, and the horns could be marketed for the manufacture of combs and buttons. Freighters in particular collected them and stacked them along the rights of way for shipment, and for years thereafter agricultural settlers were able to realize a little cash by picking up the scattered horns and bones which remained.[1]

Railroads had a profound and immediate effect on another typical frontier activity—cattle raising. They were instrumental in creating the cattle kingdom of the Plains and were of even greater significance in breaking the domination of the cattle barons.

Remnants of Spanish herds had fed and multiplied for generations in South Texas. After the war, cattle worth ten dollars a head in Texas brought forty to fifty dollars in the north central states. Restless Confederate veterans, unwilling to return to the shambles which had been their homes, began life anew as squatters on the public domain, trailing the wild stock to points on the Mississippi or to Sedalia for shipment over the Pacific of Missouri.

The trails were beset by many difficulties. Herds moving to Mis-

---

[1] Robert M. Wright, *Dodge City, the Cowboy Capital*, 75, 186–87, 192–93; Martin S. Garretson, *The American Bison*, 108–26, 156–69; Everett Dick, *Vanguards of the Frontier*, 431–41.

souri had to cross the territory of ruthless gangs who terrorized southeastern Kansas and southwestern Missouri. The more fortunate who ran afoul of the bushwhackers merely had their herds stampeded, then paid well to have them rounded up and returned; more often they lost their stock and quite often their lives. Irate citizens attempted to block by physical force or legislation the movement of Texas stock because of widespread infection from Texas fever. Stampedes were an ever present threat, and swollen streams frequently added to the woes of the drovers. The fact remained, however, that regardless of the route chosen, there was a fortune waiting for those with the courage, the resourcefulness, and the good fortune to overcome the hazards of the trail and the legal obstacles of the states.

At this point the Kansas Pacific reached Abilene. Joseph G. McCoy made it the meeting place of the cattleman and the eastern buyer, and with the arrival of the first herd on September 5, 1867, the first true cowtown was born. During the next five years, one and one-half million cattle were trailed to lawless Abilene. The railroads bestowed this prosperity, and the railroads took it away, assisted by farmers of eastern Kansas. Railheads pushing deep into the cattle country afforded more convenient shipping points. Ellsworth, Hays, and then Ellis succeeded to leadership along the Kansas Pacific, but the Santa Fe, crossing the state below the route of the Kansas Pacific, was more favorably located, and it was along this railroad that the true successors of Abilene appeared—for a short time Newton, followed by Wichita, then Great Bend, and finally Dodge City, the most fabulous of all. Termini along the Indian Territory line—Baxter Springs, Chetopa, Coffeyville, and, later, Caldwell and Hunnewell—also handled much livestock. Meanwhile the Katy, after crossing the Indian Territory and reaching Denison, diverted thousands of head from Kansas. Soon railroads were creeping into West Texas, spelling the end of the great drives, the last one to Dodge City being made in 1881. The cost of shipping by rail was almost as great as trailing, but the cattleman was relieved of a two months' drive and the loss of stock from theft, stampede, and accident; then, too, the trails were virtually closed by state law.

From its meager beginnings in the mid-fifties, the cattle industry had spread with amazing speed until it covered the Great Plains by 1876. Fat profits and favorable conditions, of which accessible railroad shipping points were not the least, led to the investment of eastern and foreign capital, the illegal use of the public domain, and the advancement of settlement into the Indian country. In 1871 a few adventurers entered southwestern Kansas and wrested it from the Plains Indians. To the southeast, Texas drovers made use of the lush prairie grass of the Indian Territory as they moved their herds slowly northward from the Red until the protests of the Indians led to a system whereby millions of acres were leased to the cattle barons of Texas and Kansas.

It is impossible to separate the development of railroads, the range cattle industry, and meat packing. Each was dependent on the other two. The Santa Fe could scarcely have survived its early days without its revenue from livestock. Most of the Katy's business in Indian Territory and Texas was handling cattle, while the Atlantic and Pacific operated its Sapulpa line, built somewhat later, only during stock-shipping seasons. The cattle trade furnished the railroads entering West Texas with their chief source of revenue. The centers of the meat-packing industry, in turn, were fed by the railroads and developed into cities in a few short years.

The early railroads made a conscious effort to improve their methods of handling livestock. There had always been a heavy loss of animals because of inferior cars, inadequate accommodations, and faulty traffic management. Probably the most notable advance came in the spring of 1873 when the Katy completed the first of its "Palace Stock Cars," with feed boxes, hayracks, and water tanks, the longest and most commodious cars of that day. This, however, was merely one outstanding incident in the evolution of stockcars. Many of the innovations took place in the Southwest, mainly because of its paramount interest in livestock breeding. Gradually the railroads began to supply conveniences, as well as bare necessities, at shipping points and terminals.

Railroads also contributed the refrigerator car. The first was patented in 1867, and by 1871 they were being used rather extensively. Joseph McCoy stated that in 1874 the Atlantic and Texas Refrigerating Company of Denison had one hundred cars, and could accommodate a daily slaughter of five hundred animals. The following year, three carloads of refrigerated meat moved from Kansas City to the Atlantic seaboard—the first long haul of fresh meat. By the eighties, refrigeration had become truly effective, and the transportation of fresh meat was quite common.

Conditions were now ripe for a tremendous expansion in the meat-packing industry. Cities demanded food; plains conditions were ideal for beef production; promoters recognized the economic possibilities. Railroads furnished transportation facilities to link the producer with the processor and the processor with the consumer, while refrigeration extended inestimably the possibilities for handling fresh meat.

Rail connections determined which cities would reap the harvest from the meat-packing industry. St. Louis was important, but in due time it was overshadowed by Chicago and Kansas City. The Katy, with a direct connection to Chicago, helped northern railroads boom that city; after it secured entrance into Kansas City, it participated in that traffic also. The Kansas Pacific, the Santa Fe, the Missouri River, Fort Scott and Gulf, and the Leavenworth, Lawrence and Galveston fed Kansas City from the boisterous cowtowns in western Kansas or from along the Indian Territory line. Denison, Texas, not only was an important shipping point where the Katy maintained extensive holding pastures and stockpens, but also had its own meat-packing industry after 1874.

The range cattle industry reached its peak from 1882 to 1885, then collapsed. Its entire structure was highly speculative, and the rush for quick profits resulted in an overstocking of the range. Homesteaders criticized the illegal use of the public lands and the extralegal leasing of Indian lands, which, in time, led to the cancellation of many Indian leases and attempts to reform the administration of the public domain. State quarantine laws became more rigid. The bitter winter of 1885–86, followed by scorching winds and drouth the following summer, exacted a terrific toll, but it was mild compared to the frightful losses of the winter which followed. This marked the end of the range cattle industry. It had already begun to crumble before an accumulation of hostile forces, no one of which spelled its end with such complete finality as the intrusion of the agricultural frontier.[2]

The agricultural frontier pressed rather closely behind the railroads as they pushed into lands readily adaptable to tillage methods employed in the settled portions of the United States. It advanced even farther when central Kansas enjoyed exceptionally favorable weather conditions for a number of years. This territory of erratic rainfall was alternately the hope and the despair of its residents. The farming frontier faltered when it reached the semiarid stretches, un-

[2] McCoy, *Historic Sketches of the Cattle Trade of the West and Southwest*, 30, 50–53, 95, 111–34, 307, 330, 418–20, 427, 432–35; "Agriculture," *Tenth Census*, III, 43; Frank Andrews, "Cost and Method of Transporting Meat Animals," USDA *Yearbook for 1908*, 227–30; Rudolf A. Clemens, *The American Livestock and Meat Packing Industry*, 86, 211–24; Walter P. Webb, *The Great Plains*, 207, 216–23, 232–40.

able to push on to the Great Plains until new crops and new techniques could be developed.

The vast fields of wheat which would in time spread across western Kansas, the Texas Panhandle, and western Oklahoma were in an embryonic state at this time. They represented an indirect triumph for the Santa Fe railroad. While there had been earlier attempts to cultivate a hardy variety of wheat, all efforts had failed because mills could not handle it and the product had a bitter taste. The Mennonites whom the Santa Fe had induced to come to central Kansas brought with them a few bushels of the variety known as hard red Turkey winter wheat, and one of their number, Bernhard Warkentin, built a small roller mill designed to process it. From Kansas its cultivation spread over all the Southwest.

Railroads gave every encouragement to these pioneer farmers. The first direct aid programs were the results of crises which left to the railroads the alternative of giving assistance or suffering tremendous losses of settlers along their lines. The drouth-ridden, grasshopper-plague year of 1874 was a striking example. The twin evils wiped out the crops of Kansas and with them the hopes of many. Railroads furnished free transportation for those wishing to leave the state. Co-operating with the Kansas State Relief Commission, the Santa Fe transported free of charge almost 5,000 tons of food and clothing donated throughout the nation to the "grasshopper sufferers," and brought in grain and coal at a rate covering only the actual cost of handling. It granted a moratorium to purchasers of railroad lands and bought 100,000 bushels of seed wheat, which it distributed to settlers on both railroad and government lands, taking unsecured notes in exchange. The Santa Fe followed the same system of seed distribution after the drouth of 1879.[3]

The economic activities of settlers following railroads into sparsely populated or wholly uninhabited areas necessarily revolved about readily exploitable resources. Few of the treasures locked in the earth were utilized at first. Coal deposits were known to exist in Missouri, Kansas, Arkansas, and Indian Territory before the days of rail transportation, but only in Missouri was there any production, and that only a few hundred tons for local consumption. Since the most satisfactory operation of locomotives required a greater volume of steam than wood could produce, railroads searched eagerly for coal, and were its largest consumers. Their needs gave it local importance until

[3] *Memorial . . . Kansas*, 27–30; Bradley, *The Story of the Santa Fe*, 125, 129–34.

such time as the requirements of industry widened the demand. With the coming of railroads, mines were opened along the lines wherever there were coal deposits. J. J. McAlester may or may not have influenced the course of the Katy when he hauled a wagonload of coal to Parsons, Kansas, in order to convince Katy officials that their road should pass near his Bucklucky Store. Whatever the cause, the fact remains that the Katy did follow that route, and almost immediately McAlester promoted extensive mining operations in the Choctaw Nation.[4]

As part of a nation in the throes of an industrial revolution, the Gulf Southwest was of low estate. On the eve of the Civil War, with thirty-four states and territories ranked, Kansas was last; Arkansas, thirty-second; Texas, twenty-ninth; and Louisiana and Missouri, twenty-second and eleventh, respectively. Twenty years later the situation had changed but little. Missouri had risen to eighth among thirty-eight states in the value of its industrial output, but the others still lagged, comparable only to the recent Confederate and newly created western states. Industrial activity, practically all of which was concentrated along the railroad lines, was typically frontier in nature—lumbering, blacksmithing, and the primary processing of agricultural products by small local establishments. With the notable exception of St. Louis, and to a less degree New Orleans and Kansas City, it was to be many years before the new transportation facilities could boast that they had attracted extensive industrial activity to the Southwest.[5]

---

[4] "Report on Indians Taxed and Indians not Taxed," *Eleventh Census*, XX, 1261–62; 45 Cong., 3 sess., *S. Rep. 744*, 250–51; Nesbitt, "J. J. McAlester," *Chron. Okla.*, Vol. XI, 758–64.

[5] "Manufactures," *Eighth Census*, III, 727; "Report on Manufacturers," *Tenth Census*, II, xii, xxv.

CHAPTER 14

The Lusty Country

SOUTHWESTERN RAILROADS building beyond established settlements penetrated a region unique in its appeal to primitive violence. No untamed country is hospitable. The Southwest was certainly no different in this respect from the ever recurring frontiers which preceded it. The difference was in the type of hostility which it exhibited towards man. The vast sun-baked sweep of treeless and waterless plains, frequently scourged by howling blizzards from the north or scorching gales from the southwest, did not invite occupation. In popular thinking the entire region was still a part of the "Great American Desert." The natives were no friendlier than the land. The nomads of the plains, with no intention of giving up their hunting grounds without a struggle, were resourceful and implacable foes.

The Southwest shared with other frontiers those conditions which placed such a premium on self-reliance that antecedents were of little consequence. When a crisis arose, nothing in one's ancestry or personal background was of particular worth; his value lay in his ability to handle the immediate situation. The administration and enforcement of the law was as primitive as other social institutions; justice was necessarily a personal matter. Within rather broad limits, private quarrels were left to the individuals concerned. Such a society appealed to the adventurous; it also appealed to the lawless.

These conditions, common to all frontiers, in themselves bred lawlessness; geography and the time element accentuated it in the Southwest. The country was ideally suited to raising livestock, an occupation always associated with hardiness and physical courage. Reckless

The Lusty Country

bravery was the rule in handling the wild stock during roundups and on the drives. Besides, the barest of law regulated the relations of a handful of cattlemen strewn over thousands of square miles of land. Those who were not strong enough to hold that which they claimed had chosen the wrong environment in which to live.

The location was ideal for anyone with a past which might rise up to haunt him. A man could not only lose himself in this wild country, but he could also find refuge in near-by havens. Between Kansas and Texas lay the Indian Territory, which was attached to no federal judicial district and in which the laws of the Indian nations prevailed, and "No Man's Land," the public land strip which was attached neither to a state nor to a federal judicial district. Both could be reached without great effort from northern Texas or southern Kansas, and from more distant points by dint of hard riding. Texans desirous of leaving the state in a hurry could also break for the Río Grande, with the security of Mexico beyond.

The time of occupancy added an element which set the southwestern frontier apart. A great fratricidal conflict had just ended. Many chose to leave their homes and start anew in the virgin land to the west, particularly Texas. There they did not find conditions entirely to their liking, for the Reconstruction government was in control. Some of the select names from the long list of Texas gunmen, both native and immigrant, received their initial training in battling Governor Edmund J. Davis' hated State Police.

The Civil War, as fought in Missouri, Kansas, and Arkansas, produced its own brand of "hard cases." The wanton brutality of irregular guerrilla bands was more savage than battlefield combat. Some of the ablest of the riding, robbing, and killing fraternity developed their prowess under the able tutelage of William C. Quantrill, Bill Anderson, and George Todd. Loyalties to a cause did not have to be too complete. While the activities of Kansas jayhawkers and Missouri bushwhackers were associated with the cause of the Union or the cause of the Confederacy, there were always those who were impartial in their looting. Too, Appomattox did not end all the activities, as many unwary travelers learned to their sorrow.

Under these conditions, violence and lawlessness flourished. The classic remark, "West of ——— there is no law; west of ——— there is no God," could be and was applied with equal truth, whether the blanks were filled with the names of Junction City and Hays City, Newton and Dodge City, or the Pecos and El Paso.

Then Came the Railroads

In addition to supplying bridges, which furnished convenient gallows in a treeless country, railroads were intimately associated with this untamed society at three points. The "end of track" attracted human beings as wild as the country through which the rails passed; strewn along behind were the cowtowns, which furnished a meeting ground for explosive elements; once they were operating, railroads were the prey for probably the most spectacular of all criminals—the train robber.

The "end of track," a source of disorder under the best of conditions, was doubly so when the scene of operation was beyond the frontier, ungraced by law, and traversing a country not yet entirely freed of roving bands of hostile Indians. The name "hell on wheels," applied to the vicious tent and shack community which followed the Union Pacific, could be used with equal propriety to describe the end of track of all western railroads. The construction camp was definitely a man's world, and a young man's world at that. It attracted all the unsavory elements capable of satisfying such a society. Cold-eyed gamblers, purveyors of cheap liquor, hangers-on capable of any crime, women with certain merchantable commodities which would bring a price in an undiscriminating market—all flocked to the end of track. With each relocation of field headquarters, proprietors of the various establishments hastily struck their tents or dismantled their rough-lumber shacks and set them up again at the new center of activity. The same drinking dives, the same gambling houses, the same tawdry dance halls, with the entertainers carrying on a brisk business on the side, were there to greet the construction gangs at each new location and separate the workers from their earnings as quickly as possible. Many of the men were willing victims because it represented their sole source of amusement. A construction worker, gingerly nursing an aching head after "relaxing" from the back-breaking toil of grading, tying, or laying iron, philosophically dismissed the prodigal waste of his wages with, "Easy come, easy go!"

The story was the same for all railroads. The Katy differed from the others only in attracting an unusually disreputable collection of gamblers, thieves, murderers, and prostitutes to follow it across the Indian Territory. Conditions were ideal for the "terminuses," the name applied to this choice assortment of camp followers. The country was practically without law: ineffective Indian courts and the most tenuous of federal control over individuals who had no right to be where they were. Each new camp had its own stories of violence

The Lusty Country

and death until, at Eufaula, a detachment of troops escorted the worst of the cutthroats out of the country. The relief was only temporary. On April 11, 1872, O. B. Gunn, chief engineer for the railroad, reported, "All Perryville slept on their arms, having word that the town was to be sacked and burned."[1] When the Katy reached Red River, it spewed the "terminuses" across into Texas, where they gave Denison a reputation rivaling that of the most lurid Kansas cowtowns. Here also came the denizens of Preston, with a reputation for depravity extending back many years. In time, "Red" Hall, the famous marshal, assisted the worst element in moving on.[2]

The wild Kansas cowtowns which sprang up along the Santa Fe and the Kansas Pacific and at the tips of the roads leading down to the Indian Territory have supplied fiction writers with some of their most stirring tales and have given world-wide meaning to the term "wild West." Without their railroads, these towns would never have blossomed at the end of the cattle trails.

Abilene was the first. The arrival of six hundred head of wild Texas stock, driven from the vicinity of Lockhart by M. A. Withers, marked the birth of a rowdy boom town at the site of a dusty, sleepy Kansas village. During the years of its cattle drives, Abilene supported four hotels and a relatively large number of clothing stores, restaurants, and miscellaneous establishments to care for the needs of its transient population. Saloons, gambling houses, and dance halls were by far the most numerous and most popular of all business houses, particularly in "Texas Abilene" south of the tracks. The Alamo was the best known of the saloons, but the Bull's Head, operated by Phil Coe and Ben Thompson, was the most popular with the cowpunchers. The "sporting" district was made up of some twenty-five houses, most of which moved to the southeast edge of town to a section known henceforth as Devil's Addition.

Twenty-five hundred cowboys would sometimes be in town at the height of the shipping season. With his wages burning his pocket, the typical hand headed for a barbershop, stopping en route at a convenient bar or two, had himself trimmed by the barber (frequently the least painful trimming he would receive), then visited a clothing store for a complete outfitting. He was then ready to see the town. Months of range life, during which he had none but fellow hands for

---

[1] Foreman, *A History of Oklahoma*, 183.
[2] *Ibid.*, 181–83; Debo, *The Road to Disappearance*, 231; Edward King, *The Great South*, 175–78; "Reminiscences of R. P. Vann," *Chron. Okla.*, Vol. XI, 843.

companions, had to be compensated for in the few days before he returned to his lonely existence. He mingled with others having the same intentions, and after a few drinks the situation could become highly explosive.

Relations between the permanent residents of Abilene and their best customers, the Texans (all cowboys being so designated), were not the friendliest. The townspeople blamed the Texans, who were accused of shooting up Abilene, riding on its board walks, and generally disporting themselves in a vicious fashion. There was an element of truth in the accusations. Mixed with the happy-go-lucky pleasure-seekers were cowboys with tempers as quick as their draws. The great majority were strongly sympathetic to the Confederate cause. Some nursed a grudge against all Northerners, which carried over to the residents of the town, most of whom were Unionists who merited further contempt because of their sedentary life.

On the other hand, the Texans were convinced that they were victims of collusion between the townspeople and the law. Resident gamblers and many of the saloonkeepers were substantial citizens, usually active in setting up local government and backing the forces of law and order. The cowboys complained that too frequently only one side of a quarrel was ever heard, and that so-called law enforcement was merely the strong arm of local interests.

An imagined slight, a suspicion of crooked dealing at a gaming table, rivalry for the favors of a lady of the evening, or just unprovoked belligerence could, in a moment, create a tense situation which could quickly turn into deadly gunplay. The answer was a marshal who was just as tough as the wild bunch he had to control. There is common agreement that Tom Smith was such a marshal. Overshadowed by more spectacular figures, he took the job when no one else could hold it. He was not a killer and rarely used a gun, keeping the peace with his hamlike fists until he was murdered. "Wild Bill" Hickok, one of the most controversial figures of the cattle country, became marshal of Abilene in April, 1871. Unlike Smith, who faithfully patrolled the streets to prevent disorder, Wild Bill could usually be found in the Alamo Saloon; nevertheless, his reputation was enough to assure a fair degree of order.[3]

The Abilene boom collapsed in 1871. Already, however, similar

[3] McCoy, *Historic Sketches of the Cattle Trade of the West and Southwest*, 111–47, 202–10, 291–95; William E. Connelley, *Wild Bill and His Era*, 138–61; Wayne Gard, *Frontier Justice*, 236–39; Louis Pelzer, *The Cattlemen's Frontier*, 53–56; Edward Everett Dale, *Cow Country*, 19–39.

Courtesy Fort Worth Chamber of Commerce

Wood-burning Katy locomotive of the seventies.

St. Louis, Iron Mountain & Southern locomotive of the eighties.

Courtesy Missouri Pacific Lines

Courtesy Fort Worth Chamber of Commerce

Wood-burning Texas & St. Louis locomotive in 1884.

St. Louis, Arkansas & Texas locomotive in 1886.

Courtesy Fort Worth Chamber of Commerce

The Lusty Country

towns had risen farther west. Everywhere the story was the same—townsmen and gamblers versus Texans, plus the interfraternity gunplay of hot-blooded cowpunchers carried away by the excitement of their celebrations.

Newton won undying notoriety as the scene of one of the bloodiest encounters in a region in which bloodshed was not uncommon. Mike McCluskie, a railroad agent of proved ability with pistols, was hired as town marshal by local gamblers, and in the course of duty he killed a Texas gambler. A few nights later McCluskie, followed by a youthful hero-worshipper named Riley, made the mistake of stopping at the gaming tables in the Tuttle Dance Hall. The room was soon filled with hostile Texans, and the marshal had no chance in the gunfight which followed. Maddened by the killing of his idol, mild-mannered Riley seized two guns, and in a matter of seconds six Texans and two innocent bystanders (reputedly railroad workers) were dead and four others wounded. Riley was never seen again.[4]

Wichita was next along the Santa Fe. Here Ben Thompson, late of the Bull's Head at Abilene, was on hand to greet the cowhands at the end of the cattle trail. Here also came Wyatt Earp, whose reputation as a peace officer was earned as deputy town marshal. Relations between the law and the Texans were much the same as they had been at Abilene and Newton. The clanging of an iron triangle in the center of town was the tocsin rallying the citizens to unite against their guests when the situation got out of hand. The reputation of bloody Keno Corner was well established before the head of the trail moved on to Dodge City, which outdid all the others in gaining its fame as the wickedest city of the day.[5]

False-fronted, plank-walked Front Street was known throughout the nation. Dodge City's saloons, its gambling houses, its dance halls and brothels—even its first jail, a converted well into which prisoners were lowered—were as widely publicized as Boot Hill, symbol of sudden and violent departure from this world.

In 1872, the Santa Fe reached Buffalo City, located barely beyond the five-mile zone within which liquor could not be dispensed to the soldiers at Fort Dodge. Because of possible confusion arising from the prior existence of both Buffalo and Buffalo Station in Kansas, the town was renamed Dodge City.

---

[4] Stanley Vestal, *Short Grass Country*, 28–33; AGS, *Kansas*, 262.
[5] Stuart N. Lake, "The Frontier Marshal," *SEP*, Vol. CCIII (Nov. 15, 1930), 16–17, 98, 101.

Then Came the Railroads

Dodge City was not without a certain notoriety before the arrival of the first herds driven up from Texas. A large, free-spending, floating population—soldiers from the fort, buffalo hunters, and freighters to remote western posts—overflowed the town and attracted the usual hangers-on intent on living in comfort with the least possible physical effort. But the cattle drives, which became increasingly important for a few years after 1875, gave the town its lasting reputation. The frequent appearance of such names as "Lone Star," "Texas," and "Alamo" in Dodge City connoted exactly what it had in the town's predecessors—an eye for business rather than any deep affection for Texas or its residents.

Most of the famous gunmen who had survived the earlier cowtowns were connected with Dodge City in one way or another. Wes Hardin and his wild cousins, the Clements boys, and such well-known figures as the three Dixon brothers, Joe and Billy Collins, Brown Bowen, and Ham Anderson, to mention only a few, held herds of Texas cattle outside the town, waiting for stockcars. The names of the Ford County sheriffs and Dodge City marshals are equally well known: Charley Bassett, "Mysterious Dave" Mather, Wyatt Earp, Bat and Ed Masterson, and, later, Pat Sughrue and Bill Tilghman. The list of famous gamblers included Luke Short, "Doc" Holliday, and Ben Thompson, along with Ben's satellite brother, Billy. It was no mean tribute to the deadliness of Dodge City gunmen when the Santa Fe entrusted to J. H. Phillips, its local agent, the job of recruiting a force to maintain its claims to the Royal Gorge against those of the Denver and Rio Grande railroad.

Oddly enough, Dodge City was the center of some really good entertainment for that day. Many traveling shows toured the country after the Santa Fe built through. The little cowtown was a convenient break in the long haul from Kansas City to Colorado.[6]

Other railroad-cattle towns in Kansas and Texas had somewhat less gaudy reputations, yet required eternally vigilant marshals. Junction City could boast its Irish-born Tom Cullinan, who miraculously served as marshal through all the rowdy days and for many years thereafter; John Henry Brown, at Caldwell, was a highly effective officer until he was killed while attempting to escape after robbing the bank at Medicine Lodge. Down in Texas, "Red" Hall brought a

---

[6] Wright, *Dodge City, passim;* Dick, *Vanguards of the Frontier,* 433, 465–68; Bradley, *The Story of the Santa Fe,* 92–100; Lake, "The Frontier Marshal," *SEP,* Vol. CCIII (Nov. 15, 1930), 16–17; Gard, *Frontier Justice,* 240–42; Zoe A. Tilghman, *Marshal of the Last Frontier,* 131–62.

The Lusty Country

degree of quiet to Denison; Jim Courtright, the long-haired Iowan, engaged in later activities which obscured his record as a good marshal at Fort Worth; ubiquitous Ben Thompson became the hard-drinking, quarrelsome marshal at Austin.[7]

The Kansas cowtowns were born of the open range, and their youthful riotousness ended with the closing of the cattle trails. While keeping alive the memories of their lurid past, they were content to accept the more durable prosperity which came to them with a more prosaic economy.

The paths of commerce have always been beset by highwaymen. The train robber of the seventies was the modern manifestation of a type of banditry that grew up wherever goods were transported from one town to another. While train holdups were not peculiar to the Southwest alone, nowhere were they conducted in more widespread or spectacular fashion. For some strange reason, possibly because of its daring, there has always been a considerable degree of admiration and sympathy for the men who engaged in this particular brand of lawlessness. Certainly in the not too distant past, few American twelve-year-olds were not filled with anger and sorrow because the

> *... dirty little coward that shot Mr. Howard*
> *Has laid Jesse James in his grave.*

This same twelve-year-old gravely nodded his assent to the judgment pronounced against Jim Murphy for his betrayal of Sam Bass:

> *And so he sold out Sam and Barnes, and left their friends to mourn,*
> *Oh! what a scorching Jim will get, when Gabriel blows his horn!*

The train robber posed a very real and constant threat to railroads. Certain stations where conditions were exceptionally favorable became notorious for the number of their holdups. For some twenty years there was always at least one train robber on the fugitive list of the Texas Rangers. Railroad and express companies hired experienced gunmen as special officers to ride the baggage and express cars; the Pinkerton and other detective agencies were called in to stop the activities of some of the abler gangs.

Some holdups attracted considerable attention because of unusual

---

[7] Gard, *Frontier Justice*, 197, 240, 243; Eugene Cunningham, *Triggernometry*, 66–89, 203–206.

Then Came the Railroads

circumstances. Such was the robbery of a Santa Fe train at Kinsley, Kansas, by the Dave Rudabaugh gang. It deviated from the normal because a posse from Dodge City, led by Bat Masterson, anticipated the movements of the gang and captured all its members at a dugout hideaway without one shot being fired.

Of all the train robbers who infested the Southwest in the seventies, none caught the public imagination so completely as the James-Younger band in the Missouri-Kansas area and Sam Bass in Texas. The Civil War furnished an excuse, if not a reason, for the subsequent activities of the Missourians. The Younger and the James families suffered injury at the hands of the jayhawkers. Both Frank James and Cole Younger rode with Quantrill, Jesse James with "Bloody Bill" Anderson. The war ended, but ruthless bands of wild, lawless Yankee-haters continued to ride.

In 1866 the James boys and the Younger brothers united their forces to create the most highly publicized gang of outlaws in American history. Their activities extended east to West Virginia, north to Minnesota, and south to Texas. The band was not narrowly specialized; its members were equally adept with trains or banks. In some ways they were more closely identified with bank robberies; they were involved in the first bank robbery in American history, made their initial reputation in that field, and the gang was eventually wrecked in an attempted bank robbery at Northfield, Minnesota. Then, too, the doubtful honor of originating the train holdup belongs to the Reno brothers of Indiana, who robbed a train seven years before the first such crime by the James-Younger gang.

The first train robbery by the James-Younger band took place in the summer of 1873 at Adair, Iowa, and was accomplished by the simple expedient of loosening a rail at a point where the train always slowed down. The wreck which followed was apparently not a part of the plan, but the removal of a gold shipment was. Shortly thereafter began the feud between the Pinkerton agency, called in by the railroads, and the outlaws. The next holdup took place on the Kansas Pacific at Muncie, just outside Kansas City, late in 1874.

The most successful of the James-Younger holdups occurred on the Pacific of Missouri at Otterville, near Sedalia, on July 7, 1876. Members of the gang were aboard the train to stop it; ties were stacked on the rails a few miles beyond Otterville, just in case they did not succeed. The train was stopped before it reached the ties. The safe yielded $14,000, and the passengers an assortment of watches, wallets, and jewelry. Two months later the gang was shattered at Northfield, Minnesota. Jesse James came out of retirement in 1879 to stop a Chicago and Alton train at Glendale, near St. Louis, but his new band was far different from the stalwarts who followed him at the peak of his career. Two robberies in 1881, one of which took place on the Rock Island at Winston, Missouri, completed the activities of the untrustworthy skeleton of the old James-Younger gang.[8]

Indiana-born Sam Bass represented a far different tradition than the James boys and the Youngers. Lacking the finesse of the more famous Missourians, he also lacked the instinct to kill. Young Sam worked as a teamster and farm hand around Denton, Texas, until he learned that the life of a gambler and horse racer was easier. He turned to train robbery in the fall of 1877 when he was a member of a gang which held up a Union Pacific train at Big Spring, Nebraska. This was his first and most profitable venture, for the take was $60,000. The gang dissolved, and Sam returned to Denton.

Sam's share took care of his needs for a while. On January 26, 1878, a stage was held up between Fort Worth and Weatherford, the first of a series of such crimes. On February 22, four men robbed a Houston and Texas Central train at Allen Station; the following month three men repeated the crime at Hutchins Station. On April 4 it was a Texas and Pacific train at Eagle Ford, and six days later another Texas and Pacific train at Mesquite. Four holdups had taken place within a span of two months, all within twenty-five miles of Dallas! Like the stage bandits, the masked men had always ridden off in the direction of Denton County.

The Texas Rangers were called in after the fourth holdup; June Peak, a former Dallas peace officer, was given a temporary commission as lieutenant and authority to raise a force of thirty men. United States Marshal Stillwell H. Russell came over from Tyler. Railroads and express companies dispatched their special agents; the Pinkerton agency sent a squad of picked operatives. It has been estimated that more than 150 officers and private detectives flocked to Dallas to join the chase.

Sam Bass and his friend, "Sebe" Barnes, were already suspect. In a short time they, with some associates, went into hiding in the creek bottoms. The remainder of Sam's short career was one of flight, which ended with his death at the hands of a Ranger at the little town of Round Rock. In spite of the widespread publicity, the Bass holdups

[8] Homer Croy, *Jesse James Was My Neighbor*, 22–40, 74–77, 82–99, 105, 147.

Then Came the Railroads

netted only small sums. In the first it was $1,280; the second $497; the third, only $52; and the last, $150.[9]

By the eighties, much of the Southwest was beginning to settle back to a somewhat more placid existence. There were many more tales yet to be told of "end of track" turbulence, of boom towns, and of train robberies, but the area was more restricted, with the Indian Territory and West Texas the chief centers of activity.

[9] Walter P. Webb, *The Texas Rangers,* 371–90; Gard, *Frontier Justice,* 229; Cunningham, *Triggernometry,* 285–95.

CHAPTER 15

The Waters Cease Running

THE ATTENTION of railroad promoters turned in the seventies to lands in the Indian Territory. Two major questions awaited solution. One was the status of the conditional land grants in Indian Territory; the other, whether the treaties limited to two the number of railroads which could cross the lands of each of the Civilized Tribes. Both problems originated with the Reconstruction treaties, and both were to wait many years for final settlement. In addition, railroad builders were interested in incidental legislation under consideration by Congress, the outcome of which would have a direct bearing on the answers to the two major problems.

Certainly there was no possible way to read into any of the treaties the consent of the Indians to anything more than a bare right of way, and that only because of circumstances and against the will of the tribes. Considering the acts making conditional land grants in their territory, the Indians had every reason to regard all bills to modify their tribal governments or any additional railroad bills as assaults on their land titles. Probably no action by Congress in the entire history of Indian Territory legislation did so much to interfere with the advancement of the Indians or to strengthen them in their determination to keep their lands inviolate than the enactment of the conditional land-grant measures.

In Congress, it was the easterner who viewed the Indian lands as a trust, with the United States pledged to keep the territory free from white influence. This position was not entirely altruistic because there was some jealousy of the growing power of the West. It was also

Then Came the Railroads

much easier for representatives of states far removed from the frontier to consider the matter philanthropically. From the standpoint of new western states, the Indians were an alien influence retarding progress. It was preposterous that there should be landless people, or even those with less desirable lands, so long as Indians occupied areas in excess of their needs. These same Indians stood as a barrier to the commercial expansion of the Southwest. To uphold "outworn treaties" and land patents which stood in the path of civilization was nothing short of "insipid sentimentality." These conflicting points of view cropped up every time the Indian problem was under consideration.

The two railroads which first penetrated the Indian Territory had no sooner entered than they began to agitate for the validation of their land grants. Even before the Katy had won its right of way across the Territory, it had made arrangements for mortgaging any lands it might acquire there, and on February 1, 1871, issued consolidated mortgage bonds including these lands. The Atlantic and Pacific acted with only slightly less celerity. C. J. Hillyer, attorney for the company, published a pamphlet demanding the extinguishing of Indian title with the statement:

> We insist that this clause of the treaty contains a promise to us which it is the duty of Congress to fulfill. Although coupled with conditions which permit the exercise of a certain degree of discretion, it is certainly not meaningless, nor is its meaning doubtful. Congress intended and agreed, as part of the inducement to build this road, that the Government should at some time, at its own expense and for our benefit, procure the cession by the Indians of their title to these lands. . . . Good faith to us requires that Congress should act at once. . . . The words "and only by their voluntary cession" were not intended and cannot be construed to destroy the previous promise to *extinguish* the title.[1]

In October, 1871, the Atlantic and Pacific mortgaged all of its property, including its rights to lands in Indian Territory.

The execution of the mortgages by both the Katy and the Atlantic and Pacific introduced another group—the bondholders—into the fraternity intent on extinguishing Indian title. The effect of conditional land grants on the status of Indian title was reflected in the fluctuation in the value of railroad securities. Atlantic and Pacific

[1] C. J. Hillyer, *Atlantic and Pacific Railroad and the Indian Territory,* 7–8; 45 Cong., 3 sess., *S. Rep. 744,* 28–31, 50–51, 231; App., 9, 44.

The Waters Cease Running

bonds tumbled to five cents when the commissioner of the General Land Office held that the railroad was not entitled to any lands in Indian Territory. He had carefully distinguished between this road and the Katy, however, and the market value of Katy securities continued to benefit from the uncertainty regarding its claims to Indian lands. Katy stocks and bonds rose and fell with the fortunes of Indian Territory bills rather than on the basis of earnings.[2]

The Indians, through their councils and their delegates in Washington, agitated for the repeal of the grants, which represented a continuous threat to the integrity of the tribes. John H. Beadle, the wandering journalist, saw in them the greatest obstacle to Indian progress.[3]

New England senators introduced a number of bills for repealing the grants, and in 1876 a House report stated: "The committee think that the contingent land grant in question [to the Katy] was utterly indefensible, without consideration, gravely injurious to the Indians, a perpetual menace, a worthless pretense of a grant in reality, which can only be made of value and substantial by the most shameless ill-faith, and that it ought to be repealed."[4]

Gardiner G. Hubbard, attorney for the Katy bondholders, while speaking before the House Committee on Territories, insisted that the United States should take the lands from the Indians and grant them to the railroads.

You then, gentlemen, representing the United States, must hold the scales fairly and equally between the parties before you—the railroad on the one hand, and the Indians on the other.

... the bondholders knew that the United States granted a vast tract of land to the corporation and agreed to extinguish the Indian title as soon as it can be done with justice to the parties interested. Relying on these pledges they loaned their money. ...

It may be said that we propose taking the land from the Indians and giving it to the railroads. If the view we have taken is correct, the United States are only fulfilling their plighted faith to both Indian and railroad, giving to the Indian three-fourths of the land in fee, and in consideration of that grant, extinguishing their title to the remainder, whereby the grant heretofore made to the railroad takes effect.[5]

---

[2] 45 Cong., 3 sess., *S. Rep. 744*, 3–4, 232–33.
[3] John H. Beadle, *The Undeveloped West*, 426–30.
[4] 44 Cong., 1 sess., *H. Rep. 299*, 7.
[5] *Argument of Hon. Gardiner G. Hubbard . . . Feb. 11, 1876*, 7–8, 10.

Then Came the Railroads

The Indians welcomed this statement because, for the first time, a railroad attorney had brought the issue into the open, uncouched in smug phraseology about bettering the condition of the Indian and promoting his civilization. They answered that they already held title to the entire area by patents granted by the President of the United States, that this title was much older than the railroad claims, and that Hubbard was appealing to Congress to dispossess the Indians for the benefit of speculators.[6]

In 1878, Daniel W. Voorhees of Indiana submitted a resolution in the Senate calling for an investigation of the issuance of railroad securities predicated upon the conditional land grants. Stephen W. Dorsey of Arkansas fathered an amendment which extended the investigation to several closely related Indian problems. This resolution led to the creation of a committee headed by John J. Patterson of South Carolina. The committee was in close touch with Gardiner G. Hubbard, attorney for the bondholders, James Baker, attorney for the Atlantic and Pacific, Judge T. C. Sears, attorney for the Missouri, Kansas and Texas, and E. C. Boudinot. Boudinot had already sent a Katy annual pass to his uncle and had advised him to help make something of the resolution.

The committee devoted itself almost exclusively to an investigation of the Indians rather than the railroads. Most of the testimony was taken in Washington. A few days were spent in the railroad towns of Indian Territory and a few more at Fort Scott, Kansas. One member of the committee spent part of one day at the Cherokee capital, Tahlequah; the other Indian capitals were never visited. The witnesses were called haphazardly, with much deference paid to the testimony of intermarried whites of questionable character, self-professed Indian authorities from Arkansas, and freedmen. On the other hand, the representatives of the Indian nations were given little advance information on when the hearings would take place.

The final committee report admitted that "the conditional land grants to railroads were ill advised and should not have been made" and recommended their repeal. It also recommended the establishment of a federal court, with both civil and criminal jurisdiction, a delegate to Congress from Indian Territory, and the extension of United States citizenship to the Indians.[7]

[6] Daniel H. Ross, *Answer . . . to Gardiner G. Hubbard*, 1–12.
[7] 45 Cong., 2 sess., *S. Misc. Doc. 30*, parts 1 and 2 and *H. Misc. Doc. 18;* 45 Cong., 3 sess., *S. Rep. 744* and *S. Misc. Doc. 52;* 49 Cong., 1 sess., *H. Misc. Doc. 3;* Phil. Coll., Correspondence of E. C. Boudinot, Series 2, II, Nos. 14 and 17.

The Waters Cease Running

Nothing was done about repealing the conditional land grants. On October 26, 1880, the attorney general ruled that a breach of condition by the railroad did not work a forfeiture of the Atlantic and Pacific lands until Congress acted; two years later the Department of the Interior reported that the Atlantic and Pacific could claim 13,170,560 acres in Indian Territory when it completed its lines. Meanwhile, J. A. Williamson, who, as commissioner of the General Land Office, had written the earlier adverse ruling on the claims of the Atlantic and Pacific, had become the attorney for that railroad and insisted that the United States was obligated to extinguish the Indian title. By this time, however, the entire Atlantic and Pacific grant was under fire.[8]

The second grave problem faced by the Indians, the demands of other railroads for rights of way through their lands, was to be settled adversely to the Indians in the early eighties. Before any railroad had earned the right to enter, the Katy had insisted that the Reconstruction treaties did not establish a maximum of two railroads in each nation. Ten years after the Katy crossed the Territory, it sent surveying parties into the Cherokee Nation to determine the best route for a branch from Muskogee, Creek Nation, through the Cherokee lands to Fort Smith, Arkansas, disregarding the fact that the Atlantic and Pacific had already crossed the Cherokee Nation from east to west. The principal chief of the Cherokees stopped the surveyors, and the Secretary of the Interior upheld the contention of the Indians that the building of the Atlantic and Pacific barred all other railroads from crossing the Cherokee Nation from east to west. This position was reaffirmed when the Atlantic and Pacific received notice that if it contemplated building a Fort Smith branch, such a line must run south of the Creek and Cherokee lands.[9]

The pioneer lines through the Indian Territory were scarcely constructed before congressmen from surrounding states began introducing bills for additional rail facilities. As more railroads reached the territorial line, the pressure grew. Early in 1881, the Indians faced the first truly serious crisis when a group of Boston promoters secured the passage of a bill through the House of Representatives which would have permitted them to build a road from Fort Smith across Indian Territory to Arkansas City, Kansas, without the consent of the Indians. The bitter protests of the Cherokees were met with the

[8] *Op. Atty. Gen.*, XVI, 572; 47 Cong., 1 sess., *S. Ex. Doc. 144*, 42; 48 Cong., 1 sess., *H. Rep. 1663*, 14–16.
[9] IAD, Creek-Railroads, 35725–30, 35754–55; *ibid.*, Creek—Principal Chief, 35590; *ibid.*, Cherokee Papers—Railroads, File IXa-4; CLPCB, V, 105–24.

argument that consent by the Indians would put it within the power of their councils to blackmail railroads or even prevent them from entering; besides, the treaties of 1866 granted rights of way. A pro-Indian bloc in the Senate, headed by Henry L. Dawes of Massachusetts, insisted that the construction of two railroads across the Cherokee Nation had exhausted the right to build. Dawes sponsored an amendment requiring Indian consent to this and all future construction. The Senate adopted the amendment the last day of the Forty-sixth Congress, which was tantamount to defeating the bill.[10]

Meanwhile the pressure for more railroads had become all but irresistible. Texas desired connections with the north, Arkansas demanded connections to the west, and Kansas urged that the laws be erased which halted the progress of its rapidly developing rail network at the Indian Territory line. St. Louis, Kansas City, and dozens of smaller cities were convinced that their welfare depended upon overriding the treaties and as much of the Indian intercourse laws as denied the railroads entrance. However, many members of Congress, particularly eastern senators, upheld the treaty rights of the Indians as a national trust which could not be set aside lightly.

The issue came to a head in 1882 when Congress was forced to determine the respective rights of the Frisco railroad and the Choctaw and Chickasaw Indians. The railroad, building at the time from Fayetteville to Fort Smith, secured permission from the United States government to negotiate with the Choctaws for a right of way from Fort Smith to the Red River, near Paris, Texas. Late in November, 1881, the Choctaw House of Representatives considered the proposal. Nine members of the body favored it; eight opposed. Speaker of the House B. F. Smallwood thereupon asserted his right to cast a negative vote. Since it was a tie, Smallwood declared the bill defeated, and an entry in the journal to that effect was approved by the House. Jackson McCurtain, governor of the Choctaws, ordered the seal of the nation affixed to the bill on the grounds that Smallwood could not legally vote, and it had therefore passed. The Congress of the United States was forced to decide if it could go behind the seal of the Choctaw Nation to determine whether the measure had been legally enacted.

Senator Sam B. Maxey of Texas had gone before the Choctaw General Council and had spoken in favor of the railroad bill while it was under consideration. He now introduced a measure in the

---

[10] *Cong. Rec.*, 46 Cong., 3 sess., 1418–20, 1904–1906, 2377–79, 2407–13, 2417; 46 Cong., 2 sess., *H. Rep. 1422*.

The Waters Cease Running

United States Senate for the purpose of recognizing the action of the Choctaw Council in granting to the railroad a right of way through the tribal lands. A spirited debate, beginning January 18, followed. Friends of Maxey's bill insisted that the opposition was inspired by Jay Gould, who wanted to assure himself a southwestern transportation monopoly.

The Choctaw delegation could have adopted no more disastrous a course than the one it pursued in attempting to defeat the Maxey bill. Whether inspired by devotion to the tribal government, as they claimed, or acting as the agent for railroad monopolists, the Indians cast enough doubt on the legality of the proceedings in the Choctaw Council for the Senate Committee on Railroads to report a substitute. Several senators had vaguely referred to the possibility of the United States' exercising its right of eminent domain in Indian Territory, but the Maxey bill was based on the consent of the Indians. The substitute approached the matter from the broader grounds. The right of eminent domain was inherent in the government and could not be abdicated; any law which attempted to do so was void. The Indian treaties and the Indian intercourse acts were therefore invalid insofar as they purported to give jurisdiction to the Indian tribes to the exclusion of the fundamental right of the United States government to have final disposition over any lands within its limits.

The bill was bound to stand or fall on moral obligation rather than legal right. The real issue was summed up in an interchange between Augustus H. Garland of Arkansas and Joseph R. Hawley. After Garland stated, "It is mere nonsense, in my humble judgment, to talk about going to the Indian Council for its leave to establish this road through that country," Hawley answered, "Is it nonsense to do it if you promised to do it, and if in this last act [ending treaty making with the Indians] you said that all previous treaties shall remain binding? It cannot be nonsense to keep your word."[11]

At the height of the debate, the Seligman brothers sold the Frisco to Jay Gould. The extension of the Frisco across the Choctaw lands would have given Texas a second railroad to St. Louis to compete with Gould's Iron Mountain–International and Great Northern combination. There was considerable force to the argument that a single, unregulated railroad monopoly should not be permitted to dominate the movement of all goods from Texas to St. Louis, but with Gould in control of the Frisco, there was no longer validity in this conten-

[11] *Cong. Rec.*, 47 Cong., 1 sess., 2571, 2574.

tion. Senator George Vest's pious suggestion that "in the providence of God, Mr. Gould may be removed from the theater of monopolies in which he now figures"[12] was scarcely an answer to the fact that Gould did control the Frisco at the time. When opponents of the bill pointed this out, its friends admitted that the primary motive was to destroy the guarantees to the Indians. In the words of Senator Garland, when Congress abolished treaty-making with the Indians, "the Government then fixed its policy with them, that they were no longer independent tribes or independent nations in any sense of the word, and it fixed the policy beyond any question or any dispute that the power of legislation for these people was and is in Congress, unrestricted and unlimited."[13] Garland failed to mention that the legislation, while terminating treaty-making, guaranteed to the Indians all existing treaty rights.

The Senate passed the bill on April 13. The significance of the action was not lost on the Indians. The upper chamber had always defended their treaty rights from the assaults of the House of Representatives, which had consistently interpreted the treaties as narrowly as possible. The combined delegations presented a protest to the Senate, but it was dismissed with the statement that none except the Choctaws were concerned with the disposition of the bill.

The fate of the Indians was determined in the intense heat of July, with barely a quorum present in the House. An eastern minority, which urged that the treaty rights of the Indians should be respected, was overwhelmed, and on August 2, 1882, the President of the United States signed the bill. The policy of securing Indian consent before permitting railroads to enter the Territory had been terminated. Construction of the railroad whose promoters had insisted that time was of the essence began five years later.[14]

The full import of the act was not immediately apparent, but a year later nine railroads sought permission from Congress to enter Indian Territory, all basing their requests on the principle of eminent domain, with the bill of the preceding session as the precedent. There was some opposition in the Senate, but most of the bills passed. The principle was firmly established when, on February 15, 1886, Senator

[12] *Ibid.*, 2803.
[13] *Ibid.*, 2804.
[14] 47 Cong., 1 sess., *S. Ex. Docs. 15* and *44, S. Misc. Doc. 18, H. Ex. Doc. 15,* and *H. Rep. 934; Cong. Rec.,* 47 Cong., 1 sess., 502–505, 2517–28, 2563–78, 2759–78, 2801–2809, 2852–57, 6582–91; OIA, Letters Received for 1881, 2703, 2712, 21482 (with enclosures), 21763–67; *U. S. Stat. at L.,* XXII, 181.

The Waters Cease Running

Dawes, reporting from the Committee on Indian Affairs, held that since Congress had granted rights of way on a number of occasions, "the committee, therefore, without waiving individual opinion upon the right of Congress to make such grants without the consent of the Indians, have considered that question settled by Congress."[15]

Dozens of Indian Territory railroad bills were introduced in the next few years. The House Committee on Indian Affairs took cognizance of the large number of "paper" railroads which were interested in speculating with their franchises rather than building. Meanwhile a new check on the indiscriminate enactment of railroad bills appeared in the form of the presidential veto. Grover Cleveland felt that whenever possible, the railroads should secure the consent of the Indians; furthermore, the prodigality of Congress was detrimental to Indian welfare. Nothing, however, could stem the flow of bills.[16]

The Cherokee Council protested as each new railroad measure was introduced, and as each passed, it solemnly dissented from the action of Congress. Failing in its appeals to Congress, the Council resorted to the courts to retard railroad penetration. The Cherokee Nation brought actions against the Kansas and Arkansas Valley and the Southern Kansas in the federal court for the Western District of Arkansas. In both cases Judge Isaac C. Parker ruled that the Cherokee Nation was under the political control of the United States and was therefore subject to any power inherent in sovereignty, a decision subsequently affirmed by the Supreme Court. Cherokee opposition came to an end when Principal Chief Joel B. Mayes, in his annual message in November, 1890, admitted that the right of the United States government to exercise the right of eminent domain in Indian Territory had been established.[17]

Much incidental legislation affecting the Indian Territory was introduced in the period following the Civil War, and, rightly or wrongly, the railroads were accused of exerting pressure to secure its passage. Allotment in severalty would create surplus lands which would eventually be thrown open to white settlement, a preliminary step in destroying the Indian nations. United States citizenship, an Indian delegate to Congress, and federal courts in Indian Territory would

---

[15] 49 Cong., 1 sess., *S. Rep. 107*.

[16] 49 Cong., 1 sess., *H. Rep. 1356;* Richardson, *A Compilation of the Messages and Papers of the Presidents,* VIII, 693-95, 777; *U. S. Stat. at L.,* XXX, 990.

[17] *Fed. Rep.,* XXXIII, 900; *U. S. Rep.,* CXXXV, 641; *Indian Citizen* (Vinita), Nov. 13, 1880.

all strike at the root of the policy of recognizing the autonomous status of the Indian nations; the creation of a regularly organized territory would destroy political control by the tribal government with a single blow.

Forces diametrically opposed in principle united to support the various measures. Philanthropists saw the solution of the Indian problem in elevating Indian culture to the same plane as that of whites through individual landholding, education, and ultimate citizenship. The railroad attorney saw increased settlement, with added revenue traffic, and the validation of the conditional land grants. The speculator saw a new field of activity in Indian lands because, granting that the lands would be inalienable for a period of years, there would undoubtedly be opportunities for evasion. Another group was also interested—the bona fide settlers who desired to enter and make homes, the group behind which speculators so often hid while making their pleas that sturdy empire builders should not be denied lands which rightfully belonged to the white race.[18] Pressed from all sides, the Indians naturally opposed legislation which endangered their security by changing their status.

The first successful assault on Indian land title came in 1871 with the termination of treaty-making. Unquestionably, many wrongs were committed under the treaty system, and there was much in it that was inherently vicious. Its abolition was inevitable, and much good flowed from its destruction. The circumstances surrounding its demise, however, were such that the tribes could well believe that it was engineered as a raid on their lands. The time was particularly ill chosen because of the approach of railroads; furthermore, its leading advocates were associated with railroads. The measure had scarcely been enacted when an Atlantic and Pacific attorney wrote: "It is not a mere prohibition of the making of future treaties with these tribes. It goes beyond this, and *destroys the political existence of the tribes*. It does not strip from tribal organization one of its attributes, but, so far as the Government is concerned, blots out from existence this tribal organization in which the right to make treaties inhered."[19]

By 1872 the forces were marshaled for the coming battle over establishing regular territorial government. Congress considered a num-

---

[18] Hillyer, *Atlantic and Pacific Railroad and the Indian Territory*, 8, 54–59; Indian Rights Assn., *Fifth Annual Report*, 9–10; *Rep. Comm. Ind. Aff., 1876*, vii; *ibid., 1869*, 73; Bd. Ind. Comm., *Annual Report* (1885), 13.

[19] Hillyer, *Atlantic and Pacific Railroad and the Indian Territory*, 27.

The Waters Cease Running

ber of territorial measures introduced by representatives from Missouri, Arkansas, and Kansas. Indian delegates protested that the bills were railroad inspired to validate conditional land grants and fill the Territory with white settlers. Proponents admitted that territorialization might facilitate railroad penetration, but that question could be left to the honor and discretion of later Congresses. John Taffe of Nebraska expressed a widely accepted western interpretation of the Indian treaties with his statement: " 'Forever' appears in nearly all the treaties setting apart reservations. That means until the white men want the lands, or rather, the obstacles removed. Such has been the practical interpretation of that word in such connections, and it had just as well be passed into legal definition."[20] Only "mawkish sentimentality" permitted any other interpretation.

George C. McKee of Mississippi directed the opposition to the most prominent of the bills. He secured the adoption of an amendment which would repeal the conditional land grants in the event the measure passed. He posed this question: If the bill merely provided for civil government, with no change in the system of land tenure, why did the St. Louis Board of Trade, the land-grant railroads, and prospective settlers support it so actively? He considered the railroads with conditional land grants as "villainous heirs seeking to encompass the death of the parent in order to come more quickly into their inheritance."[21]

While this bill did not pass either house, it represented the opening volley in a battle which was to continue for many years. A lull occurred in the mid-seventies, but near the end of the decade, bills to organize Indian Territory, to grant Indian citizenship, to give the Territory a delegate to Congress, and to establish a federal court flooded both houses. Two measures in particular, those of Benjamin J. Franklin of Missouri and Jordan E. Craven of Arkansas, drew fire from the Indians. James Baker of the Atlantic and Pacific admitted before the Patterson Committee that he had helped prepare the Franklin bill. The Baltimore *Gazette* attacked it as "a fraud and swindle upon the Indians for the benefit of a railroad monopoly."[22] It was eventually reported adversely from committee. Meanwhile, the Indian delegates in Washington were disturbed by the report of the Patterson Committee, which recommended the immediate adop-

[20] *Cong. Globe,* 42 Cong., 3 sess., App., 14.
[21] *Ibid.,* 649; see also, *ibid.,* 611–20, 648–58; App., 12–14, 31–33, 217–18.
[22] *The Vindicator* (Atoka), April 5, 1876, quoting *Baltimore Gazette,* March 27, 1876.

tion of most of the principles incorporated into the various measures under consideration.

By 1880, bills to establish a federal court in the Indian Territory were receiving the widest attention. The Creek delegates wrote to their principal chief: "It is thought that the Court establishment method of solving the Indian Territory question is ominous of a change of policy by the Railroad powers that were its projectors."[23] For four years the Indians and their friends in Congress resisted court bills, only to see them merge with other proposals in 1884. It was generally understood that the purpose was the dissolution of the tribal governments.

The course of events had proved that the Indian opposition to the various bills was not simply factious, but was based on the realization that their tribal existence, along with their land titles, was in grave danger of extinction.

[23] IAD, Creek Nation—Federal Relations, 29811; also, Cherokee Papers, Washington Delegation, File Ic-17.

CHAPTER 16

Jay Gould Invades the Southwest

THE ECONOMIC PARALYSIS of 1873 gradually relaxed its grip. In a few years hesitant encouragement of new projects gave way to a resurgence of confidence, culminating in the greatest decade of American railroad building. It ended only after the nation's transportation system was substantially complete except for certain areas in the Gulf Southwest.

On the eve of the building revival the Gulf Southwest had some seven thousand miles of railroad operated by a large number of companies, most of which had never paid dividends and were in receivership. The easing of credit and the rebirth of optimism in the later seventies restored confidence in the future of these railroads in spite of their perennially drab financial reports. They attracted capital and were soon in an era of expansion which eclipsed the earlier construction programs.

The building wave of the eighties was accompanied by overambitious projects, unscrupulous promotional schemes, and other abuses which were sometimes woven into the fabric of legitimate enterprise; however, certain elements which had lowered the moral tone of the immediate postwar period were absent. The discontinuance of the federal land-grant policy and more careful attention to local aid, the separation of railway construction from political reconstruction, the chastening effect of the panic, and a new, critical attitude in the West saved the period from the extreme abuses of the earlier one. Many areas were still prodigal in giving their money and their credit, and many towns in central Kansas or Texas impatiently awaited the com-

Then Came the Railroads

ing of the railroad, which would lift them above the obscurity which surrounding towns would suffer, but there was less tendency to mortgage their future completely to secure this blessing. Perhaps, too, builders were somewhat more cautious, and certainly bondholders, for a time at least, were hardly begging for unknown western securities.

Another aspect of the period was the movement towards the consolidation of smaller roads into systems. Later magnates were to succeed where Joy had failed. Rival financial groups began to gather into their fold strategic lines which would render their positions impregnable in their own fields. There were still many local enterprises, but most of those which had value were to be absorbed; if unwisely developed, they quietly succumbed. The number of corporate charters applied for and actually carried to completion was not indicative of the number of separate projects, because major lines preferred to build extensions and feeders through subsidiaries rather than to amend their original charters.

The Santa Fe increased in stature during the period. Charles Morgan was to build a system along the Gulf while Collis P. Huntington was making much of Texas his dominion. A powerful force, the Rock Island, was stretching down from the northeast into Kansas to enter into competition with the earlier arrivals. Towering above all others was Jay Gould, who established a virtual monopoly of transportation in most of the Southwest.

By the mid-seventies Gould was free of entanglements with the Erie and was looking towards the West, specifically towards the Union Pacific, which he was determined to encircle and force into acceptance of such terms as he might dictate. The possibilities for stock manipulation were enormous, even though the profits from operating railroads in the sparsely settled West were remote. Furthermore, with his control of the Texas and Pacific, there was always the chance that he could become the dominant figure in transportation to the Pacific Coast.

Starting with the bankrupt Kansas Pacific, Gould added roads to the east and to the west, as well as securing partial control of the Pacific Mail Steamship Company. In the Southwest he acquired the Missouri Pacific, around which to organize his system, with the Wabash leading east from both St. Louis and Kansas City. In perfecting his holdings, Gould secured the St. Louis, Iron Mountain and Southern, the Missouri, Kansas and Texas, and the International and Great Northern. He forced the Union Pacific to come to his terms,

Jay Gould Invades the Southwest

then disposed of his Colorado railroads at a substantial profit when he realized that he would never be able to eliminate all competition.

The southwestern railroads remaining in his possession, Gould's next move was to strengthen his position in that area by building lines radiating from his basic ones, thus creating as tight a monopoly as possible from Kansas and Missouri to the Gulf. Unfortunately, for both the railroads and the public, Gould's primary concern was in operating for quick profits rather than building an integrated system of transportation. He added to his personal fortune, but left a legacy of hopelessly tangled finances and public ill will.[1]

The Missouri Pacific consisted of a main line from St. Louis to Kansas City, a branch from Kirkwood to Carondelet, and two short leased lines which jointly linked Kansas City with Atchison. Gould added by purchase a narrow-gauge line between Kansas City and Lexington, a local enterprise conceived and completed in 1878 and 1879, then under separate charter built from Pleasant Hill to Nevada, Missouri. He created the St. Louis, Kansas and Arizona, under whose charter one railroad was built from Paola to Le Roy and another from Osawatomie to Ottawa, seventy-nine miles in eastern Kansas. He consolidated all of these under the name Missouri Pacific Railway Company of 1880. During the next six years he added several short branches.

Some Gould properties retained their original identities, even though they were a part of the Missouri Pacific. The old Osage Valley and Southern Kansas was reorganized as the Boonville, St. Louis and Southern, extended to Versailles, and operated under lease by the parent corporation. The Sedalia, Warsaw and South Western, a narrow-gauge railroad from Sedalia to Warsaw; the Nevada and Minden, built by the Missouri Pacific from Nassau Junction, Missouri, to Chetopa, Kansas; the Joplin and Western, running between Joplin and Grand Falls; and the Kansas City and Southwestern, a forty-eight-mile line from Cecil, Missouri, to Paola, Kansas—all were operated under their original names until 1909.[2]

In northern Kansas, Gould railroads stretched north to Nebraska and west to Colorado. Most of them eventually consolidated as the Central Branch Railway Company. A network of subsidiaries entrenched Gould in southeastern Kansas and gave him a central route

[1] Riegel, "The Missouri Pacific, 1879-1900," *MHR*, Vol. XVIII, 175-78 and *The Story of the Western Railroads*, 160-78; Matthew Josephson, *The Robber Barons*, 194-200.
[2] ICC, *Val. Rep.*, XL, 404, 408, 451, 487, 497-500, 505-15, 558-61, 568, 573-74.

across the state from Paola to the Colorado line, where it connected with an affiliate to Pueblo. Construction was pushed in the mid-eighties, and on January 10, 1891, these lines were consolidated as the Kansas, Colorado and Pacific Railway Company. This trans-state railroad had branches north to Topeka and Salina, and south to Great Bend. Another major line swung northwest in a crescent from Chetopa through Coffeyville, Winfield, and Kingman to Larned, with a branch from Dexter to Arkansas City. A road from Fort Scott through El Dorado and Wichita to Hardtner intersected this crescent at Conway Springs. A branch from El Dorado extended to McPherson, and another from Wichita extended through Hutchinson to intersect the Colorado line at Geneseo. Short connecting lines tied these roads together at strategic points.

The Missouri Pacific controlled several short roads in southern and eastern Kansas which were not a part of the Kansas, Colorado and Pacific. They all dated from the period after 1885. One joined Roper with Peru, another Olcott with Iuka, a third centered at Fort Scott, with one line running south to Cornell, Kansas, and another northeast to Rich Hill, Missouri.[3]

Before he ever developed his Kansas network, Gould had entered the area by leasing the Missouri, Kansas and Texas. Gould strengthened the Katy's position by leasing the short Kansas City and Pacific, which extended from Coffeyville to Paola. This gave the Katy a direct line from Texas to Kansas City by way of the Missouri Pacific north of Paola. Gould then disposed of his Katy stock after leasing the railroad to his own Missouri Pacific.[4]

The Missouri Pacific dominated Arkansas and southeastern Missouri by controlling the Iron Mountain, by purchasing the Little Rock and Fort Smith, and by securing an interest in the Memphis and Little Rock. The short Doniphan and Jackson branches in Missouri were placed in operation in 1884 and 1885. Gould used the Iron Mountain and, to a less extent, the Little Rock and Fort Smith as axes around which to expand, concentrating on southern and eastern Arkansas, with extensions into Louisiana. He took over the Little Rock, Mississippi River and Texas Railway, which was really the old Texas, Mississippi and Northwestern under a new name. This road now extended southeast from Pine Bluff to Halley, where it turned west to terminate at Warren, with branches from Trippe Junction to Arkansas City and

[3] *Ibid.*, 405–407, 515–17.
[4] *Ibid.*, XXXIV, 395, 475–77; *Poor's Manual, 1881*, 746–49; *Ry. W.*, Vol. VI, 1113.

from Varner to Cummings Landing. Gould extended it from Pine Bluff to Little Rock and made minor changes at the southern end. Another of his properties, incorporated as the Houston, Central Arkansas and Northern, built north in 1893 from Alexandria, Louisiana, to McGehee, Arkansas, near the southern end of the Little Rock, Mississippi River and Texas.

Gould secured the Arkansas Central, which by this time had reached the Memphis and Little Rock at Forrest City. Two years later he constructed a line from Forrest City to Knobel, on the main line of the Iron Mountain in northern Arkansas. A branch of the Arkansas Central served Brinkley.

Between 1883 and 1890 a branch from the Iron Mountain extended to Cushman by way of Batesville, while another stretched east from Bald Knob to Bridge Junction, on the Mississippi opposite Memphis. In south central Arkansas, one subsidiary built from Gurdon to El Dorado, and others penetrated the timber elsewhere. Far to the southwest, Gould took over a struggling narrow-gauge line which linked Hope and Washington, renamed it the Arkansas and Louisiana Railway, changed it to standard gauge, and extended it through the forests to Nashville, Arkansas.

Fort Smith was a center of activity. The Kansas and Arkansas Valley, incorporated in 1885 in the interest of the Iron Mountain, cut across Indian Territory from Fort Smith to Coffeyville, where it joined Gould's Kansas network. This road was finished in 1889, the same year that the Iron Mountain built a branch from Fort Smith to Greenwood.[5]

There were two threats—one actual, the other potential—to Gould's monopoly of traffic moving northeast from the Gulf. The St. Louis and San Francisco ran midway between the Missouri Pacific and the Iron Mountain, the key prongs in Gould's southwestern railroad empire. A newly developed railroad, the Texas and St. Louis, was a possible competitor for the trade of Texas and would undoubtedly drain off some local Arkansas traffic because it paralleled the Iron Mountain from Texarkana to Birds Point and planned to build all the way into St. Louis.

The Frisco was a matter of immediate concern, for it had thrown off the lethargy which marked its earlier years. The Memphis, Carthage and Northwestern, operating the connecting line between Pierce

---

[5] ICC, *Val. Rep.*, XL, 409–11, 595, 604, 606–13, 632–34, 640–49; *Ry. W.*, Vol. VI, 972; David Y. Thomas, *Arkansas*, 426–27.

City, Missouri, to a new Kansas terminus at Columbus, had added branches from Oronogo Junction to Joplin and from Columbus to Oswego. This road became the property of the Frisco in 1879. Strangely enough, until this time there was only one short line reaching Joplin, a booming mining town. It was a recent local project, the creation of John B. Sergeant and E. R. Moffet, who secured a charter for the Joplin Railroad Company and in 1879 constructed a railroad to connect with the Missouri River, Fort Scott and Gulf at Girard, Kansas. The Frisco purchased this property and added eight miles from Joplin to Galena, Kansas.

The activities of the St. Louis, Arkansas and Texas Railway Company, a Frisco subsidiary, were even more disturbing to Gould's peace of mind. Incorporated in 1880, it built rapidly from Plymouth (now Monett), Missouri, to Fayetteville, Arkansas, was pushing south towards Fort Smith, and was seeking permission to cross a corner of Indian Territory to the Texas line. The Frisco already had a Texas charter for the Paris and Great Northern, which would build from the Red River terminus of the St. Louis, Arkansas and Texas to Paris. If completed, these lines would give the Frisco a Gulf connection.[6]

The Frisco also threatened Gould from a quarter outside the Gulf Southwest. Huntington and Gould had agreed that Gould's Texas and Pacific would meet Huntington's Southern Pacific at some point in western Texas. Their only potential rival was the Frisco, which had succeeded to the rights of the Atlantic and Pacific in the thirty-fifth-parallel route. A weak Frisco would never have the money to build from Vinita, Cherokee Nation, to the West Coast; besides, the outlook was dismal for operating profitably across Indian Territory, the uninhabited Texas Panhandle, and the uninviting territories of New Mexico and Arizona. The activities of the Atchison, Topeka and Santa Fe changed the picture.

The Santa Fe had rested for a time at Pueblo before turning south from La Junta, Colorado, towards New Mexico. It routed the Denver and Rio Grande in a battle for possession of Raton Pass and on April 15, 1880, reached Albuquerque. It had already made preliminary arrangements with the Frisco whereby the two roads would jointly construct and operate the Central Division of the Atlantic and Pacific from Vinita to Albuquerque and the Western Division from Albuquerque to Needles. The agreement further provided for joint ownership of any new lines in Kansas, for immediate construction of

[6] ICC, *Val. Rep.*, XLI, 302, 305, 500–503, 506–16, 797.

a connecting link between the two railroads in eastern Kansas, and for division of traffic for thirty years.

By July, 1881, two hundred miles of the western division were in operation west of Isleta, New Mexico, and construction crews were moving steadily towards Needles, California. Meanwhile, operating under the charter of the St. Louis, Wichita and Western, the Frisco built the connecting line in Kansas from its terminus at Oswego to the Santa Fe at Wichita. There was some activity on the Central Division. Surveying parties charted its course west from Vinita by way of the Arkansas to the Cimarron, and a little building took place in 1881.[7]

Gould immediately laid plans to block this formidable combination. The obvious solution was to get control of the Frisco. He and Huntington quietly began to purchase its stock, and in February, 1882, they bought the interests of the Seligman brothers, dominant figures in the road after its reorganization. They were then in a position to block Santa Fe expansion effectively. Huntington built across California to Needles in order to place the Santa Fe at his mercy and divert trade to the southern route, while Gould found himself in control of another southwestern railroad, around which he could tie additional feeders and extensions to secure an even firmer grip on the region.[8]

Building on the Central Division through the Indian nations continued in spite of an unusual number of petty but vexatious annoyances. One in particular was the subject of much official correspondence and an irritation to both the railroad and the Cherokee Nation. One Patrick Shannahan, described by Agent John Q. Tufts as "an Indian from Dublin," established himself on a parcel of land directly in the line of the railroad, claiming it as an intermarried Cherokee. He demanded such an exorbitant sum for a right of way that the railroad resurveyed in order to bypass Shannahan's land. The Irishman was equal to the occasion. He extended his claim and his fences to block the new route, fortified his home, and, surrounded by armed friends, threatened to shoot any trespassers. Jurisdiction over the affair fell to the Cherokee courts. The controversy resolved itself abruptly when a commission appointed by Chief Dennis W. Bushy-

---

[7] *Ibid.*, 305, 516–18; *Cong. Rec.*, 46 Cong., 3 sess., 1313; Bradley, *The Story of the Santa Fe*, 216–21, 237–39; Riegel, *The Story of the Western Railroads*, 188–93.

[8] *Comm. & Fin. Chron.*, Vol. XXXIV, 60, 99–101, 113, 116, 175, 263, 488, 573; Bradley, *The Story of the Santa Fe*, 221–23; Haney, *A Congressional History of Railways in the United States*, II, 119–20.

head discovered that Shannahan's marriage to a divorced Cherokee woman was not valid under tribal law, and that Shannahan was subject to expulsion as an intruder.[9]

In 1882 the line reached the Creek Indian village of Tulsa. Four years later it was extended to Sapulpa to provide irregular service during the cattle-shipping season. The St. Louis, Arkansas and Texas was put in operation between Fayetteville and Fort Smith in 1882 and within five years was extended across the Choctaw Nation to its connection with the Paris and Great Northern on the Red. A number of branches, all built by subsidiary corporations to serve lumber interests, grew up along this line southwest from Plymouth.

Gould strengthened and extended the Frisco in Missouri and Arkansas. He freed it from future dependence on his own Missouri Pacific by constructing a line into St. Louis from Franklin. He added branches from Springfield south to Chadwick and north to Bolivar. In Kansas, Gould purchased the St. Louis, Kansas and Southwestern from its organizers while they were building from Beaumont Junction to Indian Territory. This road, which intersected Gould properties at Beaumont, Winfield, and Arkansas City, he leased to the Frisco, then extended it from Arkansas City to Anthony. The Kansas Midland, while it was still in the process of building from Wichita to Ellsworth, also came within the orbit of the Frisco.[10]

The Texas and St. Louis originated in 1871 as a narrow-gauge line to serve local interests. It was incorporated as the Tyler Tap Railroad. Its express purpose was to give Tyler, Texas, a connection with the Texas and Pacific at Big Sandy, twenty-one miles away. Local promoters finally completed it after a six-year struggle. Two St. Louis capitalists, J. W. Paramore and R. C. Kerens, became interested in the Tyler Tap as the nucleus for a road to serve the cotton-growing regions of Texas, Arkansas, and southern Missouri. In 1879 they renamed it the Texas and St. Louis. Within three years Paramore's own construction company extended it from Big Sandy to Texarkana and from Tyler through Corsicana and Waco to Gatesville, a total of three hundred miles.[11]

Before the Texas and St. Louis finished its line to Gatesville, it had already entered Missouri and Arkansas. It pushed its building program vigorously and took over the Little River Valley and Arkansas

[9] IAD, Cherokee Nation—Railroads, 2656–63, 2666–70; CLPCB, X, 325–35, 363–70; OIA, Letters Received for 1882, 9133 and 21116 (with enclosures 1–17).
[10] ICC, *Val. Rep.*, XLI, 304–309, 426–36, 519–39, 558–60, 793–805.
[11] ICC, *Rep.*, CXLIX, 545–49.

Jay Gould Invades the Southwest

Railroad Company, whose physical assets consisted of a narrow-gauge line between New Madrid and Malden, Missouri. By midsummer of 1883 the Texas and St. Louis operated a main line from Texarkana to Birds Point, 417 miles, with a Missouri branch from Lilbourn to New Madrid and an Arkansas branch from McNeil to Magnolia. It was reorganized in 1886 as the St. Louis, Arkansas and Texas Railway Company and was converted to standard gauge. Subsidiary corporations constructed branches from Altheimer to Argenta, in Arkansas, and from Lewisville, Arkansas, to Shreveport, Louisiana. In 1888 an extension was planned from Malden to Grand Tower, Illinois, but it never extended beyond Delta, Missouri.

Meanwhile, the St. Louis, Arkansas and Texas Railroad Company of Texas was expanding by construction and by the acquisition of an existing road, the Kansas and Gulf Short Line. This railroad had a predecessor with a history similar to that of the Tyler Tap. When the International and Great Northern built through Cherokee County, it missed the town of Rusk, favoring an archrival, Jacksonville. To protect their trade territory, the citizens of Rusk organized the Rusk Transportation Company to tap the International and Great Northern. They reluctantly built towards Jacksonville, the nearest railroad town, because they lacked the capital to do otherwise. Eventually they completed the line, but because of its inferior roadbed and heavy indebtedness, no one was willing to assume responsibility for its operation. Late in 1880 certain Tyler businessmen organized the Kansas and Gulf Short Line, which took over the bankrupt Rusk project and extended it as a narrow-gauge line from Tyler to Lufkin before it went into the hands of receivers. Almost from its inception the Kansas and Gulf Short Line was closely affiliated with the Texas and St. Louis and was transferred outright to its successor in 1887. Additions by construction, all completed in 1887 and 1888, included lines from Mount Pleasant to Sherman, Corsicana to Hillsboro, and Commerce to Fort Worth, a total of almost two hundred and fifty miles.[12]

Jay Gould could not avoid alarm at the threat of a road which boldly paralleled his Iron Mountain for almost its entire length, particularly since it penetrated deeply into Texas and could divert much through tonnage from his system. Nor was there any doubt that his competitor had the sympathy of those who were subject to Gould's will. Roger Mills of Texas, while speaking in favor of a bill to permit

[12] *Ibid.*, 42, 390, 441, 482, 494–502, 536–40, 545–55.

the Texas and St. Louis to bridge a number of Arkansas rivers, stated: "The object sought in chartering this road was to obtain a competing line so as to cheapen freight from Texas to St. Louis, and to prevent the success of the combination between the Gould line running through the Indian Territory and these other lines, so that people could have their freight transported cheaply."[13]

There is some question concerning the time at which Gould gained control of the St. Louis, Arkansas and Texas. It is quite possible that its weak financial structure made it impossible to reorganize in 1886 without his assistance. There is no question that he gained control by December 26, 1888, when his agent bought a large block of its securities. Regardless of when he brought it within his dominion, Gould had eliminated a resourceful, energetic rival.[14]

The St. Louis, Arkansas and Texas went into receivership in 1889. Two years later it was reorganized as two corporations with identical interests, the St. Louis Southwestern Railway Company for the lines outside Texas and the St. Louis Southwestern Railway Company of Texas for those within that state. The official corporate name has long since given way to the more familiar "Cotton Belt Route."

Several minor Arkansas properties became identified with the Cotton Belt during the reorganization period. The Pine Bluff Arkansas River Railway, representing the consolidation of several local enterprises of the eighties, was a logging road operating out of Rob Roy. Another short line, the Stuttgart and Arkansas River, was constructed from Stuttgart to Gillett between 1888 and 1892, while a third, the Paragould Southeastern, was another logging road.[15]

The Cotton Belt represented only a fraction of Gould's Texas railroad empire, for control of the routes through that state to the Gulf was the heart of his monopoly. At the height of his power, Gould possessed the Texas and Pacific, the International and Great Northern, the Galveston, Houston and Henderson, the Missouri, Kansas and Texas, and the Fort Worth and Rio Grande. These roads operated one-third of the total railroad mileage in Texas.

The most highly publicized of Gould's Texas activities was the Texas and Pacific. When he assumed control, the herculean struggle between Huntington and Scott for control of the southern route to the West Coast had been resolved in favor of the Southern Pacific.

[13] *Cong., Rec.,* 47 Cong., 1 sess., 4997.
[14] ICC, *Rep.,* CXLIX, 481, 484, 540.
[15] *Ibid.,* 419–20, 441, 472, 482, 502, 576–80.

Jay Gould Invades the Southwest

The Texas and Pacific was without resources, and until 1875 it did nothing. It then revived to add lines from Brookston to Texarkana, and from both Sherman and Dallas to Fort Worth, finally uniting the two segments which represented the activities of its most remote ancestors.

Final half-hearted litigation between the Texas and Pacific and the Southern Pacific was settled out of court by the Huntington-Gould agreement of November 26, 1881. The Texas and Pacific transferred its franchises and corporate privileges west of El Paso to the Southern Pacific, a settlement later voided by Congress. The agreement further provided that the tracks of the Texas and Pacific and those of the Southern Pacific would join at some point east of El Paso, with Huntington guaranteeing Gould trackage rights into that city. The Texas and Pacific was already pushing rapidly across the uninhabited area west of Fort Worth, and within a month reached the Southern Pacific at Sierra Blanca.

The Texas and Pacific expanded into Louisiana by purchasing existing lines and completing them. The New Orleans Pacific, dating from February 19, 1876, acquired the roadbed of the long since defunct Red River Railroad two years later. Early in 1881, it purchased the "Backbone Company" and the New Orleans, Mobile and Chattanooga line between Westwego and Bayou Goula. On June 20, 1881, the New Orleans Pacific merged with the Texas and Pacific. After constructing its own line from Westwego to New Orleans, the Texas and Pacific pushed northwest from Bayou Goula to Shreveport.

A combination of circumstances forced the Texas and Pacific into receivership in 1885, but Gould retained controlling interest. The road was not in a position to expand, but, nonetheless, it started building from Port Allen, Louisiana, toward Ferriday and added minor branches in Louisiana and Texas.[16]

The International and Great Northern was another of Gould's basic Texas railroads. He gained possession as it emerged from receivership and extended it from Austin to Laredo by way of San Antonio. It absorbed two local projects, which gave it branches from Overton to Henderson and Round Rock to Georgetown. With eight hundred miles of track, it had the most extensive mileage of any Texas road.

When the International and Great Northern completed its expansion, Gould leased it to the Katy. He then leased the Galveston, Houston and Henderson, in which he had acquired an interest, to the Inter-

[16] ICC, *Val. Rep.*, XXIX, 527, 546, 552, 582–84.

Then Came the Railroads

national and Great Northern. The International and Great Northern was allowed to deteriorate; the sections which were important links to the Gulf were operated in the interest of other lines, while the remainder was reduced to local service. Gould forced it into receivership, divested the Katy of all control, then reorganized it in 1892.[17]

The Katy provided Gould with another ingress into Texas. This road penetrated the state from its terminus at Denison before Gould entered into its management. In 1877, the Katy secured a charter for the Denison and Southeastern and built to Greenville. It then acquired a recently completed line between Denison and Gainesville. These properties were consolidated in March, 1880, as the Missouri, Kansas and Texas Extension Railway.

Six months later the Katy passed to Gould. He gave it trackage rights for ninety-nine years over the Texas and Pacific between Fort Worth and Whitesboro. Gould purchased the East Line and Red River, converted it to standard gauge, and extended it from Greenville to McKinney, after which he turned it over to the Katy. A Dallas railroad, projected to reach supposedly rich coal fields on Red River, bogged down some twenty miles north of Dallas in 1878. Gould secured possession of it through the Texas and Pacific, extended it to Denton, then transferred it to the Katy. The Katy also fell heir to the Trinity and Sabine, a logging road built by lumbermen of Trinity, Texas, and added to by Gould until it reached Colmesneil. This short line was called the "orphan branch" because it was well over one hundred miles from the nearest part of the parent road. The Katy added two major extensions under its own corporate name in 1881 and 1882—from Greenville to the Texas and Pacific at Mineola and from Fort Worth to the International and Great Northern at Taylor, with a branch from Belton to Echo.

Local economic conditions and state regulation halted Katy activities for a short time following the rapid expansion of the early eighties. Under more favorable circumstances, construction was resumed in 1886. Branches were added from Gainesville to Henrietta, Warner Junction to Ray, Greenville to Dallas, Dallas to Hillsboro, and Lockhart to San Marcos, 340 miles in the aggregate.[18]

The last of Gould's Texas properties was the Fort Worth and Rio Grande, incorporated in the interest of the Frisco and completed between Fort Worth and Brownwood in 1890.[19]

[17] ICC, *Rep.*, CXLIX, 607, 610, 629, 638, 646; Reed, *Texas Railroads*, 321.
[18] ICC, *Val. Rep.*, XXXIV, 396, 529–33, 625–46.
[19] *Ibid.*, XLI, 695–716.

Jay Gould Invades the Southwest

Before Gould had perfected his system, there were rumblings of discontent. The intricate system of leasing and the complicated interrelationships of the various roads were susceptible to much abuse. Gould's control was not through outright ownership, but by ownership extensive enough to determine policies of the companies, by leasing arrangements, and by other devices too devious to unravel. Any part of the network could be systematically drained of its resources for the benefit of favored lines.

He secured the Katy long enough to perfect a leasing agreement to the Missouri Pacific, after which he quietly rid himself of its stock, then looted it. He dismembered the International and Great Northern and permitted deterioration of those parts which did not fit into his plans, equally indifferent to the interests of security holders and the public. He manipulated his properties to serve his own uses, overcapitalized them, juggled them, and in the process made himself one of the most hated men in America. Railroads represented a medium for stock manipulation, not the arteries of transportation in an expanding national economy. Gould undoubtedly did much good in accelerating the construction of railroads in certain areas, but that was incidental to his own uncontrolled bid for wealth and power. His structure was never to suffer the complete collapse of the earlier Joy roads, but was to crumble enough to break his tight grip on the Southwest.

The Katy was the first to go. Gould disregarded the interests of its security holders until their protests forced a reckoning. In 1888 disgruntled stockholders demanded an investigation of the management of the Katy, and a committee reported that the railroad had been operated in the interest of the Missouri Pacific rather than its owners. Members of the board of directors petitioned successfully for a receivership and Gould lost all control.[20]

The road was still beset by difficulties growing out of the period of Gould's domination. Attorney General James S. Hogg of Texas, a bitter opponent of the Gould monopoly, brought an action against the Katy while it was still within the dominion of the Missouri Pacific to divest it of control over the International and Great Northern and the East Line and Red River. The specific charges were that the Katy, as a foreign corporation, could not legally take possession of these Texas properties, and that it had permitted them to deteriorate. Hogg demanded cancellation of the leases.

[20] *Comm. & Fin. Chron.,* Vol. XLVI, 171, 371, 413, 511, 538, 543–44, 609, 650, 678, 699, 739, 771; Riegel, "The Missouri Pacific, 1879–1900," *MHR,* Vol. XVIII, 184–93.

Then Came the Railroads

The Katy legalized its position by consolidating all its Texas holdings except the East Line and Red River as a single company, the Missouri, Kansas and Texas Railway Company of Texas. The Katy of Texas then created a subsidiary, the Sherman, Shreveport and Southern, to take over and operate the East Line and Red River, which it extended from Jefferson to Waskom. Other additions dated from the creation of the Katy of Texas. In 1890 Denison and Sherman were linked, in 1892 the stem terminating at Boggy Tank was completed to Houston, and in 1893 a line from Lockhart to Smithville tied the San Marcos–Lockhart branch to the rest of the Katy.

All Katy properties outside Texas were restored to the owners in July, 1891, and continued to operate under the original name. The Katy freed itself from dependence on the Missouri Pacific for an entrance into St. Louis by building a link from Bryson to Holden, then, following the north bank of the Missouri from Franklin to Machens, entered St. Louis by virtue of a trackage agreement. It added minor branches in Kansas and Missouri and, in 1899, absorbed the Kansas City and Pacific, which it had operated under lease for twelve years.[21]

The Frisco was another road lost to the Gould system. It slipped away to pass briefly into the orbit of the Santa Fe, but that road, involved in its own miseries, lost it in 1893. A committee of bondholders conveyed it to the newly created St. Louis and San Francisco Railroad Company on June 30, 1896. The next year the Frisco again gained control of the Central Division of the Atlantic and Pacific, the bankrupt segment of railroad lying partway across Indian Territory.[22]

No other radical changes took place in the Gould roads, with the exception of those in the International and Great Northern and the Galveston, Houston and Henderson. They were vital Gulf connections for the Katy as well as the Missouri Pacific, but Gould controlled them under a leasing agreement. A compromise settlement on December 18, 1889, gave the two interested roads joint control over both. The other Gould properties remained under the same management, although not so closely knit. The cracking of the structure weakened a fairly complete monopoly but left the associated lines as a potent factor in the Southwest. In the midst of the crumbling, the ruthless genius of Jay Gould was removed by death.[23]

[21] ICC, *Val. Rep.*, XXXIV, 394–400, 477–81, 533, 620–24, 632; Reed, *Texas Railroads*, 383–84.
[22] ICC, *Val. Rep.*, XLI, 442, 459–67, 477–79.
[23] *Ibid.*, XXXIV, 439–41.

CHAPTER 17

Jay Gould's Rivals

JAY GOULD was never able to eliminate all competitors. In Kansas, and later in Texas, the Santa Fe was active and resourceful. In Texas, it was the powerful Huntington interests. Smaller companies operating in various parts of the Southwest were irritations rather than actual threats to his control.

The Atchison, Topeka and Santa Fe was a perennial rival of the Gould interests. In the early eighties William B. Strong and A. A. Robinson, dominant figures in the Santa Fe, were devoting their energies to New Mexico, where the railroad followed the Río Grande to Rincon, then split to tap the Southern Pacific at Deming and the trade of northern Mexico at El Paso. Meanwhile, the Santa Fe faced a grave danger in Kansas. It was a shoestring stretching across the state, vulnerable as long as it did not send out tentacles to claim with finality the area which it penetrated. The management was aware of this situation, and in the seventies it started a system of feeders in spite of financial conditions which rendered construction all but impossible.

In 1880 the Santa Fe secured the remnants of the Joy lines stretching south from Lawrence, added other lines which joined Harper with Lawrence, Olathe with Holliday, Ottawa with Burlington, and Wellington with Hunnewell, and consolidated them in 1883 to form the Southern Kansas Railway Company. Other subsidiaries built from Chanute to Girard, Ottawa to Emporia, and Harper to Attica, then merged with the Southern Kansas in 1885. The Southern Kansas added extensions from Attica southwest to the Indian Territory line near Kiowa and west to Medicine Lodge and minor connecting lines in southeastern Kansas. In 1879 the Kansas City, Emporia and Southern penetrated from Emporia as far south as Howard, while the Santa Fe and the Union Pacific jointly built from Burlingame to Manhattan. Two years later the Walnut Valley feeder was revived to extend from El Dorado to Douglas and, later in the decade, to Winfield.

The Wichita area was also the scene of much activity. Subsidiaries of the Wichita and Southwestern extended south to Mulvane, then split to run southeast to Arkansas City and west through Wellington to Caldwell. The Wichita and Western built from Wichita through Pratt and thirty-five miles beyond, but was soon abandoned west of Pratt. Northeast of Wichita an important hundred-mile branch, the Marion and McPherson, ran from Florence, on the main line, west to Ellinwood.

Towards the close of the decade Santa Fe construction was carried on through a number of subsidiaries. All were eventually united as the Chicago, Kansas and Western, which sprawled over the entire state by 1887. In eastern Kansas connecting segments joined Chanute and Longton, Independence and Cedarvale, Colony and Yates Center, Benedict Junction and Madison Junction, and Quenemo and Osage City, while a new branch reached from Burlington to Gridley; in central Kansas a prong from Strong City ran north into Nebraska. New short lines linked Augusta with Mulvane and Little River with Holyrood. A cutoff in western Kansas extended to Kinsley from Hutchinson, while projections west from Great Bend to Selkirk, Larned to Jetmore, and Mulvane to Englewood opened another virgin territory.

Another westward Santa Fe extension was carried out in the name of affiliates of the Southern Kansas. In 1887 and 1888 they crossed the Cherokee Outlet from Kiowa and went into Texas as far as Panhandle City. Two years later the Santa Fe leased a short railroad running from Panhandle City to Washburn on the new Fort Worth and Denver City Railroad.[1]

By the late eighties the Santa Fe and the competing Missouri Pacific had interlacing lines in southern and eastern Kansas. Except for its brief alliance with the Frisco, a situation Gould and Huntington soon remedied, the Santa Fe did not contest the Missouri area.

The Santa Fe operated mileage which extended from eastern Kansas to Needles, Deming, and El Paso, with a web of feeders across

[1] ICC, *Rep.*, CXXVII, 207–19, 378–87, 398–408, 501–32, 777, 789–99.

Kansas, but its position was vulnerable because it depended on the Southern Pacific in order to reach the West Coast and on several other roads in order to reach the Mississippi. It was well on its way towards assuming the position of an intermediate carrier. Eventually, by lease, purchase, and construction, the Santa Fe reached both Chicago and the West Coast over its own tracks.

The Gulf offered another possible outlet. The Santa Fe's position was especially enviable because, with Indian Territory virtually opened to all railroad projects at this late date, it was ready to enter from Coffeyville, Arkansas City, Caldwell, and Kiowa. To cross Indian Territory and build to the Gulf would place the Santa Fe in competition with the Missouri Pacific in another strategic area.

An opportunity for the Santa Fe to enter the Texas field came about through the activities of a group of Texans building a railroad north under a name coincidentally similar to its own—the Gulf, Colorado and Santa Fe. It was conceived and financed by Galveston businessmen to overcome Houston's control of the upstate trade.

The Gulf, Colorado and Santa Fe was incorporated May 28, 1873, for the purpose of building to Santa Fé, New Mexico, but the panic delayed all activity until the spring of 1875. It was in constant financial difficulties, but through the resourcefulness of George Sealy, it finally reached Temple and branched, one line running north to Fort Worth, the other west to Lampasas. In 1883, Sealy acquired two roads by purchase. One was a narrow-gauge line from Dallas to Cleburne which was built for bonuses rather than for operation. Dallas businessmen got possession of the defunct property and rebuilt it to standard gauge before selling it to Sealy. The other was a logging road, the Central and Montgomery, which Sealy extended from Somerville to Conroe. Ironically, the first branch actually constructed by the Gulf, Colorado and Santa Fe ran from Alvin to Houston. An extension from Lampasas to Ballinger, with a branch to Coleman, was being constructed when the Sealy road became an affiliate of the Santa Fe.

In July, 1884, Congress granted the Southern Kansas permission to build across Indian Territory from Arkansas City. Construction was delayed two years, after which the road crawled across the Cherokee Outlet and into the Oklahoma District. At this time George Sealy offered to sell his railroad to the Santa Fe. The proposal met with instant favor, for the Santa Fe would have been dependent on competing lines to reach the Gulf from Red River; furthermore, the Texas road already had Congressional permission to cross into Indian Territory.

Then Came the Railroads

Railroads of the Gulf Southwest in 1880

Based on a map from the Association of American Railroads

Jay Gould's Rivals

By the terms of the agreement, Sealy guaranteed to complete lines from Fort Worth to Purcell, in the Chickasaw Nation, from Dallas to a connection with the Frisco at Paris, and from Cleburne to Weatherford, a Texas and Pacific station. The Santa Fe was then to purchase the Texas road. The terms were of particular interest to the chief engineer of the Gulf, Colorado and Santa Fe; with no preliminary preparation or even right of way, he was responsible for laying several hundred miles of track within a year. It was, however, imperative to build immediately because the time limit for completion of the Indian Territory extension was running out. The Gulf, Colorado and Santa Fe complied with all the terms, meeting the Southern Kansas at Purcell on April 26, 1887, and completing the Texas branches. The Santa Fe added a line from Ballinger to San Angelo in 1888, then rested until 1902. The only addition in the intervening period was the acquisition of a short logging road extending from Conroe to the Trinity River.[2]

The purchase of the Gulf, Colorado and Santa Fe was of tremendous importance to the Santa Fe. The Texas road and its important feeders served a well-settled, prosperous region which produced large local revenues. Not only did it furnish an outlet to the Gulf, but it also gave access to Fort Worth, Dallas, Houston, and Galveston. Acquisition of this road at the time it was gaining entrance into Denver and Chicago established the Santa Fe as one of the great railroads in the nation.

The long-time result of its rapid expansion was undoubtedly beneficial; it could have followed no other course without sacrificing its place in the Middle West, but the activity took its toll. Some of the branches proved unprofitable. Strong resigned the presidency in 1889; the new management adopted a conservative policy until new interests demanded further expansion, leading to the acquisition of the Colorado Midland, the Frisco, and some California lines. A reshuffling of the directors in 1893 put the Santa Fe in the hands of an irresponsible, speculative, and wildly extravagant management which insisted on the soundness of its practices at the same time that it drove the railroad towards bankruptcy through gross irregularities. Ruinous competitive practices added their strain, and Kansas experienced general crop failures. The Santa Fe was in no position to withstand the acute business depression of 1893 and went into receiver-

[2] *Ibid.*, 214, 694–95; Bradley, *The Story of the Santa Fe*, 248–52.

ship. A committee worked out a plan of reorganization in the next two years whereby the company relinquished control of the Colorado Midland, the Frisco, and many unprofitable branches.[3]

Another contender appeared in the Southwest in the mid-eighties: the Chicago, Rock Island and Pacific, which had its roots in Illinois. Incorporated in 1847 as a local line to run from La Salle, on the Illinois and Michigan Canal, to Rock Island, on the Mississippi, it expanded and in 1879 reached Kansas City.

A subsidiary corporation, the Chicago, Kansas and Nebraska, built the early Rock Island lines in Kansas. It reached Topeka in 1887, bent southwest to Herington, then south to Caldwell, near the Indian Territory line, with branches northwest from McFarland to Belleville and from Herington to Salina. The next year it built a line from Herington to Liberal. Dodge City residents financed a railroad from their city to Bucklin, on the Rock Island; this the Rock Island purchased.

In 1889 the Rock Island started south from Caldwell, running about thirty miles west of, and roughly parallel to, the Santa Fe through the Cherokee Outlet to Minco, in Oklahoma District. A short time later this road was extended south to Red River and, under the name Chicago, Rock Island and Texas, on to Fort Worth. The panic stopped further construction while the Rock Island was a potential rather than a real rival. Not until the turn of the century did it become a major factor in the Gulf Southwest.[4]

A segment of the Joy lines, the Missouri River, Fort Scott and Gulf, was a minor competitor. It was reorganized in 1879 as the Kansas City, Fort Scott and Gulf. A number of closely affiliated short lines in southeastern Kansas and southwestern Missouri were under construction following the business revival in the late seventies. They formed a little network connecting the mining communities of Edwards, Coalvale, Weir City, and Baxter Springs, all in Kansas, and Joplin and Webb City in Missouri, with more ambitious undertakings resulting in lines from Arcadia, Kansas, to Ash Grove, Missouri, and from Cherryvale to Weir City, Kansas. The Kansas City, Fort Scott and Gulf was consolidated with these lines in 1888 to form the Kansas City, Fort Scott and Springfield Railroad Company. Other corpor-

[3] ICC, *Rep.*, CXXVII, 207, 364; Marshall, *Santa Fe,* 208–10, 242–51; Moody, *The Railroad Builders,* 161–63.

[4] ICC, *Val. Rep.*, XXIV, 923–28, 933; Wright, *Dodge City,* 319; Carl Nyquist, "A Pioneer in the West," *RIM*, Vol. XVII, No. 10, 50; William E. Hayes, *Iron Road to Empire,* 114–17.

ations developed a railroad from Ash Grove through Springfield and across the northeast corner of Arkansas to Bridge Junction. In 1888 they were consolidated with the Kansas City, Fort Scott and Springfield as the Kansas City, Fort Scott and Memphis. In the same year, the subsidiary Current River Railroad completed the eighty-two-mile branch from Willow Springs to Grandin, Missouri.[5]

Two independent railroads worked closely with the Kansas City, Fort Scott and Memphis. The Kansas City, Clinton and Springfield was a railroad with a complicated corporate background. It acquired its first physical properties by buying the Pleasant Hill and De Soto Railroad, and in 1886 it built from Raymore Junction to Ash Grove. The second of the independent roads, the Kansas City, Osceola and Southern, had been in existence under a number of different names for thirteen years when, in 1885, it finally built from the Katy at Osceola, Missouri, to East Lynne and later to Kansas City. It had already been leased to the Frisco when, in 1898, it extended from Osceola to meet the Frisco at Bolivar.[6]

These roads, lying along the Missouri-Kansas line and stretching across southern Missouri and northeastern Arkansas, constituted no immediate threat to Gould's railroads except in eastern Kansas, because they cut diagonally across the Missouri Pacific affiliates to serve a sparsely settled, noncompetitive area; nevertheless, they had achieved a position of some importance and were to become of even greater significance after they later merged their interests with those of the Frisco.

In the St. Louis area, the St. Louis, Kansas City and Colorado Railroad became a potential threat to the Missouri Pacific when it started building from St. Louis in the general direction of Kansas City. It progressed slowly, but by 1890 it had over one hundred miles of track, which terminated at Belle.[7]

Gould was forced to share Texas and Louisiana with Collis P. Huntington, who fashioned a powerful system of permanent importance. Huntington dominated transportation in California by controlling both the network of railroads within that state and the Sierra Nevada passes suitable for railroad use. The terms of the Texas and Pacific charter authorized Huntington's Southern Pacific to meet the Texas road on the eastern border of California. Without benefit of

[5] ICC, *Val. Rep.*, XLI, 369–72, 634–84, 729–33.
[6] *Ibid.*, 530–33, 727, 743–47.
[7] *Ibid.*, XXIV, 925, 931; Nevins, "Seventy ... Service," *RIM*, Vol. XVII, 71.

federal legislation or land grants, Huntington started building along the thirty-second parallel beyond California's eastern border in 1876. After his agreement with Gould, he extended his railroad to Sierra Blanca, Texas.

Construction between El Paso and Sierra Blanca had been under the charter of the Galveston, Harrisburg and San Antonio, a road in which Huntington apparently bought an interest in 1879 or 1880 and which he had certainly helped financially. He did not stop at Sierra Blanca, but continued to build towards San Antonio as construction crews from that city raced to meet the road coming in from the west. All the work was done by Huntington's own companies, which took payment in securities of the Galveston, Harrisburg and San Antonio. The lines met west of the Pecos in January, 1883, to form a route from the Pacific coast to Harrisburg. Huntington added ten miles in order to secure access to Houston over his own lines, and then, by a trackage agreement with Gould, got into Galveston over the Galveston, Houston and Henderson. He immediately strengthened the Houston–San Antonio line with branches from Glidden to La Grange and Harwood to Gonzales; west of San Antonio he added a branch from Spofford to Eagle Pass, the result of his struggle with Gould for the trade of Mexico. In 1884, Huntington created the Southern Pacific Company, a Kentucky corporation, as a holding company for his various southwestern interests.[8]

Charles Morgan had already developed an important system along the Louisiana coast and in East Texas. Morgan used the New Orleans, Opelousas and Great Western and the New Orleans, Mobile and Texas, both acquired by purchase, as the basis for his Louisiana lines. The second, cutting diagonally across the state towards Shreveport, he sold to the New Orleans Pacific, but the first, running from New Orleans to Brashear City (renamed Morgan City), he kept and called Morgan's Louisiana and Texas Railroad and Steamship Company. He extended the main line to Vermilionville, then turned north to Cheneyville. Short branches served Raceland, Thibodaux, Salt Mine, and Cypremort.

Meanwhile, Morgan had made two important moves. In order to feed his Gulf steamship lines more effectively than he could through his Gulf, Western Texas and Pacific, Morgan purchased controlling

---

[8] ICC, *Val. Rep.*, XXXVI, 399, 401, 433; "Transportation," *Eleventh Census*, XV, Part 1, 104–105; Haney, *A Congressional History of Railways in the United States*, II, 120–22, 128–30; Reed, *Texas Railroads*, 197–98.

interest in the Houston and Texas Central and incorporated the Louisiana Western Railroad Company to extend from Vermilionville to the Sabine River. Late in 1878 he entered into an agreement with the Texas and New Orleans whereby his road would meet the Texas road at the Sabine. Both parties fulfilled their construction obligations, the Texas and New Orleans building under the name Louisiana Western Extension Railroad. The line was completed July 1, 1881.

Under Morgan, the Houston and Texas Central added mileage in the form of branches. In 1879 it appeared to be on the verge of extending the branch from Ross into the Panhandle under the name Texas Central, but construction extended only to Albany, far short of the goal. The Texas Central charter was also used to develop a short line in North Texas which had no physical connection with the parent road. The original purpose had been to reach the Frisco at Paris. Starting from Garrett, three miles north of Ennis, it ran through Terrell to Roberts, then stopped. Morgan gave financial assistance to the little Waxahachie Tap and in time took it over. This short road, running from Waxahachie to Garrett, was built by residents of the inland town of Waxahachie after they became alarmed at the rapid rise of the neighboring railroad town of Ennis.

If he could secure the Texas and New Orleans and Morgan's railroads, Huntington would have a ready-made line from Houston to New Orleans and a railroad across Texas from the Gulf to Red River. Shortly after the agreement between Morgan and the Texas and New Orleans, Huntington bought the Texas road. The Morgan lines passed piecemeal. The Gulf, Western Texas and Pacific was the first. When Morgan dropped Indianola from his regularly scheduled steamship calls, the railroad was of no particular value to him. In April, 1878, he conveyed it to Huntington. In 1884, Morgan sold almost half of his stock in the other railroad properties to Huntington, and the following February he leased them to the Southern Pacific. Within a month the Houston and Texas Central and its subsidiaries went into the hands of receivers, largely because of a series of disastrous wrecks.[9]

The New York, Texas and Mexican, a railroad with a picturesque history, passed to Huntington at almost the same time as the Morgan lines. It was built by an Italian nobleman, Count Joseph Telfener, with the financial backing of J. W. Mackay, his brother-in-law, of

[9] ICC, *Rep.*, LXXV, 73; ICC, *Val. Rep.*, XXXIV, 600, 647; *ibid.*, XXXVI, 399, 428, 432, 509–12, 537–39, 551, 578–80, 607, 622, 625–27, 670–72, 691.

Then Came the Railroads

Comstock Lode fame. Using imported Italian laborers, Telfener completed the road from Victoria to Rosenberg in 1882. He sold it to Huntington two years later.[10]

In five years Huntington had secured his ready-made railroad. He added considerable mileage, chiefly by purchase. He had already embarked on a policy of buying short lines penetrating strategic areas when, in 1882, he secured the recently completed Sabine and East Texas, a hundred-mile timber railroad running from Sabine Pass through Beaumont to Rockland. Huntington turned it over to the Texas and New Orleans. The Fort Worth and New Orleans was a Fort Worth enterprise designed to reach the Houston and Texas Central at Waxahachie. The line was completed in 1886, and control immediately passed to the Houston and Texas Central. A narrow-gauge railroad, the Austin and Northwestern was a local project extending northwest from Austin to Burnet. The Houston and Texas Central secured control sometime before 1888, rebuilt it to standard gauge, and extended it to Marble Falls, with a branch from Fairland to Llano.[11]

The Houston and Texas Central experienced considerable difficulty with one branch. Mrs. Hetty Green, of Wall Street fame, was a heavy investor in the Houston and Texas Central. She held Huntington responsible for its receivership. Knowing that Huntington needed the Waco and Northwestern to carry out his plans for Central Texas, she outbid him when it was sold at foreclosure on December 28, 1892. She became involved in litigation over the road's land grant and the sale was set aside. At resale Huntington recovered the property. He made no effort to secure the Texas Central, which Mrs. Green held in lieu of the payment of interest on her Houston and Texas Central bonds. The western segment went to the newly organized Texas Central Railway Company, the eastern part to Mrs. Green, who operated it as the Texas Midland. She extended it south to Ennis and north to Greenville in 1894. Two years later she secured trackage rights over the Cotton Belt from Greenville to Commerce and built from Commerce to Paris in order to have a through line from Ennis to Paris.[12]

The Texas Trunk, the San Antonio and Aransas Pass, the Houston East and West Texas, the Galveston, Houston and Northern, and the

[10] ICC, *Val. Rep.*, XXXVI, 399, 429; Reed, *Texas Railroads*, 264–66.
[11] ICC, *Val. Rep.*, XXXVI, 510, 534, 579, 625–27.
[12] ICC, *Rep.*, LXXV, 72–73, 93; Reed, *Texas Railroads*, 219–20.

San Antonio and Gulf became part of Huntington's Texas system in the nineties.

The Texas Trunk was originally projected to run from Dallas to Beaumont, but it was bankrupt by the time it reached Kaufman, only thirty-eight miles from Dallas. Fourteen years of receivership during which it was extended fifteen miles to Gossett terminated with its sale to Huntington in 1895.

Uriah Lott, professional promoter, conceived the idea for the San Antonio and Aransas Pass. After securing generous subscriptions from San Antonio and the towns clustered about Corpus Christi Bay, enlisting the support of Captain Miflin Kenedy, and calling on the genius of a young assistant named B. F. Yoakum, Lott started construction from San Antonio in 1885 and completed the line to Corpus Christi the following year. He then built from San Antonio northwest to Kerrville and from Kenedy northeast to Houston. Between 1887 and 1891, Lott extended the road from the new town of Yoakum north to Waco, at the same time building branches from Skidmore to Alice and from Gregory to Rockport. In 1890, Huntington bought most of Kenedy's interest since the San Antonio and Aransas Pass served so much Southern Pacific territory.

The Houston East and West Texas became a part of the Southern Pacific as the century closed. It originated in 1875 as a narrow-gauge line promoted by Paul Bremond and financed largely by the men who sold the Houston and Texas Central to Charles Morgan. Its primary objective was to penetrate the East Texas timber belt. Slowly the road crawled northward and was only a few miles beyond Nacogdoches when Bremond died in 1885. Shortly thereafter it went into receivership but was completed to the Sabine. The Houston East and West Texas built under a Louisiana charter from Shreveport to a connection with the Texas road at the Sabine River. These roads changed ownership several times, the Southern Pacific eventually gaining control.

In 1898, Huntington organized the Galveston, Houston and Northern to take over and operate a locally built line between Galveston and Houston. It was of real importance because it gave the Galveston, Harrisburg and San Antonio an entrance into Galveston free of dependence on Gould's road. The San Antonio and Gulf was another local enterprise absorbed by the Galveston, Harrisburg and San Antonio. Projected to run from San Antonio to Velasco, it was

Then Came the Railroads

only thirty miles east of San Antonio when dissension broke out among its directors, and Huntington took it over. It remained a spur leading nowhere for many years.[13]

Huntington added relatively little to his holdings by construction. In 1889 he joined two of his properties by extending the Gulf, Western Texas and Pacific from Victoria to Beeville, on the San Antonio and Aransas Pass. The former Morgan lines benefited by half a dozen short branches in Louisiana, but the total was well short of one hundred miles.[14]

The Southern Pacific was not brought to as sharp a halt as other lines in the depression years following 1893. Little construction took place, but the purchase of a number of short lines had progressively strengthened the roads in Louisiana and Texas. When E. H. Harriman purchased controlling interest in the Southern Pacific after Huntington's death in 1900, the extensive properties were protected by numerous feeders and connecting lines.[15]

A number of other railroads date from the eighties and early nineties. Some were fairly prominent, but were not well known to the country at large because they did not encroach on the battlefields of the giants. Others were temporary timber lines into the forests or tap roads connecting inland towns with near-by carriers. Many succumbed and are now all but forgotten; some were absorbed into great systems; a few survived under their original names and in some cases emerged as roads of considerable importance.

The Fort Worth and Denver City was an independent company which was instrumental in opening up the virgin Texas Panhandle, a region virtually barren of population and considered equally barren of opportunity except as rangeland. The primary purpose of the railroad was not to serve the Panhandle, however, but to reach General William J. Palmer's Denver and Rio Grande narrow-gauge line, which stretched southwest from Denver to Pueblo by the summer of 1872.

A group of Fort Worth residents incorporated the Fort Worth and Denver City to build from their city to a connection with the Palmer road at the Texas–New Mexico line. The panic of 1873 put a stop to all activity, but in 1881, General Grenville M. Dodge became interested in the project and offered to build it, taking company secur-

[13] ICC, *Val. Rep.*, XXXVII, 811–13; *ibid.*, XXXVI, 398–401, 437–44, 462, 472, 510, 539–41, 640, 656; Reed, *Texas Railroads*, 242–47, 255; J. L. Allhands, *Uriah Lott*, 26–59.
[14] ICC, *Val. Rep.*, XXXVI, 400, 432, 672.
[15] *Ibid.*, 448, 478.

ities in payment for his services. By September, 1882, he had completed the line to Wichita Falls, where construction ceased for several years. Prospects for continuing were discouraging because of the absence of revenue freight on the plains; besides, the Denver and New Orleans Railway, a Colorado corporation which was to build southeast from Pueblo to meet the Texas road, was in financial difficulties.

Conditions being somewhat more favorable by 1885, Dodge proceeded with his building once more. Two years later he and Governor John Evans, of the Colorado corporation, organized the Denver, Texas and Fort Worth to take over the unfinished line from Pueblo, and in March, 1888, it reached the Fort Worth and Denver City at Texline.

The Fort Worth and Denver City did not have sufficient business to operate profitably and therefore became one of the earlier victims of the panic of 1893, passing briefly under the control of the Union Pacific before its association with the Colorado and Southern.[16]

General Dodge promoted another railroad in West Texas. This he called the Wichita Valley. As originally projected, it would have extended four hundred miles southwest from Wichita Falls, but it only succeeded in reaching Seymour, a distance of fifty miles.

Laredo secured two railroads at this time. One, the Texas Mexican, originated as a narrow-gauge line connecting Corpus Christi with San Diego, Texas. In 1881 the Mexican National Railway took it over, gave it its present name, and completed it to Laredo. It was later converted to standard gauge. The other Laredo line was built by Alexander C. Hunt to reach the Santo Tomás cannel coal mine, about thirty miles to the north. The railroad was in constant financial difficulties, was finally divorced from the mining interests, and was reorganized as the Rio Grande and Eagle Pass.[17]

The Vicksburg, Shreveport and Pacific was the most important of the independent lines in Louisiana. Organized in 1879 to take over the Vicksburg, Shreveport and Texas, which had never been able to get beyond its ante bellum terminus at Monroe, the new organization extended the line to Shreveport by 1884 and gave northern Louisiana its only trans-state carrier. Another important northern Louisiana railroad, known after 1890 as the New Orleans and Northwest-

---

[16] ICC, *Rep.*, CXXXIV, 747–49, 797; Richard C. Overton, *Gulf to Rockies*, 31–37, 50–60, 70–191, 289–310.
[17] ICC, *Rep.*, CXIV, 677–98; *ibid.*, CVIII, 781–804.

ern, stretched from opposite Natchez to the Arkansas line, a distance of 118 miles.[18]

Southern Louisiana had its new lines. The New Orleans, Fort Jackson and Grand Isle, later called the New Orleans and Lower Coast, ran from Algiers along the west bank of the Mississippi to Buras. In the southwest, two small railroads consolidated in 1887, and before the collapse of 1893 were operating an important link in the Louisiana transportation system under the name Kansas City, Watkins and Gulf. This road connected Lake Charles with Alexandria.[19]

A number of independent railroads were operating in Arkansas in the eighties. The best known was the Hot Springs Railroad, familiarly known as the Diamond Jo Line. It was a twenty-five-mile narrow-gauge road built by "Diamond Jo" Reynolds, a rheumatic millionaire who objected to the stage ride from Malvern to Hot Springs, where he took medicinal baths. In 1889, apparently because of pressure from Jay Gould, Reynolds rebuilt the railroad to standard gauge. It remained in the Reynolds family until 1901, when it became a bone of contention between the Iron Mountain and the Choctaw, Oklahoma and Gulf. Farther east, the White and Black River Valley Railway developed into a fairly long feeder for the Memphis and Little Rock by extending north from Brinkley to Jacksonport. Besides these longer railroads, tap lines served the towns of Augusta, Dardanelle, and Bentonville.[20]

Southeastern Missouri had several lines which were of considerable economic significance. The Mississippi River and Bonne Terre served the lead mines and gave them an outlet on the Mississippi at Riverside. In the course of time it developed a considerable web of branches and for a time operated a barge line from Riverside to St. Louis. The Missouri Southern varied from the typical logging road only because it assumed greater importance than similar projects through its numerous and frequently changing branches. In the extreme "swamp-eastern" corner of the state, Louis Houck was developing a system of railroads leading from Cape Girardeau towards Poplar Bluff, with several short branch lines and extensions into the boot-heel lying between Arkansas and the Mississippi River.[21]

---

[18] ICC, *Val. Rep.*, XXVI, 507, 516–19, 536–48; *ibid.*, XL, 672–81.

[19] *Ibid.*, XL, 410, 621–24; ICC, *Rep.*, CXIX, 270–83.

[20] ICC, *Rep.*, CX, 756–66; *ibid.*, CXXXIII, 374–93; ICC, *Val. Rep.*, XXIV, 848–49, 1062; *ibid.*, XLI, 303, 539; Fred A. Bill, "The Hot Springs Railroad," *RIM*, Vol. XVII, No. 10, 84–85.

Citizens of Hutchinson, Kansas, financed a railroad which held enough future possibilities that the Union Pacific toyed with it on occasion. In 1889 its backers took over two previously granted charters and reorganized as the Hutchinson and Southern. It struggled from Hutchinson through Kingman and Anthony to the Indian Territory line by 1890, but could go no farther.[22]

The Choctaw Coal and Railway Company was the only independent company to enter the Indian Territory, and its railroad activities were at first subordinated to the development of coal mines. The company was incorporated in Minnesota, the state which furnished the original promoters, but control soon passed to Philadelphia. The first section of the railroad began at Wister, near the Arkansas line, and extended through coal fields to South McAlester. At the same time, the Choctaw Coal and Railway Company built a line in Oklahoma Territory from El Reno to Oklahoma City. The two disconnected segments, one of which reached the Katy at South McAlester, the other the Rock Island at El Reno and the Santa Fe at Oklahoma City, had a physical connection only in these roads down through Fort Worth, Texas.[23]

[21] ICC, *Rep.*, CIII, 317, 325; *ibid.*, CVI, 502; *ibid.*, CVIII, 141, 149; *ibid.*, CXIV, 795–811; ICC, *Val. Rep.*, XLI, 303, 596–613.
[22] ICC, *Rep.*, CXXVII, 208, 215, 449–53.
[23] James F. Holden, "The B I T: The Story of an Adventure in Railroad Building," *Chron. Okla.*, Vol. XI, 644–54; Nevins, "Seventy . . . Service," *RIM*, Vol. XVII, 30.

CHAPTER 18

Interlude in the Nineties

THE DEPRESSION of 1893 terminated a period of railroad building in the same manner in which similar circumstances had halted construction twenty years before. This time it was not an interlude to be followed by larger and more ambitious undertakings but one which stopped abruptly a development which otherwise would have tapered off simply because there were no other places to build. The nation as a whole had reached the saturation point.

The twenty years between the two depressions was the most remarkable period of railroad expansion the world had ever known. Development in the Gulf Southwest proceeded at a pace in excess of that in the remainder of the country. From less than five thousand miles of track in 1870, this area had almost twenty-eight thousand in 1890. Missouri, with 40 per cent of the total in 1870, showed the smallest increase, yet it had multiplied three times. Louisiana increased fourfold, Kansas more than five, Arkansas six, and Texas eleven. The mileage in the twin territories lying between Kansas and Texas had multiplied ten times since the completion of the Katy.

The movement towards consolidation was second only to the tremendous physical expansion of the railroads. In 1873, the Missouri, Kansas and Texas and the St. Louis, Iron Mountain and Southern were the only railroads operating a substantial mileage in more than one state. All the others, in spite of ambitious designs, remained local concerns and could be grouped quite easily by locality. By 1890, with few exceptions, the railroads had been gathered together by powerful economic groups, each serving a number of states, while some served every state and territory in the Gulf Southwest.

Only one major railroad was actually conceived and carried to completion in the nineties. This was the Kansas City, Pittsburg and Gulf, which could boast that during its period of construction it contributed one-third of the total new mileage in the United States. The railroad is a monument to the promotional genius of one man—Arthur E. Stilwell.

Stilwell was a resourceful, dynamic salesman who accumulated wealth by promoting a new type of insurance, an amusement park, a suburban railroad, and the Guardian Trust Company. In 1890 he conceived the idea of building a railroad to the Gulf, serving coal fields at Pittsburg, Kansas, lead and zinc deposits at Joplin, and the timberlands of Arkansas and East Texas. Originally settling on Galveston as his Gulf terminus, Stilwell changed his mind and developed his own town of Port Arthur at a site he felt to be less vulnerable to tropical storms.

Under the corporate name of Kansas City, Nevada and Fort Smith, the road moved steadily south from Grandview along the western border of Missouri, crossing briefly into Kansas at Pittsburg. At this time Stilwell changed the name of the company to Kansas City, Pittsburg and Gulf. While the depression was forcing many lines into bankruptcy, Stilwell's road continued to push forward. At Joplin it absorbed the Splitlog Railroad, the by-product of a questionable railroad and mining promotional scheme which did build a line from Joplin to Sulphur Springs, Arkansas, with a branch from Goodman to Splitlog. The Kansas City, Pittsburg and Gulf then wandered over into Indian Territory at Watts, back into Arkansas near Page, and finally reached Winthrop.

Stilwell bought the Texarkana and Fort Smith, a logging road stretching from Ashdown, Arkansas, to Texarkana, and extended it north to Winthrop and south to the Louisiana line. Under this charter he also built from Port Arthur to the Sabine River. In the meantime he secured a Louisiana charter for the subsidiary Kansas City, Shreveport and Gulf, and closed the 222-mile gap which separated the two segments of the Texarkana and Fort Smith. On September 11, 1897, in spite of financial difficulties, floods, and yellow fever, the Kansas City, Pittsburg and Gulf opened its line from Kansas City to Port Arthur.

Stilwell secured one branch by purchasing a narrow-gauge line operating between Lockport and Edgewood, Louisiana. This he extended at one end to De Quincy, at the other to Lake Charles. He built other branches from his main line to Fort Smith, Jenson, Christie, and to cement clay and chalk deposits on Little River.

With obstacles to construction overcome and the road barely completed, Stilwell was preparing to enjoy his profits when he was again beset by troubles. A factional struggle threw the railroad and the Guardian Trust Company into receivership. Stilwell and his clique were forced out, and on March 22, 1900, the Kansas City Southern, a new company dominated by the fabulous John W. "Bet-a-Million" Gates, took possession of the Kansas City, Pittsburg and Gulf.[1]

The Choctaw Coal and Railway Company expanded through the depression years. Following the panic of 1893, the Philadelphia owners reorganized the property under the name Choctaw, Oklahoma and Gulf, with Franklin I. Gowen as president. Except for coal shipments, the unconnected segments, joined circuitously through Fort Worth, afforded meager financial returns. Gowen immediately closed the 120-mile gap between South McAlester and Oklahoma City. Three years later, in 1898, the western terminus was pushed to Weatherford, the eastern from Wister to Howe, on the newly built Kansas City, Pittsburg and Gulf.[2]

All other construction in the Southwest was of a minor nature. Only after the restoration of confidence at the close of the century was there a renewal of widespread activity.

[1] ICC, *Rep.*, LXXV, 276, 289–95, 300–303, 346–48, 364–67, 374, 381, 387–89, 395, 403, 408–12, 435; Arthur E. Stilwell, *Cannibals of Finance,* 46–54, 68–95, 107.
[2] Holden, "The B I T . . . Building," *Chron. Okla.,* Vol. XI, 656–61.

CHAPTER 19

The Passing of Aids

IN DUE TIME congressmen from the Southwest learned that their requests for additional railroad land grants were out of tune with the times. Gradually they joined the spokesmen from the Old Northwest in agitating for forfeiture. As early as 1879, Kansas and Missouri congressmen were demanding that certain grants within their states be turned back to the government. By 1884 both of the major political parties demanded cancellation of all grants which had lapsed because of noncompliance by the railroads.[1]

The first successes came with the forcing of individual railroads to restore their unearned lands. Between 1884 and 1886, the Iron Mountain, which had diverged completely from its original route, lost its lands in Arkansas, and the Texas and Pacific and the Atlantic and Pacific lost all those lands coterminous with uncompleted portions of their lines.

The Texas and Pacific, as successor to the New Orleans Pacific, was forced to relinquish lands in Louisiana in 1887. These had originally been granted to the Backbone Company, but its interests had passed to the New Orleans Pacific after a complicated legal and financial history unsullied by any attempts to build a railroad. The Texas and Pacific, after taking over the New Orleans Pacific, claimed the entire grant, although the railroad ran west of the Mississippi whereas the original act provided that it should follow the east bank of the river from New Orleans to Baton Rouge. Congress confirmed the Texas and Pacific in its ownership of more than one million acres but took

[1] *Cong., Rec.*, 46 Cong., 1 sess., 63, 1060.

away all lands east of the Mississippi and those coterminous with sections not completed before 1882.²

Cleveland consistently prodded Congress to act. In his first annual message he expressed disapproval of the operation of the grants. "It has been charged that these donations from the people have been diverted to private gain and corrupt uses, and thus public indignation has been aroused and suspicion engendered. Our great nation does not begrudge its generosity, but it abhors peculation and fraud."³

The railroad grants now assumed the appearance of a gigantic conspiracy to defraud the government and the people. Both houses of Congress discussed general forfeiture. Proposals ranged all the way from the loss of all lands because of noncompliance to restoration to the public domain of lands which might remain unearned at such time as a general forfeiture act should take effect. The milder view prevailed in the legislation finally enacted on September 29, 1890. Many railroads had already disposed of all their lands, and the remainder of those in the Southwest held only remnants.⁴

Conditional land grants in the Indian Territory remained a live issue. The Atlantic and Pacific was in no position to contend seriously that its grant had not been forfeited, but the Katy was. In May, 1897, attorneys for that railroad notified the Dawes Commission that they would claim the grant because allotment in severalty had extinguished Indian title. The agreements between the government and the Indians, however, were all predicated on the theory of a trust relationship, with the lands not attaching to the public domain. A notice from the Katy to the principal chief of the Cherokees, to the effect that he should not convey to Indian allottees any of the lands lying within the grant because the railroad claimed it, availed nothing.

In 1907 the Katy brought an action against the United States government in the sum of $61,287,800 for damages suffered as the result of its failure to recover any Indian lands. The claim was disallowed by the Court of Claims, and the railroad appealed to the Supreme Court, which, on November 9, 1914, affirmed the decision of the lower court on the grounds that Indian title had never been extinguished and the lands had never passed into the public domain.⁵

[2] Haney, *A Congressional History of Railways in the United States*, II, 25–29, 130–33; David M. Ellis, "The Forfeiture of Railroad Land Grants, 1867–1894," *MVHR*, Vol. XXXIII, 39–42.

[3] Richardson, *A Compilation of the Messages and Papers of the Presidents*, VIII, 359.
[4] Ellis, "The Forfeiture ... 1867–1894," *MVHR*, Vol. XXXIII, 27–60.
[5] *Fourth Ann. Rep. Comm. to Civ. Tribes*, 37–38; IAD, Creek Nation—Railroads, 35819; *Court of Claims Rep.*, XLVII, 59; *U. S. Rep.*, CCXXXV, 36.

The Passing of Aids

Congress enacted legislation to remedy various grievances arising out of the land-grant policy. An act of 1881 protected settlers who had made improvements in good faith on disputed lands by permitting them to retain their property on payment of $2.50 per acre. In 1887 a general adjustment law restored lands to bona fide settlers whose titles had been canceled because of conflicts with railroads claiming under their grants. Those who had bought such lands were allowed to perfect their titles by paying the purchase price to the railroads, which, in turn, paid to the government.[6]

Tax dodging, an outgrowth of the land-grant policy, led to ill feeling, which remained after the ultimate solution of the controversy. The Supreme Court had ruled that lands remained a part of the public domain until they were officially patented. By delaying patenting, railroads avoided the payment of taxes. This was particularly galling because the lands were withdrawn from entry, and the roads issued bonds predicated upon their ownership; furthermore, state and local governments were loaded with a heavy bonded railroad indebtedness which the beneficiaries refused to share. Finally, in June, 1886, Congress subjected all railroad lands to taxation.[7]

In lieu of public land grants, counties and towns in areas without railroads continued to give financial assistance unless they were absolutely forbidden to do so by their state constitutions. Minor political units in Kansas were particularly generous. Local governments along the line of the Chicago, Kansas and Nebraska donated $33,000 and exchanged $1,318,000 of their bonds for railroad stock. The various railroads which eventually merged with the Santa Fe received well over $500,000 in municipal, county, and township bonds and, excluding the Leavenworth, Lawrence and Galveston, exchanged some $3,500,000 in securities. Predecessors of the Missouri Pacific were endowed even more generously, and those lines which later became a part of the Frisco exchanged about $1,500,000. Many shorter lines also benefited.

The Kansas Board of Railroad Commissioners fixed the railroad indebtedness of local governments at more than $9,500,000 in 1883, but the total increased later in the decade. In one sixteen months' period in 1885 and 1886, political subdivisions voted more than $10,-000,000 in railroad bonds. It has been estimated that 80 per cent of

---

[6] Haney, *A Congressional History of Railways in the United States*, II, 31–33.

[7] *Cong. Rec.*, 44 Cong., 1 sess., 1520–22; *ibid.*, 49 Cong., 1 sess., 3717–21, 4954–58; Haney, *A Congressional History of Railways in the United States*, II, 181–82.

Then Came the Railroads

the municipal debt of Kansas at this time was contracted to aid railroads.[8] The antirailroad sentiment which swelled in Kansas during the late eighties almost put an end to this type of aid, but as late as 1915, sixteen local units in three Kansas counties aided the Anthony and Northern to the amount of $567,500.[9]

At the turn of the century, Louisiana was the only state giving aid very generally. Locally it took the form of subsidy, or bonus, taxes. Special inducements were offered at the state level in the constitution of 1898, which provided that all railroads meeting certain conditions and completing their lines by 1904 would be granted tax exemption for a period of ten years. The last direct aid measure enacted in Louisiana extended this provision to 1909.[10]

Repeal by the various states of the acts permitting local units to make donations or lend credit did not halt all aid, for private donations replaced bond issues. Private donations became particularly popular in Texas after the exhaustion of the public lands. The Gulf, Colorado and Santa Fe received about $500,000, ranging from $70 from the town of Nickleville to Fort Worth's $85,000. The Katy, the Frisco, the Cotton Belt, and the San Antonio and Aransas Pass all benefited. This type of assistance declined as each area developed its network, but always along the fringe, where there was inadequate, if any, service, it continued. The course of private donation carried westward as the substitute for local bond issues in a new West which state legislatures protected from its own eagerness. By the early part of the new century, private donation was confined largely to Oklahoma and West Texas.

The spirit of the people had changed, even as the aid program was drawing to a close. Enthusiastic approval and unbounded optimism had given way to bitter disillusionment and furious resentment. Memory is often short, and some of the most vociferous later critics, with their neighbors, had demanded that encouragement in the form of land grants be given to railroads, that their communities meet the demand for local assistance, and that state and local governments subscribe to the plans of promoters who could induce investors to finance construction. Struggling with mortgages, increasing costs of

---

[8] Kansas Bd. of RR. Comm., *First Ann. Rep.*, 42–46; Hallie Farmer, "The Economic Background of Frontier Populism," *MVHR*, Vol. X, 406–27; Hicks, *The Populist Revolt*, 69. The valuation dockets contain long lists of donations to the various companies.

[9] ICC, *Rep.*, XCVII, 531.

[10] ICC, *Val. Rep.*, XXIX, 751, 754, 767, 777; *ibid.*, XXXVI, 447; Const. of Louisiana (1898), Art. CCXXX and Amendment 7.

production, falling prices of farm commodities, and the ever present railroad bonds which had not brought them the prosperity they had bargained for, the disgruntled and the disappointed were willing to place all the blame on the railroads.

CHAPTER 20

Indian Territory Succumbs

SUCCEEDING WAVES of western migration swirled about the Indian Territory for years before finally engulfing it. The first recognized breach had come with railroad penetration. The second came with the destruction of natural resources once transportation facilities were available. The final step was the wholesale intrusion of whites, which meant the end of a distinct Indian area.

Spoliation of natural resources was a matter of deep concern to both the Indians and their agents. Timber was the first to suffer, and before the first railroads were completed, some areas were practically denuded. The Indians accused the railroads of removing timber from the Territory for construction elsewhere, buying from unlicensed traders, and refusing to pay for ties. The Choctaw agent reported that the Katy was making no effort to avoid such illegal timber transactions. The Cherokees passed laws in 1881 and 1883 prohibiting individuals from speculating in timber, but they were unenforceable.

Coal was another resource which excited the cupidity of both railroads and white intruders. The building of the Katy made the Choctaw mines accessible at a time when surrounding states were in need of fuel. The Osage Coal and Mining Company, whose officers were largely those of the Katy, engaged in extensive mining operations and was constantly at war with the Choctaw Nation. Eventually the controversy over the mining activities was merged with complaints that the railroad had refused to pay for stone and timber. A quasi-judicial proceeding conducted by the Department of the Interior ended in the dismissal of all claims against the railroad.

Indian Territory Succumbs

The Choctaw Coal and Railway Company was the most persistent offender in executing fraudulent leases of coal lands. The union agent, Leo Bennett, reported that E. D. Chadick, acting for the company, had leased over one million acres of Creek land and even more in the Choctaw Nation. Chadick readily admitted that he had entered into illegal leasing agreements, but justified himself because he had found Indian law arbitrary in its regulation of mineral lands. The railroad company turned to Congress for relief, as did the holders of other illegally executed leases. An act of March 1, 1889, permitted the leasing of Indian lands for a period of ten years, and the Choctaw Coal and Railway Company was the beneficiary of a joint resolution which validated its thirty-year leases on eleven tracts of coal land.[1]

The ever present danger of white intrusion was the most serious problem faced by the Indians. Their opposition to railroads stemmed largely from the knowledge that, once built, the new lines would insist that there was no profit in operating through an uninhabited country and that the Territory should therefore be opened. Difficulties over mining operations and timber depredations could probably have been solved, but the activities of railroads in encouraging intrusion was of much greater consequence, a threat to the very existence of the Indian nations. Illicit incursions into the Indian country had preceded the railroads; the great invasion, however, did not take place until rail transportation made the land highly desirable.

By 1872 the campaign to legalize entry was under way. Except for those associated with the cattle industry, most of the congressmen from the southwestern states staunchly supported the demands for the opening of Indian Territory. In the words of Representative Thomas T. Crittenden of Missouri, "This whole country was set aside for the Indians at one time by God, but we have driven them out, and I say let us keep driving them if they stand in the way of the civilization of the country.... Let us make the Territory what God designed it should be, the home and abiding place of the American citizen."[2]

Sporadic attempts to force the opening of the Territory evolved into an organized movement under the aggressive leadership of David L. Payne in the late seventies. Presidents Hayes and Arthur attempted to stem the movement, first by warnings, then by the use of troops, and finally by requests for legislation which would enable the execu-

[1] 45 Cong., 3 sess., *S. Rep. 744*, 225–31, 240–78; App., 195; 46 Cong., 2 sess., *S. Misc. Doc. 100;* 47 Cong., 1 sess., *S. Ex. Docs. 80* and *89;* 48 Cong., 1 sess., *H. Ex. Doc. 14;* 49 Cong., 1 sess., *S. Rep. 1278*, part 2, 266–73; 50 Cong., 2 sess., *H. Ex. Doc. 22.*

[2] *Cong. Rec.*, 45 Cong., 3 sess., 314.

tive branch to enforce the intercourse laws more adequately. Meanwhile, the boomers were indignantly protesting that they were mistreated by the soldiers. They demanded the immediate withdrawal of troops and the organization of Oklahoma Territory to "guarantee our plain and undeniable rights under the laws and constitution of our country."[3] Senator Preston B. Plumb became very irate because honest citizens of the United States were persecuted for what at worst was an innocent mistake.

President Cleveland took a vigorous stand against the intruders. Nine days after he took office, he issued a proclamation warning trespassers that he would remove them by force. In July he dispatched two regiments of cavalry and one of infantry to see that this order was obeyed, but he was unable to secure the passage of laws for the punishment of the intruders.[4]

There is no doubt that the railroads played an important but, at times, obscure role in encouraging trespassing. Railroads advertised Indian Territory as a "land of Paradise." The editor of the Wichita, Kansas, *Eagle* reported that railroads and commercial interests of near-by cities had devoted large sums of money to their unsuccessful campaign to induce the Indians to open their lands.[5]

E. C. Boudinot was the most active resident of the Territory in supporting efforts to open it to settlement. Never a leader among his own people, he chose his associates from among railroaders and boomers. His sympathy for railroad interests had been apparent from the days of the Fort Smith Council. He moved from place to place in the character of promoter and newspaper editor.

In August, 1875, he was a dominant figure in a convention of white "boosters" in the Territory. Two months later he was in Muskogee as co-owner of *Indian Progress,* a pro-railroad newspaper. One of his associates in the enterprise was George A. Reynolds, who was an employee of the Katy at the time. Boudinot admitted that he had discussed with a railroad the advisability of founding a newspaper at Vinita. He carried on an extensive correspondence with T. C. Sears, attorney for the Katy, and conferred with David L. Payne and with Robert T. Van Horn and Sidney Clarke, both prolific authors of ter-

---

[3] *Ibid.,* 48 Cong., 2 sess., 504.

[4] Richardson, *A Compilation of the Messages and Papers of the Presidents,* VII, 521, 548, 577, 598; *Rep. Comm. Ind. Aff., 1885,* lix–lx; 46 Cong., 1 sess., *S. Ex. Doc. 20,* 13; 47 Cong., 1 sess., *H. Ex. Doc. 45* and *S. Ex. Doc. 111.*

[5] *Rep. Comm. Ind. Aff., 1871,* 468; Wichita *Eagle,* Feb. 13, 1879.

Indian Territory Succumbs

ritorial bills. Later Boudinot was an inquisitor in the interests of the railroads during the Patterson investigations.

The climax of his journalistic endeavors was a letter to the Chicago *Times* in February, 1879. He stated that there were over fourteen million acres of "unassigned lands" in Indian Territory, ceded by the Civilized Tribes but never assigned to "blanket" Indians; therefore they were subject to entry as public domain. He supplied all interested parties with maps and information and soon aroused great interest.[6]

T. C. Sears was the most active agitator employed by the railroads. He frankly stated that he was a lobbyist for the Missouri, Kansas and Texas and that he tried to influence Indian Territory legislation. Shortly after Boudinot's letter appeared in the Chicago *Times*, the Sedalia *Daily Democrat* carried a news report that Judge Sears, recently returned from Washington, said that if Congress did not open the Indian Territory, the people would. His mission in Washington, so he stated, was to keep in touch with the organization of the House and Senate committees on Indian affairs and on territories.[7]

The activities of David Payne were probably guided largely by railroads. Although he had no private fortune, he spent large sums of money in securing recruits. Payne boasted that he was closely associated with powerful interests in Washington, St. Louis, and Kansas City. Captain Thomas B. Robinson, who arrested Payne in the summer of 1880, concluded in his report that "the majority of them [the boomers] are temporarily employed to go with Payne on this expedition and are unquestionably remunerated by some agent acting for the A. T. and S. F., M. K. and T., and the St. L. and S. F. railroads, and the L. L. and G. railroad."[8] Payne was tried in November, 1880; James Baker of the Frisco was his attorney. Five years later General William T. Sherman advised the War Department that "the belief exists that their interests were not actual settlement but to call the attention of Congress to the opening up of Indian Territory, and that money was subscribed for this purpose by interested corporations."[9]

The major allies of the Indian were the cattle syndicates which grazed their stock in Indian Territory. Just as the railroads supported

---

[6] 44 Cong., 1 sess., *H. Misc. Doc. 167*, 71–86, 124; 45 Cong., 3 sess., *S. Rep. 744*, 173, 187–96, 417–19; 45 Cong., 2 sess., *S. Misc. Doc. 30*, parts 1 and 2; 46 Cong., 1 sess., *S. Ex. Doc. 20*, 6–8; Phil. Coll., Correspondence of E. C. Boudinot, Series 2, VI, Nos. 41–51 and 64 and Series 2, VII, Nos. 70 and 81.

[7] 46 Cong., 1 sess., *S. Ex. Doc. 20*, 10–12.

[8] Dept of War, Adjutant General's Office, Document File 2653, 4765/1880.

[9] *Rep. Sec. of War, 1885*, I, 60.

the boomers because increased population meant increased revenue traffic, so the cattlemen supported the resistance of the tribes to a movement which would replace the vast pasturelands with farms. Both parties maintained powerful lobbies to protect their interests.[10]

By 1884 it was freely admitted that the southwestern states were determined to destroy the tribal organizations that stood in the way of their commercial development. Senator Preston B. Plumb took the lead in advocating the opening of the "unassigned lands" and the allotment of Indian lands in severalty. Kansas and Missouri representatives deplored a situation which forced railroads to operate at a loss through unpopulated but fertile areas. An amendment to the Indian Appropriation Act of 1884 did authorize the President of the United States to negotiate with the Indians for the sale of the "unassigned lands," but the President refused to act.[11]

The debate over various bills which would change the status of Indian Territory continued for five more years, with interest concentrated chiefly on territorial bills and the "unassigned lands." Early in 1889 the Creek and Seminole nations agreed to the removal of any restrictions in the use of lands which they had ceded in 1866. Four years later the Cherokees relinquished control of the Outlet. Within a few years all the lands except those of the Five Civilized Tribes were subject to entry.[12]

Meanwhile, in 1889, Congress created a federal court with civil jurisdiction in Indian Territory, and by 1897 all Indian courts were suspended. The Indian Appropriation Act of 1893 provided for the appointment of a committee to induce the Civilized Tribes to take their lands in severalty, paving the way for the Dawes Commission. The termination of tribal autonomy occurred with the passage of the Curtis Act of 1898. Later legislation simply perfected that which had already been accomplished.[13]

Railroads were in attendance at both of the famous "runs" into Oklahoma. The Santa Fe had just finished its line from Arkansas City to Texas when President Benjamin Harrison announced that

[10] Carl C. Rister, *Land Hunger*, 133.
[11] *Cong. Rec.*, 48 Cong., 2 sess., 33–35, 861–68, 892–96, 935–47, 1746–50, 2062–64, 2391–95, 2466–68; *ibid.*, 49 Cong., 1 sess., 154–55, 345–46; *U. S. Stat. at L.*, XXIII, 384; Richardson, *A Compilation of the Messages and Papers of the Presidents*, VIII, 355–58.
[12] *U. S. Stat. at L.*, XXV, 757, 1004; *ibid.*, XXVII, 640; Richardson, *A Compilation of the Messages and Papers of the Presidents*, IX, 202–203, 236, 325, 406–24.
[13] *U. S. Stat. at L.*, XXIV, 388; *ibid.*, XXX, 495–518; *ibid.*, XXXI, 848, 1447; *ibid.*, XXXVII, 645; *ibid.*, XXXIX, 340.

Indian Territory Succumbs

Oklahoma District would be thrown open to homeseekers, who would race for their claims. On the day of the run, April 22, 1889, the Santa Fe had eleven trains on the north line of the Territory and five at Purcell, just south of the Canadian River boundary. At the sound of the bugle at twelve noon, these trains slowly moved over the line, disgorging passengers as they approached Oklahoma Station from opposite directions. All sidings were lined with the goods of homeseekers, and to this the railroads soon added carloads of food and building materials and tanks of drinking water.[14]

The Santa Fe shared with the Rock Island the opening of the Cherokee Outlet on September 16, 1893. Secretary of the Interior Hoke Smith did not issue the order permitting railroads to enter the Outlet during the run until three days before it took place. Trains were limited to a speed of fifteen miles an hour and were to stop at every station and at least once every five miles. The railroads obeyed so far as they were able, but, as one official remarked, "I am afraid that Mr. Hoke Smith has not the proper conception of the aggressiveness of one Oklahoma boomer, to say nothing of ten or twelve thousand of them."[15]

On the morning of the run there were 100,000 people poised on the borders of the land of promise—30,000 at Arkansas City, 15,000 at Caldwell, and lesser numbers at Kiowa and Hunnewell. Down in Oklahoma there were 25,000 at Orlando and 10,000 at Hennessey. At exactly twelve o'clock, ten trains of ten boxcars each moved out of Arkansas City and into the Outlet, a train of forty-two boxcars pulled out of Orlando, and another of thirty-nine from Hennessey. The passengers were in every conceivable state of disarray as they scrambled madly for space; every car in every train swarmed with humanity—inside, on top, or hanging precariously from the sides. Outrun initially by horses, bicycles, and all types of horse-drawn wagons and buggies, the locomotives puffed steadily onward past heavily guarded bridges which rumor had it would be fired to prevent the trains from crossing. While speculators cursed their slowness, the trainmen religiously observed the regulations, and at each stop hundreds of people tumbled off to seize the best available quarter-section or town lot.[16]

---

[14] Foreman, *A History of Oklahoma*, 241.
[15] Joe B. Milam, "The Opening of the Cherokee Strip," *Chron. Okla.*, Vol. IX, 464.
[16] *Ibid.*, 115–37; Foreman, *A History of Oklahoma*, 253–56.

Then Came the Railroads

Two runs were enough. Later openings were by public drawings to determine which among the thousands of hopeful registrants would secure lands.[17] Thus ended the struggle for control of the area which had been dedicated as the permanent home of the red man.

[17] Foreman, *A History of Oklahoma,* 249–50, 268–69.

CHAPTER 21

The Restricted Wild West

THE TOWNS STRUNG along the railroads building west from San Antonio and west and northwest from Fort Worth were worthy successors to those which sprang up on the plains of Kansas in the seventies. The ends of track which crept through the short grass of the Panhandle or wormed through the desert vegetation towards El Paso were just as alluring to lawless, rowdy elements. The railroads created most of the towns; they rescued a few villages from further stagnation. All the new or revived frontier settlements passed through a stage of youthful abandon before reaching a maturity which frowned upon lawlessness. The vast region served by these railroads was capable of sustaining only the sparsest of populations, and the law which protected the inhabitants was of the typical frontier variety.

The Texas and Pacific, racing west to meet the Southern Pacific, had its difficulties with the hundred or so gamblers and ruffians who followed the progress of the road, seeking easy money. The tough little settlements which had grown up around frontier posts and had served as rendezvous for buffalo hunters lost some of their gaudier citizens to the lure of "end of track." Falling within the far-flung territory patrolled by the Texas Ranger frontier battalion, the Texas and Pacific requested its protection. From November, 1880, Company B had been stationed at Hackberry Springs, some thirty miles from the tent-town of Colorado City, built on the banks of the Colorado River in anticipation of the railroad's coming. The tracks crossed the river in April and moved on towards Big Spring. The country became wilder and the riffraff more unmanageable. After the chief engineer

Then Came the Railroads

of the railroad requested that Rangers be furnished to maintain order, with a promise of wagons and locomotives as necessary for Ranger use, Company B moved on to Big Spring. Lawlessness continued until the Texas and Pacific joined the Southern Pacific at Sierra Blanca and for a considerable period thereafter.[1]

Conditions on the Galveston, Harrisburg and San Antonio were even wilder. It was scheduled to meet the Southern Pacific, building southeast from Sierra Blanca, a few miles west of the Pecos. Tracklaying was delayed at the Pecos while the stream was bridged. A tent and shack community called Vinegaroon, much more poisonous than the whip scorpion whose name it bore, flourished. Violence increased daily, and the situation became even more tense as the Southern Pacific tracks closed in from the west. Construction hands were being laid off, and many of them joined the "hard cases" who had trailed the railroad from San Antonio; the inclusion of large numbers of Chinese in the crews of the Southern Pacific added the possibility of racial outbreaks. Eight thousand men were concentrated between Vinegaroon and Eagle's Nest, a town some twenty miles west of Vinegaroon, and almost equally disreputable. On June 6 the railroads called for Rangers, and six came. Captain T. L. Oglesby, their commander, who spoke with the authority of an experienced peace officer on a wild frontier, advised his superiors that Vinegaroon had the worst bunch of toughs he had ever encountered.

This was the environment in which "Judge" Roy Bean prospered, without whose story no account of the construction of the line from San Antonio to El Paso would be complete. His early career, interesting though it was, had not been particularly fruitful. "Beanville," in San Antonio, was certainly not a show place of the chamber of commerce variety. Neither was its leading citizen an outstanding civic leader. At the age of fifty-six, Bean determined to sell his San Antonio properties and try his fortune along the railroad, which was nearing the Pecos. The $900 he received from his worldly possessions was sufficient to cover the cost of a wagon, a tent, a barrel of whiskey of questionable quality, and some bottled beer. These were his material goods; of much greater significance were certain intangibles—a shrewd mind, an elastic conscience, an uncommon ability to outbluster competitors, and a flair for self-advertising. The real mystery of his life was how fortune had eluded his grasp for so long.

Roy tried Eagle's Nest, Vinegaroon, and even Strawbridge (now

[1] J. Evetts Haley, *Jeff Milton*, 42–45, 57–58; Webb, *The Texas Rangers*, 452.

The Restricted Wild West

Sanderson), some eighty-five miles west of the Pecos, before establishing himself a few hundred yards from Eagle's Nest at a point which combined two attractive features: water and a level stretch following a long, steep grade. The railroads were supposed to meet near this point. Cold-blooded realists insist that the new creation was named for a Southern Pacific construction foreman; others still treasure the belief that Roy named it for the current rage of the theatrical world, Lily Langtry, the "Jersey Lilly," as he was wont to spell it.

It has remained a source of considerable wonderment that a squatter on railroad right of way, in the center of the extensive landholdings of the powerful Torres family, was able to seize and hold control of the town which that family had planned to operate. A long-time feud resulted, but Roy was never dislodged. He was too closely associated with the railroad, which was indebted to him for certain services he had rendered at Vinegaroon.

The wanderings of Roy Bean had come to an end. The Rangers at Eagle's Nest asked for a justice of the peace, and on August 2, 1882, Roy Bean received the commission. Everything was legal and official about the justiceship; the "law West of the Pecos" was all that he added. His methods of making change for an impatient passenger whose train was about to pull out were as unorthodox as his court procedures. Bean's name and his fame spread with his legal holdings, and they were certainly more widely known than the decisions of somewhat more erudite justices such as those of the United States Supreme Court, who professed to exercise a somewhat wider jurisdiction. "Judge" Bean became so widely known that even Jay Gould and his daughter interrupted an inspection tour of Gould's railroads to be entertained at Langtry. Although the Jersey Lilly, Bean's place of business, was somewhat isolated by the straightening of the tracks, the establishment and its proprietor remained a feature attraction on the Southern Pacific for many years.[2]

Sanderson, Murphysville (now Alpine), and Marfa on the Southern Pacific and Baird, Abilene, Sweetwater, Colorado City, and Big Spring on the Texas and Pacific had their boom-town history which fitted the general pattern of the frontier. The region produced its quota of train robbers, the stretch between the Pecos and Sanderson being the scene of particular activity. Captain Fred Jones of the

[2] C. L. Sonnischen, *Roy Bean*, 67–86, 95–105; Gard, *Frontier Justice*, 264–65; Haley, *Jeff Milton*, 69–70; Robert J. Casey, *The Texas Border*, 199.

Rangers trailed one such band from the Pecos area up the Río Grande, crossing back and forth across the international boundary and doubling back until, eight weeks later, he ran them down in Crockett County. This holdup involved only a small sum of money, but it gave rise to a buried-treasure legend which persisted for years. Meanwhile, train robbers became so active that a troop of Rangers under Captain J. F. Hughes was detailed to stop them. By 1900 this particular form of criminal activity had almost stopped.

Some of the more heroic frontier tales came out of the terminal cities. San Antonio was already old and had a very considerable population before the extension of the Galveston, Harrisburg and San Antonio farther west. It retained an air of permanence and maturity, yet at the same time it was attracting a population which added a new type of notoriety. The Menger Hotel was justly famous, and Scholz's Palm Garden attracted an elegant clientele, far different from that of the Buckhorn, the most popular hangout for the cowhands. San Antonio became a theatrical center when the railroads came, mixing really good entertainment with cheaper dance-hall and variety-theater attractions.

There was yet another side to the city. The rapid growth which followed its emergence as a railroad center brought the usual array of gamblers, prostitutes, swindlers, and killers. The Vaudeville Theatre was at the location called "the Fatal Corner" because of its reputation for bloodshed. The establishment was a gambling and variety house. It was here that Ben Thompson finally met his end. All the principals were killed in a gunfight involving Thompson, King Fisher, his notorious companion, and Joe Foster, proprietor of the Vaudeville Theatre.[3]

No city had a more lurid history in the eighties and the early nineties than El Paso. A Mexican border village of 736 inhabitants in 1880, it was converted by three rail connections into a brawling town of 10,000 within a few years. Never particularly tame, it became the wildest town in the West—with all the lustier forms of amusement wide open. Rangers brought temporary order after the mayor of the town called them in. The bloody feud between the more prominent gamblers and City Marshal Dallas Stoudenmire, which ended with the killing of Stoudenmire, can scarcely be called a continuation of

---

[3] Webb, *The Texas Rangers*, 438–41; Casey, *The Texas Border*, 296–97, 301–303; Cunningham, *Triggernometry*, 241–43.

The Restricted Wild West

that order. Jim Gillett, former Texas Ranger and former guard of Santa Fe Railway money shipments, held the town in check, as did Jeff Milton, whose background was quite similar to that of Gillett's. Nevertheless, the city compiled a lengthy list of violent casualties (including such eminent names as Wes Hardin, John Selman, and Bass Outlaw) before it outgrew its adolescent exuberance.[4]

The Indian Territory was also a retarded area, not so much because of its geographical location, as of the policy which had dedicated it to the Indians at a time when it had been considered as unfit for white occupancy. Consequently, both the lands of the Civilized Tribes and those assigned to Plains tribes were being occupied by white settlers after Kansas had already reached an advanced stage of agricultural maturity. Historians have seen fit to refer to the Indian Territory as the last American frontier. Conditions justly entitled it to the appellation.

Town building did not follow the first railroads across Oklahoma and Indian Territory because these areas were closed to white settlement. With various openings which allowed piecemeal occupation of Indian lands, town promoters naturally followed the course of the railroads. These new communities, springing up on the plains in the course of a day, attracted many adventurers who flocked in to take advantage of free lands. All had to be tamed.

This new country produced an exceptionally large number of outlaws intent on preying on railroad and express shipments. The Daltons, the Doolin gang, and the Jennings brothers all rose and fell within a period of seven years.

The Dalton brothers—Bob, Grat, and Emmet—began their criminal careers as horse thieves around Baxter Springs, and broke into train robbing in California. Their maiden effort landed them in the penitentiary, but they escaped and returned to Oklahoma Territory. Late in May, 1891, Bob and Emmet, accompanied by a cowboy named Charlie Bryant, held up a Santa Fe train at Wharton, in the Cherokee Outlet. Almost exactly a year later, and but a few miles from the scene of the previous crime, the Daltons and three other men held up a north-bound and a south-bound train simultaneously at a passing switch south of Red Rock. Within six weeks they robbed a Katy train at Adair, in Indian Territory. At this point they turned

[4] "Population," *Fifteenth Census*, I, 1056; Haley, *Jeff Milton*, 209–52; Cunningham, *Triggernometry*, 171–88, 201–202; Casey, *The Texas Border*, 187–94, 314–26.

to banks, but not for long. They were trapped in an attempted bank robbery at Coffeyville, Kansas, in October; Emmet alone survived the battle which followed.

Bill Doolin and a killer named George Weightman, commonly known as Red Buck, had ridden with the Daltons until the gang became too unwieldly, at which time they split away. Tall, lanky, and amiable, Doolin was a product of the Arkansas backwoods who came to Indian Territory and became a top cowhand before turning outlaw. He and Red Buck gathered about them some ten men, who conducted their raids from a hideout at Ingalls, in Oklahoma Territory. Their first train holdup took place at Cimarron, Kansas, on May 28, 1893.

After a pitched battle at the hideout in October, in which three United States deputy marshals were killed and a member of the gang, "Arkansas Tom," taken, three deputy marshals—Bill Tilghman, Chris Madsen, and Heck Thomas—were given the job of running down the Doolin band. A rash of train robberies occurred in 1894 as the peace officers were doggedly following the gang.

The luck of the Doolin gang ran out early in 1895. The robbery of a Rock Island train at Dover, Oklahoma Territory, in May resulted in the killing of one member of the gang and the flight of the remainder. One by one they were captured or killed. Doolin, afflicted with rheumatism and tired of outlawry, was captured by Bill Tilghman while taking medicinal baths, escaped, but was shot to death while attempting to get in touch with his wife.

The Jennings boys were the most overrated of all the train-robbing gangs which infested Oklahoma Territory. They were active for a period of about sixteen weeks and engineered only one successful holdup during that time. The band had five members. With the exception of "Little Dick" West, who had been with Bill Doolin, they were all amateurs. Al and Frank Jennings, sons of a probate judge, had moved to Tecumseh after being involved in certain difficulties around Woodward. The two remaining members were the O'Malley brothers, Pat and Morris.

On August 18, 1897, a band of robbers stopped a Santa Fe train at Edmond, Oklahoma, but became frightened and fled without loot. They were immediately identified as the Jennings brothers and their associates, and warrants were issued for their arrest. Their second attempt was an even more dismal failure; they were unable to stop a Katy train near Muskogee, Indian Territory. Success finally came after they forced a switchman to flag down a Rock Island train in the Chickasaw country. The safe did not respond to a dynamite blast, but the gang did get some bananas, a jug of liquor, and some seven hundred dollars in cash and jewelry from the passengers.

The Jennings and O'Malley brothers were caught on December 5 and given prison sentences. "Little Dick" had withdrawn from the gang after its one successful robbery; he was shot down by a posse three weeks after the capture of his recent partners.[5]

Train holdups were peculiarly suited to unsettled frontier conditions, and the frontier was passing. New boom towns would still mushroom, but with the exception of the twin territories, the Texas Panhandle, and the South Plains, their prosperity was not primarily due to the arrival of railroads. By the turn of the century, the lawlessness so closely associated with railroad penetration was practically at an end.

[5] Tilghman, *Marshal of the Last Frontier*, 188, 196, 205–30, 240–43; Evan G. Barnard, *A Rider of the Cherokee Strip*, 193–95, 209–12.

CHAPTER 22

Peopling the Plains

SOME HAVE asserted that the United States developed too rapidly and the criminal waste of resources was a disproportionate price to pay for rapid settlement. Others, equally sincere, answer that only by such development did this nation grasp and retain the position it now holds. The debate is academic. Rightly or wrongly, the nation followed a course of rapid occupation and reduction of the great West.

The Gulf Southwest reached the peak of its railroad building in the eighties and passed the peak of its ability to absorb newcomers. Although the population continued to increase, the rate of growth showed a precipitous decline.

Railroad construction in Missouri had been fairly well concentrated along the western border, with some additions in the region directly tributary to the Missouri River and in the extreme southeastern corner of the state. The lines radiating from Springfield had a notable effect on the number of new inhabitants. The population of the region west of Springfield, already partially served by railroads, increased 50 per cent; that to the southeast, which previously had neither effective water transportation nor railroads, doubled. Deep in the southeast, the timbered swamplands experienced a resurgence with new railroads. Never particularly attractive, this area was increasing its population at a rate almost double that of the state average.

The most notable development in Arkansas was in the northeastern corner of the state, where the population of the interior counties served by the Iron Mountain, the St. Louis, Arkansas and Texas, and the Kansas City, Fort Scott and Memphis increased by two-thirds.

Peopling the Plains

Northwestern Arkansas also benefited from railroads. Already fairly well settled by seepage from southwestern Missouri, the population grew rapidly with the coming of the Frisco.

Nowhere was the fallacious assumption that settlement would automatically follow a new railroad more thoroughly disproved than in the case of those Louisiana lines building along the Mississippi. At best the parishes grew very slowly, while north of the Red the population had stabilized and was stationary. Farther west, however, along the new southern rail route to Texas, population increased at a progressively higher rate. The Red River country, an area of older settlement now served by the Texas and Pacific, drew new residents at a rate roughly one and one-half times that of the rest of the state.

Kansas was unique in the amazing speed with which it completed its railroads. Only five counties clustered in the southwest corner were without rail lines, and most could boast two or more.

Kansas remained the fastest growing state in the Gulf Southwest throughout the eighties. The rate of growth had dropped rapidly in the eastern section of the state, but it increased uniformly towards the west, rising spectacularly in the newly opened semiarid sections. Nature capriciously supplied an abnormally heavy rainfall during the period of railroad construction in western Kansas, luring the unwary homesteader farther and farther west. The area circled by the great bend of the Arkansas expanded tremendously. To the north of the Arkansas, development was almost as great—an astonishing proportionate gain, but only one or two thousand persons per county.

The region between Kansas and Texas became an important center of white migration for the first time. There had always been a few settlers in the Indian Territory, but in 1880 the number had reached only 7,000, and these were located almost entirely along the Katy. After the Indians who opposed further railroad construction had their legal arguments cut from under them in 1884, several new lines entered their territory, and the white population swelled rapidly. The country of the Civilized Tribes was so infiltrated along the railroads that the 110,000 whites reported in 1889 represented approximately two-thirds of the population. The opening of Oklahoma Territory was responsible for a mass migration to the lands lying between those occupied by the Civilized Tribes and those ceded for the concentration of "blanket" Indians. Settlement in Oklahoma ran the total population of the two territories to about 250,000, practically all of which was located along the railroads.

Then Came the Railroads

Although northern and eastern Texas added creditable mileage during the eighties, the most striking development came from the three roads which boldly built across semiarid or desert lands to reach the western edge of the state. Immediately beyond Waco and north and west of Fort Worth, the counties had already profited from their proximity to railroads, and each had several thousand population, but all increased during the eighties by 50 per cent or more. The second tier of counties, with fewer settlers, showed a greater increase, often doubling.

The Fort Worth and Denver City offered a most conspicuous example of variation in the speed of development, for it penetrated an unsettled region. Counties with railroads grew several times more rapidly than those without such facilities. Farther northwest, in the Panhandle proper, there were about 1,900 residents in the twenty-seven counties in 1880. Ten years later the Panhandle was still practically uninhabited, but the fourteen railroad counties had 7,600 of the 9,500 population. The same general pattern was followed by the Huntington and Gould roads. West Texas proved two points indisputably. One was that a railroad alone could not attract settlers—there had to be some means of livelihood along the line before it could draw population, and the Panhandle and South Plains looked so desolate that few people came. The other point was that those who did come settled along the lines of transportation.

The influence of railroads on population shifts was generally less pronounced after 1890. Kansas demonstrated the correlation inversely by struggling to hold its residents after its rail network was complete. There was, however, a distinct relationship between recent railroad construction and population movements in parts of Arkansas. The three counties which had rail transportation for the first time with the coming of the Kansas City, Pittsburg and Gulf added 20,000 inhabitants, a 70 per cent increase. Southwestern Louisiana, with two railroads where none had been before, grew more rapidly than any other section of the state. Railroad building also stimulated population growth in two of the older Texas counties. Matagorda secured its first railroad, and Wharton its first not paralleling the coastline. These two counties doubled, although neither had grown out of proportion to the surrounding areas before.

The mad rush into Oklahoma and Indian Territory continued through the nineties. In 1900 their combined population was barely under 800,000, almost equally divided between the two. The decade had been one of rapid liquidation of the Indian nations as political and geographical entities. The white population of Indian Territory had risen to over 300,000, most of it concentrated along the Santa Fe and the Katy and in the coal fields. In Oklahoma Territory the counties with railroads had grown at approximately twice the rate of those without.[1]

By far the greater number of newcomers to the Southwest were native stock, usually drawn from near-by states. The flood of European immigrants reaching the shores of America in the eighties did not influence the Southwest as much as it did other sections of the nation. The larger cities did attract some aliens, but vast areas of the Gulf Southwest enjoyed little of the flavor imparted by the foreign-born. In some places the social structure was such that it discouraged immigrants, whose opportunities were limited by the presence of a recent slave group; in others the promise of the land itself was insufficient to induce settlement. Land-hungry Europeans had already established a pattern of moving to the upper Mississippi Valley, and industrial cities lured the bulk of the later immigrants. Furthermore, the South and parts of the Southwest did not generally encourage foreign settlement. Towards the end of the century, with somewhat greater diversification in agriculture, more complete exploitation of timber resources, and better transportation facilities, more European laborers and agriculturists did arrive.[2]

Prospective settlers were not abandoned to their own devices in learning the advantages to be gained by migrating to the Southwest. States large with ambition and bonded indebtedness but small in population organized boards of immigration and agriculture, whose primary purpose was to people unoccupied lands. Each newly platted town created its own organization to inform the world that the fastest-growing city in the state was now a reality. The local editor alternately spread the gospel of unparalleled opportunity in the community and railed at newspapers in rival towns for misleading honest settlers into mushroom developments with puny possibilities. If, on occasion, a railroad excursion passed through the town after dark, such an insult would furnish material for heated editorials for several weeks.[3]

[1] "Population," *Twelfth Census*, I, 10–11, 19–20, 22–23, 27–28, 38, 40–42.
[2] *Ibid.*, I, 494, 502–506, 509–11, 517, 521–24, 765–67, 777–78, 783–89; Caroline E. MacGill, "Immigration into the Southern States," *SBN*, VI, 584–94.
[3] Rupert N. Richardson and Carl C. Rister, *The Greater Southwest*, 347–50, 389; Hicks, *The Populist Revolt*, 17–20; Frank Andrews, *Railroads and Farming*, 25.

Then Came the Railroads

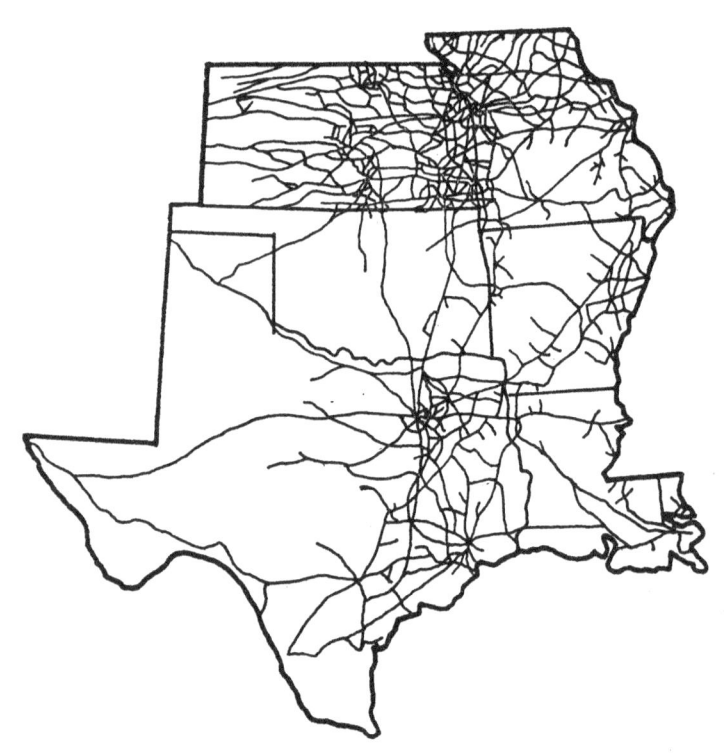

Railroads of the Gulf Southwest in 1890

Based on a map from the Association of American Railroads

Peopling the Plains

No other agencies, however, accomplished as much in advertising the entire Southwest as did the railroads. The organization of the land and immigration departments of land-grant railroads became fairly uniform. Each was under the direction of a single individual, variously designated as land commissioner, general immigration agent, or colonization agent, assisted by district and traveling agents who were full-time, salaried employees. Actual sales were made by local representatives, who sometimes received small salaries but who normally worked on a commission basis.

Two types of local representatives were needed: those in "homeseeker territory" and those in "non-homeseeker territory." If they operated in homeseeker territory, the agents were assigned near-by railroad lands, and the company referred all local land correspondence to them. In non-homeseeker territory, the area of recruitment, the agents were usually realtors or bankers who personally, or through sub-agents, solicited prospective land buyers to go west and look at the railroad lands. If the potential customers made the trip, they were turned over to the resident agent, who showed them the land. If a sale resulted, the two agents split the commission.[4]

Railroads always advised land buyers to inspect personally the tracts in which they were interested before buying them. To encourage this practice, they introduced special excursion rates, effective on certain days. In due time the first and third Tuesdays of each month were popularly recognized as excursion days. If the number warranted such action, a railroad would run a special train, supervised by a traveling immigration agent who would wire ahead to each local agent the number of buyers interested in looking at his lands. Liberal stop-over privileges prevailed in areas with vacant lands, and some railroads supplied temporary housing for homeseekers. One of the largest of these was the two-story Immigrants' Home, built and operated by the Texas and Pacific at Baird, Texas. Passenger fares on excursions were very low, usually one-half or three-fifths of the regular round-trip fare, while the Rock Island at one time had a flat rate of twenty-five dollars, round trip, from Chicago to any point on its lines where there were unoccupied lands. If a prospect bought land from the railroad, the cost of his ticket was frequently credited on the purchase price.[5]

---

[4] Information from Arthur W. Large, general agricultural agent, Rock Island Lines.
[5] Andrews, *Railroads and Farming,* 24–25; information from Arthur W. Large and J. B. Shores, director of public relations, T & P Ry Co.

The family moving to a new home in the West could secure cheap, adequate transportation by engaging an "emigrant" or "zulu" car. This was simply a boxcar which could be loaded with household goods (except pianos), farming equipment, and livestock, with one attendant to look after the stock. The arrangement was highly convenient and the rate very low. An emigrant outfit could move from Kansas City to western Kansas for less than one hundred dollars. Settlers from the South were frequently routed over the poorly equipped Memphis and Little Rock, and were often held up for days until equipment was available. The railroad built bunkhouses, where the emigrants were fed and housed until their outfits could be moved.[6]

Every railroad had a liberal budget for advertising its lands. The newspaper was the most effective means of propagandizing. Particular attention was given to rural county-seat papers, which circulated widely in agricultural sections; on occasion, however, a railroad would take an entire page in leading metropolitan newspapers. Regional guidebooks and state almanacs could always depend on railroads for advertisements.

Vast quantities of printed material originated in the land and colonization departments of every railroad. Elaborate homeseekers' guides profusely illustrated and running to forty or fifty pages, descriptive circulars, and brochures were distributed widely throughout the eastern United States and in Europe. These were carefully prepared by professional publicity men. The favorable features were emphasized, but colonization departments soon found that the impression had to be fairly accurate, or settlers would be dissatisfied. Before learning this, the Santa Fe actually moved several disgruntled families from Kansas back to their eastern homes free of charge.

The spoken word was also used to good effect. A number of railroads employed lecturers to tour the East, giving talks on lands in the West and distributing literature.

Local colonization agents became adept at exploiting every possible advertising opportunity. One common practice was to talk to each newcomer and find out how many friends he had promised to write. The agent would secure a wealth of intimate personal detail and write the letters himself, weaving in a considerable amount of information about the climate and the soil and adding that he hoped to see his old neighbors soon in this great new country. Sometimes he

---

[6] Kepler Johnson, "Bob Wilder Talks about Early Days in Arkansas," *RIM*, Vol. XVII, No. 10, 87; information from Arthur W. Large.

would write as many as forty letters for a single family, after which he would have members of the family sign them. The names of all those to whom he had written were forwarded to the land commissioner, who sent representatives to interview each one personally.

The enterprising local agent built good will in many ways. He never failed to provide special services in the name of the railroad at every public gathering. He preceded the railroad agricultural agent in encouraging fairs, disseminating information on better farming methods, and working up displays of agricultural products to advertise his area. All this he did while fighting vigorously to keep his prospective buyers from coming under the influence of agents of rival railroads.[7]

Colonization activity did not stop with the disposal of railroad lands, nor was it confined solely to land-grant railroads. R. A. Cameron, commissioner of emigration for the Fort Worth and Denver City, surveyed the resources of the Panhandle and then concentrated his attention on Iowa as a source from which to draw. The Choctaw and Memphis, successor to the Memphis and Little Rock, advertised widely to attract settlers to the line which it built from Little Rock to Indian Territory at the end of the century. S. S. Cary, land agent for the Southern Pacific, was responsible for settling many families from the upper Mississippi Valley around Jennings, Louisiana. Arthur E. Stilwell insisted that the agricultural resources along the Kansas City, Pittsburg and Gulf be surveyed as the road was built, and as soon as enough of the road was opened to justify excursions, he began to run them south from Kansas City. He put land agents in middle western and eastern states and advertised through circulars and news stories. Stilwell went so far as to recruit colonists who arrived in advance of the railroads to form the nucleus for the towns he promoted.[8]

The recruitment of foreign immigrants, particularly for settlement in Texas, was a very delicate problem. It is alleged that General Dodge suggested to Jay Gould that an active colonization program was necessary to secure settlers in the Texas and Pacific territory and that Gould budgeted $400,000 to promote immigration from northern Europe. The fund was never used for that purpose, however, because prominent Texans protested that the introduction of foreigners would

---

[7] Edward Hungerford, "Railroads as Colonizers," *Annalist*, Vol. III, 746–47; Andrews, *Railroads and Farming*, 41; Hicks, *The Populist Revolt*, 11–12, 15; information from Arthur W. Large, J. B. Shores, and Harry M. Bainer, general agricultural agent, Santa Fe System.

[8] Tascosa *Pioneer*, April 14, 1888; information from J. M. Prickett, vice-president of KCS; AGS, *Arkansas*, 363; AGS, *Louisiana*, 406.

Then Came the Railroads

be detrimental to the interests of the state. The Galveston, Harrisburg and San Antonio and the International and Great Northern were exceptional in successfully promoting foreign colonization in Texas several years before it was generally acceptable in the state. They were fortunate in serving a territory in which there were already fairly large numbers of European-born. Count Telfener accounted for some six hundred Italians, whom he imported to build his "Macaroni" Railroad. Most of them settled along the line and became American citizens.

No later movement of foreigners approached in numbers the Russo-German Mennonite migration to Kansas, but railroads were responsible for a number of less well-known colonization experiments. The Little Rock and Fort Smith gave lands and financial assistance to the Benedictine Order for a theological seminary at Subiaco, Arkansas, in order to attract German Catholics from their native land and from the community in Indiana from which the original group came. The same railroad induced a group of two hundred Polish families to purchase railroad lands just north of Little Rock. Arthur E. Stilwell, with the help of his Dutch financial backers, carried on an extensive recruitment program in the Netherlands.[9]

With the exception of some local opposition to the colonization of Europeans, the residents of thinly populated areas generally welcomed the efforts of railroads to introduce more settlers. There were a few exceptions, even to recruiting in the United States. Frequently, a town which prospered because of its location at the head of a cattle trail was hostile to landseekers, who represented a threat to its importance as a shipping point. Areas devoted to livestock resented the intrusion of farmers.

Some Texans opposed the securing of settlers from northern states for political reasons. C. F. Rudolph, editor of the Tascosa *Pioneer*, reported that he had heard considerable criticism of the Fort Worth and Denver City for its attempt to recruit Republicans to settle in the Panhandle. Rudolph himself was broad minded. He had known people from Iowa and Nebraska, and he liked them, but he qualified his position somewhat. "If you love us don't plant your agencies in Kansas,—we draw the line at Kansans, and they have been told of it. . . . No doubt there are good men in Kansas, but they stay so close

---

[9] Perkins, *Trails, Rails and War,* 260–61; Andrews, *Railroads and Farming,* 20–21; Reed, *Texas Railroads,* 264–65; AGS, *Arkansas,* 86, 286–87; Fletcher, *Arkansas,* 281; information from Mo. Pac. Ag. Dev. Dept. and J. M. Prickett.

to home that we despair of ever finding them." Rudolph was carrying on a feud with certain small-town Kansas editors when he made this half-serious suggestion.[10]

By 1900, colonization work had passed its peak, but it was to remain an important railroad function in the Gulf Southwest until well into the twentieth century.

[10] Tascosa *Pioneer*, Oct. 27, 1888.

CHAPTER 23

Stillborn Towns and Growing Cities

THE CITIES and towns of the Gulf Southwest developed remarkably during the last two decades of the nineteenth century. The two which were of national significance in 1880 were joined by Kansas City. Several others achieved regional importance and were capable of becoming great cities. The area was dotted with agricultural trading centers. Too, numerous villages with no future maintained a precarious existence, many the disappointing end product of ambitious promotional schemes.

These were the years in which New Orleans revived. By 1900, four bales of Arkansas cotton were shipped to St. Louis or Memphis for every bale that went down the river to New Orleans. But railroads could also bestow favors, and it was the river trade which suffered; exports could survive if products reached the city.

Two railroads were serving New Orleans at the end of the Civil War; fifteen years later it had five trunk lines, and in 1883 it gained its first connection with the Pacific. The Southwest was booming, and these railroads penetrated country which had never been tied to New Orleans by water. In 1900, with export trade double that of twenty years before, almost 80 per cent of the exports—cotton, grain, pork, and lumber—reached the city by rail, representing a sixfold increase in rail tonnage in a score of years. New Orleans recovered her old confidence, and with that, her population began to swell. North of the city wharves the Illinois Central had its mile-long terminal to serve the export trade; across the river, at Westwego, the Texas and Pacific operated five general-merchandise wharves and two more with

Stillborn Towns and Growing Cities

elevators having a storage capacity of one and one-third million bushels. The Southern Pacific maintained less extensive facilities at Algiers and Gretna. In 1908, New Orleans was entrenched as first port in the South, with Galveston its only near rival.[1]

St. Louis belatedly recognized that river traffic was destined to play a subordinate role in the city's future. By 1887, when nine-tenths of the raw products reaching St. Louis were carried by rail, the identification of local prosperity with western railroads was complete. The city now worked zealously to open new territory to the southwest and to encourage even more rapid rail penetration of the frontier.[2] Kansas City, never misled into depending solely on its waterway, continued to make remarkable progress.

Many budding towns from an earlier period continued their growth. The experiences of Wichita and Topeka, Kansas, and Springfield, Missouri, were parallel. All enjoyed periods of speculative growth ending in inevitable crashes. Each suffered temporary eclipse followed by steady, but less spectacular, recovery. Railroads were vital to that recovery. Wichita depended upon the rail network which radiated into every part of its fine trade territory; the other two leaned heavily on their railroad payrolls—Topeka on the Santa Fe, Springfield on the Frisco. Little Rock, with satellite Argenta (now North Little Rock), became the industrial center of Arkansas as it spun its web of rails to tap the resources of the state. Shreveport doubled its population in twenty years as it acquired two through rail lines.[3]

Several Texas cities continued their rapid rise to prominence, bearing out the promise of the seventies. Houston's railroads gave it an advantage over rival Galveston which it never relinquished. In 1900 the city secured federal assistance in improving the ship channel to tighten its grip further. At the end of the century, however, Galveston achieved a most important success when Collis P. Huntington settled on it as the port to handle the interchange of traffic between his railroad and steamship lines. The city made a serious blunder by adopting an apathetic attitude, which caused Huntington to shift his activ-

---

[1] Frank Andrews, *Crop Export Movement and Port Facilities on the Atlantic and Gulf Coasts,* 74–78; from *SBN:* Solomon S. Huebner, "The Foreign Commerce of the South," V, 397, "The Development of Foreign Commerce in the South," VI, 351–57, and "The Development of Interstate Commerce in the South," VI, 359–61 and Burr H. Ramage, "The Growth of Southern Ports," VI, 363–66 and "Transportation by Water in the South," VI, 325–26.

[2] *Rep. Int. Comm., 1887,* part 2, 58.

[3] AGS, *Kansas,* 296–98; AGS, *Arkansas,* 176–77; AGS, *Missouri,* 329–33; "Population," *Fifteenth Census,* I, 20–21, 102, 401, 456, 600.

ities to Sabine Pass. Fortunately the president of the Galveston Wharf Company, George Sealy, saved the city from its error when he reopened negotiations with Huntington and succeeded in drawing the Southern Pacific back.

Just west of the city-owned properties of the Galveston Wharf Company, which served the Santa Fe, the Katy, and the Galveston, Houston and Henderson, the Southern Pacific Terminal Company took over 3,300 feet of water front and built its piers, freight houses, slips, and tidewater terminal facilities. By 1905 an average of 20,000 tons of freight reached the city weekly over this single railroad, with 40,000 tons weekly during the heavy shipping seasons. Despite buffetings by tropical storms and epidemics of yellow fever, it developed into a major port. By 1908 the exports were thirteen times as great as in 1885; imports valued at a third of a million dollars in 1895 swelled to $5,693,000 by 1908. Primarily a shipping center, Galveston never enjoyed the complete diversification of neighboring Houston.[4]

The two bitter rivals to the north were enjoying a remarkable growth. With six railroads and an infant cotton-milling industry in 1890, Dallas was almost four times as large as it was at the last official census. The produce of a rich agricultural area poured into the city over a complete network of railroads, which carried away the processed articles as well as those of many distributors who made Dallas their headquarters. Fort Worth revived with the coming of the Texas and Pacific; the Gulf, Colorado and Santa Fe assured its growth. Citizens of Fort Worth had outbid Dallas for the road from the Gulf, giving a right of way through Tarrant County and an $85,000 cash bonus raised in mass meetings. The next year the same people backed the Fort Worth and Denver City. In the mid-eighties, Fort Worth residents built a connecting line to reach the Houston and Texas Central at Waxahachie. During the 1880's, Fort Worth almost quadrupled its population, becoming a meat-packing and milling center in the process.[5]

San Antonio almost doubled its population between 1880 and 1890 as new railways connected it with El Paso, Kerrville, Austin, Laredo, and the Gulf. It was the only city in Texas whose population exceeded

---

[4] "Population," *Fifteenth Census*, I, 18–19; ICC, *Val. Rep.*, XXXVI, 699–714; Andrews, *Crop Export Movement and Port Facilities on the Atlantic and Gulf Coasts*, 78–80; AGS, *Texas*, 294–96; Reed, *Texas Railroads*, 242, 253–54.

[5] "Population," *Fifteenth Census*, I, 18–19; Sherman Rogers, "Strikeless Fort Worth," *SCJ*, Vol. I (March 1, 1923), 14; *Fort Worth, 1849–1949*, 15.

Stillborn Towns and Growing Cities

50,000 by 1900. Both Austin and Waco enjoyed a substantial growth which paralleled the elaboration of their rail networks.[6]

El Paso, located in the region of earliest settlement in Texas but of relatively recent origin itself, lay just across the Río Grande from the important Mexican border town of El Paso del Norte (now Ciudad Juárez). First known as Magoffinsville, then Franklin, it remained an isolated adobe village until 1881. Then everything came at once. In the spring and early summer, the Southern Pacific came in across the desert from the west, and the Santa Fe came down the Río Grande from Albuquerque. A few months later the Texas and Pacific reached Huntington's road at Sierra Blanca to give El Paso a connection with Fort Worth and Dallas. In 1883, El Paso secured a Gulf connection. The sleepy Spanish-American village became a brawling, lawless border town of ten thousand. Laredo's first century and a quarter had been relatively uneventful, and its development was slow. With four new railroads, its population tripled in the eighties; the first hesitant steps in vegetable growing by means of irrigation also came with the advent of rapid transportation.[7]

Alexandria, with the first railroad west of the Mississippi, was, ironically, the last of the larger towns in Louisiana to achieve important rail connections. In spite of its age, this old river town had fewer than two thousand residents in 1880. With the arrival of railroads in the eighties and in the early years of the new century, Alexandria became a city of eleven thousand, while neighboring Pineville awakened and was growing steadily. Monroe remained almost stationary for fifteen years after the Civil War, which had destroyed the city's one railroad. With the rehabilitation and extension of that road and the addition of three others, Monroe was, in 1910, five times larger than it was thirty years before.[8]

Fort Smith, Arkansas, had its origin in the military post first established there in 1817. The fort and the village which grew up around it played a prominent part in the history of western Arkansas and the Indian Territory, yet the railroad stretching towards it from Little Rock in the late seventies reached a town of less than three thousand. Three years later the St. Louis, Arkansas and Texas reached Fort Smith from Plymouth, Missouri. This made the city. Near-by coal

---

[6] "Population," *Fifteenth Census*, I, 18, 1056–57.
[7] *Ibid.*, 20–21, 1057; AGS, *Texas*, 243–48, 306–309.
[8] "Population," *Fifteenth Census*, I, 456.

Then Came the Railroads

mines supplemented its agricultural economy and firmly entrenched Fort Smith as the major city in western Arkansas and second only to Little Rock in the state. During its half-century of service to its cotton planters, Pine Bluff had grown to a prosperous river town of two thousand by 1880. Railroads tripled that number in ten years. The new transportation facilities added lumber milling to the older cotton economy. More important, with the establishment of the Texas and St. Louis shops, the railroad payroll became, and remained, the largest in the city.[9]

The major industry of Joplin, Missouri, was partially developed before railroads came. It had already emerged as the most important of several lead-mining towns by the early seventies. Rail transportation and improved extraction processes led to the development of zinc mining, and by 1900, Joplin's population exceeded 26,000. Nearby Pittsburg, Kansas, became important as a coal-mining and zinc-smelting center only after it was tied to Joplin by rail, and it, too, developed with the arrival of new railroads, particularly the Kansas City, Pittsburg and Gulf.[10]

Many somewhat smaller cities waited for railroads to develop them. Jonesboro and Blytheville, in northeastern Arkansas, and Warren, in the southeast, date their rapid growth, first in the exploitation of timber resources and later agriculturally, from the coming of the railroads, as do Helena, at the tip of Crowley's Ridge, and Fayetteville, across the state. Railroads also sustained El Dorado until oil made it a boom town. In Louisiana, Mechanicsham (renamed Gretna), New Iberia, Lafayette (which until 1884 was Vermilionville), and Opelousas stagnated until railroads revived them. Lake Charles began to exploit its tremendous wealth of natural resources only after Morgan's line passed through. Tyler, Texas, between the headwaters of the Neches and the Sabine, was deeply indebted to railroads for its revival.[11]

Every little Kansas village had its railroad enthusiasts; indeed, it was an unusual Kansan who fell outside that category. All the towns were of recent origin, none were large, and few had locations which particularly fitted them for future greatness. Those which got rail-

[9] *Ibid.*, 102; 51 Cong., 1 sess., *H. Ex. Doc. 6,* Part 1, 72; AGS, *Arkansas,* 142–48, 189.
[10] "Population," *Fifteenth Census,* I, 400, 600; AGS, *Missouri,* 233–38; AGS, *Kansas,* 504–505.
[11] "Population," *Tenth Census,* I, 197–99; *ibid., Twelfth Census,* I, 452, 609, 618; *ibid., Fifteenth Census,* I, 102, 456, 466, 1057; AGS, *Arkansas,* 133, 165–66, 347–53; AGS, *Louisiana,* 268–69, 273–74, 280–83, 312–13, 345–48.

Stillborn Towns and Growing Cities

roads would become the distributing and trading centers for the region. If a town were to realize its dreams of greatness, it was not only necessary to get a railroad, but to be the first to obtain one. The ultimate goal was not one, but three, or four, or five roads, all radiating from the town. In the eighties, Arkansas City and Wellington were the most successful in joining such little cities as Emporia, Fort Scott, and Coffeyville, all of which had realized a measure of success in the preceding decade.[12]

The process of shifting influence and population from one town to another continued. In Arkansas, the old ferry crossing on the St. Francis River at Chalk Bluff disappeared as St. Francis, on the Texas and St. Louis, took its place. Powhatan, an important county seat, refused to give right of way to the railroad crossing the northeastern corner of the state to Memphis; the road missed Powhatan by two miles. Powhatan all but disappeared as Black Rock and Portia drew away its residents. Newly built Rogers, on the line from Plymouth, Missouri, to Fort Smith, successfully challenged Bentonville for its half-century-old dominion in northwestern Arkansas. In due time Bentonville got a branch, but it never recaptured its lost leadership.[13]

The completion of the link of the Vicksburg, Shreveport and Pacific from Monroe to Shreveport relocated the trading centers of partially settled north central Louisiana. Trenton disappeared as West Monroe took its trade. The railroad towns of Ruston and Gibsland drew the people from old Vienna and Mount Lebanon, and the parish seat of Sparta lost much of its population to Arcadia and most of the remainder to Bienville with the coming of the Louisiana and North West. St. Martinville, on Bayou Teche, settled into a period of gentle stagnation when it was unable to attract one of the first lines. It stood still while the railroad towns grew.[14]

The Gulf, Colorado and Santa Fe created Temple, Texas, when Belton refused to bid high enough for the line, and the railroad town finally outstripped the older city. The Texas and Pacific replaced Buffalo Gap as the seat of Taylor County with its own Abilene, and the Texas Central destroyed Fort Griffin by building Albany.[15]

Kansas, too, had its casualties. Many townsites died in embryo, and a few established communities failed to survive. In the southwest,

[12] "Population," *Tenth Census*, I, 183; *ibid.*, *Twelfth Census*, I, 452; *ibid.*, *Fifteenth Census*, I, 400.
[13] AGS, *Arkansas*, 255, 307, 377.
[14] AGS, *Louisiana*, 350-51, 357, 483, 486, 602, 632-33.
[15] William Curry Holden, *Alkali Trails*, 188; Reed, *Texas Railroads*, 286.

Then Came the Railroads

Springfield, confident that the Rock Island could not miss a town lying directly in its path, refused to vote aid. Its people learned how mistaken they had been when the railroad built around them and on to rival Liberal.[16]

New towns were born with each new rail extension. Theirs was frequently a story of conflict, of violent boom days, and of county-seat wars as new towns crowded out older ones and rival groups of speculators fought for supremacy. It was a struggle for survival, with quick profits for successful promoters and a reasonable guarantee of some future prosperity for their creations. It was a mixture of sound promotion and chicanery, public service and private avarice. More often than not, the railroad, its officials, or a subsidiary was involved in the townsite schemes.

The Texas and St. Louis added its settlements through Arkansas along a line south of the Cairo and Fulton. Towards the end of the century, Arthur E. Stilwell paid tribute to his Dutch backers with De Queen, Mena, and Vandervoort, all in Arkansas, Amsterdam in Missouri, De Ridder, De Quincy and Zwolle in Louisiana, and Nederland in Texas. He honored himself in naming Port Arthur, on the marshy banks of Lake Sabine. After he lost control of both his railroad and his town, Stilwell saw Port Arthur develop under the guidance of John W. Gates.[17]

Ruston and Gibsland, in Louisiana, came into existence with the extension of the Vicksburg, Shreveport and Pacific to Shreveport, and Crowley and Jennings with the building of the Morgan lines west to Texas. Count Joseph Telfener's New York, Texas and Mexico laid out most of the towns inland between Rosenberg, Texas, and Victoria. Another promoter, B. F. Yoakum, opened the half-settled area between San Antonio and the Gulf. When he and Uriah Lott built the San Antonio and Aransas Pass, they created a number of new towns, including Yoakum. In the nineties, lumber camps deep in the timber grew up along the railroads. Some grew into substantial communities, others disappeared with the timber.[18]

It was in West Texas and Kansas, however, that railroads built beyond the frontier, with a prayer that settlement would follow. The

---

[16] AGS, *Kansas*, 422.

[17] AGS, *Arkansas*, 166, 235–36, 254–55, 261–63, 269, 292, 318, 320, 347–48, 371–72; Reed, *Texas Railroads*, 434–35; Stilwell, *Cannibals of Finance*, 57–67; AGS, *Texas*, 314–18.

[18] AGS, *Louisiana*, 350–51, 404–406; Allhands, *Uriah Lott*, 33–59; Reed, *Texas Railroads*, 265.

Stillborn Towns and Growing Cities

Texas and Pacific from Fort Worth to Sierra Blanca had to build most of its towns as it went. Abilene, Sweetwater, and Colorado City were platted by the railroad. There was already a tiny settlement at Big Spring, but beyond, the railroad had to make its own stations. The Galveston, Harrisburg and San Antonio, building towards the Pecos from both the east and the west, had to adopt the same expedient.

The Fort Worth and Denver City was also desperate for settlers as it built towards the high, arid plains of the Panhandle, leaving behind a string of hopeful fledglings. It paused at Wichita Falls, already a mature settlement of four hundred, to help dispose of some lots, from which the railroad received half the proceeds. Northwest of Wichita Falls the process of town building continued. At Wild Horse Lake, nondescript Ragtown took the name Amarillo, unaware that it would become the most important city in the Panhandle with the coming of the Santa Fe and the Rock Island.[19]

The Chicago, Kansas and Nebraska added many new towns as it stretched across Kansas to the southwestern corner of the state. The railroad altered its course completely as it became involved in town making. Council Grove businessmen diverted it from its proposed course through the villages of Delaware and Lost Springs. Before any arrangements were final, M. D. Herington, who had induced the Missouri Pacific to build through his ranch the year before, offered to pay for a survey, guarantee the bonds of two counties, give outright eighty acres of land for terminal purposes, and surrender half of his interest in the townsite of Herington to the railroad if it would cross the Missouri Pacific there. The railroad agreed, and the town of Herington was born. From there the railroad resumed its original route as far as McPherson, but instead of proceeding to Trinidad, Colorado, it changed its course once more and passed through Hutchinson and newly platted Pratt on a Santa Fe extension, eventually terminating at its own town of Liberal.[20]

Widespread construction by the Missouri Pacific and additional branches of the Santa Fe led to the establishment of many new places in Kansas, a process largely paralleling the Chicago, Kansas and Nebraska activities.

While railroad construction was responsible for many permanent

---

[19] James Cox, *Historical and Biographical Record of the Cattle Industry*, 697; T & P Ry. Co., *From Ox-Teams to Eagles*, 27–29; AGS, *Texas*, 160–64, 363–68, 614–16.

[20] August H. Pronath, "The Billowy Plains of Kansas," *RIM*, Vol. XVII, No. 10, 69–71; Nevins, "Seventy ... Service," *RIM*, Vol. XVII, 35–36; Hayes, *Iron Road to Empire*, 118–19.

Then Came the Railroads

towns, it was also responsible for several score which never got beyond the driving of the stakes marking their limits or which started and then withered away, along with the hopes of their optimistic creators. Some were bypassed, others were victims of paper projects which never materialized, and others simply had nothing to offer. The names of such towns are forgotten or are but vaguely remembered by the oldest of the old-timers. Tascosa, Texas, was one of these, unique only in that it was already established; it has lived in the literature of the cattle country, and the running account of its history is preserved in the pages of its weekly newspaper.

The Tascosa *Pioneer*, self-styled "Official Journal of Oldham, Hartley, Dallam, Sherman, Moore, Potter, Randall, Deaf Smith, Parmer, and Castro Counties," was also the enthusiastic spokesman for its own town, which had already reached the ripe age of nine years and had expanded to a population of one hundred or so when the issue of July 17, 1886, carried the rumor that the Fort Worth and Denver City planned to run through the city. By the end of the year, Editor C. F. Rudolph was optimistically predicting the possible arrival of seven other railroads. The first rumor was verified, and in November, 1887, Tascosa got its railroad, but with one embarrassing qualification—the town was on one side, the railroad on the other, of the quicksand which was the Canadian River.

Tascosa was duly elated over its good fortune and formally extended the hand of fellowship to other towns along the line while observing that Tascosa was "alone in her rather provincial dignity and importance" by virtue of her age.[21] The railroad marked the beginning of a new era in which there would be "no more of the frontier life, frontier ways, frontier denials, and frontier prices." The town was leaving behind its "unassuming sociability and the easy financial status of everything," but, nevertheless, "there is nothing like being a railroad city, with a prospect of being a railroad center."[22] The same issue of *The Pioneer* carried a statement that there was little doubt that the Rock Island would cross the Denver road at Tascosa within the year.

When the Fort Worth and Denver City failed to build a permanent station across the river from Tascosa and the citizens appealed to the courts to compel the company to act, the editor hastened to explain in his issue of December 17 that this did not mean friction between the

---

[21] Tascosa *Pioneer*, Nov. 12, 1887.
[22] *Ibid.*, Nov. 5, 1887.

Stillborn Towns and Growing Cities

town and the railroad, but was merely a business deal; two weeks later it was because the roadbed had not been accepted west of Clarendon. When the Southern Kansas was lost to Tascosa beyond all hope, Rudolph consoled his fellow townsmen by informing them that that railroad had dingier equipment and poorer management than their own and that it was notorious for playing favorites among towns.

But the Rock Island was the choice subject for discussion. Other railroads— the North Platte, Lakin and Tascosa, the Mountain and Texas, the Kansas, Nebraska and Texas, the Omaha, Dodge City and Southern, and, until it built in a different direction, the Southern Kansas—merited some consideration, but Rudolph always returned to the Rock Island, stalled for a time at Liberal but still intent on reaching El Paso.

He was usually optimistic, but on occasion he expressed some concern that the Rock Island would go by Texline or Folsom if the people of Tascosa did not evince more interest. Once, after a particularly disheartening rumor was floating through the town and rival editors had been unusually pointed in their remarks that Tascosa, after all, was not really on a railroad, Rudolph, in a fit of despondency, wryly commented: "Come to Tascosa because we are sufficiently far from the tracks to be clear of all annoyances from the noise of trains and the scent of smoke dust. No other Panhandle town is so far off its railroad."[23] By the next week, however, the mood had passed, and once more he was optimistically planning for the future, "when the Rock Island comes."

The years 1889 and 1890 rolled on, and towards the end of that second year, he became somewhat gloomier. "Very soon it will be the year '91—and, sir, the Rock Island hain't come yit." Bouncing back in 1891, he began to speak of Tascosa as "Rockislandville" and continued to plan for "when the Rock Island comes"—but the Rock Island never came. Today Tascosa is the site of Amarillo's Boys' Ranch.

Town development in the twin territories was unique. Prior to 1889 there was no legal white settlement, but with the opening of the "unassigned lands" and the various reservations, followed by allotment of Indian lands in severalty, the territories filled rapidly. By that time there were a number of railroads operating in both Oklahoma and Indian Territory.

Towns inevitably grew up along the course of those railroads which

[23] *Ibid.*, Dec. 15, 1888.

entered Indian Territory following the overriding of treaty guarantees in the eighties. Talihina and Tuskahoma, in the rugged area traversed by the line from Fort Smith to Paris, Texas; Nowata, on the Kansas and Arkansas Valley, and Wagoner, where that road crossed the Katy; Wister, Wilburton, Holdenville, Wewoka, and Seminole, on the Choctaw, Oklahoma and Gulf, were a few of the more important towns. Late in the century, the Kansas City, Pittsburg and Gulf's Spiro attracted residents from the old Choctaw village of Scullyville. Farther west, in the Chickasaw Nation, a chain of new settlements—Marietta, Ardmore, Davis, and Purcell—grew up along the Santa Fe.

Of eighteen Indian Territory towns listed as having a population of more than one hundred in 1890, sixteen were the products of railroads. Only Tahlequah, the old Cherokee capital, retained a measure of prominence without a railroad, but McAlester, Krebs, Caddo, and Ardmore exceeded it in size, and Vinita and Muskogee were its equals. The other inland town, Okmulgee, was a Creek village of little more than one hundred inhabitants.

The position of the residents of the Indian Territory towns was somewhat dubious. Intruders could not establish legal title to their holdings because titles were vested in each Civilized Tribe collectively rather than in individual Indians. Certain whites did induce a few of the Indians to enclose tribal lands for proposed townsites and convey such title as they had to the instigators of the schemes. Such arrangements were clothed in the barest shadow of legality, but only by such subterfuge could intruders settle and hold lands. It was only in the early twentieth century, after legislation permitted title to real property to be vested in individuals, that really large-scale town building could take place.[24]

West of the territory occupied by the Civilized Tribes, half a dozen telegraph offices lay along the routes of the Rock Island and the Santa Fe in the Cherokee Outlet. The Santa Fe extended across the Oklahoma District, and the Rock Island built across it the year of the opening. Restless land speculators and homeseekers had alternately appealed to Congress and boldly defied its laws in attempting to force the opening of all the Indian lands, particularly those in the Okla-

[24] "Report on Indians Taxed and Indians not Taxed," *Eleventh Census*, XII, 260; AGS, *Oklahoma*, 125-30, 287, 299-309, 323-29, 362-65; Richard J. Hinton, "The Indian Territory—Its Status, Development, and Future," *Rev. of R.*, Vol. XXIII, 455; Debo, *The Road to Disappearance*, 281, 366; Holden, "The B I T . . . Building," *Chron. Okla.*, Vol. XI, 649-50, 657-58.

Stillborn Towns and Growing Cities

homa District, the name given to the "unassigned lands." They were more susceptible to townsite speculation because there were no such obstacles to acquiring title as existed in the Indian Territory.

Guthrie, Edmond, Oklahoma City, and Norman came into existence along the Santa Fe when the Oklahoma District was opened to white settlement on April 22, 1889. Hennessey and Kingfisher sprang up along the proposed course of the Rock Island the same day. Reno City was established on the route of the Rock Island, but refused to pay a bonus. The railroad bypassed Reno City by four miles, whereupon the town moved to the railroad and, under the name El Reno, became a Rock Island division point and the temporary terminus for the western segment of the Choctaw Coal and Railway Company.

The Santa Fe's Oklahoma Station had been the only point between the Canadian River and the Kansas line which was not a "prepay only" agency. Here the government sent supplies for the garrison at Fort Reno and for distribution by freighters through the reservations to the west. Here, also, the railroad handled shipments of cattle grazing extralegally on Indian lands. An estimated ten thousand persons settled at this point, renamed Oklahoma City, on the day of the opening. The residents maintained a precarious existence as the population decreased to four thousand. It was apparently destined to remain that size. In 1895, however, the Choctaw, Oklahoma and Gulf built the long link between McAlester and Oklahoma City to connect its eastern and western segments, giving to both towns the incentive for renewed growth and furnishing Oklahoma City with a direct connection with the coal mines of the Choctaw Nation and a more direct route to St. Louis.[25]

The opening of the Cherokee Outlet on September 16, 1893, lacked the drama of the run into the Oklahoma District only in the single detail that the earlier opening represented the breach presaging the flow of white settlement through all the Indian lands. It had its thousands of speculators and bona fide homeseekers waiting on the borders for the signal to pour into the Outlet and fight for choice locations; furthermore, those thousands knew that the opening would immediately precipitate a war between the government and the railroads over townsites. Prior to the opening, some seventy Cherokees, most of them apparently intermarried whites, had settled in the Outlet and

---

[25] "Population," *Fifteenth Census*, I, 18–19; AGS, *Oklahoma*, 156–57, 165–71, 226–29, 358–65, 370–71; Holden, "The B I T . . . Building," *Chron. Okla.*, Vol. XI, 658; Arthur W. Dunham, "A Pioneer Railroad Agent," *Chron. Okla.*, Vol. II, 50–53.

Then Came the Railroads

were given permission by the government to retain allotments there rather than in the Cherokee Nation proper. Instead of remaining on the lands they had improved, they came to terms with the railroads and selected new locations in the vicinity of railroad stations. The Secretary of the Interior thereupon platted the government townsites on public lands a couple of miles from existing stations.

Enid was the most famous case. For a year after the opening the battle continued there, with trains stopping at North Enid but refusing to serve "government Enid." While Congress debated a bill designed to end the conflict, the feud culminated in the wrecking of a Rock Island train after settlers on the government townsite had sawed through the bridge timbers at a river crossing. The most violent period eventually ended after citizens of "government Enid" paid the railroad $3,500 to stop trains at their town. Similar battles took place between the Rock Island's Round Pond and the official townsite of Pond Creek, the Santa Fe's Wharton and the government's Perry, and between Cross, Ponca City, and the Santa Fe town of White Eagle in a three-cornered affray.[26]

Alva, Waynoka, and Woodward, all of them along the Santa Fe line to the Texas Panhandle, also sprang into existence on September 16, 1893.

It is quite easy to overgeneralize the influence of railroads on town building. Obviously there were many more settled places with the advent of railroads, and those towns which were successful in attracting several lines normally developed into fairly large cities. Elements other than transportation, however, helped to shape their growth. Railroads were only the carriers. There had to be some economic basis for the community: fertile lands, timber, minerals, or a peculiarly advantageous location. Ambitious, farsighted businessmen had to be present to induce railroads to come, but at the same time they were compelled to turn their energies to developing to the fullest the resources at hand. Those towns which had the resources and the leadership necessary to embark on a course of industrial expansion were to become the great cities of the Gulf Southwest.

[26] *Cong. Rec.*, 53 Cong., 1 sess., 1893–95, 2713–17, 2734; Milam, "The . . . Strip," *Chron. Okla.*, Vol. IX, 123, 133–34; Preston George and Sylvan R. Wood, "The Railroads of Oklahoma," R&LHS *Bull. No. 60*, 23–24; AGS, *Oklahoma*, 136–41, 188, 243, 245–50, 369, 376; Hayes, *Iron Road to Empire*, 135–42.

CHAPTER 24

A Changing Economy

AT THE TURN of the century fundamental changes had taken place in the economy of the Gulf Southwest. More complete exploitation of natural resources—soil, timber, and minerals—gave the area an added importance in the national scene. Embryonic industrial development, largely the primary processing of its own raw products, gave promise of greater economic diversification in the new century.

Following closely behind as railroads stretched towards the western borders of Kansas and Texas, pioneer farmers arrived in ever increasing numbers. Barbed wire, used by ranchers in the eighties to enclose those sections of the public domain which they had usurped, now served to set off the holdings of small agricultural landowners. The cattlemen did not relinquish their position without a struggle, but the outcome was inevitable as hordes of farmers followed on the heels of those who had already started the fight for control of the Plains.

The monopoly of the cattle kingdom was broken. Interspersed among the great ranches which replaced the open range were many farmers, who stayed and multiplied in spite of efforts to dislodge them by violence or guile. In the fall of 1887, Colonel Charles Goodnight, in a widely quoted interview, advised the *Kansas City Star* that the Panhandle was unfit for agriculture and that those who attempted to farm were even then trying to get out. To which the pugnacious editor of the Tascosa *Pioneer* answered that the Colonel "deliberately libelled the fairest and most fertile domain under the sun, but he was only living up to the traditions of his class. It is what the cattlemen have invariably and always done."[1]

It would have been impossible to prevent agricultural development even had the railroads themselves opposed it; they, however, had every reason to encourage farming. The cattle kingdom stood for a sparsely settled Great Plains, unable to support railroads adequately except for one brief, hectic period each year. Agricultural settlement, on the other hand, meant large numbers of people, trading centers, and a year-round movement of commodities. This did not mean the end of the cattleman, but rather the growth of farming alongside ranching in areas susceptible to the change. As late as 1910 the Frisco invested rather heavily in a hundred-mile fenced lane equipped with holding pastures and windmills to facilitate the movement of livestock from Sutton County to the railroad at Brady. The lane traversed a section devoted almost exclusively to livestock.[2]

The impact of industrialization converted farming from a way of life to an occupational status. Growing cities demanded food and clothing; a growing industrial system needed raw materials. Agrarian resistance to change weakened. Reapers and moldboard plows, twine binders and cultivators, and, finally, the steam thresher revolutionized the mechanics of farming. Developments in the field of soil chemistry and successful experimentation in selective plant and animal breeding added dignity and wealth. The new farmer lived in a world different from that of his father. He farmed more extensively and depended on cash crops. There was no alternative because he competed within the framework of a mechanized agriculture which required large capital outlays.[3]

He had made one sacrifice in return for his new status. He was no longer the complete individualist. The farmer depended on others to buy what he produced and to produce the things he needed. The same system that elevated him in the social scale, and in the course of time extended luxuries previously denied him, exacted this one concession —that he become an interdependent member of society.

What was the place of railroads in revolutionizing American agriculture? Alone, the railroads would have achieved nothing, but the change could not have taken place without them. Their greatest con-

[1] Tascosa *Pioneer*, Nov. 26, 1887.
[2] Webb, *The Great Plains*, 232–40; Edward Everett Dale, "Those Kansas Jayhawkers," *Ag. H.*, Vol. II, 171–83; Hafen and Rister, *Western America*, 572–75, 578.
[3] Louis Bernard Schmidt, "The Agricultural Revolution in the Prairies and the Great Plains of the United States," *Ag. H.*, Vol. VIII, 171–72.

A Changing Economy

tribution was in supplying adequate, fast, and relatively cheap transportation. Without railroads, profitable farming was confined to areas served by natural means of transportation; with railroads, the productivity of the land itself or other uses to which it might be put became the limiting factors.

On occasion railroads gave direct relief in order to save an area from serious loss of its agricultural population. The early days of Oklahoma Territory were similar to those first few years on the plains of Kansas. The Santa Fe brought in seed wheat and released it on unsecured notes at the time of the opening. The next year, debt-ridden farmers watched their crops burn when the rains did not come. Once more the Santa Fe and the recently arrived Rock Island rescued them by selling seed wheat at cost and on credit. With slight variations, this same story has been repeated many times, the railroads furnishing credit or guaranteeing bank loans for seed in order to hold the settlers.[4]

The railroads sustained the newcomers as they began their new lives in the West in still another way. Railroads often represented the sole source of cash income until a settler reduced his quarter-section to a state of cultivation. In timbered sections he found them ready buyers of cordwood for use as locomotive fuel. Throughout the West farmers worked as tracklayers or section laborers. Many homesteaders were able to establish themselves permanently simply because railroads offered them enough work to tide them over during the lean years.[5]

Railroads played an important though ill-advertised part in the introduction of windmills to the Plains. The absence of water and timber was an all but insurmountable obstacle to their successful operation. That accounts for the gullibility of otherwise hard-headed business executives who would support the most fantastic of rain-making schemes. Railroads popularized windmills when they first appeared by using them at water tanks. Small towns followed, then ranchers, and finally farmers.[6]

In supporting fairs, railroads engaged in an activity which popularized new and better agricultural methods. One of the earliest and most ambitious of the southwestern fairs, the Fort Worth Spring Palace, was conceived by a railroader. R. A. Cameron, colonization

[4] S. R. Overton, "When the Rock Island Came to the Rescue of Oklahoma," *RIM*, Vol. XVII, No. 10, 182–83; Marshall, *Santa Fe*, 236.
[5] Barnard, *A Rider of the Cherokee Strip*, 159; information from Arthur W. Large.
[6] Webb, *The Great Plains*, 339, 348, 382.

director of the Fort Worth and Denver City, suggested an annual agricultural fair to advertise both the ambitious little city of Fort Worth and the opportunities in the state of Texas. The idea took hold immediately, and in May, 1889, the Spring Palace opened. The Palace was a big enclosure, covered on the outside by split ears of corn; inside, each county in the state maintained a booth to exhibit its products. The first fair proved highly successful, and the city made plans for another the following year. It began auspiciously, but was cut short on the night of May 30, 1890, by a great fire which completely destroyed the building.[7]

The unfortunate termination of the Spring Palace was one of the few cases in which a fair succumbed before it developed sufficiently to become a tradition. More often it became an important event in the life of the town, an opportunity for local people to display the choice results of a year's activity. The excitement of the horse races, the carnival midway, and the exhibits at the county fair brought to the rural county seat an interlude of holiday which interrupted the normal routine.

None have supported fairs more ardently through the years than the railroads, which recognized their worth as a gentle prod to greater effort and an opportunity to acquaint large numbers of persons with the most recent trends in agriculture. They have given generously of money and have assisted in preparing exhibits and programs. They have moved registered livestock for exhibit purposes at half-rate to encourage their showing. The motives were not purely altruistic but were representative of sound business practice. Not only did these activities build good will, but they also offered the opportunity to teach by observation the value of better methods, careful seed selection, and well-bred livestock. This meant revenue to the carrier.[8]

Although it was by far the most important, agriculture was not the sole foundation of southwestern economy. Some types of industry inevitably followed the course of the rails. Every new village had its blacksmith shops and its gristmills. Then, too, railroads naturally followed the routes most susceptible to rapid development—normally through fertile valleys, but not infrequently to mineral deposits or timber. The first embryonic industrialization was in extractive endeavors—the exploitation of the resources at hand, including the utilization of farm products.

[7] *Fort Worth Magazine* (July, 1949), 12, 43.
[8] Andrews, *Railroads and Farming*, 23–24, 43.

Courtesy Southern Pacific Lines

Southern Pacific freight train at Painted Cave, Texas, about 1900.

Shooting buffalo on the Kansas-Pacific Line.

From Frank Leslie's Illustrated Newspaper, June 3, 1871

Courtesy Kansas City Southern Lines

Kansas City Southern passenger train about 1900.

Missouri Pacific locomotive of the early 1900's.

Courtesy Missouri Pacific Lines

A Changing Economy

Timber was the basis for several major industries. Vast forests stretched west from the Mississippi as far as East Texas and eastern Indian Territory, but Texans secured most of their lumber from Florida prior to the railroad expansion of the seventies. Small mills operated in Louisiana and Arkansas as early as 1836, but it took railroads to make lumbering the great industry it was to become later. Jay Gould was acutely aware of the millions of acres of timberland his railroads served.

The decade of the eighties was one of expansion for the lumber industry and the railroads. Major lines cut through the forests, and branches probed deeply into the woods, leaving behind a string of lumber camps as they worked their way into virgin timber. Between 1870 and 1907, the years of railroad penetration, the southwestern lumber industry redoubled over twelve times, and Louisiana, Texas, and Arkansas ranked second, third, and sixth, respectively, in lumber production.

Related industries followed in the wake of sawmills. The manufacture of barrel staves and tool handles, sashes and doors, and coffins and unassembled furniture inevitably grew up where lumber was available. Carriage making became an important industry; veneering and wood-preserving plants sprang up. The extraction of turpentine and resinous substances was an industry of no little importance. At a later date pulp and newsprint and Kraft paper mills would overshadow the other forest industries.[9]

Bulky minerals were another form of wealth which could be utilized only with effective transportation systems. Coal furnished the Katy with a large portion of its meager tonnage originating in the Indian Territory, as well as a field for speculative activity by its officers and directors. The Choctaw Coal and Railway Company was purely a coal road designed to serve the same area. In western Missouri, western Arkansas, and eastern Kansas, mines opened with the coming of railroads.

Southeastern Missouri, with access to the Mississippi, had a flourishing lead industry from early in the century. The Iron Mountain stimulated activity when it reached these deposits, but all earlier production was dwarfed after the St. Joseph Lead Company built the Mississippi River and Bonne Terre, which provided a rail outlet on the Mississippi. Smelting immediately assumed a new importance. The rich lead and zinc deposits around Joplin were known before

[9] The valuation dockets summarize lumber industries along each individual carrier.

1850, but were scarcely touched for years because the long overland haul to Boonville, Lime Creek on the Osage, or Fort Smith discouraged operations. The railroads which pushed down through eastern Kansas boomed this tri-state area. Much of the smelting gravitated to Kansas, which had transportation facilities and, later, natural gas.[10]

Salt, an age-old necessity, gave the Southwest an important industry. The working of salt deposits antedated the coming of the white man, but successful large-scale operations had to wait for adequate, cheap transportation. Hutchinson, Kansas, and the Five Islands district south and east of New Iberia, Louisiana, became major producers once they secured railroads. Rock salt furnished northwestern Louisiana with an important industry, while in the interior of Texas several towns, notably Grand Saline, were built on salt mining.[11]

Second in point of time in all areas, and first in those which had no readily exploitable resources other than fertile soil, the processing of agricultural products became and remained a basic part of the economy.

While there was no complete uniformity in the order of development, livestock raising was almost invariably of primary importance in frontier areas. With the coming of railroads and the development of refrigerator cars, it served as the foundation for a major industry. There was a pronounced tendency to relocate packing houses near the source of supply and ship meat rather than live animals.[12]

Certain agricultural products attracted processing industries from very early times. Cotton had been grown for generations as a cash crop throughout the South, as had rice and sugar cane in restricted areas. Wheat became a major product of the Plains. All required some kind of processing.

With the advent of railroads, rice culture became more prominent. Large-scale production began in Louisiana about 1870; in the eighties, with more attention given to irrigation and with both the state and its railroads encouraging immigration from the Middle West, rice growing made tremendous strides. By 1914 production was eighty times as great as it had been immediately after the Civil War. Arthur E. Stilwell was instrumental in promoting its culture in Texas as a byproduct of his railroad promotion. Cleaning and polishing mills grew alongside this agricultural development.[13]

[10] AGS, *Missouri*, 450–52.
[11] Edward Bennett Matthews, "The Products of Minor Mineral Industries in the South," *SBN*, VI, 250–52; AGS, *Louisiana*, 20, 71; AGS, *Kansas*, 90, 201–202.
[12] Andrews, "Cost . . . Animals," USDA *Yearbook for 1908*, 244.

A Changing Economy

Cotton was potentially the basis for extensive industrialization in much of the Gulf Southwest. The textile industry had not developed greatly even though incipient activity at New Orleans, Dallas, and a few other towns dated from the later nineteenth century.[14] Cottonseed gave the Southwest an industry of real importance, but rapid development did not take place until well after the Civil War. New Orleans, with eight mills in 1885, dominated the industry, but other equally important establishments were located at Little Rock, Pine Bluff, and Texarkana. Texas entered the field somewhat later, but by the turn of the century cottonseed crushing was second only to lumber in the value of the product.[15]

Small flour mills and gristmills existed on even the most primitive frontiers, but the rise of a major flour-milling industry awaited revolutionary changes in processing and the conversion of much of the Mississippi Valley into a vast granary. Minneapolis became the great center, but many southwestern cities shared such importance to a limited degree. This activity was of prime importance in the rise of most of the larger towns in Missouri, Kansas, Oklahoma, and West Texas.[16]

Unlike the industrialized Northeast, with its concentration of wealth, the Southwest did not draw raw materials to the region. It did process those products of its own territory which required relatively little refining or which, by their bulk, could be converted more easily near the source. Most of the relatively minor industrialization which occurred came in the last twenty years of the century. A general business revival followed the bleak seventies, and sectional animosity was beginning to ebb.

The gross value of the manufactured products of Arkansas and Texas in 1890 represented forty-two- and sixtyfold increases, respectively, over 1850. In spite of its very considerable prewar industry, Missouri increased ninefold during this period, while Louisiana's production was eight times as great. During the nineties Arkansas and Louisiana doubled the value of their output, and Texas increased its productivity by 70 per cent. In spite of the impressive gains, however,

---

[13] K C P & G Ry. Co., *Ann. Rep., 1898*, 8–9; AGS, *Louisiana*, 70.
[14] Victor S. Clark, "Modern Manufacturing Development in the South," *SBN*, VI, 282–83.
[15] *Ibid.*, 290–92; AGS, *Arkansas*, 70; AGS, *Louisiana*, 69–70; Cox, *Historical and Biographical Record of the Cattle Industry*, 708.
[16] Andrews, *Crop Export Movement and Port Facilities on the Atlantic and Gulf Coasts*, 18–20; information from Arthur W. Large.

at the turn of the century only Missouri ranked as a major industrial state.[17]

The greatest single contribution by railroads to the industrialization of the Gulf Southwest was furnishing a type of transportation which permitted the concentration of bulky raw materials at processing points and the distribution of the finished products to widely scattered markets. Railroads not only made it physically possible to transport commodities in great quantity, but they also reduced the cost in so doing. The normal cost of freighting averaged about 20 cents per ton-mile. In 1873 the average railroad rate per ton-mile in Texas was 5.13 cents. It was down to 1.76 cents by 1883. The average speed of freighters was roughly twenty miles a day; railroads soon attained that much an hour. Cheaper, faster transportation speeded the overall process of economic development.[18]

Railroads destroyed some local industry while paving the way for new endeavors. Those activities connected with overland freighting were necessarily crippled as stage and freight lines were forced out of business. Industries dependent upon local resources and local consumption sometimes found that they were unable to compete with outside producers who invaded the field. Saddle and harness shops, salt and wagon works, and flour and grist mills were frequently forced to close. In Arkansas competition from northern mills drove the small local textile industry completely out of business for a time.[19]

Railroads were instrumental in attracting outside capital into much of the Gulf Southwest. The chaotic economic and political conditions which followed the Civil War discouraged investment in the recent Confederate states. The war and reconstruction left them hopelessly in debt; by 1880 state credit was in low repute, while taxes were ruinously high. The first substantial postwar investments in Louisiana, Arkansas, and Texas were in railroads. The opening of virgin territory and the desire of railroad promoters to realize a profit from their operations helped to restore the flow of outside credit so sorely needed in the South and the Southwest.[20]

Carriers were also responsible for determining the point at which

---

[17] Clark, "Modern . . . South," *SBN*, VI, 265–66, 291–99, 303.
[18] Albert C. Simmonds, Jr., "A History of the Texas and Pacific Railway Company, 1871–1924" (Thesis, Harvard University, 1925), 177, 180; Reed, *Texas Railroads,* 182.
[19] AGS, *Arkansas,* 70–71.
[20] Paul H. Buck, *The Road to Reunion,* 180; Walter L. Fleming, "The Economic Results of Reconstruction," *SBN,* VI, 12.

A Changing Economy

new investments would take place. One of the grievances about which the West complained so bitterly—place discrimination—gave certain cities an initial advantage which they continued to hold, first as distributing, then as industrial, centers. All ambitious towns could not become cities; therefore, every special favor which any one of them could secure gave it an advantage over its rivals. Shipping points served by two or more railroads occupied particularly choice positions, since the ruthless competition for traffic gave them very low rates, with recoupment in the form of higher rates at noncompetitive stations. Once a city had achieved considerable importance, local groups were frequently able to bring pressure to secure even more favorable rates and services.[21]

The points at which railroads touched deep-sea ports frequently determined the later location of industries. The tremendous increase in exports from Gulf ports between 1880 and 1900 naturally encouraged industrial development. In 1884 only 2 per cent of the wheat exports originated at Gulf ports; twenty years later the figure had risen to 55 per cent. Galveston and New Orleans together handled more than half of the entire cotton exports of the nation. Other products soon followed. Practically all arrived at the export point by rail. Wharves, warehouses, and elevators sprang up along the water front, as did a web of industrial trackage to serve them; thousands of waterfront workers added to the population of these cities to furnish the incentive for increased industrialization.[22]

The most direct and definitely conscious effort of railroads to promote industrial development was in determining the resources of their respective territories. The Texas and Pacific reputedly spent $500,000 as early as 1874 in exploring the possibilities along its line, an endeavor involving 15,000 miles of reconnaissance. The Kansas City, Pittsburg and Gulf made a similar survey of mineral, timber, and agricultural resources before the road was built. It purchased timber tracts of from 20,000 to 50,000 acres; these it leased to four lumber companies which began operating immediately. Stilwell also employed a geologist, who located building stone and rock, which in 1898 was being shipped to Kansas City for building purposes and street con-

[21] Haney, *A Congressional History of Railways in the United States,* II, 304–305; Riegel, *The Story of the Western Railroads,* 224.

[22] Andrews, *Crop Export Movement and Port Facilities on the Atlantic and Gulf Coasts,* 10–16, 21–28, 30–37 and "Freight Costs and Market Values," USDA *Yearbook for 1906,* 373–80; Harold Sinclair, *The Port of New Orleans,* 303–306.

struction and to Port Arthur for use in improving the harbor and canal.[23]

In earlier days, railroads carried on extensive industrial activities of their own, particularly in the extractive fields. They were the owners and operators of coal, lead, and zinc mines, lumber mills and granite quarries, cotton gins and grain elevators, coke ovens and iron works. Popular hostility to such activities eventually forced railroads to divest themselves of many of their industrial properties; the railroads themselves tended to absorb the bulk of the output of those which they retained.[24]

The thousands of railroad employees who came to the Southwest were an important contribution to the economic prosperity of the region. In many rural areas the agent, the section foreman and his crew, and an occasional bridge and building outfit were the most important salaried groups; they were therefore of real importance to the small-town merchants. The labor forces at terminals attracted merchants, professional people, and craftsmen to fill their needs.

By 1880 the railroads of St. Louis employed more than 3,200 workmen, those of Kansas City more than 1,300. New Orleans, still clinging to the river, listed only 468, one-fourth the number employed in steamboating. At the turn of the century the number in St. Louis and East St. Louis was approaching 5,000, in the two Kansas Citys, 3,000, and New Orleans more than 2,000. Railroad employees swelled the labor force of Houston by 1,500, of Little Rock by 1,200. Fort Worth, San Antonio, Dallas, and Galveston each added several hundred more. Engineers and firemen, conductors and brakemen, switchmen and yardmen, baggage handlers and freight workers, and boilermakers and engine hostlers added to the number profitably employed. The total in the Gulf Southwest was well over 75,000.[25]

Another labor force, usually considered separately, was tied much more directly to industry than most transportation workers. It was made up of those engaged in the construction and repair of rolling stock. In all the Southwest in 1880, four railroads operated a total of one passenger car, six baggage and express cars, thirty-eight boxcars, sixty-two flatcars, and twenty stockcars which had been built in their own shops. Ten years later railroad car and shop construc-

[23] K C P & G Ry. Co., *Ann. Rep., 1898*, 7–8; MS history of T & P, general office, Dallas, 4.
[24] Listed in the valuation dockets and annual reports of various railroads.
[25] "Population," *Tenth Census*, I, 881, 891, 900; *ibid., Twelfth Census*, I, Part 2, 514, 524–25, 534–35, 545, 552–601.

A Changing Economy

tion ranked as a major industrial activity in every southwestern state, with 103 railroad companies and 4 private establishments employing more than 11,300 workers. In 1900 the number passed 26,000.[26]

Railroads introduced complicated labor problems into the Gulf Southwest, never before fully cognizant of the revolutionary social and economic implications of the industrialization and urbanization of the East. In practically the entire area, railroad employees were more nearly the counterpart of industrial labor than any other group. Labor organization made its appearance and spasmodically participated in politics, even influencing the course of some scattered legislation.

Labor conflict first touched the Southwest in the form of railroad strikes. Those of 1877 spread to St. Louis, Kansas City, Topeka, and Emporia. A successful strike on the Gould lines in 1885 in protest of unwarranted wage reductions had the sympathy of the governors of the states involved and of the public in general. Another strike was precipitated in 1886 when the Texas and Pacific went into receivership. Several Knights of Labor locals insisted that the railroad had been forced into insolvency to destroy the wage settlement of 1885 and weaken labor organization, an argument bolstered by Gould's unquestioned discrimination against union members. The discharging of a prominent union foreman in the Texas and Pacific shops at Marshall was the immediate cause of the walkout, which quickly spread through all the shops and yards of the Gould lines. The railroads were forced to suspend operations, even though the operating trainmen, with separate unions, held aloof from the strike. There was much violence, particularly around St. Louis.

Gould made no effort to operate his southwestern lines, and the public, which had been warmly sympathetic to the strikers at first, changed its attitude as the price of coal rose from five to forty dollars a ton and as the shutdown of the railroads threatened to paralyze all economic activity. Terence V. Powderly, Grand Master of the Knights, attempted to end the conflict, but the bitter workmen turned to Martin Irons, their more radical local leader in St. Louis. Eventually they were completely defeated and discredited. The Knights of Labor never recovered, and it was to be many years before railroad labor regained its lost prestige in the Southwest.[27]

[26] "Statistics of Railroads," *Tenth Census*, IV, 1572–73; "Manufactures," *Twelfth Census*, VIII, 24, 258, 298, 473, 863.
[27] Terence V. Powderly, *The Path I Trod*, 114–39; James Ford Rhodes, *History of the United States*, VIII, 269–77.

CHAPTER 25

Grievances

ONCE THE rail network was well on its way towards completion, the Southwest found it a mixed blessing. Unfortunately, the region suffered from real abuses, and these gave color to the half-truths, distortions, and outright fabrications which added to the disrepute into which railroads were steadily falling. The full weight of the agrarian revolt, however, came only after the disastrous drouth which struck the Plains in 1887 and persisted for a decade. A rage of despair swept the area. Helpless farmers watched as hot winds swept the parched land, driving out all but the hardiest settlers. Added to existing difficulties arising from increased costs of production, sagging prices, heavy indebtedness, and a rigid monetary policy, the drouth completely shattered the dreams of the agricultural pioneer and land speculator alike.[1] The situation did not lend itself to moderation. The farmer struck blindly at the railroads, the nearest tangible evidence of what to him was the agent of his misfortunes. The railroads thus became the whipping boy for all the accumulated woes plaguing the West. Shortsighted railroad management did little to improve public relations at this critical time.

Charges and countercharges, many of which were the outgrowth of circumstances over which neither party had any control, were made in efforts to place the blame, but these frequently failed to touch the roots of the problem. On the other hand, neither the railroad nor the farmer was blameless; neither was entirely responsible for the resulting tensions. Both were motivated on occasion by selfishness and

[1] Farmer, "The . . . Populism," *MVHR*, Vol. X, 416–25.

Grievances

a complete absence of social and ethical responsibility, the railroad more often than its adversary simply because of its preferred position. Both had been guilty of errors in judgment, the farmer in mortgaging his future to hasten the westward progress of transportation, the railroad builder in overestimating the potential revenue traffic.

An even more fundamental antagonism lay behind the reaction to immediate conditions. Bred in the tradition of self-sufficiency, the western farmer was only vaguely aware that he was being integrated into an emerging industrial society in which he had to produce larger surpluses, invest larger sums in equipment, and depend increasingly upon others for credit, for transportation, for machinery, and for markets. He was an individualist trapped by the course of events into a position of increasing dependence on others. The significance of his position became fully apparent only when economic conditions depressed the value of his product to a point where he faced ruin. At this point he resisted, and the railroads were near at hand to bear the brunt of the agrarian attack on the industrial system.

Other than the reaction against the policies which had bestowed great tracts of land on railroads and weighted western communities with huge public debts, excessive rates furnished the most obvious point of attack. Noncompetitive areas usually suffered from the higher rates imposed by the railroads to offset losses sustained in the struggle for the traffic of towns fortunate enough to have more than one carrier. Commodity discrimination, often justifiable but frequently dictated by powerful economic interests, also worked to the disadvantage of the farmer.

The West suffered from both of these discriminatory practices. Few towns were located on more than one railroad, agricultural commodities furnished the bulk of their produce, and the great majority of shippers did not merit special consideration. Furthermore, extensions into virtually uninhabited areas burdened the carriers with lines which would be unable to pay their way for years to come. Under the best of circumstances rates would have been high; in the absence of any restraining force they were all but unbearable. The railroads did not deny the fact that rates in the West were much higher, but attempted to justify them as necessary in sparsely settled areas.

Dependence upon competition as the proper regulatory medium gave rise to pooling, another western grievance. Ruinous rate wars were not new, but the overexpansion of western railroads forced them into a feverish race for traffic which could lead only to bankruptcy or agreements. The latter prevailed.

In April, 1871, following a struggle for control of the cattle trade, the major railroads of Missouri and Kansas agreed on a flat rate of $115 per car from specified competitive points to Chicago. A few years later the abortive Southwestern Railway Rate Association briefly united a number of lines in an effort to stabilize rates from Chicago and St. Louis to certain points in Missouri. The Gulf and the Trans-Missouri divisions of the Western Traffic Association, the Transcontinental Association, and the Southern Interstate Association operated in the Southwest. The Texas Traffic Association, informally organized in 1882, took shape in 1885 with nine Texas and eight connecting carriers as members. Many southwestern roads also had bilateral agreements with their competitors. In Texas the traffic arrangement between the Morgan interests and the Texas and New Orleans preceded by four years the more famous Huntington-Gould agreement. The Katy admitted to being a party to no less than eight such agreements, involving all of its competitors, in 1880.

These mutual understandings, entirely unofficial, were never too successful because the gentlemen in agreement were not in complete accord with respect to how far each was bound when his own personal interests were at stake. Even before state and federal legislation outlawed pooling, the participants evaded the terms.[2]

The West regarded pooling with misgiving. In practice it circumvented a deeply imbedded economic principle, smacked of "monopoly," and potentially gave to a few directors of corporations the power to control rates upon which the economic life of a great region depended. The evils flowing from evasion of the pooling agreements evoked more bitter denunciation. Rebates and drawbacks added to the hostility already engendered by easily observable favoritism in furnishing cars and facilities and in sudden changes in unposted rates.

Absentee ownership bred suspicion and distrust. Conceived locally and with local interests predominant at first, the railroads soon passed under the control of those who were able to transform dreams into reality. Absentee financiers determined policy. The resulting hostility was not merely prejudice toward outside control, although that un-

---

[2] Robert E. Riegel, "Western Railroad Pools," *MHVR*, Vol. XVIII, 364-77 and *The Story of the Western Railroads*, 162-59, 219-23, 301-304; Potts, *Railroad Transportation in Texas*, 79-82; "Statistics of Railroads," *Tenth Census*, IV, 596, 599.

doubtedly played an important part, but toward the complete loss of sympathetic contact. There was no agreement regarding the primary reason for the existence of a railroad. To the agrarian West it was the vital transportation which sustained its economy; to the absentee owner it was an investment for profits. To one it was a basic social instrument; to the other, a privately owned company. Neither understood the problems of the other or had any desire to increase that knowledge. With financial control determining policy, the western point of view had little chance for a hearing.

Absentee owners controlled not only the railroads but also, either directly or indirectly, the marketing facilities. Even without actual ownership, railroad management would exercise much control over these facilities, since it could furnish cars and services as it saw fit. Through favoritism to certain grain and livestock buyers it could determine the extent to which competition would be permitted at a particular shipping point.[3]

Wholesale abuses in construction and operation were the least defensible of all malpractices. It is true that western railroad building progressed at a rate which exceeded immediate needs and spread over a vast area that would require years for development. There was no hope for profits from operations alone, but to use such an argument as a justification for unethical practices was nothing more than an apology for corruptness, an effort to salvage something from losses incurred because of bad judgment. It is also true that the unscrupulous peripheral speculator, interested only incidentally in actual construction, gave the legitimate promoter an undeserved repute, but, unfortunately, many of the railroad builders mixed elements of both. Many fine railroads were to suffer losses—in both money and public esteem—because of irresponsible financing.

The policy of letting construction contracts to companies whose directors were largely the same as those of the railroads smacked of collusion. It is now immaterial whether or not the Katy's Land Grant Railway and Trust Company, the Texas and Pacific's California and Texas Construction Company, the Choctaw, Oklahoma and Gulf's Choctaw Construction Company, and the numerous subsidiaries of other southwestern railroads were guilty of corrupt practices. The situation itself gave color to the general western belief that the profits

[3] Hicks, *The Populist Revolt*, 75–76; Allan Nevins, *The Emergence of Modern America*, 165.

were in building, not in operating, railroads. Poor construction and bad equipment often seemed to verify these suspicions.[4]

Weak railroads, unable to enlist support otherwise, drastically discounted their securities. It was a common practice to donate stock to purchasers of bonds. Quite often the subsequent issuance of preferred stock wiped out the value of the common stock. Such arrangements frequently accompanied consolidations and mergers.[5] The West was particularly violent in its attitude toward such stock watering, which resulted in tremendous overcapitalization. "Sockless Jerry" Simpson's estimate that the railroads of Kansas were capitalized at six times the actual cost of construction might be dismissed as the wild guess of a highly prejudiced critic, but the estimate in *Poor's Manual* for 1883, fixing the capitalization of all railroads in the United States at considerably more than double the cost of construction, is certainly worthy of serious consideration. The exact amount of "water" in the financial structure of western railroads is unknown. Proof is not necessary because their management readily admitted the practice, justifying it as a legitimate means of financing extremely hazardous investments. The justification neither assuaged the indignation of the western farmer nor saved the railroads from later grief.[6]

Railroad interference in politics was in many respects the most serious complaint of the West. By the end of the Civil War responsible congressmen were greatly concerned about the increasing pressure from private interests in shaping the course of legislation. President Johnson saw a grave threat to democratic institutions in the alliance of government and business; E. L. Godkin's *Nation* was alarmed over the apparent decline in public morality resulting from railroad interest in politics.[7]

The scene at Washington was reproduced in miniature in state capitals. Writing of the period after the frenzy of building had passed from the north central states to the Gulf Southwest, John D. Hicks comments:

---

[4] See "construction" and "corporation finance" in each valuation docket.

[5] Riegel, *The Story of the Western Railroads*, 118, 131–35, 160–78, 306; Hicks, *The Populist Revolt*, 68; Buck, *The Agrarian Crusade*, 84; Davis R. Dewey, *National Problems, 1885–1897*, 91–96.

[6] Hicks, *The Populist Revolt*, 29, 65–66; Haney, *A Congressional History of Railways in the United States*, II, 309.

[7] Claude G. Bowers, *The Tragic Era*, 115, 268, 283–84; Haney, *A Congressional History of Railways in the United States*, I, 313.

Grievances

It is not unfair to say that normally the railroads,—sometimes a single road—dominated the political situation in every western state. . . . Railway influence was exerted in practically every nominating convention to insure that no one hostile to the railways should be named to office. Railway lobbyists were on hand whenever a legislature met to see that measures unfavorable to the roads were quietly eliminated. Railway taxation, a particularly tender question, was always watched with the greatest solicitude and, from the standpoint of the prevention of high taxes, usually with the greatest of success. How much bribery and corruption and intrigue the railroads used to secure the ends desired will never be known.[8]

Apparently, the words of Jerry Simpson could well have been applicable in most of the Southwest if the name of the state and the company were changed. He said: "Fellow citizens, we have come today to remove the seat of Government of Kansas from the Santa Fe offices, back to the State-house where it belongs."[9]

There was some reason, if not justification, for the interference of railroads in politics. The inevitable answer of the railroads was that it was a common practice of the times, accepted as a part of lawmaking, and was necessary for survival. Railroads were not alone in employing lobbyists to look after their interests. Furthermore, antirailroad laws were often punitive. Sometimes they represented the well-meaning efforts of amateur reformers, sometimes the work of demagogues, and in some cases the machinations of opportunists as a type of legalized extortion. Subsequent apologists have suggested that the willingness to assume the risk of building western railroads entitled the promoters to use all means at their command to assure the success of their ventures. It is quite easy to rationalize a defense, but it is doubtful whether the early builders would have been greatly concerned about rationalization. They would probably have agreed bluntly that given a weapon, they used it. Bribes, favors, and judicious distribution of free passes to legislators, judges, and publicists were a small cost to pay when compared with the results.

Irresponsibility, recklessness, and ruthlessness were peculiar neither to the West nor to the railroads. The era was notable neither for high ethical standards nor for a sense of social responsibility. Western railroads appear in sharp relief, however, because they were the most extreme examples of concentrated capital in a region dedicated to agriculture, a region ever suspicious of corporate wealth.

[8] Hicks, *The Populist Revolt,* 69–70.
[9] Barr, "The Populist Uprising," *Kansas and Kansans,* I, 1122.

CHAPTER 26

The Temper of the Times

THE AGRARIAN reform movement in the north central states gradually seeped into the Southwest, coloring local politics more and more. By 1880 railroad development had advanced far enough in the state of Kansas for the Republican party to advocate mild state regulation, and three years later Kansas secured a Board of Railroad Commissioners with very limited powers. A prolonged drouth, a steady decline in the price of agricultural commodities, and the pinch of farm mortgages, however, were required to spawn radical farm leadership in the state.[1]

In 1879 a farmers' alliance appeared in Parker County, Texas. The organization was interested primarily in local problems, but agitated incidentally for federal control of interstate commerce and more adequate taxation of railroad property. This incipient agency of reform, as well as the Louisiana Farmers' Union and the Agricultural Wheel of Arkansas, was not particularly vigorous until the mid-eighties, when declining prices and the return of hard times gave it an economic reason for reviving. Planks calling for state regulation of railroads took on meaning, along with other proposals which were shortly to become identified with Populism. Demands for strict regulation of rates and services placed on the defensive those who advocated innocuous legislation to woo the roads and at the same time meet popular demand for control.[2]

[1] Buck, *The Agrarian Crusade*, 19, 30–32; Barr, "The Populist Uprising," *Kansas and Kansans*, I, 1126–34; Stene, *Railroad Commission to Corporation Commission*, 11–17, 98–99.

[2] Buck, *The Agrarian Crusade*, 112–17; Hicks, *The Populist Revolt*, 100–114.

The Temper of the Times

The Agricultural Wheel put an entire slate of candidates in the Arkansas state elections of 1886. Although its candidates were all defeated, much of their program was adopted by the victorious Democrats, who enacted drastic regulatory legislation. The Wheel soon passed into the orbit of the Texas movement and, along with other cotton-belt states, developed into the Southern Alliance. James S. Hogg, attorney general of Texas, was waging a vigorous crusade for state control of railroads which was soon to become the heart of his gubernatorial platform.

The flagging Kansas movement revived, largely through the medium of the Winfield *Non-Conformist,* edited by the Vincent brothers. The first annual meeting of the revived Kansas Alliance stated that one of its objectives was "to secure the enactment of state laws auxiliary to the interstate commerce laws, and to establish equitable relations between the people and the roads, making the rights and duties of each depend, not upon doubtful discretion, but upon positive enactment." The Alliance grew rapidly. By 1890 it claimed 130,000 members, and entered a full slate of candidates in the election.

The political campaign of 1890 was reminiscent of camp-meeting techniques, with the Alliance members spurred on by parades, songs, and cheers and exhorted by a host of speakers at picnics, in rural schools, and on small-town streets. Railroad regulation was basic in the appeals to revolt against those in power. While many farm leaders asked for more stringent control over rates, services, and political activities of railroads, others demanded government ownership. Jerry Simpson was a leader among those advocating the more radical course. Probably the most frequently quoted attack on railroads from the radical camp was Mrs. Mary E. Lease's statement: "Kansas suffers from two great robbers, the Santa Fe Railroad and the loan companies. . . . We want money, land, and transportation."[3]

The State Alliance convention at Emporia in March, 1890, adopted resolutions condemning the bonding of any local political units for railroad purposes. As election day drew near, there were demands for a general reduction in freight rates and passenger fares.

When the returns were in, the Alliance had five Congressional seats, the lower house of the state legislature, the attorney-generalship, and control of a number of county governments. The Republican party barely held the governorship. After the election, Alliance members charged that the railroads provided free transportation to many out

[3] Quoted by John D. Hicks, *The Populist Revolt,* 160.

of state voters, who were eligible to vote under the lax suffrage laws of the times.

The Alliance, soon to be associated with the national Populist party, was able to enact practically none of its program. Bills to reduce freight rates and passenger fares, to prohibit subscriptions to railroad stock by municipal corporations, to inflict severe penalties for corrupt practices, and to limit the use of the blacklist passed the House, only to die in the Senate. The only major victories were an act limiting alien ownership of land and the unseating of United States Senator John J. Ingalls by William A. Peffer, a picturesque Populist newspaper editor.

Two years later a Populist-Democratic fusion ticket elected six congressmen, secured control of the state senate, and won the governorship for Lorenzo D. Lewelling. It lost control of the lower house but claimed fraud in the returns, again accusing railroads of bringing in voters from outside the state. The election was marked by continuous attacks on railroad influence in politics and demands for regulation. The state Populist convention, held at Wichita in June, censured the Senate for defeating regulatory measures in the preceding session and called for legislation prohibiting the issuance of railroad passes to anyone but company employees. W. F. Rightmire popularized statistics purporting to show that Kansas produced $49,000,000 worth of wheat and oats but paid $59,000,000 in transportation, taxes, and interest. On the night of the inauguration Jerry Simpson addressed a Populist rally with the words: "The struggle in this state was not between the People's Party and the Republican Party, but between the People's Party and the railroad corporations. You have beaten the Santa Fe Railroad and you must take charge of the government." Populists spoke seriously of moving the state capital to the village of Kanopolis in order to escape railroad pressures.

Governor Lewelling recommended the direct election of railroad commissioners, extension of the authority of the commission to the regulation of freight rates and the prohibition of unjust discrimination, and restrictions on the issuance of free passes. Again the Populists failed to enact their program.

The Populist-Democratic fusion, never popular with the more aggressive Populists, led to internal dissension, and in 1894 the Republican party regained control of the state administration and increased its majority in the lower house of the legislature; the Fusionists kept control of the Senate simply because it held over from 1892.

Courtesy Union Pacific

Laying track 600 miles west of St. Louis, 1867.

Driving bridge piles on the Kansas City Southern about 1900.

Courtesy Kansas City Southern Lines

Courtesy Kansas City Southern Lines

Early-day Kansas City Southern freight train passing Butler's Bluff, near Noel, Missouri.

Kansas City Southern's *Southern Belle* passing Butler's Bluff.

Courtesy Kansas City Southern Lines

The Temper of the Times

From almost half of the total vote cast in 1892, the Populists dropped to less than 39 per cent in 1894. In 1896, however, the Fusion ticket, headed chiefly by Democrats, won its most complete victory, gaining control of both houses of the legislature and electing John W. Leedy to the governorship.

In spite of its political success, the Democratic-Populist majority did nothing; it split on how railroads should be regulated. Only after a decisive Republican victory in 1898, which permanently destroyed the Populists as a factor in Kansas politics, did a last-minute special legislative session create the "Court of Visitation" with supervisory powers over railroads. The return of prosperity so blunted the demand for regulation that within a few years Kansas elected a railroad contractor as governor.[4]

While no other state embraced Populism as enthusiastically as Kansas, there were elements in other southwestern states which stood for similar programs. This was particularly true in Texas, where the party was strong in spite of the fact that the Hogg faction in the Democratic party stood for agrarian reform. As attorney-general, Hogg attacked railroad abuses and special privileges, winning the governorship in 1890, with Alliance support, on the strength of his record in prosecuting railroad cases. He drew many Populist votes in his race for re-election in 1892.[5]

The Texas election of 1890 illustrated perfectly the conflict between the areas with railroads and those without. The editor of the Tascosa *Pioneer* was an inveterate foe of "Jim" Hogg. He insisted that Hogg's regulatory program was politically inspired and that its adoption would blight all hopes for railroads in the Panhandle. When he became convinced that there was no hope of stopping the Attorney General's gubernatorial boom, he lamented: "Hogg will be governor and the Rock Island won't come just now. Hurrah—for—Hogg."[6]

The strength of the agrarian movement in Missouri can scarcely be measured in terms of the third-party vote because Alliance members preferred to work within the framework of the two-party system. Alliance sympathizers did gain control of the state assembly in 1890. In Arkansas and Louisiana, where Populists fused with Republicans,

---

[4] Barr, "The Populist Uprising," *Kansas and Kansans*, I, 1137, 1140–64, 1170, 1178–92; Stene, *Railroad Commission to Corporation Commission*, 22–25; Hicks, *The Populist Revolt*, 140–42, 162, 178–80, 261–63, 268, 274, 333, 337; from *Kansas and Kansans*: Edith Connelley Ross, "John W. Leedy," II, 845–46 and "Walter Roscoe Stubbs," II, 857.

[5] Hicks, *The Populist Revolt*, 63, 249, 393, 395.

[6] Tascosa *Pioneer*, Sept. 27, 1890.

there was no strong antirailroad sentiment. After the silver issue rose to overshadow all others, the relationship between state regulation of transportation and partisan politics dwindled in importance throughout the Southwest.[7]

[7] Melvin J. White, "Populism in Louisiana during the Nineties," *MVHR*, Vol. V, 1–19; Frederick E. Haynes, "The New Sectionalism," *QJE*, Vol. X, 278–79; Buck, *The Agrarian Crusade*, 149–51, 188–89.

CHAPTER 27

The Course of State Legislation

RAILROAD REGULATION, following in the wake of political agitation, was confused and contradictory. There were several reasons for its checkered course. The completeness of the rail network determined the degree to which such legislation received favorable consideration. Legislatures frequently failed to distinguish between regulation and vindictiveness. The problem was further complicated by demagogic appeals for political reasons. A more serious confusion, however, resulted from the inconsistencies prevailing in western economic thought. Competition was accepted as the most salutary type of regulation. A unique plan to achieve such a result was the proposed Gulf and Interstate Railway, apparently conceived in Texas in the early nineties and enthusiastically endorsed in Kansas. A railroad running from Minnesota to the Gulf would be constructed by the ten states involved, each to own the section operating within its borders. This line would automatically set all rates by maintaining moderate charges. This project, however, would simply have added another road to share the revenue in an area which did not supply enough for lines already operating.[1]

The establishment of basic rate schedules and minimum standards of service was a definite part of the regulatory legislation, but it was contradictory to the whole theory of competition. This peculiar contradiction frequently appeared in the West, and it explains the emphasis on regulation in a region renowned for its individualism. In-

---
[1] Haney, *A Congressional History of Railways in the United States*, II, 311; Hicks, *The Populist Revolt*, 284.

dividualism represented the right to enter forbidden territory, legalize title, and improve the land. But the West believed in law, even while flouting it, and frequently called on the government for relief. When the frontier farmer found himself at the mercy of a force which controlled his economic fortunes, he became aware of the necessity for holding such a force legally, as well as morally, responsible and demanded legislation to effect such a result. The concept of positive regulation was conceived in large part in the Middle West, and later found ardent advocates in the Southwest.

Although the agrarian movement, which culminated in the Populist party, did not assume real prominence until the late eighties, the regulation of railroads became a moderately important political issue much earlier. Rate making drew some attention in the Kansas elections of 1882, and in the next two years the state brought about a few reductions in rates. Arkansas was experimenting with passenger fares, working on a plan of valuation for tax purposes, and adopting laws to prevent consolidations. In Texas the legislature reduced passenger fares to three cents per mile, and in 1882 a special session considered the problem of more rigid regulation. Shortly thereafter, interest shifted to the vigorous campaign waged by Attorney General Hogg against questionable financial policies, discrimination, and pooling.[2]

Regulating the participation of railroads in politics was an all but impossible task. It was generally known that they exerted tremendous influence, but obviously there would be no open admission by a legislator or administrative official that he was a creature of outside influence, nor would the railroads admit such control. One practice, however, which inherently placed public officials under less or greater obligation to railroads was the wide distribution of free passes. Arkansas and Missouri provided heavy fines for issuing passes or reducing fares for judges, legislators, or public administrators quite early, but Kansas and Texas did not follow until much later.[3]

Much of the formal code governing incorporation and financial restriction also preceded the most active period of antirailroad agitation. The Missouri, Arkansas, and Texas constitutions of the mid-

---

[2] Stene, *Railroad Commission to Corporation Commission*, 9–13; Moore, "State ... in Arkansas," AHA *Pub.*, Vol. III, 23–26; Potts, *Railroad Transportation in Texas*, 115.

[3] ICC, *Rys. U. S. 1902*, Part 4, 298, 300; Moore, "State ... in Arkansas," AHA *Pub.*, Vol. III, 24, 29; Stene, *Railroad Commission to Corporation Commission*, 38; Reed, *Texas Railroads*, 728.

seventies established many of the basic principles, but all were elaborated by legislative action during the next several decades. All the southwestern states adopted general incorporation laws which provided for the filing of articles including information about the company making the application. The problem of controlling stock manipulation was met in part by requiring a detailed statement of the proposed issue and by providing for the maintenance of a stock book, which was to be open for inspection by state officials or stockholders. Texas and Arkansas required that a majority of the directors be residents of the state, with the further provision in Arkansas that one-third of the total number of directors be required to reside in counties which the railroad served. All the southwestern states except Louisiana joined in the movement requiring railroads to make annual reports.

Various rules were adopted to insure that the corporation would actually construct and operate a railroad. Missouri and Arkansas both required that it be completed within ten years; Texas, that at least ten miles be completed within two years and twenty miles annually thereafter; Kansas, that it begin "active operations" within five years, a period reduced in 1898 to one year.

The various states dealt with the subjects which had so long been sources of bitter controversy. Even the scant Louisiana statutes forbade extortionate rates, unjust discrimination, and agreements in restraint of trade. Most of the states forbade railroad officials to contract to supply materials to their own lines, and Kansas denied to railroads the right to engage in any other type of business.

In spite of the agitation for rate control, none of the southwestern states adopted a comprehensive plan before the turn of the century. Only in the matter of passenger fares did all adopt laws. Missouri and Texas had certain general legislation on freight rates, but sound rate making was not developed until later.

Laws providing for public safety and convenience were generally much less adequate in the Southwest than in areas more widely acquainted with railroad operation. All, however, had minimum requirements for the maintenance of public crossings and warnings of approaching trains. Kansas and Missouri provided that railroads must fence their rights of way; Texas and Louisiana held them accountable for stock killed on unfenced right of way. Somewhat more comprehensive rules guaranteed minimum standards of convenience. Trains had to operate on a posted schedule; Arkansas and Texas required daily train service. All states insisted that adequate waiting rooms be maintained and Arkansas, Louisiana, and Texas that separate accommodations be provided for Negroes.

Each state had certain laws peculiar to itself. Texas required any line running within three miles of a county seat to pass through it, and Kansas that railroads stop one train each way each day in every county they served. A Missouri statute provided that all bridge construction had to be approved by army engineers.

There was nothing particularly striking in the law governing construction and operation of railroads in the Southwest except that it was piecemeal. The region as a whole had not gone as far in regulation as most states, and Louisiana was an outstanding example of almost complete absence of restrictive legislation. The Southwest was conspicuous in one respect only: the severity of the penalties for violation of such law as it had.

The time element accounts for the lack of comprehensive legislation, the penalties, and the peculiar position of Louisiana. Although the Southwest was not highly developed, its rail network was unbelievably complete in most areas. Economic ills and substantial completion of the railroads came at almost the same time and were thereby joined in the thinking of the people. Much of the legislation, which had been passed in an atmosphere of marked hostility, prescribed penalties reflecting both a belief that stern measures would discourage violations and a spirit of animosity. At the same time, railroads were too new for legislators to know which of their activities should be controlled. Louisiana, with only a few railroads and the desire to attract others, was not interested in imposing rigid restrictions or heavy penalties.

The specter of monopoly haunted the West. Pooling, with all its possibilities for abuse, was the partial answer of railroad management to destructive rate wars. Consolidation was an alternative to pooling, but it was even more obnoxious in an area where the word "monopoly" was anathema. A regulated monopoly would fit neither the prevailing economic theory nor the facts. There was no satisfactory solution. The course adopted by the state legislatures was, however, the only one which could have been followed in view of all the circumstances. All the southwestern states except Louisiana forbade the consolidation of parallel or competing lines, while Texas refused to sanction the consolidation of a domestic line with a connecting foreign road.[4]

The Course of State Legislation

State legislation did not prevent consolidation. Some of the more notorious monopolies were forced to divest themselves of certain properties in the early nineties, but the trend was in the opposite direction. The logic supporting combination was unanswerable. Consolidation would effect many economies and eliminate many costs which would ultimately have to be borne by the shipper. The problem then became one of guarding the public interest from an abuse of power, a balancing of the concepts of private ownership and public interest. This problem, however, was largely reserved for the next century.

Demands for regulation raised the difficult problem of the method by which it could best be accomplished. Failure to set up any administrative machinery for enforcement in such a technical field was a fatal defect. State railroad commissions could be the answer. The advisability of establishing commissions and the extent of their powers in the event of their creation were among the most bitterly fought issues in southwestern legislative history.

Railroad commissions were not new. Rhode Island created a short-lived commission as early as 1836; Connecticut and Massachusetts had them before the Granger states attracted nationwide attention by creating similarly named administrative agencies. There was reason enough, however, for the general interest in the Granger commissions, for they differed drastically from their New England counterparts. Those in the East were advisory and depended upon publicity alone; those created by the Grangers exercised quasi-judicial powers. The Granger commissions, crippled by court decisions and weakened by returning prosperity, had run their course by 1880. Those which remained no longer exercised much regulatory power.

Missouri's Railroad and Warehouse Commission of 1875 preceded such agencies in the remainder of the Southwest by a number of years. It was charged generally with administering all laws relating to common carriers and public warehouses.[5]

The most heated campaign for a powerful railroad commission took place in Kansas. In 1883, Democratic Governor George Glick recommended to his Republican legislature that it consider the creation of an agency with extensive rate-making and regulatory authority. A measure which finally did secure legislative approval provided for a

---

[4] The summary of state legislation is based on the tables of state regulation in ICC, *Rys. U. S. 1902,* Part 4, 23–30, 118–305.
[5] Riegel, *The Story of the Western Railroads,* 19–20.

Board of Railroad Commissioners with advisory power only, except for authority to investigate specific rates under certain conditions. The board was rendered virtually impotent by unfavorable court decisions.

As the decade wore on and economic unrest in Kansas became more pronounced, spokesmen for the farmers demanded regulatory powers for the board. The Populist-controlled lower house passed a measure in 1891 which gave the commission power to prescribe maximum freight rates, but the bill died in a Senate committee. The legislative history of this bill became a major issue in the election of 1892, but the restoration of conservative control in the legislature and the choice of a Populist governor created another stalemate. Meanwhile, the Populist-dominated Board of Railroad Commissioners adopted rate schedules which the railroads ignored.

Following the Fusion victory of 1896, a split in the Populist ranks prevented action. Governor Leedy recommended that the commission be given judicial power in adjusting rates; a moderate wing wished the power of the commission increased, but with no authority to establish maximum rates. The more conservative view prevailed in the legislature, but Governor Leedy vetoed the measure as a violation of his campaign promises.

After the Fusion ticket suffered a complete defeat in 1898, Leedy called a special session to consider railroad regulation before the victorious Republicans took over. This time the legislature acted. It replaced the existing board with the Court of Visitation, made up of three elected judges. It was a court of record sitting in perpetual session, vested with full common law and equity jurisdiction in matters involving railroads. A popularly elected solicitor represented the state in all cases. The court could issue decrees concerning the reasonableness of rates and could force the appointment of receivers when railroads refused to conform, but the defendant had six months in which to appeal.

The unique Court of Visitation had been in existence less than two years when the Supreme Court of Kansas declared it unconstitutional, leaving the state with no regulatory agency. The legislature immediately created a second Board of Railroad Commissioners, with power to supervise and regulate services and to fix rates on complaint of another carrier, certain municipal officials, or shippers. In 1903 it was made elective, and two years later it began to establish maximum rates, which were based on a study of other states.[6]

The Course of State Legislation

The constitution of Texas imposed upon the legislature the duty of establishing maximum rates and controlling abuses and discriminations. Such legislation was not passed until 1883, when slight administrative authority was vested in the state engineer. Governor Sul Ross blocked an attempt to transfer this power to a commission in 1887, but in his successful bid for the governorship, "Jim" Hogg so popularized the idea of a railroad commission that the people of the state overwhelmingly adopted a constitutional amendment providing for its creation.

The elective Texas Railroad Commission had among its various powers the right to fix rates, subject to the right of appeal to the state courts. Its early days were stormy. Failing in attempts to have the federal courts declare it unconstitutional, opponents of the commission were no more successful in attempting to defeat Hogg for re-election. Meanwhile, John L. Reagan, the most famous name in the Southwest with respect to the development of railroad regulation, became its first chairman. He exercised his authority so conservatively that all major criticism soon subsided.[7]

Arkansas and Louisiana belatedly followed the example of the other states. The Arkansas constitution of 1874 made possible the creation of a regulatory body, but conservative anticommission Democrats controlled the state until a split occurred in their ranks in 1896. The following year the legislature provided for a State Board of Construction, made up of the governor, the state auditor, and the attorney general, to control any railroads which the state of Arkansas might build.

In 1899 two more regulatory agencies were added. The State Board of Incorporators, entirely ex officio, approved proposals for new construction; the Arkansas Railroad Commission, consisting of the members of the Board of Construction and three elected members, determined the reasonableness of rates.

Jeff Davis, a highly publicized Arkansas politician, made capital of the conservative Democratic split and became attorney general in 1898 on a strong antitrust and regulatory platform. He then served three consecutive terms as governor. His talk exceeded his accomplishments. In 1901, Arkansas abolished the Board of Construction

---

[6] ICC, *Rys. U. S. 1902*, Part 4, 31–33, 48–49, 54–55, 62, 66–71, 80–81, 92–93, 98–99, 102–103, 106–107; Stene, *Railroad Commission to Corporation Commission*, 14–47, 98–100.

[7] ICC, *Rys. U. S. 1902*, Part 4, 52–53, 60–61, 64, 68–69, 72–73, 90–91, 96–97, 100–101, 104–105, 112–13; Potts, *Railroad Transportation in Texas*, 115, 132–37, 156–74.

and gave additional rate-making power to the Railroad Commission, but state courts declared the added powers unconstitutional.[8]

Louisiana created its commission in 1898, with the state divided into three districts, each of which elected a member. It had rate-making powers in theory, but as a matter of actual practice, it was simply advisory during its first few years.[9]

At the turn of the century all the states of the Gulf Southwest had railroad commissions, and within three years thereafter all had the so-called strong type, with rate-making power. Louisiana was the only state in the region which did not give general supervisory powers to its commission. By the terms of the highly controversial Stock and Bond Law of 1893, Texas gave its commission the right to determine the physical value of railroads and limit mortgage indebtedness to that value. Rail service degenerated so rapidly that within a few years the Railroad Commission was authorized to approve the issuance of securities equal to the reasonable value of proposed extensions.[10]

Although the powers and duties of all commissions have been elaborated since, the basic theories and organization were established in the last twenty years of the nineteenth century and the first few years of the twentieth.

One of the most serious permanent effects of railroad regulation was the persistence of a tradition of natural antagonism between railroads and the public. Since early railroad development had been marred by ruthless self-interest, planned mismanagement, and arrogant disregard of the rights of both the public and the security holders, personal vindictiveness and demagoguery were mingled with sincere efforts to correct abuses. Once the orgy of wild building and the desire for speculative profits subsided, however, railroads began to operate on the basis of legitimate returns from actual operation. They recognized a community of interest with their patrons. Sound long-term policies had to rest upon good public relations with prosperous communities along their lines. Unfortunately, the tradition inherited from the past remained strong, and it was to take many years of sustained effort to recover public confidence.

[8] ICC, *Rys. U. S. 1902*, Part 4, 31, 46–47, 54–55, 66–67, 70–71, 76–77, 92–93, 98–99, 102–103, 106–107, 160; Fletcher, *Arkansas*, 288, 290–93, 300–301, 313.

[9] ICC, *Rys. U. S. 1902*, Part 4, 48–49, 56–57, 62, 68–71, 82–83, 93, 98–99, 102–103, 108–109; Nat B. Knight, Jr., "The Louisiana Public Service Commission," *TLR*, Vol. XVI, 1–10.

[10] ICC, *Rys. U. S. 1902*, Part 4, 14–16, 19–22, 28; Potts, *Railroad Transportation in Texas*, 140–55; Lewis H. Haney, "Railway Regulation in Texas," *JPE*, Vol. XIX, 450–51, 455; William Z. Ripley, *Railroads: Finance and Organization*, 302–306.

CHAPTER 28

B. F. Yoakum, Entrepreneur

THE EFFECTS of the panic of 1893 gradually wore off, and railroad building was gathering momentum in limited sections of the Gulf Southwest as the century ended. A few corporations were entering the field, but those already established were to carry on the bulk of the construction. A few individuals were to make names for themselves as railroad builders, but they were exceptions because the individual was normally subordinated to the corporate whole.

B. F. Yoakum was by far the most spectacular builder in the Gulf Southwest during the early twentieth century. Texas-born Yoakum represented the tradition of the earlier giants more than anyone else of his day, and the collapse of his rail empire in 1913 revealed that many of his methods were those he learned in his younger promotional days. A combination of circumstances put it within Yoakum's power to help mold the destinies of three major carriers. One, the Rock Island, was a shoestring from Kansas City to Fort Worth; a second, the Frisco, stretched into a virgin field but was handicapped by a tradition of impotence as it was tossed from one to another of its more powerful rivals; the third, the Gulf Coast Lines, was the creation of Yoakum himself in a bold bid for partial control of the Gulf region of Louisiana and Texas.

Although Yoakum was already interested in both, the Rock Island and the Frisco each developed along its own separate path in the first years of the business revival. Charles B. Eddy, a New Mexico promoter, was influential in securing the extension towards El Paso of the Rock Island line terminating at Liberal, in southwestern Kansas. He conceived the idea of building a railroad northeast from El Paso as part of an ambitious scheme involving the development of mines, resort areas, timberlands, and townsites. Eddy was able to interest the Phelps-Dodge Corporation, which, in turn, secured a commitment from the Rock Island to build southwest through the old Public Land Strip (which had become Beaver County, Oklahoma Territory), the northwest corner of the Texas Panhandle, and into New Mexico to meet the road building northeast from El Paso. The two roads joined at Santa Rosa, New Mexico, late in 1901. The Rock Island had traversed a practically uninhabited territory, with Old Optimo, in Beaver County, and the XIT Ranch headquarters the only white settlements in 263 miles.

The Rock Island line crossing Oklahoma Territory in 1889 and 1890 furnished a central trunk for branch lines. Enid to the north and Chickasha to the south were the chief centers for feeders. One ran northeast from Enid to Billings. A Rock Island affiliate built west from Enid for some twenty miles and then paralleled the parent road south as far as Lawton, rejoining it at Waurika. This gave the Rock Island parallel lines almost all the way across Oklahoma. In addition, it built a line from Chickasha to Mangum.

In July, 1902, the Rock Island changed hands. Two former railroaders, William B. Leeds and Daniel Reed, the "tin-plate kings" who had recently sold their holdings to the United States Steel Corporation, chose this railroad as the instrument through which to enter the transportation field. A syndicate made up of these two men and W. H. and J. H. Moore secured control, organized a holding company and the subsidiary Rock Island Improvement Company in New Jersey, and entered into a period of expansion and outside speculation which proved disastrous to the railroad.[1]

The Frisco was enjoying a rare interlude of independence at the end of the century. In June, 1896, it was reorganized after being severed from the Santa Fe, and under Yoakum's guidance it expanded rapidly, chiefly by acquiring semidependent short lines. In 1898 it took over the operation of the Kansas City, Clinton and Springfield and the Kansas City, Osceola and Southern. Three years later the Kansas City, Fort Scott and Memphis, which had added considerable mileage to its already extensive holdings, passed under

[1] ICC, *Val. Rep.*, XXIV, 924, 928, 930, 940–42; O. P. Byers, "The El Paso Line," *RIM*, Vol. XVII, No. 10, 88–89; Guthrie Smith, "William Ashton Hawkins," *NMHR*, Vol. XIV, 306–308.

B. F. Yoakum, Entrepreneur

Frisco control. A branch from South Greenfield was extended to Aurora, Missouri, and the original main line was thrust to the Neosho River at Miami, Indian Territory. The Kansas City, Fort Scott and Memphis controlled, through stock ownership, short railroads from Joplin to Webb City, Missouri, and between Deckerville and Luxora, in northeastern Arkansas. A total of 760 miles of operating railroad in Kansas, Missouri, Arkansas, and Indian Territory passed to the Frisco under this leasing agreement. The Frisco added a little more by building from Miami to Afton.

The Frisco took over the Kansas Midland and purchased a number of recently built short lines. The Arkansas and Choctaw, running from Ashdown, Arkansas, to the Indian Territory line at Arkinda, passed to a Frisco construction company when it resumed building in 1901. The Bentonville Railroad, in Arkansas, expanded to Grove, Indian Territory, under the name Arkansas and Oklahoma Railroad and became a Frisco property.

Five Oklahoma railroads, all originating locally with an eye to eventual absorption, did follow that course as the Frisco took over their construction. The St. Louis and Oklahoma City pushed the terminus of the old Atlantic and Pacific from Sapulpa to the thriving town of Oklahoma City; the St. Louis, Oklahoma and Southern ran south from Sapulpa to Denison, Texas. The Oklahoma City Terminal Company was what its name indicated, and the Oklahoma City and Western ran southwest to Lawton. To the north, enterprising Blackwell citizens built from Arkansas City, Kansas, to Blackwell, then sold to the Frisco.

Local Texas interests started the Red River, Texas and Southern Railway from Sherman to Carrollton; it passed to the Frisco in 1901 before it was completed. It had access to Fort Worth over the Rock Island by virtue of a trackage agreement; it then tied to the Kansas, Oklahoma and Gulf by building from Red River to Denison and getting trackage rights over the Houston and Texas Central between Denison and Sherman. In the same year, the Frisco legally took over the Fort Worth and Rio Grande, which it had always operated.

Rock Island control in no way hampered the Frisco's growth in its logical field. It continued to spread over Oklahoma and Indian territories. The opening of the Kiowa-Comanche reservation furnished the incentive for extending from Lawton, Oklahoma, to Quanah, Texas, in 1903, which was the final link in a line extending diagonally across the twin territories from northeast to southwest.

Then Came the Railroads

The Arkansas and Choctaw pushed from its terminus at Arkinda along Red River to Ardmore. Farther north three subsidiaries, eventually united as the Ozark and Cherokee Central, stretched from Fayetteville, Arkansas, across parts of the Cherokee and Creek nations to Okmulgee, on the Sapulpa-Denison line. The subsidiary Arkansas Valley and Western, completed in 1903, extended 175 miles west from Tulsa to a juncture with the Santa Fe at Avard; the next year another line extended from Blackwell through Enid and southwest across Oklahoma to Vernon, Texas. In its brief period under Yoakum influence, and primarily between 1900 and 1903, the Frisco added more than eleven hundred miles in the twin territories, crisscrossing them in every direction.[2]

Frisco expansion in Arkansas and Missouri included the acquisition of the Houck lines, the leasing of two short Arkansas roads, and minor construction. Louis Houck had added to his lines until, at the time of their incorporation into the Frisco as the St. Louis, Memphis and Southeastern, they represented some twenty-five predecessor corporations which formed a network stretching southward from Cape Girardeau and Poplar Bluff into Arkansas. The Frisco extended them from Poplar Bluff to Pocahontas and from Cape Girardeau to Southeastern Junction, near St. Louis. The only other important Frisco construction in Arkansas was the connecting line from Hope to Ashdown, to the southwest.[3]

With the exception of the stubs which jutted south to Texas termini along Red River, expansion of the Frisco in Texas was confined to a fifty-mile addition to the Fort Worth and Rio Grande from Brownwood to Brady.[4]

The Rock Island enjoyed an expansion comparable to that of the Frisco, with the bulk of its development likewise confined to the purchase of existing lines, but with considerable construction in Oklahoma and Indian territories. The greatest increase in mileage in the territories came from the absorption of its keenest rival, the Choctaw, Oklahoma and Gulf. This road had increased its mileage tremendously by taking over the Memphis and Little Rock, the pioneer railway of Arkansas. Once it reached Little Rock, the Memphis and Little Rock built no farther and for twenty-five years stumbled

[2] ICC, *Val. Rep.*, XLI, 223–24, 302–309, 368–72, 438, 527–30, 539, 545, 552–57, 560–65, 613–17, 622–24, 678, 699, 766, 782, 785–91.
[3] *Ibid.*, 305, 307, 370–72, 410–18, 566–613; ICC, *Rep.*, CIII, 317, 325–27.
[4] ICC, *Val. Rep.*, XLI, 700.

through various receiverships. In 1898 it passed to the newly organized Choctaw and Memphis, whose interests were identical with those of the Choctaw, Oklahoma and Gulf. Construction in the direction of Indian Territory was already underway, and in 1899, the two roads joined at the Arkansas state line.

The Choctaw, Oklahoma and Gulf continued to expand in Arkansas and the twin territories. A complicated struggle with the Missouri Pacific for a monopoly of the Hot Springs traffic ended with the Choctaw in possession of the Diamond Jo Line, with a connecting line from Butterfield to Haskell added to the original road. In 1900 the Choctaw leased the White and Black River Railroad and bought a line linking Searcy with Des Arc.

Meanwhile the western end of the Choctaw was pushing through Oklahoma and the Texas Panhandle to Amarillo. It built a line in Indian Territory from Haileyville to Ardmore to facilitate the movement of coal from the Choctaw Nation to Central Texas. A local company passed to it under the name Choctaw Northern. This road ran from Geary, Oklahoma, to Anthony, Kansas, with a branch from Ingersoll to the Santa Fe at Alva and an extension from the main line to Homestead. The Choctaw also took over the five-mile Tecumseh Railway Company and extended it to Asher.[5]

The Rock Island was acutely conscious of this rapidly expanding road because of the intense rivalry which developed between the two. The obvious solution was to secure control of the Choctaw, a step which the new Rock Island owners lost no time in taking. Soon thereafter they built a branch from Guthrie to Chandler.

The Leeds-Yoakum interests embarked on an impressive building program along the Choctaw in Arkansas. A connecting line from Des Arc to Mesa attached the disconnected Searcy and Des Arc to the parent company. In 1907 a new branch was extended from the main line at Ola to Dardanelle. A more ambitious project extended the Rock Island from near Little Rock to Alexandria, Louisiana. In the mid-nineties the Arkansas Southern Railroad and its affiliates built from El Dorado, Arkansas, to Winnfield, Louisiana. Late in 1902 the Rock Island came into possession of this trackage and organized subsidiaries which constructed lines from Haskell to El Dorado,

---

[5] *Ibid.*, XXIV, 819, 930, 939, 999, 1018–21, 1066; Holden, "The B I T . . . Building," *Chron. Okla.*, Vol. XI, 649, 661–64; Nevins, "Seventy . . . Service," *RIM*, Vol. XVII, 30, 39; Bill, "The . . . Railroad," *RIM*, Vol. XVII, 84–85.

Arkansas, and from Winnfield to Alexandria, Louisiana. All were consolidated as the Rock Island, Arkansas and Louisiana early in 1906. An extension from Alexandria to Eunice was soon added.

While developing its Arkansas network, the Rock Island entered the Missouri field by buying the St. Louis, Kansas City and Colorado, which had resumed construction and by 1902 had reached Strasburg, less than forty miles from Kansas City. The Rock Island closed the thirty-three-mile gap between Strasburg and its road at Leeds, thus giving itself a railroad across the state and an entrance into St. Louis. This road was operated after 1904 by the subsidiary Kansas City Rock Island Railway Company.

Texas was another field of activity. In the Panhandle the Rock Island crept westward from Amarillo to tap its El Paso road at Tucumcari, New Mexico, by 1910. Along the Fort Worth line a spur pushed from Bridgeport to Jacksboro, hesitated, then moved west to Graham. Meanwhile, the Rock Island had gathered its Texas roads, one across the northwest corner of the Panhandle, another the extension of the Choctaw through Amarillo, and a third from Red River to Fort Worth, into a single corporation, the Chicago, Rock Island and Gulf, with headquarters at Fort Worth.[6]

All other Rock Island projects in Texas were subordinated to Yoakum's desire to reach the Gulf over his own railroad. In 1902 he secured an amendment to the Rock Island charter to permit the building of a branch from Fort Worth to the Gulf. He built to Dallas and was grading beyond when E. H. Harriman offered what virtually amounted to one-half interest in major Southern Pacific subsidiaries leading to the Gulf in return for Yoakum's abandonment of his project. The state of Texas intervened, refusing to permit the two to unite any of their interests. Yoakum then turned his attention to a new railroad, the Trinity and Brazos Valley, which a group of Houstonians promoted to reach Fort Worth from their city. They built from Cleburne to Mexia before the Boston syndicate which was financing them lost confidence and withdrew. The Houston backers offered it to the Colorado and Southern and the Rock Island. Yoakum was on the board of directors of both corporations. When completed, the Trinity and Brazos Valley would give Yoakum his Gulf connection, so, with the backing of both companies, he took it over and

[6] ICC, *Val. Rep.*, XXIV, 711, 828, 855, 926, 930, 938, 999, 1034, 1044; Nevins, "Seventy ... Service," *RIM*, Vol. XVII, 31, 99; Reed, *Texas Railroads*, 407–409.

B. F. Yoakum, Entrepreneur

completed it from Mexia to Houston, with an extension north from Teague to Waxahachie and with trackage rights into Fort Worth and Dallas.[7]

Yoakum's third project was the Gulf Coast Lines. He hoped to build a line from Memphis to Brownsville by way of New Orleans and Houston and enter Mexico. The two basic lines were the Colorado Southern, New Orleans and Pacific Railway Company in Louisiana and the St. Louis, Brownsville and Mexico Railway Company in Texas.

The Texas corporation began building in August, 1903, from a point on the Texas Mexican at present Robstown, moving south to Brownsville and north to Algoa, a total of 350 miles along the Gulf Coast. Twenty-five miles north of Brownsville, at a point called Rattlesnake Junction, a fifty-mile branch followed the Río Grande to the town of Sam Fordyce. On this branch Yoakum purchased the unincorporated San Antonio and Rio Grande Valley extending from San Juan to Edinburg. Yoakum's original plan was to build from Houston to the Louisiana line, but he secured trackage rights into Houston, then purchased the Beaumont, Sour Lake and Western, a Beaumont project extending to the oil field at Sour Lake, and extended it to Houston.

The Louisiana line was delayed somewhat. In 1905, Yoakum secured a charter for the Colorado Southern, New Orleans and Pacific, providing for a road from Anchorage, opposite Baton Rouge, to the Texas line. He built almost the entire distance across Louisiana, but secured trackage rights over the Kansas City Southern from De Quincy, Louisiana, to Beaumont, Texas, to avoid the expense of bridging the Sabine. A trackage agreement with the Illinois Central gave him entrance into New Orleans from Baton Rouge, and with that he possessed a Gulf Coast road from New Orleans to the southernmost tip of Texas. The only branch in Louisiana was a line from Eunice to the Southern Pacific at Crowley. He purchased an East Texas lumber feeder, the Orange and Northwestern, and extended it to Newton.[8]

The first break in Yoakum's holdings occurred in 1909 when the Rock Island ran into financial difficulties. Yoakum dissociated himself from that company and formed a syndicate which took over the

[7] ICC, *Rep.*, CXLIX, 301, 318, 325, 335.
[8] ICC, *Val Rep.*, XXIX, 677, 685, 703, 729, 783, 800; Reed, *Texas Railroads*, 336–37.

Then Came the Railroads

Frisco and the lines along the Gulf. His ambition to expand continued, unabated, as he added mileage in Texas and Louisiana.[9]

The Colorado Southern, New Orleans and Pacific was reorganized as the New Orleans, Texas and Mexico in 1910, and a branch was added near its eastern end from Erwinville to Mix. Yoakum's next move was to organize the New Iberia Syndicate, which built two short lines centering at New Iberia. The southern coast of Texas was the scene of further activity. Yoakum added a number of branches in the Matagorda Bay area. At Brownsville he advanced funds to a local man, S. A. Robertson, to build a tight system of feeders radiating throughout that section to guard against outside intrusion, while allied interests took over the pioneer railroad from Point Isabel to Brownsville.

Yoakum did not ignore West Texas entirely. He extended the Fort Worth and Rio Grande to Menard. He took over and completed the Brownwood North and South, a local enterprise which bogged down before it reached its objective, the inland town of May, eighteen miles north of Brownwood. The Quanah, Acme and Pacific was another West Texas road in which the Frisco had an interest. It originated as a connecting link between the Frisco at Quanah and the Fort Worth and Denver City at Acme; in 1910, in building to Mac-Bain, it took the first step towards what was hoped to be a line to El Paso.[10]

The collapse of the Yoakum empire occurred in 1913. It was the inevitable result of extravagance and overexpansion. Yoakum's own construction syndicates did much of the building, reaping large profits which saddled the roads with heavy debts. Ill-advised branches sapped the profits from sound portions of the road. It was simply a matter of time until these twin burdens broke the back of the system. The Frisco went into receivership on May 27, 1913, and was ordered to divest itself of its coastal lines. It was transferred to a new corporation, the St. Louis–San Francisco Railway Company, in 1916. St. Louis and New York interests took over the Gulf Coast Lines after their reorganization. The Trinity and Brazos Valley went into receivership about a year after the Frisco and emerged years later as the Burlington–Rock Island, with joint ownership in the two systems whose name it bears.[11]

[9] ICC, *Val. Rep.*, XXXVI, 43–61; *ibid.*, XXXV, 940–42, 1078.
[10] *Ibid.*, XXIV, 686, 700, 750, 757, 770, 810, 818, 854; Reed, *Texas Railroads*, 343, 467; Allhands, *Uriah Lott*, 147–49.

B. F. Yoakum, Entrepreneur

Between the time of its reorganization and the entrance of the United States into the first World War, the Frisco added only a nine-mile oil-field line in Oklahoma.[12]

The Rock Island did not suffer so drastic a reorganization as did the Frisco after the separation of the two. The property was returned to its owners without a sale. The road added short but important lines in Arkansas. It secured its trackage between Benton and Little Rock from the Missouri Pacific and took over short lines from Malvern to Kent and from Mesa to Stuttgart.[13]

[11] ICC, *Rep.*, XXIX, 139–209; *ibid.*, CXLIX, 318; ICC, *Val. Rep.*, XLI, 309–12; Reed, *Texas Railroads*, 343; Ernest R. Dewsnup, "Recent Financial Investigations of the Interstate Commerce Commission," *AAA*, Vol. LXIII, 205–207.

[12] ICC, *Val. Rep.*, XLI, 304, 619–20.

[13] *Ibid.*, XXIV, 840, 1034; *ibid.*, XL, 651–53; Stuart Daggett, "Recent Railroad Failures and Reorganizations," *QJE*, Vol. XXXIII, 463, 485–86.

CHAPTER 29

Approaching Maturity

THE GIANTS of the Gulf Southwest added proportionately fewer miles of railroad than some of their smaller competitors in the first years of the twentieth century. The Missouri Pacific served an area already matured. The only additions to its lines were the construction of two short links in Missouri and the leasing of the Kiowa, Hardtner and Pacific in western Kansas.[1]

There was more activity along the Iron Mountain, which pushed an extension of the Cushman branch through the Ozarks to Carthage, Missouri, with a branch from Crane to Springfield; built a connecting line between Benton and Pine Bluff and an extension from Crossett to the Mississippi at Luna Landing; and acquired by purchase the Arkansas Central, which ran from Fort Smith to Paris. Early in the century it built from Little Rock to Hot Springs in order to compete with the Diamond Jo, but sold the trackage east of Benton to the Rock Island. A few years later the Iron Mountain tied its southeastern and northeastern Arkansas lines together with a river road from McGehee to Barton Junction.

The lines extending down into Louisiana were the most significant additions. The Iron Mountain purchased the New Orleans and Northwestern and the St. Louis, Watkins and Gulf, and through subsidiaries connected them with its lines in southern Arkansas. By 1910 the Iron Mountain and its various subsidiaries operated two prongs from opposite Natchez, Mississippi, into Arkansas, one terminating at McGehee, the other at El Dorado. Another road ran across Loui-

[1] ICC, *Val. Rep.*, XL, 463-65, 574-75.

siana from Lake Charles to Monroe, where it forked, one line extending northeast to McGehee, the other tapping the El Dorado prong at Felsenthal. A feeder from Litro to Farmerville rounded out the Louisiana lines. The only other important addition was the Arkansas cutoff from Marianna to West Memphis, completed in 1913.[2]

Two Texas roads closely associated with the Missouri Pacific added to their mileage. The Texas and Pacific constructed a line from Denison to Sherman Junction and acquired another recently completed line between Weatherford and Mineral Wells, which it extended to Graford. Its greatest expansion, however, was in Louisiana. It built its own road from Waskom to Shreveport and added branches at Donaldsonville, Bunkie, and Melville. The line from Port Allen to Ferriday was revived and completed in 1903. The Texas and Pacific purchased two new short roads joining Shreveport with Texarkana and Cypress with Natchitoches, then built a connecting link between them.[3]

The International and Great Northern revived briefly in the first three years of the new century to add considerable mileage to its system. Most of the building revolved around the Calvert, Waco and Brazos Valley Railroad, which had constructed a line from Bryan to Marlin, with a branch to Calvert, before passing to the International and Great Northern in 1901. The road was extended southeast from Bryan to Spring, with a branch from Navasota to Madisonville and another from Waco to Fort Worth.[4]

Another "Gould road," the Cotton Belt, expanded. Emerging from receivership in 1891, it remained under the guidance of Colonel Samuel W. Fordyce for thirteen years. It acquired three logging roads and connected them to create a line from Tyler to White City. In 1910 the Cotton Belt took over the Stephenville North and South Texas, which had gone deeply into debt building its original section from Stephenville to Hamilton, and added new roads from Hamilton to Gatesville and from Edson to Comanche. The Gray's Point Terminal, a connecting line between Delta and Illmo, was the most important addition in Missouri. The Cotton Belt also secured trackage rights over the Rock Island between Brinkley and Bridge Junction,

[2] *Ibid.*, 409–11, 613–15, 621, 624–26, 629–31, 635–42, 646, 649–51, 662; Thomas, *Arkansas*, 427.
[3] ICC, *Val. Rep.*, XXIX, 546–47, 584–96, 600, 608.
[4] ICC, *Rep.*, CXLIX, 609–10, 629–30, 647, 649–50.

Arkansas, and over the Iron Mountain from Delta, Missouri, to Paragould, Arkansas.[5]

Southern Pacific interests, now controlled by E. H. Harriman, made few changes which were not forced upon them by Yoakum. This rivalry was possibly the cause for an action by the Texas Railroad Commission to force the Southern Pacific to relinquish its eleven-year control of the San Antonio and Aransas Pass, a parallel and competing road which Harriman planned to extend to Alice, in the lower Río Grande Valley. Harriman complied technically by selling to friendly interests, and the extension was abandoned when it reached Falfurrias.

There were no significant Southern Pacific additions in Texas. Probably the most important was the joining of the Texas Trunk with the Sabine and East Texas by a line from their respective termini at Gossett and Rockland. This gave Dallas a direct connection with Beaumont and made the timber of East Texas accessible to the Southern Pacific. Branches from the Texas and New Orleans reached the Cotton Belt at Rusk and the newly developed Sour Lake oil field near Beaumont; the New York, Texas and Mexican added a few spurs around Matagorda Bay; the Austin and Northwestern built from Burnet to Lampasas, on the Santa Fe; and the San Antonio and Mexican Gulf pushed on to Cuero. On the eve of World War I the Texas and New Orleans acquired a logging railroad operating between Rockland and Turpentine, and the Houston and Texas Central opened a cutoff between Giddings and Hearne. A corporate change in the Southern Pacific lines had taken place in 1905 when half a dozen subsidiaries consolidated with the Galveston, Harrisburg and San Antonio.

Harriman's desire to control transportation in southern Louisiana and Yoakum's attempt to enter that area compelled the Southern Pacific to add by purchase and construction a number of branches between Lake Charles and New Orleans. Short spurs extended service to Weeks Island, Lockport, Port Barre, South End, and Mamou, while longer lines reached from Lafayette to near Anchorage, from Midland to F & A Junction by way of Abbeville, from Lake Charles to Lake Arthur, and from De Ridder to Lake Charles. With these additions, the Southern Pacific had a web across southern Louisiana.[6]

Of the earlier giants, the Santa Fe carried on the most ambitious

[5] *Ibid.*, 371, 405, 416–20, 424, 441, 472–78, 502, 509, 518, 531, 536, 550, 555, 569, 574, 576–78, 582.

[6] ICC, *Val. Rep.*, XXXIII, 811; *ibid.*, XXXVI, 339–401, 478, 510, 542, 551, 580, 630, 672, 811; Reed, *Texas Railroads*, 222–24, 247–48.

building program, primarily in Oklahoma and the Texas Panhandle. Eastern Kansas actually showed a decrease as three short spurs failed to offset abandonments. Southwestern Kansas also suffered some abandonments but made a substantial net gain because of a connecting line between Scott City and Garden City and extensions from Dodge City to Elkhart and from Kiowa to Belvidere. The Santa Fe did no building in south-central Kansas, but took over the St. Louis, Kansas and Southwestern and the Hutchinson and Southern.

In the last four years of the nineteenth century the Santa Fe began to establish itself along the northern boundary of the territories soon to be united as the state of Oklahoma. It extended the Hutchinson and Southern to Blackwell shortly before another Santa Fe property dropped almost due south from Hunnewell through Blackwell to Tonkawa. A local railroad to serve the Bartlesville oil field from Caney, Kansas, passed to the Santa Fe, which pushed construction south to Tulsa. Several subsidiaries jointly built from Guthrie by way of Enid to Kiowa, Kansas; others constructed a series of short roads forming a loop to the east of the original Santa Fe line across Oklahoma, leaving it at Newkirk to the north, passing through Stillwater and Shawnee, and then rejoining it again at Pauls Valley to the south, with an intermediate connecting link from Cushing to Guthrie. All eventually consolidated as the Eastern Oklahoma Railway. Meanwhile, new spurs along the original line furnished service to Cashion, Lindsay, and Sulphur. Shortly before World War I the Santa Fe secured an important line, the locally financed Oklahoma Central, which stretched from Lehigh to Chickasha. The Santa Fe also added some oil-field mileage in the Cushing area.[7]

Expansion in the Texas Panhandle and South Plains achieved two major objectives. One was an extension into New Mexico which gave the Santa Fe control of the Pecos Valley and a direct line from the Panhandle to the Pacific; the other was the creation of a network of feeders on the South Plains and a direct connection from West Texas to the Gulf. The first step was construction of a road from Panhandle City to Amarillo. Santa Fe plans then became closely tied to those of two New Mexico promoters, J. J. Hagerman and Charles B. Eddy, who were searching for rail outlets for the Pecos Valley. By 1894 they completed their Pecos River Railroad, from Pecos, Texas, on the Texas and Pacific, to Roswell, New Mexico. Hagerman built on to

[7] ICC, *Rep.*, CXVI, 847–54, 859–61; *ibid.*, CXXVII, 208, 211, 213–18, 311–19, 335, 448, 471, 492, 582–90, 638–45; Marshall, *Santa Fe*, 431–34.

Amarillo in 1899. Two years later the Santa Fe took over the Hagerman properties and in 1908 built west from Clovis to Dalles, New Mexico, thereby realizing a short cut from the Panhandle to the Pacific.

The first step in accomplishing the second objective was initiated in 1906 with the construction of a railroad from Canyon to Plainview, which was later extended through Lubbock to Coleman, where it joined the Gulf, Colorado and Santa Fe. It not only provided the desired Gulf connection, but furnished the backbone for feeders. The first such feeder, from Plainview to Floydada, was started as the Llano Estacado Railway and was taken over by the Santa Fe before the grading was finished. A second ran from Lamesa to Slaton. In 1912 the Santa Fe added a cutoff from Lubbock to Texico, thereby opening a new territory and giving it a trunk from Galveston to the Pacific, and three years later it took over the newly built Crosbyton–South Plains Railroad, which ran from Lubbock to Crosbyton. The previous year, it had regrouped its Texas holdings, incorporating all of those north of Coleman into the Panhandle and Santa Fe.[8]

The Gulf, Colorado and Santa Fe engaged in considerable building in East Texas, around Matagorda Bay, and in West Texas south of the Panhandle and Santa Fe territory. In East Texas it purchased two logging roads and linked them to form a continuous line from Beaumont through the timber to Longview. The new acquisition was tied into the remainder of the Santa Fe system by means of a connecting road from Silsbee to Navasota. In 1908 the Santa Fe purchased the Gulf and Interstate, which had been operating from Beaumont to Port Bolivar for the preceding twelve years, and built from Longview in the direction of Cass County iron deposits near Hughes Springs. The East Texas lines were also a means of penetrating the gloomy piney woods of Louisiana. The subsidiary Jasper and Eastern built from Kirbyville, Texas, to the Missouri Pacific at Oakdale, Louisiana. A spur from Bleakwood, Texas, reached Wiergate. Santa Fe expansion in the Matagorda Bay area involved the acquisition of the profitable little Cane Belt Railroad, which ran from Sealy to Bay City. It was extended to Matagorda.

The West Texas lines were later in developing than those in East Texas. In 1909 the increased production of livestock around San Angelo led to the incorporation of the Concho, San Saba and Llano Valley, which had financial backing from the Santa Fe. The road con-

[8] ICC, *Rep.*, CXVI, 831, 836; *ibid.*, CXXVII, 219, 590–606, 789, 799, 814–16, 827.

sisted of two disconnected segments, one from San Angelo to Sterling City, the other from Miles City to Paint Rock. Livestock development and liberal bonuses from inland towns induced the Santa Fe to build a hundred-mile extension west from Lometa to Eden to serve an area southeast of San Angelo.[9]

The Katy did not enjoy as spectacular a boom as did some roads, but it could boast a steady increase in mileage. At the beginning of the century it secured a newly built line in Missouri between McBaine and Columbia, another in Kansas running from Moran to Iola, and a third connecting Mineral, Kansas, with Joplin, Missouri, in the lead and zinc area. It added over four hundred miles in Oklahoma, constructing under the names of subsidiaries. In three years, starting from the terminus of the old Denison and Washita Valley, a line pushed northwest to Oklahoma City, turning northeast at that point to reach the Kansas boundary near Coffeyville. One branch extended southeast from Osage to intersect the original Katy line at Wybark, and another from Fallis extended to Guthrie. Another subsidiary built east from Krebs to Wilburton, and a connecting line from Kiowa tapped the Rock Island at Pittsburg, while several spurs served towns and industries a short distance off the main lines.

Development in Texas was carried on largely through the leasing of existing railroads. Under its own name, however, the Katy completed the San Marcos line to San Antonio. It took over a partially built road between Granger and Georgetown, extending it to Austin, and leased two new short lines running from Egan to Cleburne and from Denison to Bonham. It also bid for a share of West Texas trade by buying controlling interest in the Texas Central, which had been extended south from Ross to Waco and northwest from Albany to Rotan. The Katy immediately added a branch from De Leon to Cross Plains.

The most extensive of the new properties were those Texas and western Oklahoma lines centering at Wichita Falls. This West Texas city had risen to prominence in the railroad field because of the activities of J. A. Kemp and Frank Kell, a partnership which gave rise to the locally popular success formula: "Think like Kemp and work like Kell." Their initial venture into railroading was the Wichita Falls Railway, completed from Wichita Falls to Henrietta in 1895. Eleven years later they undertook the ambitious project of building from Wichita Falls along the western boundary of Oklahoma in the direc-

[9] *Ibid.*, CXXVII, 695, 712, 720, 729, 735, 744, 752, 767–69.

Then Came the Railroads

tion of Kansas. This line, the Wichita Falls and Northwestern, was finally completed in 1912 to Forgan, Oklahoma, 287 miles northwest of Wichita Falls, with a branch from Altus, Oklahoma, to Wellington, Texas. Another Kemp and Kell road, the Wichita Falls and Southern, was being built during the same period. Originally projected to reach Cisco, it actually got only as far as the coal fields at Newcastle. The Katy secured controlling interest in the Wichita Falls railroads in 1911.

The Katy leased properties in East Texas and on the Gulf. The Beaumont and Great Northern, running from Livingston to Weldon, passed to the Katy in 1914 through stock ownership and a lease. The Gulf property was much older. Completed in 1892 from Chenango to the port of Velasco, it was never a financial success because of a sand bar at the mouth of the Brazos River. It changed hands several times, finally passing to the Katy in 1915 under the name Houston and Brazos Valley. Newly discovered sulphur deposits at Freeport supplied it with revenue tonnage. Further expansion of the Katy was halted when, in 1915, it went into receivership.[10]

The Fort Worth and Denver City passed to the newly organized Colorado and Southern in 1898, with the Texas road retaining its identity. The only additions were those which were incorporated into its feeder system at Wichita Falls through affiliates of the Wichita Valley Railway Company. By 1909 the feeder to the south had reached the Texas and Pacific at Abilene, with a branch from Stamford to Spur, eighty miles to the northwest. Another feeder ran north from Wichita Falls to the Red River at Byers.[11]

The most recent of the important Southwestern railroads, John W. Gates' Kansas City Southern, made a few additions. Gates organized the Arkansas Western Railway and under its charter built from Heavener, Indian Territory, to Waldron, Arkansas, and eventually to Forester. Ten years later the little Poteau Valley Railroad, which had operated since 1900 in the Indian Territory from Shady Point to Calhoun, passed to the Kansas City Southern. Meanwhile, in 1905, Leonor F. Loree of the Delaware and Hudson began his thirty-two-year tenure as chairman of the board of the Kansas City Southern.[12]

[10] ICC, *Val. Rep.*, XXIX, 833–35, 846–50; *ibid.*, XXIV, 395, 397, 459–74, 531–33, 558–75, 581, 586, 600, 647, 672; *ibid.*, XLIV, 904, 917.

[11] ICC, *Rep.*, CXXIV, 612, 797–99, 809–11, 815, 821, 826–28.

[12] *Ibid.*, LXXV, 304, 308, 317, 400–424.

CHAPTER 30

The Newcomers

A NUMBER OF NEW railroad corporations made their appearance in the Gulf Southwest at the turn of the century. The most ambitious was the Kansas City, Mexico and Orient, a project conceived by Arthur E. Stilwell. At a testimonial dinner given in his honor shortly after his unwilling separation from the Kansas City, Pittsburg and Gulf, he outlined a plan for a railroad from Kansas City to Topolobampo, Mexico, on the Gulf of California. This line, he reported enthusiastically, would shorten the distance from Kansas City to Central and South America by sixteen hundred miles and to a Pacific Coast harbor by four hundred miles; it would tap the timber and mineral resources of Mexico and open many fertile valleys which awaited only irrigation and transportation. His enthusiasm inspired others, and on May 1, 1900, the Kansas City, Mexico and Orient was legally delivered.

Stilwell had already secured a start in Texas by discovering and buying a local enterprise which was ambitiously named the Panhandle and Gulf but which was struggling futilely to reach San Angelo from Sweetwater. Building in two directions from Sweetwater, the Orient extended south to San Angelo and north to Odell, on Red River. Meanwhile, construction in Kansas was begun at Milton, with one line building northeast to Wichita and another south through Oklahoma to intersect the Frisco at Foley. Stilwell secured trackage rights from Foley to near Clinton and gradually extended the line south to Odell, thereby giving the Orient a continuous road from Wichita to San Angelo by 1909.

Then Came the Railroads

During the next four years the Orient crept southwest in the general direction of the Big Bend country, reaching the Southern Pacific at Alpine in 1913. Meager local tonnage along the entire line, political repercussions arising from the overthrow of President Díaz in Mexico, and inability to complete the Mexican link across the western Sierra Madres spelled insolvency for the Orient before it reached Alpine. It clung to its precarious existence for years only because of the perseverance of William T. Kemper, the receiver, who secured various concessions from the national and state governments.[1]

Two railroads in Louisiana and Arkansas were to gain considerable prominence as independent companies before joining their fortunes with the Kansas City Southern. The Louisiana and Arkansas Railway was the work of William Buchanan, a Texas lumberman, who, in 1897, bought a logging road operating between Minden and Sibley, Louisiana, and extended it north to Cotton Valley. Buchanan acquired another short line running from Stamps, Arkansas, to Spring Hill, Louisiana, from the Bodcaw Lumber Company. He then created the Louisiana and Arkansas Railroad Company, merged the identity of the other roads into the new corporation, and linked them with a road from Cotton Valley to Spring Hill. In 1903 he built southwest to Jena and north to Hope, Arkansas. Later he added a branch from Packton to Pineville, Louisiana, and purchased a lumber road running west from Minden, which he extended to Shreveport. In 1913 Buchanan built from Jena to Wildsville Junction and in 1917 leased a segment of the Missouri Pacific into Ferriday, with trackage rights to Natchez, Mississippi.[2]

The Louisiana Railway and Navigation Company was the other Louisiana railroad which was to be associated with the Kansas City Southern. It was conceived by William Edenborn, who started it in 1897 as the Shreveport and Red River Valley. He constructed a line from Shreveport through Alexandria to Mansura, and was building on towards New Orleans, with a branch from Aloha to Winnfield, when he reorganized the company as the Louisiana Railway and Navigation Company. The road was completed in 1906 and became the second to cross the state diagonally from Shreveport to New Orleans.[3]

The only other new railroad in the area with a fairly extensive mileage was the Louisiana and North West, which, starting in 1890, possessed a connecting line between the Cotton Belt at Magnolia,

[1] ICC, *Rep.*, CXXXV, 205–208, 217, 229–35, 243, 246.
[2] *Ibid.*, CXXXIII, 704, 716–18, 721–23.
[3] *Ibid.*, CVI, 49, 59.

The Newcomers

Arkansas, and the Texas and Pacific at Natchitoches, Louisiana, by 1905. It has maintained a separate existence to the present, although it has suffered a number of abandonments.[4]

The Missouri and North Arkansas was the most important Arkansas line dating from this period. Originating as the Eureka Springs Railroad as early as 1883, it served that resort town from Seligman, Missouri. In 1900 it took the name St. Louis and North Arkansas and built from Junction, on the original line, southeast to Leslie, adding a branch from Freeman to Berryville. It was soon reorganized as the Missouri and North Arkansas, constructed a section from Neosho to Wayne, Missouri, and secured trackage rights into Joplin. It extended east to Helena before going into receivership in 1912.[5]

Three independent lines served Indian Territory. Between 1901 and 1903, the Fort Smith and Western built from Coal Creek, on the Kansas City Southern, to Guthrie, almost two hundred miles, and secured trackage rights over the Kansas City Southern into Fort Smith and over the Katy from Fallis to Oklahoma City. In 1906 it added by purchase the three-year-old St. Louis, El Reno and Western, which ran from Guthrie to El Reno.

A Philadelphia syndicate built the Midland Valley, second of the new Indian Territory roads. It was launched from Hartford, Arkansas, in 1903 to serve the coal mining town of Greenwood. This first line became a branch as the main line was developed from Excelsior, Arkansas, to Silverdale, Kansas, with trackage rights over the Missouri Pacific into Arkansas City. The opening of the Glenn Pool oil field, seven miles off the main line, led to the building of a branch from Jenks in 1907. By 1911 a Kansas subsidiary had extended the Midland Valley into Wichita.

The Missouri, Oklahoma and Gulf, third of the Indian Territory lines, had a number of predecessors, one of which built a railroad from Wagoner to Muskogee. By 1910 the successor corporation had built from Muskogee to Red River and from Wagoner to the Kansas line. Affiliated companies built from their respective state borders to Denison, Texas, and to Baxter Springs, Kansas, giving this company well over three hundred miles of railroad. It went into receivership in 1913 and did not emerge until after World War I.[6]

[4] *Ibid.*, CXXXV, 865–67, 880.
[5] *Ibid.*, CXXV, 639, 647, 658–60, 666–73.
[6] *Ibid.*, CXXXV, 577, 580, 596, 608–18; *ibid.*, CXLI, 389, 402, 417–20, 439–44; *ibid.*, CXLIII, 878–80, 891, 893; Holden, "The B I T . . . Building," *Chron. Okla.*, Vol. XI, 665.

Then Came the Railroads

E. J. Buckingham of St. Louis was the moving spirit in developing a railroad which extended from Crystal City, Texas, where Buckingham held much land, to a connection with the Southern Pacific at Uvalde. Control passed to a St. Louis banking syndicate, which renamed the road the San Antonio, Uvalde and Gulf and added a line which swung in a loop through Gardendale and Pleasanton to San Antonio, with a tangent from Pleasanton to Corpus Christi. What had been a profitable road was now burdened by nonpaying segments which forced it into receivership in the summer of 1914.[7]

Many short lines appeared throughout the Southwest to serve specialized local industry. Timber was the most frequent incentive. Starting from some point on a major carrier, logging roads wandered through the forests to sawmills, which they served until the timber was exhausted, after which they were shifted to other points. The region of most intense activity lay south of a line running diagonally across Arkansas, slightly north of the Missouri Pacific and flaring somewhat south of Malvern to include the southeastern corner of Oklahoma, then following the headwaters of the Sabine and the Trinity to encompass the forested areas of East Texas and Louisiana. Northwestern Arkansas also had a number of logging roads. Far to the southwest the Uvalde and Northern existed only to haul cedar posts and firewood from Camp Wood. A few lumber roads survived bankruptcy and merger, remaining as feeders for main lines along which the timber was not entirely exhausted and, in some localities, assisting in the restoration of a small agricultural economy on the cutover lands.[8]

The petroleum industry was responsible for many miles of railroad. Major carriers raced to new discoveries, notably to Spindletop and Glenn Pool in the early days. In Oklahoma, John Ringling's line from Ardmore to Healdton (later to become a part of the Santa Fe), the Oil Fields Short Line, which served the Dilworth field during its years of prosperity, and the Okmulgee Northern were the direct result of the opening of new oil fields; the Sand Springs Railway, built to serve the Sand Springs Orphans' Home, drew the bulk of its tonnage from oil refineries and related industrial development.[9]

[7] ICC, *Rep.*, CXLI, 244–46.
[8] *Ibid.*, CIII, 372, 376, 490; *ibid.*, CVI, 47–59, 689–98, 714–30; *ibid.*, CVIII, 539–53, 629–49, 721–37; *ibid.*, CX, 429–50; *ibid.*, CXIV, 626–38; *ibid.*, CXVI, 864–75; *ibid.*, CXIX, 68–80, 535–51; *ibid.*, CXXI, 166–72; *ibid.*, CXXX, 308–25; ICC, *Val. Rep.*, XXV, 165, 173; *ibid.*, XLIII, 228–40, 265–76, 319–30, 561–71; Reed, *Texas Railroads*, 482–87.

The Newcomers

Coal was another product which attracted railroads. Short lines supplemented the numerous spurs of major roads. The Fort Smith, Subiaco and Rock Island, operating between Paris and Scranton, Arkansas, is one which survived. The Texas Short Line served both the coal mine at Alba and the salt works at Grand Saline. Lead and allied products were responsible for a number of smaller railroads in both southeastern Missouri and the great tri-state field. Along the Mississippi the present Missouri-Illinois Railroad Company, successor to the Mississippi River and Bonne Terre, was the product of lead mines, while the Northeast Oklahoma and, later, the Miami Mineral Belt served the tri-state district. Both of the Oklahoma roads survived, one independently, the other as part of the Frisco.[10]

The tremendous bauxite deposits west of Little Rock, Arkansas, led aluminum interests to build the Bauxite and Northern in 1906. The Brimstone Railroad and Canal Company, in southwestern Louisiana, operated from 1905 until 1930 to serve a sulphur mine. The Texas State Railroad originated in 1894 as an auxiliary to the penitentiary at North Rusk and also as part of an unsuccessful effort to develop low-grade iron ore. By 1904 it had reached the International and Great Northern at Palestine.[11]

Many railroads came into existence to save inland towns from extinction or to guard trade territories from near-by rivals. The little Cassville and Exeter in southeastern Missouri, the Paris and Mount Pleasant in northeast Texas, and the Beaver, Meade and Englewood in the Oklahoma Panhandle served such local purposes.

Several railroads, notably in western Oklahoma, Texas, and Kansas, were the product of agricultural development, either actual or potential. Frank Kell built the Clinton and Oklahoma Western with the immediate objective of serving the farmers of the Washita Valley. The railroad crept up the river from Clinton to Strong City, but stopped before it reached Cheyenne. The Cheyenne Short Line, a project of disgruntled townsfolk who feared the loss of their county seat, eventually passed to Kell and merged with the other railroad.[12]

[9] ICC, *Rep.*, CXIV, 467–78; ICC, *Val. Rep.*, XXIX, 186–209; George and Wood, "The . . . Oklahoma," R&LHS *Bull. No. 60,* 13, 36, 57, 70.

[10] ICC, *Rep.*, CVIII, 141–53, 186–99, 758–73; *ibid.*, CXIV, 211–21; *ibid.*, CXIX, 94–111; ICC, *Val. Rep.*, XXV, 142, 151, 259; *ibid.*, XLV, 867–86; *ibid.*, XLIII, 701–10; George and Wood, "The . . . Oklahoma," R&LHS *Bull. No. 60,* 14–15, 44, 55–56, 64.

[11] ICC, *Rep.*, CXXI, 474–94; *ibid.*, CXLI, 445–63; ICC, *Val. Rep.*, XXXIV, 276–91; ICC, *Stat. Rys., 1931,* 248.

[12] ICC, *Rep.*, LXXXIV, 369, 375; *ibid.*, CIII, 631; *ibid.*, CX, 212–19; *ibid.*, CXIV, 266–73; *ibid.*, CXVI, 63–71, 260, 265, 272, 458–74; George and Wood, "The . . . Oklahoma," R&LHS *Bull. No. 60,* 17–19.

In West Texas the Gulf, Texas and Western was building west from Jacksboro; the Abilene and Southern had two disconnected lines—from Anson to Hamlin and from Abilene to Ballinger; the Roscoe, Snyder and Pacific linked Roscoe with Fluvanna; and the Pecos Valley Southern connected Toyahvale with Pecos. All of these agricultural roads were most active about 1909. The latter two still maintain an independent existence, but the others have since been absorbed. South of San Antonio the Artesian Belt Railway penetrated a potential irrigated district, permitting one C. F. Simmons to develop his lands and giving him an outside connection with the International and Great Northern at Kirk; farther south, on the International and Great Northern, the Asherton and Gulf extended from Artesia Wells to the lands of Asher Richardson at Asherton. The Sugar Land Railroad, below Houston, originated in the eighties as private industrial trackage to serve the E. H. Cunningham cane plantation, but in 1908 it passed to W. T. Eldridge, who developed it as a common carrier.

Far to the north the Garden City Sugar and Land Company, refiners and landowners in Finney and Kearny counties, Kansas, built the Garden City Western in 1915 to serve beet growers. Between 1913 and 1917 the ill-fated Anthony and Northern managed to construct a hundred miles of track through the wheat fields of Kansas before going into receivership. It struggled through another twenty years under the name Wichita Northwestern, only to succumb in 1940.[13]

World War I ended a fruitful era of railroad development. Twentieth-century building had been concentrated largely in the Gulf Southwest, with the major activity occurring before 1907. Oklahoma and Indian Territory, with a meager 1,200 miles in operation in 1890, had almost doubled by 1900 and had swelled to barely under 6,000 by 1910; the next ten years accounted for less than 600 miles. Arkansas added 1,200 miles in the last decade of the nineteenth century, 1,800 more to exceed 5,000 by 1910, and then added only 240 miles in the next ten years. Neighboring Louisiana's mileage increased from 1,660 to more than 2,800 between 1890 and 1900, almost doubled by 1910, but decreased during the next decade. Although Missouri added more than 2,000 miles between 1890 and 1910, the actual increase was considerably less than that of any Gulf Southwest state

[13] ICC, *Rep.*, LXXXIV, 488, 494; *ibid.*, XCVII, 17, 23, 29–41, 44, 51, 136, 144, 151, 524; *ibid.*, CIII, 603–607; *ibid.*, CVI, 587–97; *ibid.*, CVIII, 660–76; *ibid.*, CXVI, 71–81; *ibid.*, CXLIII, 850–61; *ibid.*, CCXLII, 613–16; ICC, *Stat. Rys., 1919*, 790; *ibid., 1940*, 548.

Courtesy Fort Worth Chamber of Commerce

The Texas Spring Palace at Fort Worth in 1889.

Fort Worth in 1849.

Courtesy Fort Worth Chamber of Commerce

Courtesy St. Louis–San Francisco Railway Company

Frisco steam locomotive.

The Santa Fe *Chief*, operating between Chicago and Los Angeles.

Courtesy Santa Fe Railway

The Newcomers

except Kansas, whose mileage was declining before 1900. Texas varied from all the other states. With the largest actual increase in each decade after 1890, its proportionate increase was less than that of any contiguous state, but after the others had reached almost complete maturity in 1910, Texas continued to add considerable mileage.[14]

With the exception of Texas and, to a less degree, Oklahoma, the mild panic of 1907 marked the end of extensive railroad building in the Gulf Southwest, just as the economic dislocation of 1893 had terminated Kansas building when it reached the saturation point. The familiar pattern of gradual recovery, followed by accelerated construction, with a depression at the time when the system was essentially complete, was re-enacted, but with one other familiar feature—future construction was more limited geographically than it had been before. Only in the very new sections of the Southwest was there a field for further expansion.

[14] Walter Williams, *The State of Missouri*, 261; Slason Thompson, *A Short History of American Railways*, App. B.

CHAPTER 31

Further Population Shifts

THE UNITED STATES increased its population by one-fifth between 1900 and 1910. Except for Oklahoma and West Texas, the Gulf Southwest was below that figure. Generally speaking, the entire sweep of land embracing Missouri and Kansas had reached agricultural maturity. The outstanding exception was western Kansas, rebounding from the effects of the drouth which had all but depopulated many counties and had drained heavily on others. Population in Orient territory increased 50 per cent, and that along Santa Fe extensions even more rapidly. It doubled around Dodge City and Garden City, and all but tripled near Scott City. Three counties in the extreme southwest, on the line from Dodge City to Elkhart, had dropped to less than 1,400 in 1900; by 1910 they had 4,800. The remarkable recovery of southwestern Kansas, destined by nature to remain sparsely settled, was undoubtedly aided by railroads. Only two counties—Stanton and Grant—did not surpass their previous top population of 1890 by substantial majorities; they were the only two without railroads.

The doubling of the population of Oklahoma between 1900 and 1910 represented the last push of the frontier into new lands. While the remainder of the state grew, western Oklahoma remained sparsely settled because of its semiaridity and its scant transportation facilities. Climatic conditions dictated sparsity, but those western counties with railroads did increase somewhat. Those which had none actually declined between 1907 and 1910.

Further Population Shifts

West Texas developed at a most startling pace as the frontier was reduced. The Wichita Falls lines and the Orient served an interstitial area. A few hardy pioneers had seeped in shortly after the Civil War, but the region had grown slowly. Seven of the sixteen counties were without railroads in 1900; only two were not served within the next ten years. From 83,000 in 1900, the population increased to 189,000 in 1910. The two counties without railroads increased from 8,000 to 12,500, while the five securing their first lines jumped from 20,000 to almost 70,000. Meanwhile, the magic of transportation and dry-land farming methods had converted the Panhandle–South Plains into the fastest-growing section of Texas, and its population increased from 80,000 to 270,000 in the decade ending in 1910.[1]

Only in West Texas and western Oklahoma were there new lines of real importance during the war decade. The effect of the railroads on both was disappointing. Much of the area was grazing land, and, after the first enthusiastic rush, there was a general decline. Railroads could neither attract nor hold settlers except in those areas susceptible to agricultural development. The Texas Panhandle counties which turned to wheat and grain sorghum grew at a comfortable rate. The South Plains area centering about Lubbock and Plainview, where ranches were being broken up into farms, also expanded. Here the counties along the Santa Fe feeders doubled their populations; those without railroads grew half as fast.[2]

Many railroads continued to maintain active colonization departments. The Kansas City Southern published a quarterly bulletin featuring its agricultural possibilities and cities. The Santa Fe's *Earth* and the Rock Island's *Western Trail* (later called *The South West Trail*) were monthly publications distributed in numbers running as high as 100,000. As late as 1912 the Santa Fe issued a bulletin, *Free Lands in the Southwest,* which included a synopsis of the Homestead and Desert Land Acts and a listing of unoccupied public lands in Kansas, Oklahoma, New Mexico, and Colorado.

The Rock Island and the successful cultivation of rice came to the Grand Prairie of Arkansas together. The railroad lost no time in advertising this new agricultural development, distributing great numbers of descriptive circulars in Illinois and Iowa. For fifteen years thereafter, German-Americans from those states streamed into Prairie

---

[1] "Population," *Fourteenth Census,* III, 91–97, 344–53, 393–98, 551–61.
[2] *Ibid.*, 817–23, 990–1014.

Then Came the Railroads

and Arkansas counties, founding their own settlements of Stuttgart and Ulm.[3]

B. F. Yoakum carried his promotional enthusiasm over into the field of colonization. His general immigration agent for the Frisco, Samuel A. Hughes, formed the Frisco System Land and Immigration Association in 1904. Although this organization was never officially a part of the Frisco railroad, its offices adjoined those of Hughes in St. Louis. The membership included realtors throughout the United States. The Frisco campaign was directed primarily towards advertising its own territory; it incidentally encouraged migration to the lower Río Grande Valley, which was served by Yoakum's St. Louis, Brownsville and Mexico. This road was also active and at times had an annual budget of $25,000 for advertising its lands. In the first eight months of 1905 it handled 251 emigrant outfits; in 1906 it brought in 11,700 homeseekers with special round-trip fares of $15, valid from Chicago, Minneapolis, or St. Louis to Brownsville. Brownsville was so crowded with potential land buyers that on occasion the hotels were forced to place as many as six persons in each room.[4]

Several railroads were built for the specific purpose of breaking up great ranches. This was true of the Asherton and Gulf and the Crosbyton–South Plains. The Farwell brothers of Chicago, dominant figures in the XIT Ranch, encouraged the Rock Island to build into the Panhandle because they wished to dispose of their surplus lands. The San Antonio and Aransas Pass, the Quanah, Acme and Pacific, the Wichita Falls and Northwestern, and the West Texas branches of the Rock Island, the Santa Fe, and the Denver, brought about the splitting up of ranches in the areas they served.[5]

Railroad influence on town growth was seldom identifiable in the more mature states of the Gulf Southwest after 1900, but was still traceable in parts of Texas and Oklahoma. One such place was the Brownsville, Texas, area. The town itself realized its most rapid growth with the building of Robertson's web of local lines and with the irrigation project which converted the valley into citrus-fruit orchards and truck farms. A tributary region experienced its first extensive town building early in the century. B. F. Yoakum returned to the area where he had promoted railroads fifteen years before and

---

[3] Fletcher, *Arkansas*, 358–59.

[4] Allhands, *Uriah Lott*, 167; information from C. B. Michelson, director of agricultural development, Frisco Lines.

[5] Reed, *Texas Railroads*, 431; ICC, *Rep.*, CXVI, 836–38; information from Arthur W. Large.

built from what eventually became Robstown to Brownsville without passing through a town which was not his own creation. One hundred and sixteen miles south of Robstown he constructed a branch from Rattlesnake Junction, now Harlingen, to newly built Mission, platting the half-dozen intermediate stations as he went.[6]

The Panhandle and South Plains areas waited for the new century, when railroads and the conversion of ranches brought dozens of towns. Amarillo redoubled its population ten times to surpass fifteen thousand in 1920. Lubbock and Plainview dominated an area farther south. Neither had been listed in the census of 1900, but both had attained populations of about four thousand in 1920.[7]

The greatest changes took place in Oklahoma. Extensive railroad building added many towns and boomed older ones. Oklahoma City became the most important marketing and distributing center in the twin territories after the arrival of its two new lines; Shawnee's three railroads, two of which maintained shops there, built it into a substantial city. Ada grew rapidly after securing its first line.

Tulsey Town was a nondescript post office in the Creek Nation before it got a railroad. Even after the Atlantic and Pacific reached the village, it remained a vicious little community, the haunt of lawless whites, enjoying the excitement of seasonal cattle shipments but having no particularly bright prospects until June 21, 1901, when the oil well across the river at Red Fork came in. Four years later fabulous Glenn Pool established the town, now dignified by the name of Tulsa, as an oil center. It became an important city by virtue of its vast oil resources, but its several railroads speeded that growth. Bartlesville, Sapulpa, and the old Creek capital of Okmulgee trace their development to a combination of transportation and oil, with oil the dominant factor.

Although such places as Henryetta, in old Indian Territory, and Carmen and Fairview to the northwest date from early in the century, greater activity was taking place southwest of Oklahoma City in an area experiencing later reservation openings. Many of the new towns were born with the coming of the railroads; others were villages denied a chance to grow without transportation. Anadarko, Duncan, and Waurika were the larger stations on the Rock Island, while Law-

[6] "Population," *Twelfth Census,* I, 461; *ibid., Fifteenth Census,* I, 600, 627, 1056; AGS, *Missouri,* 200–202, 427; AGS, *Louisiana,* 67, 481–82; J. H. Welch, "Thanks to Two Railroad Trail Breakers," *TF&C* (Dec., 1937), 5, 18; Reed, *Texas Railroads,* 331–33; Allhands, *Uriah Lott,* 129–39.

[7] "Population," *Fifteenth Census,* I, 1056, 1090; AGS, *Texas,* 160–64, 483, 522–23.

ton and Chickasha were on both the Rock Island and the Frisco. Far to the northwest, at the end of the Wichita Falls and Northwestern, Forgan was the last of the purely railroad towns in Oklahoma.[8]

Except in the most limited areas, railroads would never again dictate the movement of population and the rise of new towns. The major cities and most of the smaller communities were established. Arable lands were occupied. The role of the railroad in the future was to be that of bringing to more complete maturity an area which it had largely populated but which now no longer required an active program of colonization.

[8] "Population," *Fifteenth Census,* I, 18–19, 878; AGS, *Oklahoma,* 131–35, 142–47, 181–85, 192–96, 205–10, 224, 230–33, 250, 263–73, 288, 323–28, 345–50, 372–78, 385, 392; Carl C. Rister, *Oil! Titan of the Southwest,* 22–24, 94, 136, 142; Angie Debo, *Tulsa—From Creek Town to Oil Capital,* ch. V.

CHAPTER 32

Farming in the Dust

IT REQUIRED no particular acumen for railroad builders to conclude that their ventures were not sound unless there were patrons who needed transportation facilities. They laid the groundwork early by engaging in extensive colonization activities, but they were tardier in realizing that it was also good business to encourage the most effective utilization of the land. The agricultural departments, when they were finally developed, extended the activities of colonization agents by working with farmers who had been induced to try their fortunes in a new region.

At the same time, railroads were improving their facilities and were giving closer attention to schedule-making in the interests of faster, more convenient service. The improvement of refrigerator cars was only one notable illustration of the change which was taking place in rolling stock. The sale on eastern markets of fruits and berries from Louisiana and Arkansas, citrus fruits from the lower Río Grande Valley, and vegetables from the Texas "Winter Garden" became possible only through the development of refrigerator cars and the constant improvement in train service.

The first conscious agricultural-development work was carried on by colonization departments as incidental to the major task of peopling the country. The Fort Worth and Denver City, for example, has no record of such work until later, but newspaper reports of 1888 mention an agricultural survey of the Panhandle by R. A. Cameron,[1] that railroad's emigration agent, to determine the feasibility of irri-

[1] Tascosa *Pioneer*, March 10, 1888 and April 14, 1888.

gation on the Plains. Two of the most energetic of the railroad builders, Stilwell and Yoakum, used their colonization departments to carry on extensive agricultural programs.

No man ever worked more diligently to create revenue traffic than did Arthur E. Stilwell. As the Kansas City, Pittsburg and Gulf built south, he interested others in investing in its territory to prove the potentialities of the land. One group of promoters bought 4,500 acres of Ozark land, and within two years had 1,600 acres planted to fruit trees. In a few years other growers added 3,000 acres. Stilwell inspired another group to buy land near Port Arthur and plant rice.[2]

B. F. Yoakum was a leader in agricultural betterment on the Gulf Coast. He resurrected an earlier technique in initiating a program for the territory served by the St. Louis, Brownsville and Mexico. The area had developed very slowly, but Yoakum was convinced that it could be adapted to farming. He invited leading agricultural educators from all parts of the United States to be his guests on an excursion through the territory, with the request that they evaluate it. The majority reached the conclusion that the land was suited to orchards and truck gardens, whereupon Yoakum set aside $50,000 to carry on his campaign. Most of the money was spent on direct colonization effort, but a considerable sum was used in circulating literature combining the advertising of the country with information on truck gardening and fruit growing. This launched the highly specialized agriculture for which the area became famous.[3]

Almost all of the southwestern lines had entered the field of agricultural education by the early part of the century. They finally realized that an immediate increase in population was not necessarily the best measure of the success of their colonizing activities. In the words of a colonization agent of a later period: "A well satisfied settler is a good asset. A misplaced man is a liability. Our interest does not close with the location of the settler. We are deeply interested in his success."[4] It was simply good business for railroads to help their patrons achieve the highest degree of prosperity.

A survey conducted in 1912 disclosed that thirty-three southwestern railroads, serving counties in which 96 per cent of the farms were located, were giving attention to agricultural development. This

[2] K C P & G Ry. Co., *Ann. Rep., 1898*, 8–9; information from J. M. Prickett.

[3] "Missouri Pacific Stimulates Agricultural Program," *Ry. A.*, Vol. LXXXV, 449–51; Reed, *Texas Railroads*, 251; information from Arthur W. Large.

[4] C B & Q R. Co., *Western Agriculture and the Burlington*, 52, quoting Val Kuska.

Farming in the Dust

was the highest average in the United States. The most intensive programs were in Kansas, Oklahoma, Arkansas, Missouri, and Texas.[5]

The divorcing of agricultural work from colonization began in the early 1900's. The Missouri Pacific appointed its first agricultural agent in 1905, but the panic of 1907 terminated his activities temporarily. Soon the Missouri Pacific and the Iron Mountain each created the post of agricultural commissioner, an arrangement which continued until 1917, when the offices of the two were consolidated.[6]

The problems of newcomers to the semiarid Plains country were particularly acute. Thousands of farmers from the East faced failure simply because they were ignorant of the best dry-land farming methods. No one was more aware of the situation than C. L. Seagraves, general colonization agent for the Santa Fe. He convinced the company that it should hire an agricultural expert, and in January, 1910, J. D. Tinsley, a soils specialist at New Mexico A. and M. College, joined the Santa Fe staff. Six months later Seagraves employed Harry M. Bainer, professor of agriculture at Colorado A. and M. Both men were given the names of newcomers and were told to help them. Traveling in every conceivable type of conveyance, they pioneered educational work for four years before the Smith-Lever Act created the Agricultural Extension Service.[7]

The Frisco program was largely the achievement of C. B. Michelson; the Rock Island entered the field with H. M. Cottrell, previously associated with the land grant colleges of Kansas and Colorado, in charge. All major railroads followed and in some cases added agents in such specialized fields as dairying, marketing, poultry raising, and horticulture.[8]

Agricultural agents turned for aid to the United States Department of Agriculture and state agricultural boards, farm implement manufacturers, distributors of feeds and fertilizers, processors, and various farm organizations. Their relations with land grant colleges were particularly close. They asked personnel from agricultural colleges to participate as lecturers and demonstrators and used experiment-station findings as the basis for their own programs. After the Agricultural Extension Service was established, railroads turned over

[5] Andrews, *Railroads and Farming*, 11–18, 46–47.
[6] Information from Mo. Pac. Ag. Dev. Dept.
[7] Information from Harry M. Bainer.
[8] Information from C. B. Michelson.

many of their activities to that agency, but continued to co-operate with it very closely.[9]

The programs were multifold in purpose, but their most obvious function was to increase production. This included encouraging the adoption of the best tillage methods, popularizing new crops, and educating farmers in the values of planting good seed for higher yields. Railroad agricultural agents also worked out programs designed to eradicate the myriad of natural enemies, plant and animal, which were a constant threat to farm income. Diversification campaigns stressed the need for well-rounded land utilization.

Production programs were trimmed to fit the needs of an area. In parts of the Gulf Southwest better adapted to such pursuits as exploiting timber or minerals, agricultural education was held to a minimum until, with the exhaustion of other natural resources, the soil saved these regions from complete abandonment. In the older rural areas railroads popularized new methods, but it was in the semiarid Southwest that agricultural education achieved its most striking results. There, where settlement was new, where the possibilities were not yet appreciated, and where farmers had to adjust themselves to dry-land tillage, the opportunities for educational work were unlimited.

Marketing was second only to production in importance. Agricultural agents devoted much time to a study of marketing conditions and acquainted their patrons with the customs of local and special markets. They encouraged the grading of farm produce and advised on packaging. They helped solve complicated tariff problems, particularly those involving intermediate stops for processing before the product reached the consumer. While building good will, marketing programs added to the prosperity of communities and, incidentally, reduced the number of claims arising from haphazard packing and marketing.

Railroads were among the first to recognize the need for soil conservation. When the first lines opened broad new areas to cultivation, the wastefulness of "soil-mining" seemed of little consequence when compared to the rapid subjugation of the land. Since the farmers' goal was the highest yield with a minimum labor force, the accepted practice was to crop the land continuously, fertilize little, if at all, and move on when production declined. The census report of 1880 took

---

[9] Andrews, *Railroads and Farming,* 10–11; information from Harry M. Bainer, C. B. Michelson, and Arthur W. Large.

cognizance of the situation without becoming too concerned. "The word 'indignant' would often better express the feeling aroused in those [European] writers by their contemplation of our dealing with the soil, which from their point of view, they cannot but regard as wasteful, wanton, earth butchery."[10] The narrator agreed that the waste was economically justifiable but warned such a system could not last indefinitely. The very fact that railroads became interested in dry-land farming methods is indicative of the fact that the limits had indeed been reached and that newcomers would have to stake their future on less desirable lands.

Railroads developed a two-fold program in the development of soil resources. On the one hand, they promoted the utilization of lands which heretofore had not been occupied; on the other, they educated the landowners in the best conservation practices.

The problem of protecting the land from wind erosion was particularly important on the Plains. Since stock raising was basic to a diversified program, railroads consistently advised that much of the land either be left in native grasses or planted to permanent pastures. For cultivated fields, the primary concern was conservation of both soil and moisture. Santa Fe agricultural agents began to struggle with this problem when they were first employed, and by 1911 they were preaching contour farming. The Department of Agriculture depended on the railroads to carry this phase of conservation directly to the people.

Arid lands susceptible to irrigation were widely advertised. Many communities in western Kansas and Oklahoma, the Texas Panhandle, and the valleys of the Pecos and the Río Grande awaited only adequate development of irrigation projects to become prosperous. The Santa Fe deviated from the norm only in the extensiveness of the irrigated areas which it served and advertised. Several years before World War I it was publicizing the Pecos Valley of Texas and New Mexico and the shallow-water district in West Texas which subsequently gave Hereford, Plainview, Muleshoe, Lubbock, and other towns a major reason for existence. A few years later the Santa Fe became interested in projects at Ulysses and Scott City, Kansas. The St. Louis, Brownsville and Mexico established farms in the lower Río Grande Valley to demonstrate the best methods while irrigation was still new to that area.[11]

---

[10] "Statistics on Agriculture," *Tenth Census*, III, xxx.
[11] Harry M. Bainer, *Diversified Farming in the Southwest*, 16; A T & S F Ry. Co.,

Then Came the Railroads

Various methods were employed to sell the over-all educational program to farmers. Agricultural agents gradually took over the colonization magazines and contributed widely to rural newspapers and farm periodicals. To the many thousands of government bulletins which they distributed among their patrons, railroads added their own specialized publications. While all issued such literature, none surpassed the Santa Fe in either variety or total number. This railroad published twenty-three strictly agricultural bulletins, as well as many others which had considerable agricultural information. Distribution ranged from 5,000 to 100,000 copies. These publications discussed such topics as diversification, dairying, poultry raising, silo building, fruit and vegetable storage, pest control, and the cultivation of specific field crops.[12]

Railroads encouraged farm conferences and associations. They made the arrangements and frequently furnished lecturers. The Missouri Pacific entered the field in the fall of 1906 when it joined with the agricultural colleges of Kansas and Missouri in promoting the Farmers' Institute held that fall and winter. That same year, it helped to organize poultry associations in the two states. Every major southwestern railroad was soon engaged, assisting in the organization of local corn, cotton, rice, fig, peach, grape, and citrus growers, poultry, cattle, and swine breeders and nurserymen and beekeepers.[13]

Agricultural agents made use of visual education. Probably no one advertising medium had a greater popular appeal than the demonstration trains which were so effective in the subhumid Southwest, with its new and peculiar problems. Filled with charts, implements, livestock, and other exhibits, they stood on rural sidings for all to see. Lecturers explained the purpose for which each was run while attendants distributed literature. The first such train was operated by the Rock Island in Iowa. Professor Perry G. Holden, director of the experiment station at Iowa State College, was alarmed by the steady decline in the state's corn yield. Through field tests he verified his own theories concerning proper corrective measures. His next prob-

---

Shallow Water Country of Northwest Texas and *The Pecos Valley of Texas and New Mexico;* information from Mo. Pac. Ag. Dev. Dept. and Lee Lyles, asst. to pres., A T & S F Ry. Co.

[12] Information on distribution from Harry M. Bainer; for examples of railroad periodicals devoted largely to agriculture, see Santa Fe's *Earth,* Rock Island's *Western Trail* (later called *South-Western Trail*), and Kansas City Southern's *Current Events.*

[13] John Hamilton, *The Transportation Companies as Factors in Agricultural Extension,* 5–6; Andrews, *Railroads and Farming,* 31–32, 43; A T & S F Ry. Co., *Ag. Bull. No. 5,* 16; information from Mo. Pac. Ag. Dev. Dept.

lem was to advertise his findings. He approached the Rock Island superintendent at Des Moines with a proposal that the railroad furnish him an exhibit car to be moved from town to town. The Rock Island did better than that. It furnished a complete train, the Iowa Corn Special, and assumed responsibility for advertising its itinerary.

The Rock Island continued to run educational trains, and in the fall of 1906 the Missouri Pacific adopted the practice. In conjunction with the agricultural colleges of Missouri, Arkansas, and Louisiana, it prepared an exhibit car of poultry products and appliances to stimulate the organization of poultry raisers' associations.

Early in 1907 the Missouri Pacific ran its first full-scale educational train, the "Corn Show on Wheels," for the purpose of improving corn cultivation in southeastern Kansas. Almost immediately thereafter a dairy-development train toured Missouri and Kansas. One of its cars was a complete, operating dairy; other cars were equipped to demonstrate butter making, cream separation, pasteurization, and ripening of milk with lactic acid. The milking machine, which skeptical farmers did not believe even when they saw it in operation, was the sensation of the tour.

The Santa Fe brought the demonstration train to the semiarid regions. Early in February, 1911, one pulled out of Amarillo to popularize diversified farming along the Panhandle, South Plains, and northwestern Oklahoma lines. The railroad kept a record of attendance at the thirty-eight meetings, and, in spite of the sparse population and a blizzard, a total of 6,330 attended. In 1913 another demonstration train, arranged with farm wives in mind, toured the same area in the interests of rural home life. The "Cow, Sow, and Hen," designed to encourage diversification of farm livestock, was the most famous of the Santa Fe's early educational trains. It made more than one hundred stops on a six-week tour.

The passage of a demonstration train through a district usually resulted in an increase in the number of carloads of fertilizer purchased, improvements in pastures, or a rash of new poultry houses, depending on the purpose for which it was run. The Missouri Pacific's Soybean Special increased the soybean acreage in the territory through which it passed by 250 per cent. The Rock Island operated a wheat improvement train in 1910 which led to the planting of 300,-000 acres to improved seed. At the time, Minneapolis millers refused to take Kansas wheat because it did not meet their minimum standards. The improved strain not only sold on the Minneapolis market, but topped other Kansas wheat by ten cents per bushel on other markets.[14]

Railroads did not lose sight of the individual in the mass approach to better farming. Agricultural agents carried on extensive campaigns through private correspondence and personal interviews and referred hundreds of names to the proper agencies for specialized information which railroads were unable to furnish. Individual farm demonstrations represented another type of activity. A highly satisfactory yield for a local man from a few acres dedicated to a new crop, an improved strain of seed, or a different method of cultivation was most convincing.[15]

The Santa Fe introduced individual farm demonstrations to the Panhandle and South Plains in 1911. Each co-operator agreed to farm a minimum of ten acres according to a plan worked out by the railroad's director of farm demonstrations. During the first year a total of 148 co-operators in twenty-one widely scattered communities planted 2,738 acres to sixteen different crops. The railroad distributed seed to all participants, and the director visited each plot several times to inspect the crop and make suggestions. Scant rainfall the preceding year had made it impossible to prepare the ground in the fall, and conditions in general were not favorable; nevertheless, the demonstration plots consistently yielded larger returns than any other acreages.

To keep the program in operation, each farmer returned to the railroad as much seed as he originally received, and this was distributed to new recruits. In five years the Santa Fe co-operated with 2,000 farmers working over 40,000 experimental acres. By 1918 it had redistributed approximately 50,000 bushels of seed. Results obtained by individual dry-land farmers proved that alfalfa, barley, and broomcorn could be profitably grown if they were properly cultivated. They demonstrated that, although corn could not be considered a reliable Plains crop, there were four varieties best adapted to the country; they also established the northern limit beyond which it was unwise to plant cotton. They popularized improved methods of cultivating pinto beans, oats, Spanish peanuts, sorghums, and wheat.[16]

[14] Clifford V. Gregory, "Farming by Special Train," *Outlook*, Vol. XCVII, 919–20; Rock Island Lines, *Kansas Wheat Festival Special Train Campaign;* information from Arthur W. Large, Harry M. Bainer, and Mo. Pac. Ag. Dev. Dept.

[15] Andrews, *Railroads and Farming*, 23–24; Hamilton, *The Transportation Companies as Factors in Agricultural Extension*, 4–6.

[16] A T & S F Ry. Co., *Ag. Bull No. 5*, 16–21; information from Harry M. Bainer.

Farming in the Dust

Most of the railroads serving the Plains educated their farmers in the importance of milo and kafir after the Department of Agriculture introduced these peculiarly drouth-resistant crops. Several railroads donated seed to farmers and supervised the first plantings. Combined, the two have since become a 100,000,000-bushel crop upon which a great new processing industry developed. In order to encourage diversification, the Rock Island distributed cottonseed at every alternate station between Guthrie and El Reno, Oklahoma, a region dedicated to wheat. The wheat crop failed, the cotton crop returned good yields, and the farmers of central Oklahoma received a practical lesson in diversification. B. F. Yoakum used a similar scheme to popularize new crops in South Texas. In its program for 1911, the Santa Fe placed one thousand bushels of an improved strain of winter wheat in the hands of its patrons. Railroad agricultural agents were responsible in large part for demonstrating the value of winter-grazing wheat. They also encouraged the planting of shrubs and such ornamental trees as the hardy Chinese elm.[17]

All demonstration work was not confined to subhumid areas. In 1906 the agricultural agent for the Missouri Pacific was instrumental in getting farmers around Alexandria, Louisiana, to plant two hundred acres to Irish potatoes as part of a program to promote diversification along the Louisiana lines. In its first year of operation the Missouri Pacific Agricultural Development Department, in co-operation with the United States Department of Agriculture, set up about fifty demonstration tracts in Arkansas and Missouri. In addition, almost 1,450 Arkansas farmers participated in a program worked out jointly by the railroad, the Department of Agriculture, the State Board of Agriculture, and the state agricultural college. After the timber resources of Arkansas and Louisiana and East Texas were depleted, railroads helped to establish agriculture on suitable cutover lands, stressing dairy, poultry, fruit, and vegetable projects.

The Rock Island and the Missouri Pacific were both interested in rice culture in eastern Arkansas. The Rock Island agricultural agents helped develop the Lady Wright variety and popularized its use. The Missouri Pacific, already serving a rice-producing area at Lonoke, wished to establish it as a crop on the Helena Division. In 1906 the railroad prevailed on one farmer to plant ten acres of rice on a plot adjacent to the right of way and immediately in front of a railroad

---

[17] M. G. Cunniff, "The New State of Oklahoma," *WW*, Vol. XII, 7625; information from Harry M. Bainer, Arthur W. Large, C. B. Michelson, and Mo. Pac. Ag. Dev. Dept.

station. The experiment was so successful that many neighboring farmers began to plant rice.

During the same period, the Missouri Pacific encouraged the planting of apples along the White River Division and assisted the growing strawberry districts at Van Buren and Judsonia. Meanwhile, the Frisco was promoting some twelve varieties of commercial fruits and vegetables, notably spinach and Concord grapes, in northwestern Arkansas and encouraging soybean planting at a number of places along its lines.[18]

On occasion various railroads have made more direct contributions than simply supervising work on experimental plots. This was particularly true with regard to livestock improvement. Diversification campaigns not only stressed the necessity for beef and dairy cattle, swine, and poultry, but also aimed at replacing scrubs with purebred animals. In the early days railroads gave away foundation stock to encourage herd improvement, but this practice had all but ended by 1910 except as an award for achievement. Several railroads continued to import purebred stock and sell it at cost; a number of others, including the Missouri Pacific and the Kansas City Southern, owned outstanding sires which they moved from place to place for breeding purposes. The Frisco, in pioneering the Ozark dairy industry, brought in registered stock and placed a dairy specialist at Springfield, Missouri.[19]

Of all railroad activities, none was of greater importance than the work with farm youth. The railroads borrowed this idea from Seaman A. Knapp and his son, Bradford Knapp, two agricultural educators bent on breaking the one-crop system in the South. Their basic premise was that it was easier to demonstrate the value of certain farm practices through the activities of boys than to convince their parents by argument. The first clubs organized for this purpose were corn clubs, started in 1908. Each member planted exactly one acre of corn, keeping strict account of methods, labor, and costs, and state winners were awarded trips to Washington by the Department of Agriculture.[20]

The youth-club idea was carried to the Plains in 1912 when Harry

---

[18] Andrews, *Railroads and Farming*, 33–34, 40; AGS, *Louisiana*, 163; information from C. B. Michelson, Arthur W. Large, and Mo. Pac. Ag. Dev. Dept.

[19] Information from Arthur W. Large, C. B. Michelson, J. M. Prickett, and Mo. Pac. Ag. Dev. Dept.

[20] Frederick W. Williams, *Yesterday and Today in Louisiana Agriculture*, 63; Holland Thompson, *The New South*, 78–80.

Courtesy Santa Fe Railway

Santa Fe Pleasure Dome Lounge Car.

Ninety-eight carloads of pipe winding through West Texas.

Courtesy Southern Pacific Lines

Courtesy Southern Pacific Lines

Southern Pacific's *Sunset Limited,* operating between New Orleans and Los Angeles.

Missouri Pacific diesel-powered freight train.

Courtesy Missouri Pacific Lines

M. Bainer organized the Boys' Acre Kafir Club at Sweetwater, Texas, for the avowed purpose of advertising the possibilities of kafir and improved methods for its cultivation. The following year Bainer organized the Boys' Acre Kafir and Milo Maize clubs in Potter and Randall counties.

The organization followed that of the corn clubs, with membership open to any boy between the ages of eight and twenty. Members had to follow the instructions given by the director in soil preparation, seed testing, planting, and cultivating. A railroad representative visited each plot during the growing season. Every club member was obligated to display ten heads taken from his acre at the Boys' Kafir and Maize Show, competing for locally subscribed cash prizes. During the first year the club members averaged twenty-seven bushels per acre; their fathers averaged ten.[21]

Other railroads followed the lead of the Santa Fe. On one occasion the Rock Island invited a specialist from Oklahoma A. and M. College to speak at Hennessey on better livestock. The result was the organization of the Boys' Calf Club, with a local bank selling two carloads of purebred Holsteins to members on long-term notes. A pig program followed, then a poultry club. Within three years scrub stock was practically eliminated from a locality which had previously had little else.[22]

The basic purpose of railroad agricultural departments was to educate; consequently they rarely engaged in pure research. On occasion, however, they did assist with specific problems demanding immediate solution. Normally, the railroads furnished experimental tracts, turning the actual work over to experiment-station staffs. Less frequently they attached a research expert from a governmental agency to their own staffs for a time. Early in the century railroads subsidized the work of Hardy W. Campbell and Vernon T. Cooke, who jointly developed many of the principles of cultivation and water conservation which made dry-land farming possible.[23]

In East Texas, when the boll weevil threatened its principal source of revenue freight, the Texas Midland bought and equipped a model demonstration farm at Terrell. This it turned over to Seaman A. Knapp and J. H. Cornell, representing federal and state agricultural agencies, for experimentation in the eradication of the pest. By chang-

---

[21] Harry M. Bainer, *Boys' Acre Kafir and Milo Maize Club Contest;* information from Harry M. Bainer.
[22] W. E. Babb, "The Hens of Hennessey," *SCJ,* Vol. I (March 1, 1923), 44.
[23] Information from Arthur W. Large.

ing the methods of cultivating cotton and by developing weevil-resistant strains, these men contributed tremendously to the prosperity of cotton growers along the Texas Midland and throughout the country.[24]

The St. Louis, Brownsville and Mexico maintained an experimental farm at San Benito to work on improving crops in South Texas. Shortly after the Rock Island built its line from Arkansas down to Eunice, Louisiana, through a nonagricultural area, railroad-inspired research was a major factor in increasing sugar cane, rice, and sweet potato production in the area from Eunice to Alexandria.[25]

The American Railway Development Association is a present-day nationwide organization which co-ordinates the work of railroad agricultural and industrial departments. At its annual meetings the members exchange information, summarize their activities, and discuss plans for more effective techniques. Founded in 1906, the Association has acted as a forum for the discussion of practically every major developmental problem since that time.[26]

[24] Reed, *Texas Railroads*, 270–72.
[25] ICC, *Val. Rep.*, XXIX, 721; information from Arthur W. Large.
[26] The results of these meetings are published in the annual ARDA *Proceedings*.

CHAPTER 33

Growing Industries

THE ENCOURAGEMENT of industry was a later contribution of railroads to developmental work. The industrialization of the East had dictated the sequence of growth in the West. The final decision had been to build ahead of settlement rather than permit an inadequate transportation system to retard growth. Railroads thereupon assumed the responsibility for colonization, followed by an intensive campaign to educate transplanted farmers in the most effective use of the land. A conscious effort to extend their activities into industry occurred only after the agricultural program was well under way.

In the meantime, the Gulf Southwest was realizing some degree of industrialization because of the discovery of new resources and the more complete processing of older ones. Petroleum proved to be the greatest mineral resource of the Gulf Southwest, while natural gas attracted industries later. "Tar springs" along the coasts of Texas and Louisiana and oil accumulations at rock-salt springs in parts of Louisiana had been used for years to meet local needs for lubricants. To the north, Corsicana, Texas, boomed mildly with the bringing in of wells in 1896, but production exceeded demand for several years. A dozen eastern Kansas towns could list oil among their resources, and there was some activity in Indian Territory. The frenzied development of major fields, however, had to await the twentieth century, with its demand for fuel oil and gasoline.

Lucas' Spindletop well, brought in on January 10, 1901, ushered in the fuel oil age. Beaumont became a boom town as the field developed. Other salt domes along the Louisiana and Texas coast were exploited immediately. Interest next turned to Indian Territory, where the Bartlesville field and fabulous Glenn Pool, opened late in 1905, shifted the interest of the petroleum world to Tulsa. New fields were opened on Creek and Osage tribal lands, in the rolling hills west of Ardmore, and eventually in widely scattered areas throughout most of the new state of Oklahoma. The Caddo field in northwestern Louisiana was developing steadily, if not spectacularly. Kansas, too, benefited from new discoveries near Augusta, El Dorado, and Towanda.[1]

Much crude oil moved through pipelines, yet the petroleum industry leaned heavily on railroads, and many known productive areas had to await their coming. Railroads brought in the heavy equipment used in drilling, refining, and pipeline building; a small station located near an oil field frequently shot high above major cities in the amount of freight it handled. Furthermore, the many industries which grew up around the production of oil depended on rail transportation to serve their needs and to distribute their finished products.

The gravitation of railroads to oil fields indicated the interdependence of the two. The Bartlesville field did not mature until the Santa Fe arrived. John Ringling's road from Ardmore to Healdton and, later, Jake Hamon's Wichita Falls, Ranger and Fort Worth were built for no other purpose than to serve the petroleum industry. Big Lake kept the Orient solvent through the mid-twenties, and the Texas and Pacific enjoyed its most prosperous years with the opening of oil fields along its lines. The Midland Valley drew the bulk of its tonnage from Glenn Pool. In the Spindletop field there were 1,750 company-owned and almost 1,000 privately owned tank cars in service. The demand was so great that Beaumont built a tank-car factory.

Railroads played a vital role in creating a greater demand for fuel oil. J. S. Cullinan, a pioneer refiner, designed an oil burner which the Cotton Belt used on its passenger run between Corsicana and Hillsboro. The Santa Fe began experimenting in 1901 and within four years was using 227 oil-burning locomotives. By midsummer of 1902 the Kansas City Southern used nothing else south of Shreveport, and early in the century the Texas affiliates of the Southern Pacific Lines converted. Most of the remaining southwestern roads soon followed.[2]

[1] Rister, *Oil! Titan of the Southwest*, 22–24, 33–49, 81, 88, 94–97, 100, 119–35, 139–42, 196.
[2] *Ibid.*, 53–68, 78, 91, 278; Reed, *Texas Railroads*, 308, 372, 392; ICC, *Rep.*, CXLI, 412; ICC, *Val. Rep.*, XXIX, 537; H. F. Hoag, "A Brief History of the Kansas City Southern Railway" (MS in KCS general office), 82.

Growing Industries

The Gulf Coast is the chief source of American sulphur. It had been known to exist in southwestern Louisiana for years, but overlaying quicksands and inadequate transportation forestalled any serious activity. By 1905 engineers had solved the problem of the quicksands, and the Brimstone Railroad and Canal Company furnished transportation. That year, the United States produced over 180,000 tons of sulphur, most of it from Calcasieu Parish, Louisiana. The mines were exhausted by 1925, but 9,500,000 tons of almost pure sulphur had been taken from them. Sulphur mining developed at Jefferson Island and Grand Écaille in the early thirties, but the center of production had shifted to Freeport, Texas.[3]

Arkansas easily leads the nation in the production of bauxite, the basic mineral of the aluminum industry. In 1937 the deposits west of Little Rock accounted for 96 per cent of the nation's output. Railroads made possible the exploitation of this natural resource; at the present time the Bauxite and Northern is almost wholly dependent upon it for revenue.

Oklahoma, Texas, Kansas, and Missouri are among the nine states which produce rock asphalt in quantity. The Asphalt Belt Railway in Uvalde County, Texas, was built to break the control of a company which, by having exclusive use of the one railroad spur to the beds, maintained a monopoly.

Building stone, too, the value of which is derived largely from labor and transportation, was undeveloped without railroads; with their coming all the Gulf Southwest states except Louisiana had quarries of considerable importance.[4]

All of the railroad-transported products were not from the mines and the quarries. Clam shells, used for road building, became an important source of tonnage for the Louisiana Southern. Refrigeration and fast transportation gave Louisiana a nationwide market for oysters, shrimp, froglegs, crabs, and fish.[5]

Railroads were directly responsible for a marked degree of industrialization. During the first decade of the twentieth century, general car and shop construction and repair, the great bulk of which was carried on by steam railroads, became the fourth largest industry

---

[3] ICC, *Rep.*, CXLI, 457–59; Matthews, "The . . . South," *SBN*, VI, 246–48; AGS, *Louisiana*, 20, 71; A. B. Cox, "Resources and Industry of Texas," *U. Tex. Bus. Conf. Transp.*, 9.

[4] ICC, *Rep.*, CXXI, 489; AGS, *Arkansas*, 22–23; Reed, *Texas Railroads*, 348; George P. Merrill, "Building and Ornamental Stone," *SBN*, VI, 199–201.

[5] ICC, *Val. Rep.*, XXIX, 707; U. S. Geol. Surv., *Bull. No. 845*, Part F, 12.

in Kansas, the fifth in Texas and Arkansas, and the eleventh in Missouri. Its relative importance continued into the twenties. Railroads were also responsible for the concentrations of population which attracted industries. Not including shop- and car-repair workers, the census of 1920 listed almost 15,000 railroad employees in the St. Louis area, more than 11,000 in the Kansas City area, 5,300 in New Orleans, 3,400 in San Antonio, 3,300 in Houston, and 2,700 in Fort Worth. Dallas, El Paso, Little Rock, Oklahoma City, Wichita, Shreveport, Topeka, Springfield, Galveston, and Wichita Falls ranged from one to two thousand, and in many smaller cities the numbers ran high in the hundreds. Translated into purchasing power and consumption, railroad employees represented a local market for thousands of small shops and industries. They also meant thriving cities with adequate transportation facilities bidding for new industries.[6]

The creation of industrial departments specifically dedicated to developmental work was a later innovation in the evolution of railroad services. The Southwest was not ready for them, nor were there trained industrial engineers available. Even the eastern railroads failed to recognize the need for such activity, and until well into the twentieth century most of this work was handled through freight traffic departments.

The first true industrial departments were those of the Chicago, Milwaukee and St. Paul and the Illinois Central railroads, both of which date from the late nineties. In 1898 the Katy employed a "railroad industrial agent," Thomas Lamar Peeler, whose headquarters were at Dallas. He was charged in general with the responsibility of increasing the revenue tonnage, particularly with locating sawmills on a branch line which the Katy had recently acquired. The Santa Fe created an industrial department in 1902, and the Frisco and the Missouri Pacific did so two years later.[7]

The early work was not as highly specialized as it became later. The Katy and the Missouri Pacific combined industrial development with colonization and agricultural education for several years. By the end of World War I, however, most of the major southwestern railroads had become active in the one specialized field.

The primary purposes of industrial development departments were

[6] "Manufactures," *Twelfth Census*, VIII, 52, 368, 637, 1198; ibid., *Fourteenth Census*, IX, 64, 452, 510, 779, 1216, 1451; "Population," *Fourteenth Census*, IV, 151, 154–60, 172–78, 186, 190–96, 205–15, 243–46, 261, 267, 278, 284, 291, 302, 320–21.

[7] Memorandum from Assn. Am. R.; information from J. A. Senter of ARDA and Arthur W. Large.

Growing Industries

to attract new industries to their respective lines and to encourage sound expansion of those already in operation. Although the railroads concentrated most of their attention on those which could be expected to give them a considerable volume of business, they also encouraged the so-called "needle-goods" plants until truckers cut deeply into this traffic.

The basic activities of the earliest departments were relatively simple. Since they were in a favorable position to know the needs and resources of their territories, they supplied the information to those seeking new outlets for capital. Whenever possible, the industrial commissioner personally interviewed interested investors; otherwise, all business opportunities were included in the railroads' published lists of openings along their lines. The needs for doctors, lawyers, barbers, and blacksmiths were listed, along with requests for grain elevators, cotton gins, canneries, and sawmills. On the other hand, the industrial commissioner had the task of diplomatically discouraging investments in ventures which experience had proved unsound.

The industrial commissioner engaged in many activities, limited only by his own imagination and resourcefulness. The Missouri Pacific industrial department was particularly interested in organizing commercial clubs in its principal towns, and in 1907 it assisted with 192 of them. All railroads gave close attention to the development of natural resources. They prepared special booklets on the resources of specific localities and used their colonization magazines to advertise opportunities for investments in the towns they served.

Some of the results in the early years were amazing. The Missouri Pacific made a study of iron-ore deposits in Missouri which resulted in the organization of three new mining companies. An engineer attached to the Santa Fe's industrial development department discovered excellent limestone deposits at Iola, Kansas, and located an investor who established the town's first cement plant. By 1912 the Santa Fe was directly responsible for securing an average annual investment of more than $16,000,000 in new capital in its territory. The Frisco was instrumental in locating a large percentage of the three thousand new industries established along its lines between 1905 and 1912.

On occasion some unforeseen obstacle blocked an otherwise sound business venture. The Santa Fe made all arrangements for a pottery works at Tulsa, Oklahoma, with kaolin from Texas deposits. The enterprise had to be abandoned, however, since most of the skilled pottery workers were apparently fond of beer and Oklahoma was a "dry" state. This, at least, was reported at the time as the reason why it was impossible to recruit workmen.[8]

Railroad industrial development departments were already assuming their form when World War I suspended many of their activities. They could, and would, be revived in the twenties, and from that time forward they would assume an increasingly important place as the Southwest turned to industry.

[8] "Frisco Lines," *Harper's W.*, Vol. LVII, 22; Henry Oyen, "Making Business to Order," *WW*, Vol. XXIV, 308–12.

CHAPTER 34

Between Two Wars

WHEN PRESIDENT WOODROW WILSON placed the nation's railroads under a director general late in 1917, he was recognizing that a smooth functioning transportation system was vital to the conduct of the war. In a sense this represented the peak of American dependence on steam locomotion. When their own management repossessed them after the war, the railroads faced the competition of an embryonic highway system which at the time appeared a threat only in the field of less-than-carload short-haul shipments. The amazingly rapid growth of this competition in both freight and passenger traffic threatened railroad revenue and cut much more deeply into rail tonnage than anyone had anticipated. The remarkable extension of pipelines and, somewhat later, the increasing importance of air transportation spelled further difficulty.

Railroads were not relegated to a position of uselessness nor even replaced as the backbone of American transportation, but no longer were they completely dominant in the field. In an earlier day they were the single thread around which might be woven the cultural evolution resulting from rapid transportation. Now the time was past when in many small communities the arrival of the train was the major event of the day.

The changed mileage between 1920 and 1948 is indicative of the change in the prominence of the railroads themselves. Every one of the Gulf Southwest states registered a substantial decrease. Some of the abandonments were the result of ill-advised expansion, others the exhaustion of resources which had been responsible for the original construction. Some branches were unable to meet the competition which siphoned off enough tonnage to render profitable operation impossible.[1]

A number of important changes between the two world wars altered corporate structure without materially affecting the regions served. The group of railroads known historically as the "Gould roads" underwent radical changes. The Missouri Pacific, sold in 1917 to agents of its creditors, formally absorbed the Iron Mountain, recognizing the identity of interest which had existed for many years. It also launched a thoroughgoing campaign to rehabilitate its lines and to acquire additional ones, particularly in Louisiana and Texas. Under Jay Gould the road had maintained a tight control over the Texas lines leading north, but this control had slipped away until the Missouri Pacific found itself without Texas Gulf subsidiaries.

The International and Great Northern and the Gulf Coast Lines offered two major possibilities, and both were known to be for sale. The International and Great Northern, traditionally a Missouri Pacific affiliate, passed through two receiverships between 1908 and 1922, the second marking the end of Gould influence. The Frisco was bidding for it, but in 1924 the group of New York and St. Louis bankers who had taken over Yoakum's Gulf Coast Lines gained control of the road, known after 1922 as the International–Great Northern. They also acquired the Houston and Brazos Valley. A short time later the Missouri Pacific acquired these properties and firmly established itself in the Gulf area, with alternate routes north for perishables and with access to Baton Rouge, New Orleans, and most of the major Texas cities. Through control of the International–Great Northern, it also held half-interest in the Galveston, Houston, and Henderson and terminal railroads at Houston, Brownsville, and Texas City.[2]

The Missouri Pacific added a number of smaller Texas roads. It secured five of these from W. T. Eldridge by purchase in the name of the New Orleans, Texas and Mexico. Of these, the San Antonio, Uvalde and Gulf, the Sugar Land, and the Asherton and Gulf dated from an earlier period, while the Rio Grande City Railway and the Asphalt Belt had been constructed only recently. Eldridge and Frank Kell built the Asphalt Belt Railroad to serve asphalt deposits south of Uvalde; the Rio Grande City was an extension of the Brownsville

---

[1] ICC, *Stat. Rys., 1948*, 5.
[2] ICC, *Rep.*, XC, 262–72; *ibid.*, XCIV, 191–205; ICC, *Val. Rep.*, XL, 350, 403, 408, 475–78; ICC, *Stat. Rys., 1947*, 563–64.

web from the town of Sam Fordyce to Rio Grande City. In 1926 the Missouri Pacific bought the Artesian Belt. The same year, it built from Houston to Goose Creek. In 1940 the Port Isabel and Rio Grande Valley was abandoned, and a solitary ten-mile strip leading into Port Isabel passed to a Missouri Pacific subsidiary. The Missouri Pacific suffered misfortune by falling under the influence of the Van Sweringen brothers in their vast speculative bid for power and went into receivership after their spectacular collapse.[3]

Another of the original Gould lines, the Texas and Pacific, was controlled by the Missouri Pacific, but maintained its independent existence and made its own policies. It emerged from an eight-year receivership in 1924 and was reorganized without loss of its federal charter. During the next few years it secured the Abilene and Southern and the Pecos Valley Southern, then added the Texas Short Line, which it extended to a new oil field at Van. The Cisco and Northeastern, operating between Cisco and Breckenridge, and the Texas–New Mexico, running from Monahans, Texas, to Lovington, New Mexico, were two West Texas oil roads which became Texas and Pacific properties.[4]

A third Gould line, the Cotton Belt, passed under the control of the Southern Pacific after an attempt to unite it with the Katy and the Kansas City Southern failed. In 1929 it absorbed several short lines in northeastern Arkansas and constructed an additional thirty miles to secure a continuous line from Malden, Missouri, to McDonald, Arkansas. Despite the abandonment of several of its unprofitable lines, it was again in receivership from 1935 until 1947.[5]

The most striking single feature in Southern Pacific development was the unification of its Texas and Louisiana lines around the Texas and New Orleans; also, certain accessions and abandonments worked minor changes in the areas served. Some of the acquisitions preceded the consolidation in point of time. The San Antonio and Aransas Pass, technically severed from the Southern Pacific early in the century, was legally reunited with it in 1925. Shortly thereafter, the Southern Pacific extended it to its logical termini at McAllen and

[3] ICC, *Rep.*, CV, 35–42, 79–84; *ibid.*, CCXLII, 165–70; ICC, *Val. Rep.*, XLIII, 277–86, 877; Daniel Dodge, "An Empire in Hock," *Am. Merc.*, Vol. XXXIV, 160–74; Max Lowenthal, "The Case of the Missouri Pacific," *Harper's*, Vol. CLXX, 87–98.
[4] ICC, *Rep.*, CXVII, 447–50; *ibid.*, CXXIV, 369–72, 749–52; *ibid.*, CXLV, 639–42; *ibid.*, CL, 604–606; ICC, *Val. Rep.* XXVI, 143–60.
[5] ICC, *Rep.*, CXXIV, 401–47; *ibid.*, CL, 685–707; *ibid.*, CLVIII, 206–209; *ibid.*, CCXLI, 811; Jacob E. Anderson, *A Brief History of the St. Louis Southwestern Railway Lines*, 26.

Brownsville, abandoning unprofitable branches. E. H. R. Green's highly successful Texas Midland passed to the Southern Pacific when Green was forced to relinquish control and return to New York; it was largely abandoned in later years. The Southern Pacific leased the Texas State Railroad for a time and purchased the very profitable Dayton–Goose Creek, an oil-field road built in 1918. Short, specialized lines serving gravel pits near Houston and salt and gypsum deposits south of Austin were added in 1929 and 1935.

Before the final additions, the consolidation of the Texas and Louisiana lines had occurred. In 1927 the Texas and New Orleans leased some dozen roads under Southern Pacific control. Seven years later, despite the intervention of other carriers and several towns, the Texas and New Orleans assumed the obligations of the other corporations, and the Galveston, Harrisburg and San Antonio, the Houston and Texas Central, Morgan's Louisiana and Texas lines, the San Antonio and Aransas Pass, and several less famous roads ceased to exist, even nominally, as separate entities.[6]

The Frisco made a bid for power in Texas in 1923, but its application for control of the International–Great Northern was denied. In 1930 it secured the Gulf, Texas and Western in West Texas, but traded it ten years later to the Rock Island in exchange for trackage in Oklahoma. It added the Motley County Railroad serving Matador, Texas, and extended the Quanah, Acme and Pacific to Floydada. In general, however, the Frisco was inactive in Texas after it failed to get the International–Great Northern, preferring to strengthen itself outside that state. In 1928 the Frisco assumed formal control of the Kansas City, Fort Scott and Memphis and the Kansas City, Clinton and Springfield. Over a period of several years it secured three short lines to add more than 150 miles in northeastern Arkansas and southeastern Missouri. The Frisco expanded in Oklahoma by acquiring the Miami Mineral Belt and a Rock Island connecting line into Ardmore and by constructing a few miles of oil-field road.

The strengthening process included the elimination of costly branches. In 1926 the Brownwood North and South was abandoned, and other lines soon followed. In spite of all that was done, the Frisco was forced into receivership in 1932, and during the next four years abandoned no less than twenty-four unprofitable branches in Mis-

[6] ICC, *Rep.*, XCIV, 701–703; *ibid.*, CXVII, 504–508; *ibid.*, CXCIX, 47–58; *ibid.*, CCII, 767–70; ICC, *Val. Rep.* XLI, 130; *ibid.*, XLVII, 118, 205, 212, 226; Reed, *Texas Railroads*, 454.

souri, Arkansas, and Oklahoma. At the end of the receivership, its total mileage was considerably reduced, but the Frisco was a much sounder railroad.[7]

The combining of the Kansas City Southern, the Louisiana and Arkansas, and the Louisiana Railway and Navigation Company created a compact major system in the Gulf Southwest. William Edenborn, of the Louisiana Railway and Navigation Company, purchased the Sherman, Shreveport and Southern from the Katy in 1923. Edenborn died a short time later, and his railroad came into the possession of H. C. Couch, who had previously taken over the Louisiana and Arkansas. In 1932, Couch secured trackage rights into Dallas over the Katy, but the Couch lines needed a closer affiliation with another railroad, for they had access to few major cities. Meanwhile, the Kansas City Southern had failed in its plans to secure control of the Katy and the Cotton Belt, and was itself in need of an affiliate. In 1939 the two roads secured permission from the Interstate Commerce Commission to unite their interests. In 1945 the Louisiana and Arkansas' branch from Georgetown to Vidalia was sold to a new corporation, the Louisiana Midland.[8] Of the other major lines in the Gulf Southwest, all had two features in common—expansion on the Great Plains and abandonment of unimportant lines to the east.

The Katy underwent the greatest change. Under a reorganization plan put into effect in the spring of 1923, it was divested of many of its properties. The Trinity and Sabine and the Beaumont and Great Northern passed to the newly created Waco, Beaumont, Trinity and Sabine; the Denison, Bonham and New Orleans and the Dallas, Cleburne and Southwestern were abandoned in due time; the Wichita Falls and Southern was restored to its builders; the Houston and Brazos Valley passed to the Southern Pacific in the first of a number of rapid transfers; and the Sherman, Shreveport and Southern became a part of the Louisiana Railway and Navigation Company. The following year the line from Atoka to Oklahoma City went to a new corporation, the Oklahoma City–Ada–Atoka. The Katy retained its half-interest in the Galveston, Houston and Henderson and in 1929 acquired the Beaver, Meade and Englewood, which, after being ex-

---

[7] ICC, *Rep.*, XCVII, 445, 454, 477, 602, 604, 612; *ibid.*, CV, 729–38; *ibid.*, CXXXI, 105–13; *ibid.*, CXXXIII, 424; *ibid.*, CXLV, 110–15; *ibid.*, CLVIII, 199–201; *ibid.*, CLXII, 404–10, 427; *ibid.*, CCXXXIII, 321–31; *ibid.*, CCXXXVI, 19–21; George and Wood, "The . . . Oklahoma," R&LHS *Bull. No. 60*, 69–70.

[8] ICC, *Rep.*, CXXIV, 401–47; *ibid.*, CCXXXIII, 37–41, 123–46; *ibid.*, CCLXI, 820, 846; ICC, *Val. Rep.*, XXXIV, 295.

tended to Keyes, represented more than one hundred miles of railroad in the Oklahoma Panhandle.[9]

The Rock Island added considerable mileage in western Oklahoma and the Texas Panhandle after World War I. A line from Amarillo pushed north to Liberal, Kansas, while a connecting link joined Dalhart and Morse in the Panhandle. In Oklahoma the existing road from Enid to Billings was extended to Ponca City, and in the southwest corner of the state a branch from Lawton to Chattanooga was extended to the Katy at Grandfield. The Rock Island operated the Gulf, Texas and Western for a short time after securing it from the Frisco, then abandoned it. The Rock Island was unable to weather the depression and went into receivership, emerging early in January, 1948.[10]

A spirited rivalry developed between the Fort Worth and Denver City and the Santa Fe in the late twenties. The Panhandle–South Plains area was the scene of the struggle. The Denver's building program, concentrated in the period 1925 to 1932, was carried on through two subsidiaries. The Fort Worth and Denver South Plains was most active during the first four years, and the Fort Worth and Denver Northern in the later years. The South Plains road started from the main line at Estelline, ran southwest to Plainview, then west to Dimmitt, with branches from Sterley north to Silverton and south to Lubbock, a total of more than two hundred miles. The more northerly road, originating at Childress, crossed the Rock Island at Shamrock and reached Pampa, served solely by the Santa Fe until this time. Even before the Panhandle expansion the Fort Worth and Denver City added a line from Wichita Falls, Texas, to Waurika, Oklahoma, which, however, it abandoned in 1942.[11]

The Santa Fe added mileage out of all proportion to that of the other southwestern railroads. It had started developing its Panhandle and South Plains lines before the beginning of its rivalry with the Fort Worth and Denver City. In 1918 it added a branch from Lubbock to Seagraves, and when the Denver threatened its territory in the midtwenties, it extended another line almost due west from near Lub-

[9] ICC, *Rep.*, LXXXII, 30–32; *ibid.*, LXXVI, 84–133; *ibid.*, CLVIII, 219–33; ICC, *Val. Rep.*, XXXIV, 293–95; ICC, *Stat. Rys.*, *1923*, 282; *ibid.*, *1924*, 241; George and Wood, "The . . . Oklahoma," R&LHS *Bull. No. 60*, 15–17; Reed, *Texas Railroads*, 328, 388.

[10] ICC, *Val. Rep.*, XLVII, 421, 434; George and Wood, "The . . . Oklahoma," R&LHS *Bull. No. 60*, 43; ICC, *Stat. Rys.*, *1948*, 584.

[11] ICC, *Rep.*, CXVII, 233–82; *ibid.*, CLXII, 398–431; *ibid.*, CLXVI, 359–72; Reed, *Texas Railroads*, 400.

bock to Bledsoe. The Santa Fe penetrated newly opened wheat lands in the northern Panhandle when, in midsummer of 1920, a branch from Shattuck, Oklahoma, reached Spearman, Texas. Eleven years later it was extended to the Rock Island at Morse. The Hutchinson County oil boom accounted for branches from Panhandle City to Borger and from White Deer to Skellytown. This expansion came just before the Fort Worth and Denver City moved into the area.

The territories of the two rivals were fairly well stabilized in 1928 when the Santa Fe purchased the Clinton and Oklahoma Western and extended this Oklahoma road across the state line to Pampa, Texas, adding an oil-field branch from Heaton to Coltexo. The final building in the Panhandle occurred in 1931 when the Santa Fe built a hundred-mile line from Amarillo to Boise City, in the Oklahoma Panhandle, and extended it in 1937 to Las Animas, Colorado. This opened a new route to eastern Colorado and supplied the Santa Fe with a cutoff for its transcontinental lines.

Northwestern Oklahoma and southwestern Kansas had Santa Fe lines other than those primarily associated with the Texas Panhandle. In 1920 the Santa Fe reached the inland county seat of Buffalo, Oklahoma, from Waynoka. In the second half of the decade the line formerly terminating at Elkhart, Kansas, was extended through the Oklahoma Panhandle by way of Boise City to Farley, New Mexico, and from Satanta, Kansas, west to Pritchett, Colorado.

Elsewhere in Kansas, Oklahoma, and Texas, the Santa Fe made some minor additions: cutoffs, extensions in the Osage oil field, and short branches. Along the Cane Belt, far to the south, it added trackage to serve better the sulphur deposits in Wharton County, Texas.

In 1928 the Santa Fe annexed the Orient. It disposed of the Mexican mileage, rehabilitated the remaining lines, then extended it to the Mexican border at Presidio. The Orient charter was used to build a branch line from San Angelo to Sonora. In the same area, the Fort Worth and Rio Grande, the old Frisco property which had always been an expensive nuisance to the parent road, passed to the Santa Fe. The change of ownership benefited all parties concerned because it reduced Santa Fe–system hauls from the Brownwood area to Fort Worth and Dallas by well over one hundred miles and tied in nicely with the network the Santa Fe was developing.

The later history of the Santa Fe included many abandonments. Unprofitable branches in Kansas, Oklahoma oil-field roads which had passed their period of usefulness, and ill-conceived Texas lines were dismantled. Some of the more notable included much of the old Oklahoma Central, the road from Cherokee, Oklahoma, to Anthony, Kansas, the Port Bolivar and Iron Ore Railway, and the new line from Boise City to Farley.[12]

A new combination of earlier roads rose to considerable importance in eastern Oklahoma between the two world wars. This was the Muskogee Company, which was incorporated in 1923 in Delaware as a holding company. It organized the Oklahoma City–Ada–Atoka to take over the line between Atoka and Oklahoma City lost to the Katy. It reorganized the Missouri, Oklahoma and Gulf as the Kansas, Oklahoma and Gulf. The Midland Valley also belonged to this group. The Foraker Company, predecessor of the Muskogee Company, had built the Osage Railway, running from the Midland Valley at Foraker to Lyman, in the Burbank oil field. These roads likewise suffered extensive abandonments.[13]

The Wichita Falls and Southern, also lost to the Katy, was returned to Kemp and Kell, who had extended it from Newcastle to Jimkurn in 1921. The Wichita Falls, Ranger and Fort Worth, promoted by Jake Hamon to serve the Ranger oil field and completed from Dublin to Jimkurn, passed to the Wichita Falls and Southern in 1927. For a time the Wichita Falls and Southern leased another oil-field short-line road, the Eastland, Wichita Falls and Gulf, built by John Ringling from Mangum, on the Katy, to Ringling Junction, on the Wichita Falls and Southern, but this arrangement proved unsatisfactory, and the line was released, operating independently until its abandonment.[14]

A relatively small number of independent short lines came into existence after World War I, and even fewer survived. Several proved unprofitable: a couple of logging roads and an oil-field short-line road in Oklahoma; lines to pegmatite deposits in the Big Bend region, to timber on the Neches, and to gravel deposits in Kaufman County, in Texas; and a railroad in the livestock belt in southwestern Kansas. The Hamlin and Northwestern in West Texas, the Rockdale, Sandow and Southern in Central Texas, and the Reader and the Murfreesboro and Nashville in southwestern Arkansas remained in operation.

[12] ICC, *Rep.*, CXXXVIII, 787–92; *ibid.*, CXLV, 350–54; *ibid.*, CLIV, 171–74, 215–18, 769–78; *ibid.*, CCXVII, 659–68; Marshall, *Santa Fe*, 326, 436–43; Reed, *Texas Railroads*, 297–99, 304; George and Wood, "The . . . Oklahoma," R&LHS *Bull. No. 60*, 34, 37, 39.

[13] ICC, *Val. Rep.*, XLIII, 95–107; ICC, *Stat. Rys.*, *1924*, 246; *ibid.*, *1934*, 221; George and Wood, "The . . . Oklahoma," R&LHS *Bull. No. 60*, 48, 55, 60–62.

[14] ICC, *Val. Rep.*, XLIII, 747; *ibid.*, XLIV, 904, 917.

The Central Texas road was almost wholly dependent upon lignite, the Arkansas roads on lumber. The last addition was the seventeen-mile Point Comfort and Northern, built by the Aluminum Corporation of America in 1948 to connect Point Comfort, Texas, just outside Port Lavaca, with Lolita, on the Missouri Pacific.[15]

The first half of the twentieth century saw the completion of the southwestern rail network, largely accomplished before 1907 except for the western parts of Oklahoma, Texas, and Kansas. Probably the most striking development since World War I has been the increasingly varied and intense competition from other forms of carriers. Many branches were rigorously pared as trucks and buses took over the bulk of the tonnage. This basic change has meant that since the early twenties the contributions of railroads have been so intermingled with those of other carriers that it is no longer possible to isolate basic economic and social changes attributable directly and solely to railroad penetration.

[15] *Ibid.*, XLIII, 75–84, 118–30, 407–17, 648–58, 711–17, 795–806; ICC, *Rep.*, CCLXXI, 804, 821; ICC, *Stat. Rys., 1949*, 575; Reed, *Texas Railroads*, 454, 469–70.

CHAPTER 35

Agricultural Education Renewed

RAILROADS RENEWED their activities in agricultural education following World War I. In such companies as the Missouri Pacific, which had suspended developmental work in 1917, it was resumed; in other instances budgets were increased and more services offered.

Demonstration trains reappeared in the early twenties. They were not exactly the same as the earlier ones, however, for they employed new techniques. Motion pictures supplemented lectures; tests on soil samples brought in by farmers were run in laboratory cars; horticultural exhibits included specimens of diseased nursery stock to show how infestations could be identified in the orchard. The lessons were more pointed in their application. Thus the Rock Island Wheat Festival Train of 1927 had for its sole purpose the advertising of the Kansas State College wheat-improvement program. Other trains distributed plants in order to encourage fruit and berry growing or centered their programs around popularizing the work of county extension agents.

The Missouri Pacific was most active in the twenties, running twenty-five trains and exhibit cars embracing such varied fields as crop dusting, fertilization, improved marketing, reforestation, soil improvement, wheat storage, and malaria control. In the mid-twenties, the Missouri Pacific ran a demonstration train directed at the consumer rather than the producer. It displayed South Texas fruits and vegetables in the Middle West so effectively that there was an immediate increased demand. Broccoli in particular enjoyed a wide sale in areas where it had been previously unknown.

Agricultural Education Renewed

The nature of the exhibit determined which towns a particular train visited and how many patrons it attracted. The Missouri Pacific strawberry exhibit made only eleven stops and had a total attendance of less than 3,000. At the other extreme, the marketing-exhibit train operated for three months and made more than one hundred stops. The Dairy and Poultry Train of 1928 attracted more than 100,000 people to its sixty-six programs and set an attendance record. Harry M. Bainer of the Santa Fe fixed at 750,000 the attendance for the twenty-five demonstration trains which that road operated in Texas between 1911 and 1946. His figure was based on the records that he maintained for each demonstration train.[1]

Railroads remained ardent supporters of local fairs and instituted their own traveling Chautauquas. The Missouri Pacific, in co-operation with the American Royal Livestock Show, sponsored one for ten years to exhibit prize-winning livestock. It also had its own series of two-day Chautauquas. The railroad furnished a few exhibits, but most of them came from local farmers and livestock breeders. Program arrangements were in the hands of local committees except for speakers, who were provided by the railroad. One of the most ambitious was the Traveling Dairy Show of 1925–26, which required three carloads of equipment. During the tour the railroad sponsored contests, awarding registered bull calves through local farm organizations as prizes. In this particular case the railroad laid the foundation for a number of dairy herds along the line, but by and large, the greatest value of the Chautauquas lay in drawing townspeople and farmers together and in furnishing an additional social event for rural areas.

The Rock Island held a series of farm-prosperity Chautauquas in 1923 and 1924. Each was patterned to fit the needs of a particular area. Usually, they were operated for about two weeks, showing in selected towns for one day or less. To make the meetings more attractive, the Rock Island arranged for local merchants to have "bargain days" when the Chautauquas came to their communities.

The Rock Island also sponsored agricultural and community-life institutes in larger towns in its territory. When possible, the institutes were held in connection with some local celebration—at Fort Worth with its Diamond Jubilee, at Enid with the thirtieth anniversary of the Cherokee Strip (misnomer for Outlet) opening, or, more often, with

[1] Information from Arthur W. Large, Harry M. Bainer, and the Mo. Pac. Ag. Dev. Dept.

Then Came the Railroads

some less colorful but locally popular events, such as Marlow's annual poultry show. The institutes lasted three days. In addition to the usual agricultural specialists, the speakers represented state agencies, civic and farm organizations, and private industry. The sessions always ended with a banquet for businessmen and farmers. One at Chickasha, held on the campus of the Oklahoma College for Women in November, 1923, received wide publicity because most of the program was broadcast by radio, a daring and exciting new form of communication.[2]

With the rise of the 4-H clubs and the Future Farmers of America, railroads gave up their own youth organizations but did not lose interest in the movement. In 1924, after one company had given a trip to the International Livestock Show at Chicago as an award, Thomas E. Wilson of Wilson and Company, along with Presidents James E. Gorman of the Rock Island and William B. Storey of the Santa Fe, formulated the plan for the National Congress of Boys and Girls Club Work. The congress, financed by contributions from railroads and other interested parties, now meets annually in conjunction with the International Livestock Show. For six years carriers bore most of the expense, but commercial and industrial concerns gradually began to share more of the burden. Individual railroads still sponsor 4-H Club state winners, finance the complimentary Railroad Banquet for all members, and donate a large number of awards. Although not officially a part of the 4-H organization, the congress has come to be the climax of its year.

Railroads have similar arrangements for assisting delegates to the Future Farmers of America Congress held in Kansas City each fall. They played a most interesting role in the first congress. The congress was highly successful, but on adjournment many farm boys suddenly realized that they had not allowed for fare home. Arthur W. Large, general agricultural agent for the Rock Island Lines, was present and described the sequel: "I was one of those who paced the Union Station at Kansas City, running to the telegraph office every few minutes for word from Chicago. Finally word came over the wire from railroad headquarters in Chicago: 'Send all the boys home.' That was the greatest moment of the convention."[3]

Local problems with which they were peculiarly fitted to cope

---

[2] Information from Rock Island circulars, Arthur W. Large, and Mo. Pac. Ag. Dev. Dept.

[3] Arthur W. Large; additional information from Harry M. Bainer and J. M. Prickett.

Agricultural Education Renewed

occupied much of the attention of all railroad agricultural-development departments. The Missouri Pacific, in co-operation with government agencies, achieved one of its outstanding successes in the early twenties. Crowley's Ridge, a gently sloping upland rising above the valleys on either side, thrust northward from Helena to the northern border of Arkansas. Ideally suited to peach culture, it was used almost exclusively for cotton growing. In 1924 the railroad began its work of convincing farmers that peaches, with a harvest season between the time cotton was laid by and the picking began, would be highly profitable. A series of meetings resulted in the Crowley's Ridge Development Association to promote the planting of orchards, and the railroad hired a horticulturist to supervise the work and make suggestions.

The Missouri Pacific also hired a plant breeder from the Department of Agriculture to develop a new type of Bermuda onion for the Laredo, Texas, area after both the quality and the yield began to slip. The growers had considered turning to a different type of onion, but the new Bermuda made it possible for them to continue producing the variety for which they were famous, at the same time increasing yields from 50 to 100 per cent and reaching the market two weeks earlier because of the maturation date. The improved Bermuda also opened up another field of agricultural activity because the seed could be grown locally, whereas all seed had been imported previously. The railroad did not discontinue its research immediately, but carried on experiments until the new strain became highly disease resistant.

When the economy of Crystal City, Texas, was threatened because of difficulties in the marketing of spinach, the Missouri Pacific Agricultural Development Department demonstrated that a variety of green beans believed cultivable only in the Northwest could be grown there, encouraging a diversification which attracted canneries by offering them a longer season than spinach alone afforded.

The Texas and Pacific was particularly active in two areas in the midtwenties. Its Louisiana agricultural agent assisted in introducing truck crops, notably spinach and carrots, when a slump in the price of sugar made cane growing less profitable. The railroad carried on a similar program along its East Texas lines to release that section from almost complete dependence on cotton. The Rock Island was one of several roads which popularized the practice among cotton farmers of growing Austrian winter peas to build the soil and prevent erosion, with the peas being turned over as green manure in the spring.

Livestock was not overlooked. In 1929 the Missouri Pacific imported a carload of Jersey bulls from Canada and placed them in dairying sectors along its lines. Several railroads organized local farm groups to tour sections which had achieved reputations for successful stock or poultry breeding. The Rock Island conducted such an excursion in the early thirties, taking a group from near Oklahoma City to the finest dairying centers of Minnesota and Wisconsin. With the advent of artificial insemination, the Kansas City Southern pioneered the practice in the dairy herds of its territory.[4]

Marketing furnished railroads with a perennial problem: convincing their patrons that it was sound business practice to grade their produce, pack it properly and attractively, and learn the customs of their markets. Although livestock and major crops consumed the greatest time and energy, it was in specialized local problems that railroads frequently achieved the most striking results. This was especially true of perishables.

Watermelons had been an established crop in parts of Oklahoma for years, but haphazard marketing had so reduced the profits that the growers cut their acreage. The Rock Island, which served approximately two-thirds of the watermelon-producing section, assigned an agricultural agent to assist with experiments to determine the most marketable type of melon and to organize the growers into local associations. He also assumed responsibility for informing reliable buyers of approximate shipping dates and the stations from which the movements would originate. He then distributed, at cost, excelsior pads which would keep the melons from being bruised in transit. Incidental to preserving an important established crop, the railroad added another by encouraging the sale of watermelon seed, a specialized activity which returned an income of about $125,000 annually.

Lower Río Grande Valley producers struggled with a different problem. They found that carload shipments of a single vegetable were difficult to manage because only the largest consuming centers could absorb such quantities at one time. Since tariff restrictions forbade mixed loadings, the freight traffic departments and the agricultural departments of the South Texas roads co-operated in securing amendments to the existing regulations, then popularized the practice of shipping a variety of vegetables in one car.

[4] Information from Mo. Pac. Ag. Dev. Dept., Arthur W. Large, J. M. Prickett, and J. B. Shores.

Agricultural Education Renewed

In the same area, the citrus-fruit growers, far removed from both consuming and canning centers, were selling a perishable commodity. The Gulf Coast Lines and the Southern Pacific agitated for the development of a canning industry to take care of the surplus even before the canning of citrus fruit juices had been perfected. Although the subsequent location of such an industry in the area was not due solely to railroads, no one worked more consistently towards that end or advertised its potentialities more widely than the railroads. As much as half the annual crop is now marketed in cans, saving the growers from losses caused by underconsumption during the marketing season.

Canning was only one of the processing methods encouraged by railroads as a means of facilitating the marketing of perishables and saving a surplus which would otherwise be lost. The Frisco was instrumental in securing the establishment of six large quick-freeze poultry plants in northwestern Arkansas; the Missouri Pacific helped locate four freezing plants which in 1947 processed one-third of the strawberries from their territory.[5]

At the time of its inception, agricultural-development work was definitely subordinate to the task of attracting settlers. Since World War I the situation has been reversed. Colonization has frequently become a function of the agricultural agent as the areas seeking to attract newcomers became more limited. He was at times responsible for deciding whether a railroad would invite the occupation of undeveloped areas by building branches. He had to determine whether it was desirable to encourage newcomers with the promise of irrigation. The agricultural development department of the Missouri Pacific made a detailed study of the problem of irrigation in the subhumid zones on its Texas lines in 1923. It had to determine the feasibility of specific proposed projects and release the conclusions to the communities involved. The department also employed a geologist to make an underground water survey, a report of such merit that it was published as a bulletin of the United States Geological Survey.[6]

Pure colonization work, as understood in an earlier day, was not entirely past history, even though the great mass movement had ended. In 1926 the Santa Fe handled almost 1,500 emigrant outfits to Texas, Kansas, and Oklahoma. The same year, the Missouri Pa-

---

[5] K. E. Soder, "Watermelon Marketing Problems," ARDA *Proc., 1944,* 101–103; information from Arthur W. Large, C. B. Michelson, and the Mo. Pac. Ag. Dev. Dept.
[6] Information from Harry M. Bainer and the Mo. Pac. Ag. Dev. Dept.

cific temporarily revived the post of colonization agent in its agricultural development department to advertise southeastern Missouri, Crowley's Ridge, the White River country of the Ozarks, southwestern Louisiana, and western Kansas. The Missouri Pacific continued the intensive advertising of the lower Río Grande Valley after acquiring the Gulf Coast Lines and moved 30,000 persons in organized homeseeker parties in the peak year. In 1933 it employed an assistant colonization agent to establish a colony of Germans and Hungarians in southwestern Louisiana. Another assistant settled a considerable number of families in southwestern Missouri in 1933 and 1934.

As a result of the "dust bowl," the Kansas City Southern and the Louisiana and Arkansas revived their colonizing activities. In co-operation with the Long Bell Lumber Company, they moved Mennonite families from the stricken area to the vicinity of De Ridder, Louisiana, arranged credit for seed, fertilizer, and other supplies, and secured registered bulls for them to improve their herds.[7]

The place of agricultural development has been modified constantly to meet changed conditions. By the end of World War I the Agricultural Extension Service had taken over much of the educational work previously performed by railroads, but there was still much activity through the twenties. Depression and war years led to reduced budgets, but these departments still have important functions.[8]

The program of the Missouri Pacific is fairly typical of southwestern roads in general. In 1948 it maintained a dairy program, including pasture improvement, artificial insemination, and the elimination of scrub stock. A fruit- and vegetable-marketing program was designed to serve producers of eleven major perishable crops in five states. The railroad co-operated with the Wheat Improvement Associations of Kansas and Nebraska and popularized better strains of hybrid corn in corn-producing sections. Activities in the field of poultry raising were directed towards improving practices and extending into new territory. In co-operation with industrial concerns, the railroad promoted better means of processing and marketing perishables. The agricultural and industrial development departments worked to-

[7] C. L. Seagraves, "Colonization as a Factor in Traffic Development," *SF Mag.*, Vol. XXI (Aug., 1927), 19–20; information from the Mo. Pac. Ag. Dev. Dept. and from J. M. Prickett.

[8] John F. Benham, "New Things Being Done in Agricultural Development Departments," ARDA *Proc., 1944*, 45–54; information from Mo. Pac. Ag. Dev. Dept. and C. B. Michelson.

Agricultural Education Renewed

gether in locating freezing plants, creameries, canneries, and alfalfa dehydrators.[9]

All the aid given to farmers is not confined to agricultural development departments. At times railroads have assumed partial responsibility for supplying farm labor. From early in the century some railroads kept on file requests for farm laborers, with such information as the kind needed, prevailing wages, and working conditions. If the local agent could not fill the request, he referred it to the proper state office. The service has been used most effectively in placing harvest hands and packing-shed workers. In 1924 and 1925 American railroads established a temporary fare for farm laborers of one-half the regular fare to assist in overcoming a critical shortage of agricultural manpower.[10]

Traffic departments have made their important contributions. Between 1925 and 1928 the Missouri Pacific cut the time from Harlingen, Texas, to St. Louis, Missouri, from 118 to 72 hours. Locals picked up the produce from numerous shipping points and concentrated it at Harlingen. From there the Missouri Pacific ran trains of solid "fruit-blocks," stopping only for icing and inspection. To save still more time, the railroad established an icing station at Lexa, Arkansas, and routed the perishables around Little Rock to avoid congestion. The Southern Pacific was equally careful in handling Texas fruits and vegetables. Trains of perishables were made up at Edinburg, left there at six o'clock each morning, picked up shipments at four concentration points en route, and made delivery to the Cotton Belt at Shreveport on the afternoon of the next day. The trains then sped across Arkansas to Memphis, Tennessee, their cargoes destined for eastern markets. Special handling is not reserved for perishables alone. In 1949 the Santa Fe began operating the "Cotton Special," an all-cotton train from the Lubbock area to Houston and Galveston, for speedy delivery in the export trade.[11]

Railroads have developed a very efficient system of keeping in close touch with each locality so that facilities can be mobilized to take care of peak harvest needs. Long before the actual harvest begins, the preliminary plans have been made. By the time the wheat,

[9] Information from Mo. Pac. Ag. Dev. Dept.
[10] Andrews, *Railroads and Farming*, 32–33, 44; information from Lee Lyles.
[11] "Missouri Pacific Stimulates Agricultural Program," *Ry. A.*, Vol. LXXXV, 449–451; "Fast Service for Southeast Texas," *Ry. A.*, Vol. CVIII, 449–50, 452; "Houston's Railroads Continue to Modernize," *Houston* (April, 1950), 19.

vegetables, or fruit starts moving, the traffic departments have accurate estimates of the requirements of each shipping point.[12]

Railroads share some of their traffic problems with shippers and other interested parties through the activities of the Regional Shippers' Advisory boards, organized nationally in 1924 after being tried successfully in the Pacific Northwest. Initiated by the car-service department of the Association of American Railroads, the boards drew their membership from shippers and public officials rather than from carriers. Their original purpose was to assist the railroads in planning the distribution of their cars during the peak shipping periods, but their activities were subsequently extended to include promoting better shipper-carrier relations, compiling more complete seasonal information, and recommending modifications in regulations to fit shippers' needs.

In the first year of their operation, the second largest wheat crop in Kansas history was moved with practically no complaints, while the Southwestern District reported the best car service in that area's history. In the second year, E. I. Lewis of the Interstate Commerce Commission reported: "As a result of these new public relations [advisory boards] the heaviest traffic in the history of this country is being moved this year with less cars and fewer locomotives than in any recent previous year. Thus the shippers and the carriers, under ideals and conditions that have been created through the channels of regulation, are voluntarily, I am pleased to report, beginning to withdraw from commissions one of the most troublesome common carrier problems."[13]

After a quarter of a century the boards are an established auxiliary to common carrier services. Although not strictly agricultural in nature, many of the members are drawn from that field to meet with representatives of other economic interests in order to create a cross section of the complex society which is America.[14]

The agricultural scene has been revolutionized dramatically since bands of steel first pushed across the Plains. It was more than simply establishing good relations which prompted railroads to offer their continuously changing agricultural services; it meant survival. The

---

[12] Information from Arthur W. Large and Lee Lyles.
[13] Quoted in *Ry. A.*, Vol. LXXIX, 1019–20.
[14] "Eleven Regional Shippers Boards Now Organized," *Ry. A.*, Vol. LXXVII, 249–51; "Shippers Praise Transportation Service," *Ry. A.*, Vol. LXXVII, 848–50; RRS *M. Bull.*, VI (n.s.), 57–63.

railroads met that challenge by assuming a major role in pioneering those developments which built the agricultural prosperity of the Southwest and by continuing those services which were still of value to their agricultural patrons.

CHAPTER 36

From Strawstack to Smokestack

BY THE EARLY twenties, southwestern railroads were well aware of the importance of their industrial developmental work. Since the region was still largely agrarian, in no section of the country was there greater opportunity to pioneer such activities. The industrial department's duties, nebulous in the beginning, were more clearly defined, and its functions, along with its technically trained personnel, expanded. The primary purpose was still the location and expansion of industries, but newer methods were much more thorough. Then, too, building good will became increasingly important as competition from rival forms of transportation threatened to cut into railroad revenues. Few communities failed to appreciate new payrolls, the more complete utilization of near-by resources, and the urbanization which followed. The railroads learned that it was good policy to identify themselves with their communities.[1]

Industrial departments continued most of their earlier activities, but with refinements in technique. They advertised cities and resources by preparing detailed reports on specific towns or groups of towns. The Santa Fe issued an informative bulletin, *New Industrial Sites in the West and Southwest,* which attracted a number of investors. The Missouri Pacific's report on various Arkansas towns led to the establishment of four textile mills. Most of the other southwestern railroads supported similar enterprises. The Rock Island, the Missouri Pacific, and the Kansas City Southern advertised the

[1] Warren T. White, "Public Relations in Industrial and Agricultural Development," ARDA *Proc., 1944,* 9–15.

Ozark and Ouachita Mountain country, building up local resorts and passenger traffic at the same time.[2]

The collection of data for prospective investors became more and more important. It became highly specialized as industry itself became more complex. In addition to general information, a vast body of more technical knowledge was necessary, with great variations in the demands of specific industries. One industry might request a thorough scientific analysis of certain raw materials; another, the source, amount, and bacterial and mineral content of the water; a third, the seasonal variations in temperature. Practically all would be interested in the availability of fuel and electric power, the price of land, the tax structure, and general living conditions. In order to furnish such extensive information the industrial commissioner had to have an intimate knowledge of each city.

As requests were received, industrial departments analyzed the requirements for each proposed industry and recommended sites. This service was of unusual value, since industries planning large-scale developments often desired to make their initial investigations without publicity. Railroad industrial departments could either supply the information directly or collect it without revealing the names of interested parties.[3] The work of the commissioner did not end with the location of the industry. He continued to act in an advisory capacity as long as his services were needed. In so doing he not only maintained close relations with the various industries, but co-operated with chambers of commerce, state universities, governmental agencies, and civic groups.

The results were of great significance to the Southwest, but the full story will never be written. Some railroads did not keep a running account of their accomplishments, and many transactions were confidential in nature. The most cursory examination, however, reveals in part the importance of railroads in the location of new industries.

The Missouri Pacific lines in Texas established an industrial department for Texas and Louisiana in 1920. The first year, it aided the Jefferson Island Salt Mining Company in locating at Jefferson

---

[2] "Beating the Bushes for Freight," *Ry. A.*, Vol. CXX, 1003; information from Mo. Pac. Ag. Dev. Dept. and Arthur W. Large; summary of brochures of various southwestern railroads.

[3] William H. Manss, "The Industrial Commissioner," *Railway Organization and Working*, 44–62; William R. Wright, "Industrial Plant Location," ARDA *Proc., 1944*, 104–108; information from Mo. Pac. Ind. Dev. Dept., J. M. Prickett, and Arthur W. Large.

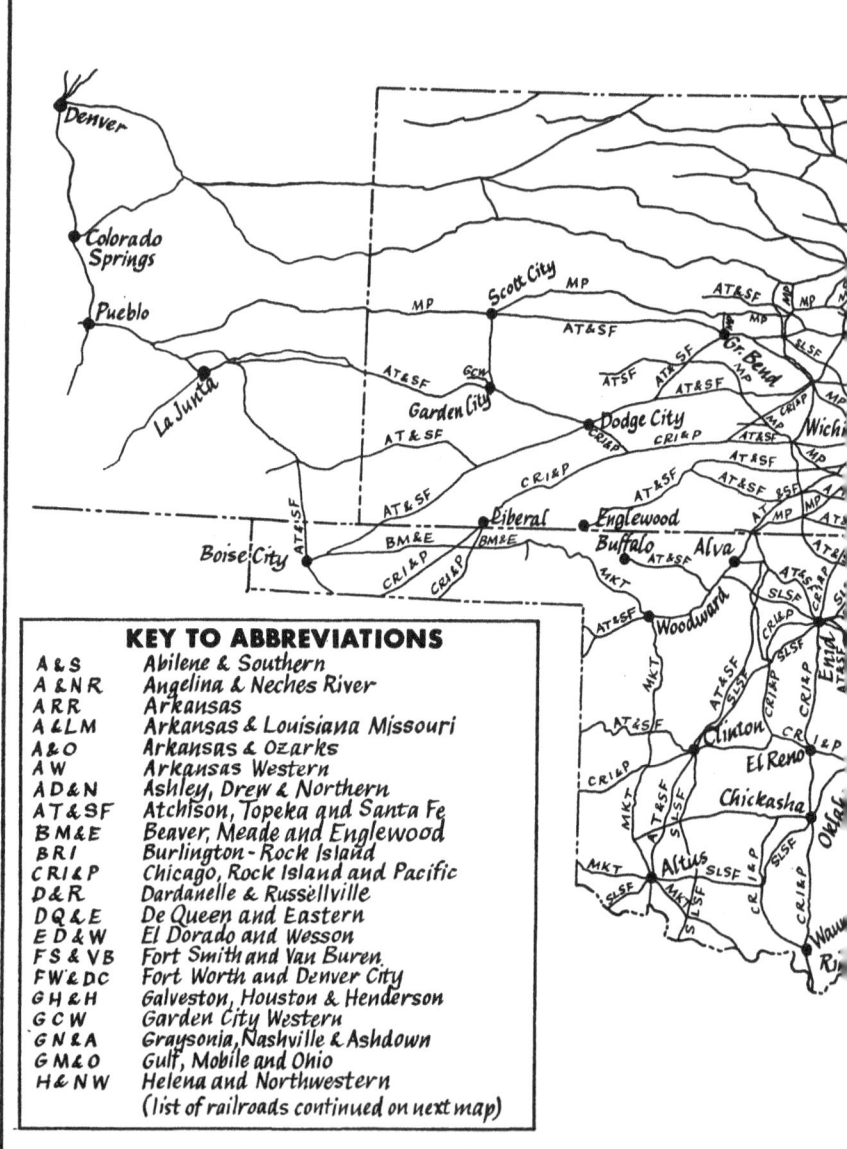

KEY TO ABBREVIATIONS

A & S	Abilene & Southern
A & NR	Angelina & Neches River
A R R	Arkansas
A & LM	Arkansas & Louisiana Missouri
A & O	Arkansas & Ozarks
A W	Arkansas Western
AD & N	Ashley, Drew & Northern
AT & SF	Atchison, Topeka and Santa Fe
BM & E	Beaver, Meade and Englewood
B R I	Burlington – Rock Island
CRI & P	Chicago, Rock Island and Pacific
D & R	Dardanelle & Russellville
DQ & E	De Queen and Eastern
E D & W	El Dorado and Wesson
FS & VB	Fort Smith and Van Buren
FW & DC	Fort Worth and Denver City
GH & H	Galveston, Houston & Henderson
G C W	Garden City Western
GN & A	Graysonia, Nashville & Ashdown
GM & O	Gulf, Mobile and Ohio
H & NW	Helena and Northwestern

(list of railroads continued on next map)

Gulf Southwes

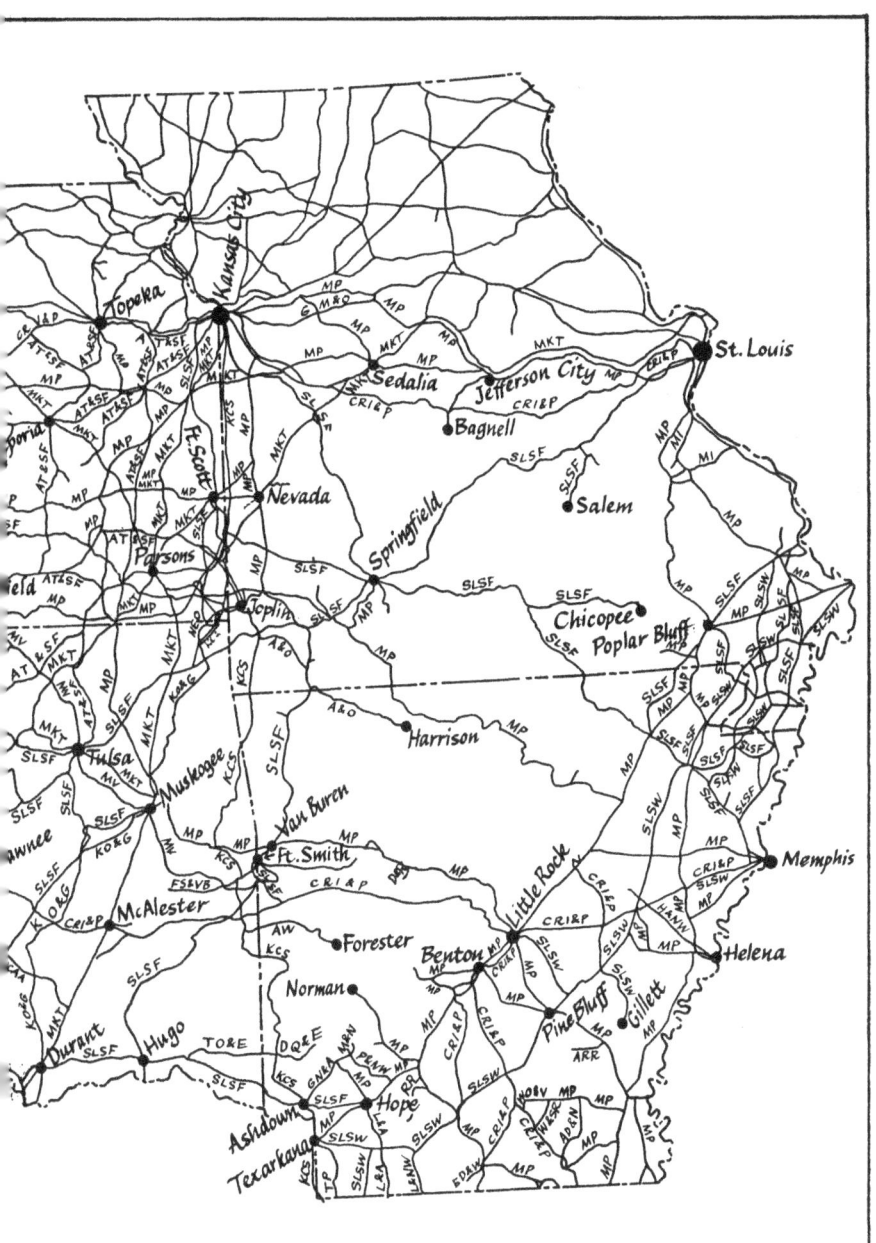

Railroads, 1950

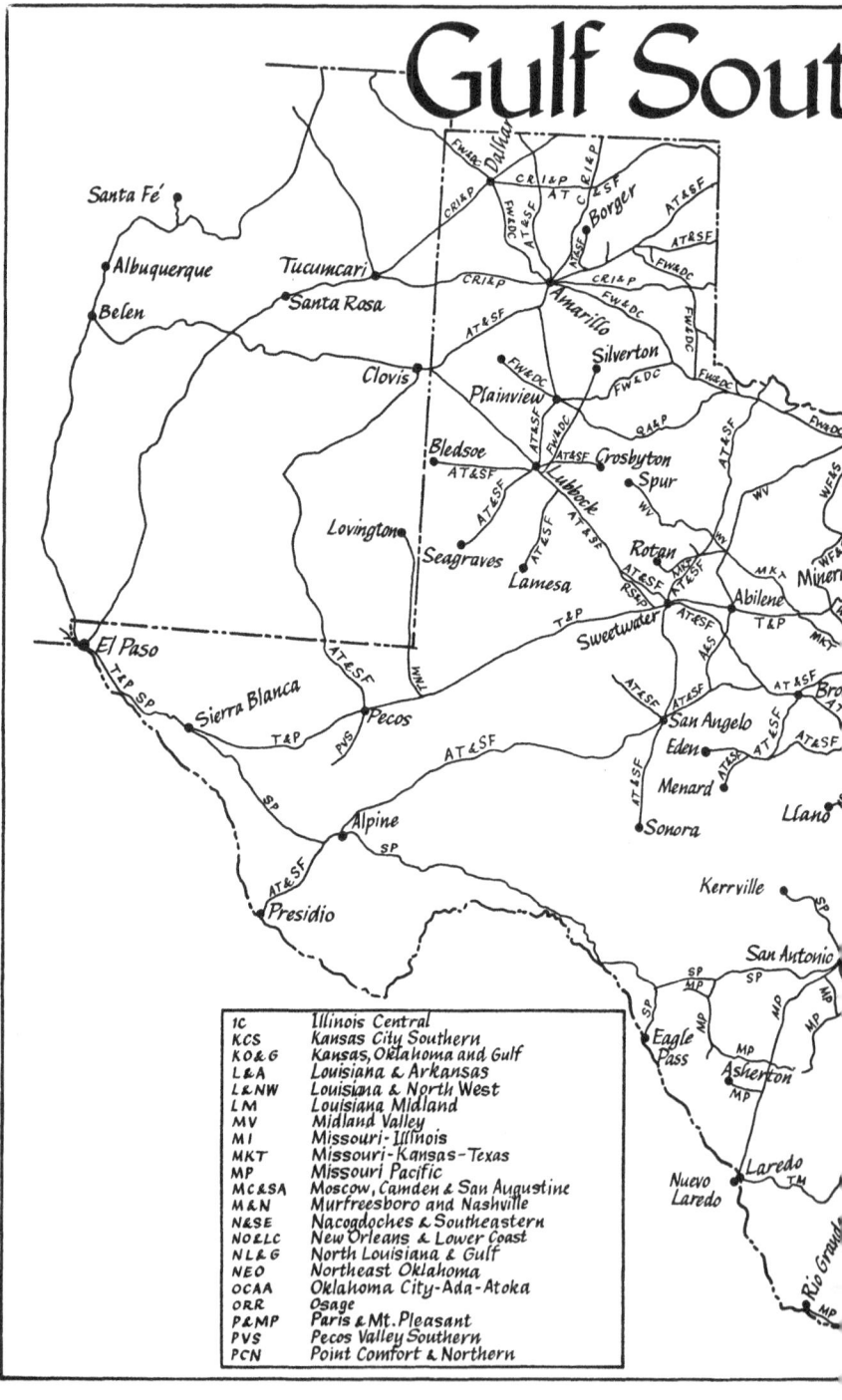

est Railroads, 1950

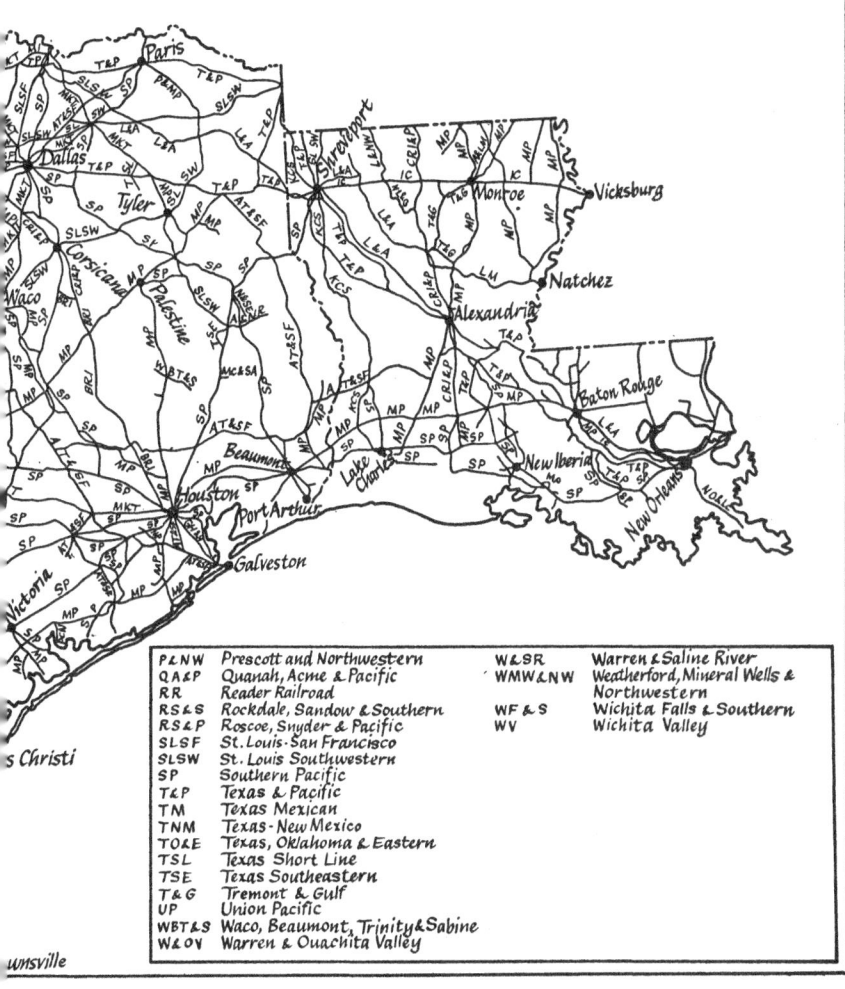

P&NW	Prescott and Northwestern	W&SR	Warren & Saline River
QA&P	Quanah, Acme & Pacific	WMW&NW	Weatherford, Mineral Wells & Northwestern
RR	Reader Railroad		
RS&S	Rockdale, Sandow & Southern	WF&S	Wichita Falls & Southern
RS&P	Roscoe, Snyder & Pacific	WV	Wichita Valley
SLSF	St. Louis-San Francisco		
SLSW	St. Louis Southwestern		
SP	Southern Pacific		
T&P	Texas & Pacific		
TM	Texas Mexican		
TNM	Texas-New Mexico		
TO&E	Texas, Oklahoma & Eastern		
TSL	Texas Short Line		
TSE	Texas Southeastern		
T&G	Tremont & Gulf		
UP	Union Pacific		
WBT&S	Waco, Beaumont, Trinity & Sabine		
W&OV	Warren & Ouachita Valley		

Island, Louisiana. Subsequently, it assisted in establishing the Southern Alkali Corporation at Corpus Christi, the Mathieson Alkali Works at Lake Charles, and the Solvay Process Company at Baton Rouge. Its most outstanding successes have been in the chemical industries, but its work with citrus-juice canners in the lower Río Grande Valley and spinach and bean canners at Crystal City was of much local significance.

The Rock Island played an important part in securing the first Kraft paper mill to operate west of the Mississippi when it helped to locate the one at Hodge, Louisiana. The Frisco assisted in establishing oil mills in the Delta area, twenty alfalfa-dehydrating plants between St. Louis and Memphis, and, later, six large poultry-dressing, quick-freezing plants in northwestern Arkansas. The pioneer work of this railroad in encouraging commercial canning not only developed that important activity, but was of material weight in attracting two can-manufacturing plants to northwestern Arkansas.[4]

Despite the efforts of industrial departments, the Gulf Southwest remained predominantly agricultural until the forties. Oil refineries and zinc smelters, brick and tile kilns, and portland cement and gypsum plants which were scattered through the area were there simply because of the fortunate circumstance of the location of basic raw materials. The percentage of persons engaged in manufacturing in 1939 was indicative of the relatively incomplete industrialization of the entire area. Missouri was twenty-third, Louisiana twenty-eighth, Texas thirty-seventh, Arkansas thirty-eighth, Kansas thirty-ninth, and Oklahoma forty-fourth among the states. St. Louis led all Southwestern cities in the extent of its manufacturing, followed by the Kansas City, the Houston, the Dallas–Fort Worth, and the Beaumont–Port Arthur districts. New Orleans, San Antonio, Oklahoma City, Tulsa, and Wichita were all of considerable importance.[5]

The forties comprised a period of rapid development in the islands of industrial activity in the agricultural Southwest. All the earlier centers grew at fantastic rates, and several new ones appeared. By the end of the decade the coastal region from Houston to New Orleans was rapidly becoming a major area of industrial concentration, and a number of inland cities were beginning to overtake the older

---

[4] Information from W. H. Hobbs, dir. of res., Mo. Pac. Lines, and from Mo. Pac. Ind. Dev. Dept., Mo. Pac. of Tex. Ind. Dev. Dept., Arthur W. Large, and C. B. Michelson.

[5] "Manufactures," *Sixteenth Census*, I, 42, 50–53, 55, 97, 116; ibid., III, 170, 332, 374, 544, 830, 982.

ones of the East and North.⁶ Two factors, the full significance of which were realized later, were responsible for the growth. One was the dispersion of industry, the retreat from extreme concentration and urbanization; the other was the realization that acids, hydrocarbons, and fresh water were present in parts of the Southwest in almost unlimited quantities, thus laying the foundation for chemical industries.

There was some tendency towards decentralization in the thirties, with the Gulf Coast and the larger cities of the interior benefiting because of their transportation facilities and raw materials. Railroads seized the opportunity to supply much of the information to those industries which were relocating. World War II stimulated the movement as the demand grew for synthetic rubber, high-octane gasoline, and other products to which southwestern industry could readily adapt itself. The Southwest possessed other advantages. Housing, transportation, and power were not such critical problems as they were in the heavily industrialized East.⁷

Discoveries in the field of industrial chemistry were of equal importance. They did not burst full blown on the Southwest. Petroleum resources in particular had been exploited for years. The period beginning with World War I and continuing through the twenties contributed new oil fields, whose boisterous, lawless boom towns were reminiscent of the mining camps and cowtowns of bygone days. The thirties added great new fields, and each year since has contributed its discoveries. The chemical industry was also established before the forties; gas, oil, and basic chemicals were already challenging the historic trinity of coal, limestone, and iron ore. Without this basic change, the raw materials of the Southwest would have continued to be siphoned off to more mature industrial areas.⁸

With the government underwriting much of the cost, industry providing technical experts, and railroads supplying information on local conditions, there was a mass movement of war industries to the coastal zone and the larger interior cities. After the war, railroads assisted in the process of converting war plants to peace-time production for civilian consumption. The impetus furnished by the war did not die, and at the meeting of the American Railway Development Association in 1949, Henry W. Coffman of the New York Central reported that

---

⁶ *1950 Census of Population,* Series PC–2, Nos. 25, 29, 33, 39, 43 Rev., 44.
⁷ See ARDA *Proc.* since 1936 for many comments on this movement.
⁸ Rister, *Oil! Titan of the Southwest,* 106, 108–18, 143–80, 196–283.

Houston, Texas, was leading the nation in the number and value of new industrial plants.[9]

The general promotional activities of railroads did not abate. In 1945 alone the Frisco's industrial department assisted in establishing 208 industries along its lines; two years later the industrial research development department of the Katy located 360 new or expanded industries in its territory, representing a new investment of $20,000,000 and more than 5,000 new jobs. Within a few months the Katy helped to bring 35 varied industries, including manufacturers of fencing materials, concrete blocks, paint products, road machinery, paper products, and oil-field equipment to the city of Houston, adding more than 2,000 to the labor force of the city. Other railroads have equally impressive records.[10]

In 1946 the Katy, traditionally a leader in advertising the Gulf Southwest to the nation, ran a special train for fifty guests, and two years later another for one hundred guests, to show off its territory. The tours lasted ten days and covered well over three thousand miles. Leading newspaper columnists, financial writers, editors, industrial engineers and analysts, and businessmen made up the parties. Civic leaders in the larger cities provided local transportation and meals and arranged tours through industrial plants, oil fields, and other points of interest. Other railroads have advertised in periodicals with national circulation; have personally established contact with possible investors, and have distributed brochures. They have also followed the example of the Kansas City Southern, which has conducted additional surveys along its lines in the search for new basic industrial materials, a list now ranging "from antimony to zinc."[11]

Once a new industry had determined to locate at a given city, it faced the problem of securing a specific site. Since heavy industries had to be in the immediate vicinity of the tracks, railroads determined their locations. In the first years this was largely a matter of chance, but in time railroads participated much more directly. They prepared maps of industrial districts, kept listings of available lands and buildings, and circulated the brochures of industrial realtors, fre-

---

[9] ARDA *Proc., 1949*, 35–44 and many articles in the *Proc.* dealing with this subject.
[10] "Beating . . . Freight," *Ry. A.*, Vol. CXX, 1003–1004; "The Katy Shows Off Its Territory," *Ry. A.*, Vol. CXXV, 895; *Galveston Mag.* (Feb. 10, 1950), 10; *Houston* (Nov., 1947), 11, 85; information from C. B. Michelson.
[11] "The Katy . . . Territory," *Ry. A.*, Vol. CXXV, 894–95; Robert K. Butcher, "For a Greater Shreveport," *Shreveport Mag.* (April, 1949), 49; information from J. M. Prickett.

quently acting as brokers in real estate transactions. This field of railroad activity expanded so greatly that most of the southwestern railroads began to develop their own industrial districts.

Douglas Island, at Shreveport, was consciously converted to this purpose by railroads serving the city. The Burlington pioneered this work in Kansas City by holding one-third interest in the North Kansas City Development Company, which provided locations for many industries. Other companies bought and cleared large acreages for such use until there were few cities which did not feel the influence of railroads in shaping the growth of their industrial districts. The Santa Fe purchased 145 acres adjacent to its tracks in Houston, all to be released to industrial concerns, and the Katy likewise held considerable real estate in Houston for that purpose. The same two railroads had similar projects in Oklahoma City. The Santa Fe improved a 140 acre tract in the northwestern section of the city; the Katy developed the 40-acre East Reno district, near the heart of the business district, for light industries interested in locating in a zoned area restricted to modern architecture.

Fort Worth and Dallas, the two North Texas cities which grew so remarkably during the forties, shared in railroad-sponsored industrial districts to an unusual degree. The Cotton Belt opened up a section in Fort Worth at North Commerce about 1920 and later secured an acreage at Hodge for general industrial development. The Frisco became interested in the Bailey District and the Santa Fe in a 220-acre site in east Fort Worth. The Rock Island held four sites, totaling almost 300 acres, which it made available by either purchase or lease to new enterprises. In 1950 the Katy was planning a new site in south Fort Worth as a modernistic, landscaped project.

Of the major industrial districts in Dallas, three were specifically of railroad origin. The Eagle Ford Land and Industrial Company, a Texas and Pacific subsidiary, acquired more than 200 acres of land and started the Eagle Ford District in 1922. The company built streets and provided for gas and electricity, but its greatest period of expansion was delayed until 1947. The Santa Fe had a 300-acre tract, bearing the name of the railroad, which in 1949 and 1950 was being supplied with industrial tracks and utilities. The Katy, in line with its work in other cities, acquired 180 acres in Dallas which it dedicated to business uses, but with restrictions against nuisance industries and unsightly buildings. By 1950 this area, called the Airlawn District, had attracted thirty-six companies, including some of the largest distributors in the United States, who had invested over $20,000,000 in improvements.

The increased cost of land began to limit the activities of railroads in acquiring industrial properties by the late forties, although they were still in the market for sites which they could buy at reasonable prices.[12]

One of the most recent services introduced by railroads in promoting industrialization has been the establishment of foreign freight departments to meet the demands of importers and exporters. Their duties are varied, but their primary functions are to furnish patrons with detailed information on shipping problems, port facilities, local marketing conditions and routings, and answers to the hundreds of questions which shippers ask. They also radio information on shipments which require extra care or equipment in handling.[13]

In their struggle for new types of economic development, the railroads did not neglect earlier industries which were declining. Their work in timbered areas was particularly noteworthy. The depletion of the forests forced the abandonment of a number of settlements, and ghost towns dotted the cutover lands as denuded areas were eroded, leaving the region barren. Attempts by railroads to introduce an agricultural economy were largely abortive because much of the pineland was a sandy soil which did not lend itself to cultivation; some of it could be converted to orchards and more to grazing, but there was a tendency for oak thickets to overrun it.

From the standpoint of continued industrialization, however, the attempts of the railroads to preserve the tonnage derived from the transportation of lumber and wood products was of greater significance than their efforts to establish an agricultural economy. The Illinois Central, still dependent on the forests for much of its tonnage in Louisiana and Mississippi, was particularly active. In co-operation with lumber companies and civic groups, it initiated a timber-conservation program. By the summer of 1949 it had graduated over 1,400 students from short courses which gave instruction in selecting trees for cutting, preventing forest fires, and handling timber sales. It has also instituted an extensive reforestation program. There is at

---

[12] ARDA *Proc., 1936,* 40; *ibid., 1950,* 135–38; Hoag, "A . . . Railway," 155–58; *Houston* (July, 1948), 12, 18; *Fort Worth Mag.* (July, 1949), 10, 14–16; information from Thomas W. Finney, Ind. Dept., Dallas Chamber of Commerce.

[13] "Beating . . . Freight," *Ry. A.,* Vol. CXX, 1000; *KCKN Railroad Radio Series No. 7.*

the present time an increasing tendency among railroads to attach foresters to their industrial departments.[14]

Industrial-development work occupies a more and more prominent place in the deliberations of the American Railway Development Association. Absorbed more with problems of agriculture than of industry in its formative years, it now serves both. The industrial development departments are also vitally interested in the work of the regional shippers' advisory boards.

With both agricultural and overindustrialized areas growing at a much slower proportionate rate than younger cities and with the continued dispersion of industry which has already been of material benefit to the Southwest, railroads have steadily extended their activities in the field of industrial development.

[14] USDA *Forest Service Bulletin No. 47, passim;* J. Walter Meyers, Jr., "The Southern Forests and What They Mean to the Illinois Central Railroad," ARDA *Proc., 1949,* 65–69.

CHAPTER 37

A Century in Retrospect

WITHIN A FEW decades after the government drew a permanent Indian-frontier line across present eastern Kansas and Oklahoma (a line beyond which the wildest expansionist was content to admit that no white man would ever care to settle), speculators were realizing large paper profits from townsites along existing or potential railroads on the Plains. Forty years after California-bound wagon trains pushed westward from the last outposts of civilization at the bend of the Missouri to cross half a continent before reaching the fringe of civilization along the Pacific, the government had officially erased the line representing the western frontier. Railroads played a major role in this and equally spectacular dramas which were to follow.

Railroads developed concurrently with a mass migration westward, a movement which they partially inspired and to which they contributed in no small degree. They were indispensable to the growth of the West, but they were only one factor. In combination with fertile soil, virgin forests, mineral resources, and other bounties of nature, they built the West. A rapidly urbanizing and industrializing nation could absorb the increased production. The operation of each factor rested on the existence of the others.

Railroads did not wait passively for the coming of settlers, but carried on an active campaign both at home and abroad to stimulate a desire in the landless to occupy the virgin country. The exact number who came to the Gulf Southwest as the direct result of railroad colonizing activity will never be known. It is quite easy to trace such

A Century in Retrospect

movements as the Russo-German Mennonites, the Iowa-bred rice farmers of the Grand Prairie, or Count Telfener's Italian laborers. The obvious migrations, however, do not include such things as railroad advertising, which increased the population along the Santa Fe west of Hutchinson, Kansas, from 2,000 to 67,000 within five years after the line was constructed. They do not include the many thousands, eager to grow up with the country, who followed railroads across the Mississippi to the plains of Kansas, Oklahoma, and West Texas, the Ozarks of Arkansas and Missouri, or the timberlands of Louisiana and East Texas.

When the railroads extended their practice of pushing into the wilderness ahead of settlement to the more speculative field of building into territory not even subject to legal entry, they determined the course of Indian policy. The early agitation for the dissolution of tribal organization and the opening of Indian Territory originated largely with railroads, supported by border cities. Congress laboriously hewed from the tangle of treaties, railroad bills, and conflicting theories regarding the status of the Indians a series of arrangements whereby the railroads could enter. They were the first to breach the territory closed to settlement. Through the wedge thus inserted, white settlers were funneled in until the number became so great that the Indian nations collapsed.

Railroads soon found themselves in conflict with those whom they had attracted to the West. Much of the ill-feeling arose because the highly individualistic settlers resented their dependence on an alien force, especially after economic conditions over which neither contending faction had any control stripped the western farmer of his profits. There were enough serious abuses on the part of the railroads to furnish the West with positive wrongs around which to crystallize its wrath. Inevitably, the politically minded frontier turned to politics for its answers.

The Gulf Southwest cannot be differentiated from other parts of the West in the tenor of its course. The true differentiation is one of time, rather than substance, since the area lagged in its development. Even within the region there were wide differences. Cosmopolitan New Orleans and bustling St. Louis had long since passed the frontier stage before Oklahoma could be legally settled. The uneven development led to a wide range of legislative answers. Proposals originating in more mature areas were usually cautiously regulatory; in the newer western communities the nature of the society dictated vigorous action.

Then Came the Railroads

Several principles emerged from the regulatory provisions. One was the right of states to exercise control over rates and services, subject to federal and state constitutional limitations and the paramount interest of the federal government in interstate commerce. Another was the relinquishment of direct legislative control in favor of commissions acting within the framework established by the legislature. Gradually, the commissions' activities were extended to embrace other public utilities, and the name of the agency was usually changed to Public Service Commission or Corporation Commission. The statement by the leading student of the Kansas agency that "state administrative regulation of public utilities was introduced into Kansas as a direct consequence of the coming of the railroads"[1] was no less applicable to other southwestern states.

Political pressures, however, were far from being the most compelling reason for a changed attitude on the part of railroad management. Largely because of their colonization efforts, the railroads gradually realized that their own prosperity depended upon that of the regions which they served. The need for a positive program had not been so evident in the earliest period because the lines penetrated a partially developed country, agricultural settlement having already pushed far up the river valleys before there were any railroads. Later the rails ran ahead of settlement and into lands which were known to be fit for agriculture but which had not fared well because of inadequate transportation. They then pushed on through a territory in which agricultural productivity was highly questionable and which certainly could not be developed without railroads. It was in these unsettled areas that colonization work was to proceed at a rapid pace, and it was here that the railroads realized that the problem of holding settlers was of equal importance with recruiting them.

The first program was one of direct relief. Few railroads fail to record the story of seed or stock feed hauled free and then sold at cost on unsecured notes in stricken areas. The work of agricultural development departments, starting as adjuncts of colonization departments and growing until they swallowed the parent activities, is a less widely known activity. Railroads educated the uninitiated in the art of making a living in the dry Southwest. Certainly no one would claim that all agricultural improvement came about as the result of railroad activities, but during much of the period of rapid advancement, their development departments operated almost alone

[1] Stene, *Railroad Commission to Corporation Commission*, 7.

A Century in Retrospect

in disseminating information on new crops, new methods, diversification, and better methods of marketing. It was only after the creation of the Agricultural Extension Service in 1914 that a government agency assumed prime responsibility for this vital service.

All the newcomers to the area did not settle on farms, nor did all take their living directly from the soil. The rural trading town was essential during the heyday of the railroads. It served as a market for farm produce and as a shopping center for near-by farmers. There is almost a drab uniformity in the history of small agricultural communities which sprang up along the railroads. Most of them grew fairly rapidly to somewhat more than their logical size, then, in the absence of unusual circumstances, became relatively static or even settled into mild stagnation, enjoying an annual revival only during the few feverish weeks when harvest hands swelled the population abnormally and long lines of loaded wagons waited their turns under gin spouts or at elevator scales. The agricultural trading centers continued to hold on until highway transportation practically put an end to their usefulness. The little town then withered; its bank, its drugstore, its barbershop, and all but one or two general stores and filling stations closed.

Most railroad towns remained of local importance only, but a rather large number became substantial cities, and a dozen became diversified commercial and industrial centers of national significance. In 1950, fifteen cities in the Southwest were larger than the New Orleans of 1850. Far out on the Plains, Amarillo and Lubbock were approximately the size St. Louis had been one hundred years before. Almost a hundred cities in the Gulf Southwest exceeded 15,000 in population, a figure which would have placed them among the important places in the nation in 1850. Most of them originated in the latter part of the nineteenth century, and some even later.[2]

Most of the larger cities were greatly indebted to railroads for their subsequent growth. They were placed in a favorable position because of the transportation facilities which drew trade to them; furthermore, the conversion of a raw new town into a railroad terminus gave it a decided advantage over its rivals. It is a far cry from the handful of workmen on short local roads to the thousands of highly specialized employees living in each of the major termini of the present great systems; the early lines, with their scant labor forces and primitive equipment, however, gave just enough impetus to the growth

[2] *1950 Census of Population,* Series PC-2, Nos. 25, 29, 33, 39, 43 Rev., 44.

of favored localities to make some of them the great industrial cities of today.

The importance of railroads in community building cannot be confined to the narrow study of their entrance into each city. It must also be measured in terms of transportation lines, extending deep into trade territories so that fertile lands could be cultivated profitably, timber cut, and zinc, coal, or sulphur mined, and products put at the disposal of processors to develop industry. These were the things which attracted population. With the growth in population, the merchant had his customers, the doctor his patients, the lawyer his clients.

The conscious effort of the railroads to develop the cities in their territories by participating in industrial-development work came somewhat later than similar activities in the agricultural field. Even the earliest colonization agent was aware of the needs of his charges, and he was compelled to assume some responsibility for fitting them into a new environment. The transition from colonization to agricultural work was most natural. This was less true of industrial departments. When railroads finally recognized the importance of industrial development, they made intensive studies of the resources at hand, the capacities of specific cities, and the trends and conditions which would encourage expansion in the Southwest. They collected information and acted as confidential agents for new enterprises. Eventually, they assumed the responsibility for developing districts for the exact location of new industries.

But railroad influence cannot be limited to material things alone. Railroads exerted a very real influence on the social growth of the Southwest. They contributed to the standardization of patterns of life and, at the same time, made possible the variations which gave a distinctive flavor to certain local cultures. They were the one contact with the outside world which tended to break down extreme provincialism before the coming of motion pictures, automobiles, and radios.

In many diverse ways railroads made direct contributions to the intellectual and aesthetic development of the Gulf Southwest. The story of the Santa Fe's Harvey girls as a civilizing influence in a harsh environment is well known. Because of the magic of telegraphy, the "depot agent" was the one source for early information on prize fights, elections, and other events attracting wide popular attention. Railroads made possible the introduction of new forms of entertain-

A Century in Retrospect

ment. In 1873, P. T. Barnum was able to take his sixty-five-car circus west of the Mississippi to perform before awed Missourians and Kansans. Two years after the Memphis and Little Rock was completed, the Arkansas capital took its place on road-show schedules. The construction of the "Opera House," at which traveling troupes, lyceums, and minstrels held forth, usually followed the entrance of a railroad into a town. To a sophisticated society, much of this would appear light fare, but it was certainly better than none.

Inevitably railroads identified themselves with their communities as the range of their activities broadened. This relationship appeared in sharp relief during floods, blizzards, tornadoes, or other crises, when railroads put their facilities at the disposal of local authorities and assisted with the work of rehabilitation. The day-to-day contacts which built up a community of interest, however, have not been publicized. The activities of development departments in helping a community and the railroad at the same time, the presence of a popular agent or section foreman or train dispatcher, the participation of railroad employees in civic affairs, the paying of taxes ahead of time to assist a financially weak school district, contributions to funds to put up stadium lights or build a ball park or send a 4–H member to Chicago—these are the small things which have integrated great corporations into the affairs of the communities they serve.

Railroads are no longer unchallenged in the field of transportation. Towns are served by buses, trucks, and automobiles; impatient tourists and harassed businessmen reduce their travel time by patronizing the airlines. Railroads are sharing their business with other common carriers more and more, but no other can boast as great an influence as they in shaping the course of economic growth, politics, and social institutions in the Gulf Southwest.

Bibliography

THE FOLLOWING abbreviations have been used in both the footnotes and the bibliography. Such generally used abbreviations as Cong. (Congress), sess. (session), *Cong. Rec.* (*Congressional Record*), and *Census* (*Census of the United States*) are used throughout, as are the following abbreviations for specific agencies: ICC (Interstate Commerce Commission), USDA (United States Department of Agriculture), U. S. Geol. Surv. (United States Geological Survey), GLO (General Land Office), OIA (Office of Indian Affairs), Dept. Int. (Department of the Interior), and Bd. Ind. Comm. (Board of Indian Commissioners). The customary abbreviations have been used for Senate and House reports and documents. In addition, the following abbreviations have been used for specific periodical publications: *Rep. Comm. Ind. Aff.* (*Annual Report of the Commissioner of Indian Affairs*), *Op. Atty. Gen.* (*Opinions of the Attorney General*), *Fed. Rep.* (*Federal Reporter*), *U. S. Rep.* (*United States Reports*), *Rep. Int. Comm.* (*Report of Internal Commerce of the United States*), *Val. Rep.* (*Valuation Reports* of the Interstate Commerce Commission), *Stat. Rys. U. S.* (*Annual Report of Statistics of Railways in the United States*), and "Stat. Pop." ("Statistics of Population" in the various census reports).

The Association of American Railroads has been shortened to Assn. Am. R., the American Railway Development Association to ARDA, and the Missouri Pacific Agricultural Development Department to Mo. Pac. Ag. Dev. Dept.

The following abbreviations have been used for periodicals: *AAA* (*Annals* of the American Academy of Political Science), AEA *Pub.* (American Economic Association *Publications*), AHA *Ann. Rep.* (*Annual Report* of the American Historical Association), AHA *Pub.* (Arkansas Historical Association *Publications*), *AHR* (*American Historical Review*), AHS *Trans.* (Alabama Historical Society *Transactions*), *ALR* (*American Law Review*), *Ag. H.* (*Agricultural History*), *Chron. Okla.* (*Chronicles of Oklahoma*), *Comm. & Fin. Chron.* (*Commercial & Financial Chronicle*), *JPE* (*Journal of Political Economy*), *KHQ* (*Kansas Historical Quarterly*), *KSHS Coll.* (*Collections* of the Kansas State Historical Society), *LHQ* (*Louisiana Historical Quarterly*) *MHR* (*Missouri Historical Review*), MSHS *Proc.* (Missouri State Historical Society *Proceedings*), *MVHR* (*Mississippi Valley Historical Review*), *NAR* (*North American Review*), *NMHR* (*New Mexico Historical Review*), *PSQ* (*Political Science Quarterly*), *QJE* (*Quarterly Journal of Economics*), R&LHS *Bull.* (Railway and Locomotive Historical Society *Bulletin*), *RIM* (*Rock Island Magazine*), RRS *M. Bull.* (Railway Research Service *Monthly Bulletin*), *Rev. of R.* (*Review of Reviews*), *Ry. A.* (*Railway Age*), *Ry. W.* (*Railway World*), *SCJ* (*Southwestern Colonization Journal*), *SEP* (*Saturday Evening Post*), *SFM* (*Santa Fe Magazine*), *SHQ* (*Southwestern Historical Quarterly*), SHSW *Proc.*

Bibliography

(*Proceedings* of the State Historical Society of Wisconsin), TAS *Trans.* (*Transactions of the Texas Academy of Science*), *TF&C* (*Texas Farming & Citriculture*), *THM* (*Tennessee Historical Magazine*), *TLR* (*Tulane Law Review*), TSHA *Quar.* (Texas State Historical Association *Quarterly*), and *WW* (*World's Work*).

In the following cases, abbreviations have been used for special collections or libraries; CLPCB (Cherokee Letter Press Copy Books, University of Oklahoma), IAD (Indian Archives Division, Oklahoma Historical Society), and Phil. Coll. (Phillips Collection, University of Oklahoma).

The Federal Writers' Project, the American Guide Series, is listed AGS, and the multi-volume *The South in the Building of the Nation* as *SBN*.

Note: For the sake of brevity, those items which contribute to several aspects of railroad influence in the Southwest are listed under the subject to which they primarily contributed.

1. GENERAL MATERIAL

In spite of the wide variation in scholarliness and reliability, the numerous state and local histories are the only available source for general local conditions. The American Guide Series (Federal Writers' Project of the WPA) and James Curtis Ballagh (ed.), *The South in the Building of the Nation* (12 volumes, Richmond, 1909) contain much information, but are of unequal merit.

2. RAILROAD AGITATION, PROJECTS, AND CONSTRUCTION

General Edmund P. Gaines' proposal: *Communication from Major-General Gaines, U. S. Army, relative to a system of Railroads* (Annapolis, 1839); *Letter of Major-General Gaines to the Governor of Mississippi, October 14, 1838* (n.p., n.d.); 25 Cong., 2 sess., *H. Ex. Doc. 311;* and 26 Cong., 1 sess., *S. Ex. Doc. 256.*

Southwestern railroad conventions: Three articles by Robert S. Cotterill: "Early Agitation for a Pacific Railroad, 1845–1850," *MVHR,* Vol. V (1919), 396–414; "The National Railroad Convention in St. Louis, 1849," *MHR,* Vol. XII (1918), 203–15; and "The Memphis Railroad Convention, 1848," *THM,* Vol. IV (1918), 83–94; and William Watson Davis, "Ante-Bellum Southern Commercial Conventions," AHS *Trans.,* Vol. V (1904), 153–202.

The Pacific Railroad issue: 30 Cong., 2 sess., *H. Rep. 145;* 32 Cong., 1 sess., *H. Rep. 101;* 34 Cong., 1 sess., *H. Reps. 273, 324,* and *358;* 34 Cong., 3 sess., *H. Rep. 264;* 36 Cong., 1 sess., *H. Rep. 428;* 36 Cong., 1 sess., *S. Ex. Doc. 56* (which is the 10-volume *Pacific Railway Surveys*); Lewis Henry Haney, *A Congressional History of Railways in the United States* (Madison, 1908, 1910); Robert Royal Russel, *Improvement of Communication with the Pacific Coast as an Issue in American Politics, 1783–1864* (Cedar Rapids, 1948); and George Leslie Albright, *Official Explorations for Pacific Railroads, 1853–1855* (Berkeley, 1921).

Railroad construction, general: The first forty-seven volumes of ICC *Val. Rep.* (Washington, 1916–1938); *Ry. A.* (1870–); *Ry. W.* (1856–1915); *Comm. & Fin. Chron.* (1865–); and *Poor's Manual of Railroads* (57 volumes, New York, 1869–1924) and the successor *Railroad Manual.* None of the general works on American railroads add any detail to southwestern railroad building, but certain regional ones are more rewarding: Robert E. Riegel, *The Story of the Western Railroads* (New York, 1926); S. G. Reed, *A History of the Texas Railroads* (Houston, 1941); Charles S. Potts, *Railroad Transportation in Texas* (Austin, 1909); R. A. Thompson, "The Development of the Present Texas Railway System," TAS *Trans.,* Vol. IV (1900), 57–80; Preston George and Sylvan R. Wood, "The Railroads of Oklahoma," R&LHS *Bull. No. 60* (1943), 7–78; Richard L. Douglas, "History of Manufactures in the Kansas District," KSHS *Coll.,* Vol. XI (1910), 81–215; Oscar Clayton Hull, "Railroads in Kansas," KSHS *Coll.,* Vol. XII (1911), 37–52; Edward J. White, "A Century of Transportation in Missouri," *MHR,* Vol. XV (1920), 126–62; and Charles H. Brough, "The Industrial History of Arkansas," AHA *Pub.,* Vol. I (1906), 191–229.

Railroad construction before 1875: Balthasar H. Meyer, *History of Transportation in*

Then Came the Railroads

the *United States before 1860* (Washington, 1917); Robert E. Riegel, "Trans-Mississippi Railroads during the 'Fifties," *MVHR*, Vol. X (1923); 153-72; Carl Russell Fish, *The Restoration of the Southern Railroads* (Madison, 1919); R. B. Oliver, "Missouri's First Railroad," *MHR*, Vol. XXVI (1931), 12-18; Lucinda de Leftwich Templin, "The Development of Railroads in Missouri to 1860" (M. A. Thesis, University of Missouri, 1913); Paul W. Gates, "The Railroads of Missouri, 1850-1870," *MHR*, Vol. XXVI (1932), 126-42; J. M. Greenwood, "Col. Robert T. Van Horn," *MHR*, Vol. IV (1909-1910), 92-105, 167-81; Robert E. Riegel, "The Missouri Pacific Railroad to 1879," *MHR*, Vol. XVIII (1923), 3-26; W. J. Thornton, "Early History of Railroads in Missouri," *Proceedings of the State Historical Society of Missouri . . . (1902)* (Palmyra, Mo., 1903), 28-43; Edward Joseph White, *Past and Future Influences of Railroads on the Development of Missouri* (Columbia, 1933); Margaret Lorene Fitzsimmons, "Railroad Development in Missouri, 1860-1870" (M. A. Thesis, Washington University, St. Louis, 1931); Andrew Forrest Muir, "Railroad Enterprises in Texas, 1836-1841," *SHQ*, Vol. XLVII (1944), 339-70; Alexander Deussen, "The Beginnings of the Texas Railroad System," *TAS Trans.*, Vol. IX (1906), 42-74; S. S. McKay, "Texas and the Southern Pacific Railroad, 1848-1860," *SHQ*, Vol. XXXV (1931), 1-27; P. Briscoe, "The First Texas Railroad," *TSHA Quar.*, Vol. VII (1904), 279-85; Harold J. Henderson, "The Building of the First Kansas Railroad South of the Kaw River," *KHQ*, Vol. XV (1947), 225-39; and D. L. Phillips, "The Early History of the Cairo and Fulton Railroad" (MS, University of Arkansas library). Contemporary accounts include: "The First Railroad in Missouri," *Western Journal and Civilian*, Vol. VIII (1852), 308-10; Atlantic and Pacific Railroad Company, *Opening of the Atlantic and Pacific Railroad and Completion of the South Pacific to Springfield, Missouri* (Springfield, 1870); Missouri, Kansas and Texas Railway Company, *Missouri, Kansas and Texas Railway Company* (New York, 1871); and Walter Prichard (ed.), "A Forgotten Louisiana Engineer: G. W. R. Bayley and His 'History of the Railroads of Louisiana,'" *LHQ*, Vol. XXX (1947), 1065-1325.

Later construction: Steven Frederik Van Oss, *American Railroads as Investments* (New York, 1893); Robert E. Riegel, "The Missouri Pacific, 1879-1900," *MHR*, Vol. XVIII (1923), 173-96; "Louis Houck, Empire Builder," *MHR*, Vol. XXIV (1930), 322-23; Charles S. Gleed, "The Rehabilitation of the Santa Fe Railway System," *KSHS Coll.*, Vol. XIII (1914), 451-68; James Franklin Holden, "The B I T: the story of an Adventure in Railroad Building," *Chron. Okla.*, Vol. XI (1933), 637-66; Otto Philip Byers, "The Conception and Growth of a Kansas Railroad," *KSHS Coll.*, Vol. XII (1912), 383-87; Arthur E. Stilwell, *Cannibals of Finance* (sixth edition, Chicago, 1912) and "I Had a Hunch," *SEP*, Vol. CC (Dec. 3, 1927), 3-4; (Dec. 17, 1927), 24-26; (Dec. 31, 1927), 24-26; and Vol. CCI (Jan. 14, 1928), 31; the following works of James L. Allhands: *Gringo Builders* (Iowa City, 1931), *Boll Weevil: Recollections of the Trinity and Brazos Valley Railway* (Houston, 1946), *Uriah Lott* (San Antonio, 1949), and "History of the Construction of the Frisco Railway Lines in Oklahoma," *Chron. Okla.*, Vol. III (1925), 229-39; Otto Philip Byers, "Early History of the El Paso Line of the Chicago, Rock Island and Pacific Railway," *KSHS Coll.*, Vol. XV (1922), 573-78; and Guthrie Smith, "William Ashton Hawkins," *NMHR*, Vol. XIV (1939), 305-308.

Histories of specific railroads: Glenn D. Bradley, *The Story of the Santa Fe* (Boston, 1920); James L. Marshall, *Santa Fe, the Railroad That Built an Empire* (New York, 1945); L. L. Waters, *Steel Trails to Santa Fe* (Lawrence, 1950); Sylvan R. Wood, "Locomotives of the Katy," *R&LHS Bull. No. 63* (1944), 8-132; V. V. Masterson, *The Katy Railroad and the Last Frontier* (Norman, 1952); Neill C. Wilson and Frank J. Taylor, *Southern Pacific, the Roaring Story of a Fighting Railroad* (New York, 1952); Richard C. Overton, *Gulf to Rockies: The Heritage of the Fort Worth and Denver—Colorado and Southern Railways, 1861-1898* (Austin, 1953); Albert C. Simmonds, Jr., "A History of the Texas and Pacific Railway Company, 1871-1924" (Thesis, Harvard University, 1925); Texas & Pacific Railway Company, *From Ox-Teams to Eagles* (Dallas, n.d.); Jacob E. Anderson, *A Brief History of the St. Louis Southwestern Railway Lines* (n.p., n.d.); William Edward Hayes, *Iron Road to Empire* (New York,

Bibliography

1953); *RIM*, Vol. XVII, No. 10 (1922); H. F. Hoag, "Brief History of the Kansas City Southern Railway System" (MS in KCS general office). Many periodical articles appeared from 1902 to 1916, particularly in *World's Work* and *Moody's Magazine*, dealing specifically with railroad finance, but incidentally discussing construction.

3. FRONTIER CONDITIONS AND INDIAN RELATIONS

General accounts: John H. Beadle, *The Undeveloped West* (Philadelphia, 1873) and *Western Wilds and the Men Who Redeem Them* (San Francisco, 1880); Edward King, *The Great South* (Hartford, 1875); Linus Pierpont Brockett, *Our Western Empire* (Philadelphia, 1881); Joseph G. McCoy, *Historic Sketches of the Cattle Trade of the West and Southwest* (Kansas City, 1874); Robert M. Wright, *Dodge City, the Cowboy Capital* (Wichita, 1913); Evan G. Barnard, *A Rider of the Cherokee Strip* (Boston, 1936); and Zoe A. Tilghman, *Marshal of the Last Frontier* (Glendale, 1949) are some of the better-known accounts by participants. The field of secondary accounts includes the notable contributions of such historians as Walter Prescott Webb, Edward Everett Dale, Everett Dick, Fred A. Shannon, Ernest S. Osgood, Carl Coke Rister, Louis Pelzer, and J. Evetts Haley and a vast field of so-called popular accounts of unequal merit.

Railroad-Indian relations, general: Annie H. Abel, *The American Indian under Reconstruction* (Cleveland, 1925); Roy Gittinger, *Formation of the State of Oklahoma* (Berkeley, 1917); Angie Debo, *The Rise and Fall of the Choctaw Republic* (Norman, 1933), *The Road to Disappearance* (Norman, 1941), and *And Still the Waters Run* (Princeton, 1940); Morris L. Wardell, *A Political History of the Cherokee Nation* (Norman, 1938); and Grant Foreman, *Advancing the Frontier* (Norman, 1933). *Ann. Rep. Comm. Ind. Aff.* gives a running account in the correspondence of the Indian agents, and the vast body of manuscript material in the archives of the OIA is indispensable in studying this relatively unexplored field. Fifty-seventh Cong., 1 sess., *S. Doc. 152* and 62 Cong., 1 sess., *S. Doc. 719* are a compilation of Indian treaties and laws.

Problems concerning the sale of Indian reservations to railroads and railroad penetration into the Indian Territory are dealt with in 40 Cong., 2 sess., *H. Ex. Docs. 59, 85*, and *310, H. Rep. 63*, and *S. Misc. Doc. 98;* 40 Cong., 3 sess., *H. Misc. Doc. 49* and *S. Misc. Docs. 33* and *34;* 41 Cong., 2 sess., *H. Rep. 53* and *H. Misc. Doc. 150;* 44 Cong., 2 sess., *S. Misc. Doc. 30* and *H. Misc. Doc. 167;* and Eugene F. Ware, "The Neutral Lands," KSHS *Coll.*, Vol. VI (1898), 147–69 deal with the Cherokee Neutral Lands and Osage Lands controversies; 47 Cong., 1 sess., *S. Ex. Docs. 15* and *44, S. Misc. Doc. 18,* and *H. Rep. 934* and 49 Cong., 1 sess., *S. Rep. 117* deal with exercising the right of eminent domain in the Indian Territory; 46 Cong., 2 sess., *S. Misc. Doc. 100;* 47 Cong., 1 sess., *S. Rep. 392* and *S. Ex. Docs. 80* and *89;* 48 Cong., 1 sess., *H. Ex. Doc. 14;* 49 Cong., 1 sess., *S. Rep. 1278;* 49 Cong., 2 sess., *S. Rep. 1898;* 50 Cong., 1 sess., *H. Reps 101* and *2860;* 50 Cong., 2 sess., *S. Ex. Doc. 22;* and 51 Cong., 1 sess., *S. Misc. Doc. 223* deal with the struggle over Indian mineral and timber lands; the manuscript acts of the Cherokee Council, Vols. CCXLVIII, CCLI, CCLII, and CCLIII and the Cherokee Papers, File IX–a–1 (IAD, OHS) deal with the abortive Cherokee Nation project of buying stock in the MK&T Railroad.

Conditional land grants to railroads: C. J. Hillyer, *Atlantic and Pacific Railroad and the Indian Territory* (Washington, n.d.); *Argument of Hon. Gardiner G. Hubbard, before the Committee on Territories . . . Feb. 11, 1876* (Washington, 1876); Daniel H. Ross, *Answer . . . to the Arguments of Gardiner G. Hubbard* (Washington, 1876); 42 Cong., 2 sess., *H. Rep. 89;* 44 Cong., 1 sess., *H. Rep. 299;* 45 Cong., 3 sess., *S. Rep. 744;* 47 Cong., 1 sess., *S. Ex. Doc. 144;* 48 Cong., 1 sess., *H. Rep. 1663; Fourth Annual Report of the Commission to the Five Civilized Tribes, 1891;* and Henry King, "The Indian Country," *Century Magazine*, Vol. VIII (n.s., 1885), 599–606.

Relation of railroads to intruders: 44 Cong., 1 sess., *H. Misc. Doc. 167;* 45 Cong., 2 sess., *S. Misc. Doc. 30;* 46 Cong., 1 sess., *H. Ex. Doc. 145* and *S. Ex. Doc. 111;* 47 Cong., 2 sess., *S. Ex. Doc. 58;* 48 Cong., 1 sess., *H. Ex. Doc. 17* and *S. Ex. Doc. 50;* 49 Cong., 1 sess., *S. Ex. Doc. 14;* 50 Cong., 1 sess., *S. Ex. Doc. 41;* Department of War,

AGO, Doc. File No. 2653, box nos. 1236-39; Phil. Coll., David L. Payne Case and the Boudinot Papers; and Carl Coke Rister, *Land Hunger: David L. Payne and the Oklahoma Boomers* (Norman, 1942).

4. POLITICAL PROBLEMS

Federal aid to railroads: 40 Cong., 2 sess., *H. Ex. Doc. 101*; 46 Cong., 2 sess., *S. Rep. 717*; 47 Cong., 1 sess., *H. Ex. Doc. 144*; 47 Cong., 2 sess., *H. Misc. Doc. 45*, Parts 1, 2, and 3; 48 Cong., 1 sess., *S. Ex. Docs. 88* and *90, S. Reps. 305* and *961*, and *H. Reps. 45, 193*, and *2443*; and 50 Cong., 1 sess., *H. Rep. 2476* and *S. Ex. Doc. 194* are a few of the more important documents dealing with this subject. In addition to the more general works of Roy M. Robbins, Benjamin H. Hibbard, and Matthias P. Orfield on public-land policies, E. H. Talbott, *Railway Land Grants in the United States* (Chicago, 1880) and John Bell Sanborn, *Congressional Grants of Land in Aid of Railroads* (Madison, 1899) are more specialized. George W. Julian, "Railway Influence in the Land Office," *NAR*, Vol. CXXXVI (1883), 237-56 and "Our Land-Grant Railways in Congress," *International Review*, Vol. XIV (1883), 198-212 and John W. Johnston, "Railway Land Grants," *NAR*, Vol. CXL (1885), 280-89 are contemporary; W. J. Donald, "Land Grants for Internal Improvements in the United States," *JPE*, Vol. XIX (1911), 404-10; Robert S. Henry, "The Railroad Land Grant Legend in American History," *MVHR*, Vol. XXXIII (1945), 171-94; Paul W. Gates, "The Homestead Law in an Incongruous Land System," *AHR*, Vol. XLI (1936), 652-81; Harold H. Dunham, "Some Crucial Years of the General Land Office, 1875-1891," *Ag. H.*, Vol. XI (1937),117-41; Roy M. Robbins, "The Public Domain in the Era of Exploitation, 1862-1901," *Ag. H.*, Vol. XIII (1939), 97-108; and David M. Ellis, "The Forfeiture of Railroad Land Grants, 1867-1894," *MVHR*, Vol. XXXIII (1946), 27-60 are thoughtful.

State and local aid: Missouri General Assembly, Joint Committee to Investigate Bonds and Accounts of the Pacific Railroad Company, *Report* (Jefferson City, 1868); *List of Acts and Resolutions Passed by the Louisiana Legislature Incorporating the New Orleans Pacific Ry. Co. and Other State Railway Corporations* (Baton Rouge, 1878); 43 Cong., 1 sess., *H. Rep. 771* (on Arkansas); Kansas Board of Railroad Commissioners, *Annual Report* (Topeka, 1883-1906); "Statistics on Railroads," *Tenth Census* and "Public Debt," Part I, *Eleventh Census;* S. G. Reed, "Land Grants and Other Aids to Texas Railroads," *SHQ*, Vol. XLIX (1946), 518-23; John W. Million, *State Aid to Railroads in Missouri* (Chicago, 1896); Edwin Lee Lopata, *Local Aid to Railroads in Missouri* (New York, 1937); Powell Clayton, *The Aftermath of the Civil War in Arkansas* (New York, 1916); Thomas S. Staples, *Reconstruction in Arkansas, 1866-1874* (New York, 1923); Ella Lonn, *Reconstruction in Louisiana after 1868* (New York, 1918); Charles W. Ramsdell, *Reconstruction in Texas* (New York, 1910); William A. Scott, *The Repudiation of State Debts* (New York, 1893); and Robert P. Porter, "State Debts and Repudiation," *International Review*, Vol. IX (1880), 556-92.

Conflict of railroads and western agrarians: the writings of Solon J. Buck and John D. Hicks are the classic studies in their respective fields. Supplementary periodical articles include: Hallie Farmer, "The Economic Background of Frontier Populism," *MVHR*, Vol. X (1924), 406-27 and "The Railroads and Frontier Populism," *MVHR*, Vol. XIII (1926), 387-97; James A. Woodburn, "Western Radicalism in American Politics," *MVHR*, Vol. XIII (1926), 143-68; Chester McArthur Destler, "Western Radicalism, 1865-1901: Concepts and Origins," *MVHR*, Vol. XXXI (1944), 335-68; Raymond C. Miller, "The Economic Background of Populism in Kansas," *MVHR*, Vol. XI (1925), 468-89; Elizabeth N. Barr, "The Populist Uprising," in W. E. Connelley's *A Standard History of Kansas and Kansans* (Chicago, 1918), II, 1113-95; Melvin J. White, "Populism in Louisiana during the 'Nineties," *MVHR*, Vol. V (1918), 1-19; and Ralph Smith, "The Farmers' Alliance in Texas, 1875-1900," *SHQ*, Vol. XLVIII (1945), 346-69.

Railroad abuses and their reform: In addition to the standard treatments by Frederick A. Cleveland and Fred Wilbur Powell, Arthur T. Hadley, William Z. Ripley, and Stuart Daggett and the frankly hostile accounts of Matthew Josephson, Gustavus

Bibliography

Myers, and Lewis Corey, specific problems are treated in John Gibbon, "Railroad Consolidation," *NAR*, Vol. CLIV (1892), 251–54; Joseph Draper Sayers, *Railroad Consolidation in Texas 1891–1903* (Austin, 1904); Edward L. Andrews, "The Watering of Railroad Securities," *ALR*, Vol. XXI (1887), 696–704; Thomas L. Greene, "Railroad Stock Watering," *PSQ*, Vol. VI (1891), 472–92; John W. Midgeley, "Railroad Rate Wars: Their Cause and Cure," *Forum*, Vol. XX (1896), 519–30 and "A New Departure in Railroad Management," *Forum*, Vol. XXVII (1899), 491–501; Martin A. Knapp, "Some Observations on Railroad Pooling," *AAA*, Vol. VIII (1896), 127–47; Simon F. Kropp, "The Struggle for Limited Liability and General Incorporation Laws in Missouri" (M.A. Thesis, University of Missouri, 1939); Edwin C. Manning, "The Kansas State Senate of 1865 and 1866," *KSHS Coll.*, Vol. IX (1906), 359–75; Hsien-Ju Huang, *State Taxation of Railroads in the United States* (New York, 1928); and Robert E. Riegel, "The Southwestern Pool," *MHR*, Vol. XIX (1924), 12–24 and Western Railroad Pools," *MVHR*, Vol. XVIII (1931), 364–77.

Articles by agrarian spokesmen include William A. Peffer, "The Farmer's Defensive Movement," *Forum*, Vol. VIII (1889), 464–73 and "The Mission of the Populist Party," *NAR*, Vol. CLVII (1893), 665–78; James Baird Weaver, "The Three-Fold Contention of Industry," *Arena*, Vol. V (1892), 427–35; Charles S. Gleed, "The True Significance of Western Unrest," *Forum*, Vol. XVI (1893), 251–60; William V. Allen, "Western Feelings towards the East," *NAR*, Vol. CLXII (1896), 588–93; James Fairchild Hudson, *The Railways and the Republic* (New York, 1886); William A. Peffer, *The Farmer's Side; His Troubles and Their Remedy* (New York, 1891); Jesse Hardesty, *The Mother of Trusts* (Kansas City, 1899); and Frank Parson, *The Railways, the Trusts, and the People* (Philadelphia, 1905). Hostile to western agrarianism are Sidney Dillon, "The West and the Railroads," *NAR*, Vol. CLII (1891), 443–52; J. Laurence Laughlin, "Causes of Agricultural Unrest," *Atlantic Monthly*, Vol. LXXVIII (1896), 577–85; and Frederick Emory Haynes, "The New Sectionalism," *QJE*, Vol. X (1896), 269–95. Relatively objective are Frank M. Drew, "The Present Farmer Movement," *PSQ*, Vol. VI (1891), 282–300; Henry C. Adams, "The Farmer and Railway Legislation," *Century*, Vol. XXI (n.s., 1892), 780–83; and William H. Glasson, "The Crusade against the Railroads," *South Atlantic Quarterly*, Vol. VI (1907), 165–76.

Analyses of state regulation: George Ticknor Curtis, "The Ownership of Railroad Property," *NAR*, Vol. CXXXII (1881), 343–55; J. M. Mason, "The Right to Regulate Railroad Charges," *NAR*, Vol. CXXXII (1881), 592–601; Frederick C. Clark, "State Railroad Commissions, and How They May Be Made Effective," *AEA Pub.*, Vol. VI (1891), 473–83; A. G. Warner, "Railroad Problems in the West," *PSQ*, Vol. VI (1891), 66–89; Frank Haigh Dixon, "Recent Railway Legislation in Kansas," *QJE*, Vol. XIII (1899), 336–38; James L. Slayden, "Railway Regulation in Texas," *AAA*, Vol. XXXII (1908), 225–34; Lewis Henry Haney, "Railway Regulation in Texas," *JPE*, Vol. XIX (1911), 437–55; M. M. Crane, "Recollections of the Establishment of the Texas Railroad Commission," *SHQ*, Vol. L (1947), 478–86; Samuel W. Moore, "State Supervision of Railroad Transportation in Arkansas," *AHA Pub.*, Vol. III (1911), 266–309; Edwin O. Stene, *Railroad Commission to Corporation Commission* (Lawrence, 1945); and Nat. B. Knight, Jr., "The Louisiana Public Service Commission," *TLR*, Vol. XVI (1941), 1–26. ICC, *Sixteenth Annual Report*, App. G, Parts 4 and 5 has a summary and analysis of all state railroad laws enacted prior to 1902.

5. POPULATION MOVEMENTS AND COLONIZATION ACTIVITIES

The census reports, supplemented by guidebooks and almanacs (both state and privately sponsored) and local histories, are the basic source of information concerning population movements. Wallace E. Miller, *The Peopling of Kansas* (Columbus, 1906) and Carroll D. Clark and Roy L. Roberts, *Peopling of Kansas: a Demographic and Sociological Study* (Topeka, 1936) treat that state.

There is no general work on the colonizing activities of the railroads. Early annual railroad reports and the publications of railroad colonization departments are still the major sources. *Memorial of the A T & S F Railroad Company to the Senate and House*

Then Came the Railroads

of Representatives of the State of Kansas (Topeka, 1881); Norris Gage, *The Relation of Kansas Railroads to the State of Kansas* (Topeka, 1884); C. L. Seagraves, "Colonization as a Factor in Traffic Development," *SFM*, Vol. XXI (Aug., 1927), 19–20; Carl B. Schmidt, "Reminiscences of Foreign Immigration Work for Kansas," KSHS *Coll.*, Vol. IX (1906), 485–97; and Forrest Crissey, "Confessions of a Colonizer," *SEP*, Vol. CLXXXV (Aug. 19, 1913), 19–20, "Pushing to Prosperity," *SEP*, Vol. CLXXXV (Aug. 26, 1913), 10–12, and "Railroads as Colonizers," *The Annalist*, Vol. III (1914), 746–47 contain materials which are primarily the work of participants.

6. AGRICULTURAL AND INDUSTRIAL DEVELOPMENT

Railroad agricultural and industrial development work is virtually unexplored. Formal organization is discussed in Chu-chang Liang, *A Study of the Industrial and Agricultural Departments* (Peiping, 1913); more informative are the annual ARDA proceedings, census reports on agriculture and industry, state yearbooks and handbooks, railroad agricultural bulletins, colonization journals, brochures on business opportunities, etc., and publications of various chambers of commerce. In addition, there are periodic summaries of the resources of various states, such as those of Sylvester Waterhouse, C. C. Hutchinson, and others.

Agriculture: Louis Bernard Schmidt, "The Agricultural Revolution in the Prairies and Great Plains of the United States," *Ag. H.*, Vol. VIII (1934), 169–95 and the standard works of Fred A. Shannon, Walter P. Webb, and William B. Bizzell are varying scholarly interpretations of general agricultural conditions, while Frederick W. Williams' *Yesterday and Today in Louisiana Agriculture* (Baton Rouge, 1940) deals with Louisiana. The standard works of Rudolph Alexander Clemen, Ernest S. Osgood, and Edward Everett Dale deal with the livestock industry. Dealing specifically with the relations between railroads and agriculture are: Edward Atkinson, *The Railroad and the Farmer* (two bulletins, New York, 1883); Harry Turner Newcomb, "Railway Progress and Agricultural Development," *Yale Review*, Vol. IX (1900), 33–57; Frank Andrews, *Railroads and Farming* (USDA, Bureau of Statistics, *Bull. No. 100*, 1912), "Freight Costs and Market Values," USDA *Yearbook for 1906*, 371–86, "Cost and Method of Transporting Meat Animals," USDA *Yearbook for 1908*, 227–44, and *Crop Export Movement and Port Facilities on the Atlantic and Gulf Coasts* (USDA, Bureau of Statistics, *Bull. No. 38*, 1905); John Hamilton, *The Transportation Companies as Factors in Agricultural Extension* (USDA, Office of Experiment Stations, *Circular* No. 112, 1911); Theodore Dreiser, "The Railroad and the People," *Harper's*, Vol. C (1900), 479–84; Clifford V. Gregory, "Farming by Special Train," *Outlook*, Vol. XCVII (1911), 913–22; and French Strother, "The Railroad War in Texas," *WW*, Vol. LI (1926), 610–15.

Material dealing with industrial development in the Southwest, other than the many brief articles appearing in such periodicals as *Railway Age* and Henry Oyen's "Making Business to Order," *WW*, Vol. XXIV (1912), 308–12, is scarce. Industrial Commission, *Report for 1898* (19 volumes, Washington, 1900–1902) has some material. Carl Coke Rister, *Oil! Titan of the Southwest* (Norman, 1949); Louisiana Forestry Commission, *Forestry Resources of Louisiana* (second edition, Baton Rouge, 1945); and Texas Planning Board, *A Review of Texas Forestry and Its Industries* (Austin, 1937) deal with specific industries. Regional Shippers' Advisory Boards are discussed in John K. Barnes, "The Silent Revolution on the Railroads," *WW*, Vol. XLIX (1925), 673–78; Henry E. Stringer, *History, Accomplishments, and Objectives of the Shippers' Advisory Boards* (Washington, 1938); and Clark Hungerford, *Address . . . before the Southwest Shippers' Advisory Board, Oklahoma City, May 28, 1948* (St. Louis, 1948).

Index

Abilene, Kansas: 65, 92, 103, 111–12
Abilene, Texas: 177, 197, 199, 250, 256
Abilene and Southern Railway Company: 256, 283
Abuses, railroad: 165, 216–21
Agitation for railroads: 12, 73, 166; in Missouri, 13–14; in Texas, 14–15, 25, 200–201; in Arkansas, 16, 31; for Pacific railroads, 18–20; in Kansas, 42ff., 196; at Kansas City, 93; across Indian Territory, 124
Agricultural Extension Service: 265, 296, 315
Agriculture: 196, 278; expands to Plains, 90, 105–106, 205, 206, 255–56, 258–59; effect on town growth, 92–93, 96, 194f.; railroad aid to, 106, 189, 207, 263–75, 290–99, 314–15; and antirailroad sentiment, 216–17
Aid to railroads: 33, 46, 73, 217; federal, 33–35, 74–75; state and local, 35–39, 75–78, 95f., 131–32, 155, 165–66, 194, 223, 249, 252; demanded in Kansas, 43f.; Cherokee Indians, 45; Confederacy, 47; Reconstruction, 48–53; reaction against, 79–81; private donations, 166; *see also* land grants
Alexandria, Louisiana: 5, 135, 158, 239f., 252, 271, 274; first railroad, 13; growth, 195
Alexandria and Cheneyville Railroad: *see* Red River Railroad
Allen, A. C.: 15
Allen, Ebenezer: 28
Allen, James R.: 14
Allen, Thomas: 25, 36, 63

Amarillo, Texas: 239f., 247f., 286f.; growth, 199, 261, 315
American Railway Development Association: 274, 307, 311
Anthony and Northern Railway Company: 166, 256
Antirailroad sentiment: 72, 74f., 78–83, 163–67, 214, 216–27, 234, 313
Ardmore, Oklahoma: 238f., 284; origin, 202; petroleum, 254, 276
Arkansas: 284; in 1850, 6–7; pre-Civil War railroad activity, 16, 19, 26, 31–32; railroad mileage, 32, 75, 160, 256; aid to railroads, 34f., 37, 74, 163; interest in Indian Territory, 45, 124, 129; railroad construction, 47, 49–50, 63, 134ff., 138f., 151, 158, 161, 237ff., 244f., 250, 252ff., 273, 288; Reconstruction, 47–48, 51; population, 48, 84f., 182ff.; railroad regulation, 82, 228ff., 233–34; townbuilding, 98ff., 193, 197f.; resources and industrialization, 106f., 209ff., 277f., 300ff.; outlawry, 109; antirailroad sentiment, 222f., 225; agriculture, 263f., 271–72, 293, 296, 312
Arkansas and Choctaw Railroad Company: 237f.
Arkansas and Louisiana Railway Company: 135
Arkansas and Oklahoma Railroad Company: 237
Arkansas Central Railway: 49f., 135, 244
Arkansas City, Kansas: 123, 134, 138, 146f., 172f., 197, 237, 253
Arkansas Midland Railroad: 32, 50

Arkansas Southern Railroad Company: 239
Arkansas Valley and Western Railway Company: 238
Arkansas Western Railway Company: 250
Artesian Belt Railway: 256, 283
Asherton and Gulf Railway Company: 256, 260, 282
Asphalt Belt Railway: 277, 282
Atchison, Kansas: 42, 44, 66, 71, 74, 133
Atchison and Topeka Railroad: 42, 44, 65
Atchison, Topeka and Santa Fe Railway Company: 101, 104f., 132, 144, 150, 159, 168, 179, 236f., 254, 316; history and construction, 44, 65–66, 71, 136–37, 145–50, 246–49, 286–88; land grants, 65, 74, 80, 89–90; state and local aid, 77f., 165; effect on population, 84f., 89, 259f.; colonization work, 87–90, 188, 259, 313; influence on town growth, 93, 97, 99, 111, 193ff., 199, 202ff.; aid to agriculture, 106, 207, 265, 267, 269f., 273, 291, 297; outlawry, 111, 113f., 180; opening of Oklahoma, 172–73; hostility in Kansas toward, 223f.; influence on industrial development, 276, 278f., 300, 309
Atlantic and Pacific Railroad: 104, 136f., 144, 237, 261; origins and construction, 56, 66–67, 70, 100, 123; land grants, 56–57, 74, 120–23, 128, 163f.
Atlantic and Pacific Railroad (Texas promotional scheme): 29f.
Austin, Texas: 8f., 29, 53, 63, 71, 96–97, 114, 141, 154, 194, 249, 284
Austin and Northwestern Railroad Company: 154, 246

"Backbone Company": see New Orleans, Baton Rouge and Vicksburg Railroad
Bainer, Harry M.: 265, 272–73, 291
Baker, James: 122, 129, 171
Bass, Sam: 115, 117–18
Baton Rouge, Louisiana: 5, 163, 241, 282, 306
Baton Rouge, Grosse Tete and Opelousas Railroad: 37, 51
Bauxite and Northern Railway Company: 255, 277
Baxter Springs, Kansas: 61, 77, 103, 150, 179, 253
Bean, Roy: 176–77
Beaumont, Texas: 7, 31, 47, 154f., 241, 246, 248; industry, 275f., 306
Beaumont and Great Northern Railroad Company: 250, 285
Beaumont, Sour Lake and Western Railway Company: 241

Beaver, Meade and Englewood Railroad Company: 255, 285–86
Benton, Thomas Hart: 13, 19f., 34, 66
Bentonville Railroad: 237
Birds Point, Missouri: 26, 135, 139
Boggs, Lilburn W.: 13
Boonville, St. Louis and Southern Railway Company: 133
Borland, Solon J.: 34
Boudinot, Elias C.: 55, 100, 122, 170–71
Bowlin, James B.: 20
Brazoria County, Texas: 28, 39
Brazos and Galveston Company: 15
Bremond, Paul: 28, 155
Brimstone Railroad and Canal Company: 255, 277
Briscoe, Andrew: 15, 27
Brooks, Joseph: 49
Browning, O. H.: 60
Brownsville, Texas: 8, 69, 240, 242, 260–61, 282, 284
Brownwood North and South Railway: 242, 284
Buchanan, William: 252
Buckingham, E. J.: 254
Buffalo Bayou, Brazos and Colorado Railway: 15, 27f., 39, 54, 94
Buffalo herds and hunting: 101–102
Burlington–Rock Island Railroad Company: 242
Butler, George: 45

Cairo, Illinois: 26, 32
Cairo and Fulton Railroad: 32, 98f., 198; history and construction, 26, 63–64; aids to, 35f., 49, 63, 74
Caldwell, Kansas: 103, 114, 146f., 150, 173
Calvert, Waco and Brazos Valley Railroad Company:. 245
Cameron, R. A.: 189, 207, 263
Campbell, Hardy W.: 273
Canadian River route: 19, 21, 23, 67, 136
Cane Belt Railway: 248, 287
Capital, eastern and foreign: 27, 33, 54, 56, 67; in Kansas, 59f., 65; in Texas, 64, 69; western hostility toward, 218–19
Carney, Thomas: 58
Cary, S. S.: 189
Cassville and Exeter Railway Company: 255
Cattle industry: 18; influence on town growth, 92ff., 95, 111–15, 138, 261; rise and decline, 102–105, 205–206; and outlawry, 108–109; and Indian Territory, 171–72, 203
Celaya, Simon: 69

Index

Central and Montgomery Railway: 147
Central Branch Railway: 133
Chadick, E. D.: 169
Challis, Luther C.: 44
Cherokee Nation: 54, 238; resists railroad penetration, 45, 62, 123, 127; Fort Smith Council, 35; right of way and conditional land grants, 55–56, 67, 164; sale of Kansas lands, 60; railroad construction, 62, 67; fear of intruders, 98; railroad towns, 99–100; Shannahan affair, 137–38; timber, 168
Cherokee Neutral Lands controversy: 59–61
Cherokee Outlet: 146f., 172, 179; opened, 173; town-building, 202–203
Chetopa, Kansas: 62, 100, 103, 133f.
Cheyenne Short Line: 255
Chicago, Illinois: 12, 19f., 63, 92, 105, 147, 149, 218, 292
Chicago, Kansas and Nebraska Railway Company: 150, 165, 199
Chicago, Kansas and Western Railroad Company: 146
Chicago, Rock Island and Gulf Railroad Company: 240
Chicago, Rock Island and Pacific Railroad Company: 132, 159, 173, 244f., 249, 287; outlawry, 117, 179f.; history and construction, 150, 235–43, 284, 286; colonization and town development, 187, 198f., 200ff., 260f.; aid to agriculture, 207, 259, 265, 268f., 271, 273f., 290–94; industrial development, 300, 306, 309
Chicago, Rock Island and Texas Railroad Company: 150
Chickasaw Nation: 55, 149, 181; grants right of way, 45; debate on railroads, 124–26
Choctaw and Memphis Railroad Company: 189, 239
Choctaw Coal and Railway Company: 159, 162, 169, 203, 209
Choctaw Nation: 55, 203, 239; grants right of way, 45; railroad construction, 62, 138; town growth, 98, 100; coal, 107, 168–69; debate on railroads, 124–26
Choctaw Northern Railroad Company: 239
Choctaw, Oklahoma and Gulf Railroad Company: 158f., 162, 202f., 219, 238–39
Cisco and Northeastern Railway Company: 283
Civil War: 212; Pacific railroad issue, 22; effect on Southern railroads, 46–47; effect on Indian Territory, 54–55; relation to outlawry, 109, 116
Civilized Tribes: 9–10, 23, 45, 54–57; see also names of individual tribes
Cleveland, Grover: 127, 164, 170
Clinton and Oklahoma Western Railroad Company: 255, 287
Coal: 106–107, 209, 255; in Texas, 142, 157, 289; in Indian Territory, 159, 162, 168, 198; in Kansas, 161, 196; in Arkansas, 195–96
Coates, Kersey: 58f.
Coffeyville, Kansas: 62, 97, 103, 134f., 147, 180, 197, 249
Colonization activities of railroads: 87ff., 210, 259–60, 263f., 275, 295–96, 312–13; in Europe, 88–89; methods, 186–91
Colorado and Southern Railway Company: 157, 240, 250
Colorado Southern, New Orleans and Pacific Railroad Company: 241f.
Concho, San Saba and Llano Valley Railroad Company: 248–49
Consolidation, movement towards railroad: 132, 160–61, 230–31
Conventions, railroad: 18–21, 25, 44
Cooke, Vernon T.: 273
Cooley, Dennis M.: 55
Cornell, J. H.: 273
Corpus Christi, Texas: 8, 47, 155ff., 254, 306
Corruptness in railroad building, charges of: 70, 131, 149, 236; Texas, 29–30, 40, 76; during Reconstruction, 48–53; Missouri, 63, 70; federal land grants, 75, 163–64; local aid, 77; Arkansas, 82; Jay Gould, 132, 142ff.; methods, 219–20, 228; B. F. Yoakum, 242
Cotton Belt Route: see St. Louis Southwestern Railway Company
Cottrell, H. M.: 265
Couch, H. C.: 285
Craig, James: 23
Creek Nation: grants right of way, 45; railroad building, 62, 238; town growth, 98, 100, 261; opposition to railroads, 130; resources, 169, 276
Crittenden, Thomas T.: 169
Crosby, Josiah F.: 54
Crosbyton–South Plains Railroad Company: 248, 260
Cullinan, J. S.: 276
Cunningham, E. H.: 256
Current River Railroad: 151

Dallas, Texas: 63, 68, 96, 141, 149, 155, 195, 240f., 246, 285, 287; growth, 7, 95,

98, 194; aid to railroads, 53, 142, 147; outlawry, 117; industrialization, 210, 278, 306, 309
Dallas, Cleburne and Southwestern Railway Company: 285
Dalton gang: 179–80
Dancy, John W.: 15, 27
Davis, Jeff (of Arkansas): 233–34
Davis, Jefferson: 19, 21, 23
Dawes, Henry L.: 124, 127, 164, 172
Dayton–Goose Creek Railway Company: 284
Denckla associates: 49
Denison, Texas: 100, 142, 144, 237, 245, 249, 253; origins, 62f.; cattle trade, 103ff.; outlawry, 111, 114–15
Denison and Southeastern Railway Company: 142
Denison and Washita Valley Railway Company: 249
Denison, Bonham and New Orleans Railroad Company: 285
Denver and New Orleans Railway Company: 157
Denver and Rio Grande Western Railroad Company: 114, 136, 156
Denver, Texas and Fort Worth Railway Company: 157
Depression: of 1837, 13, 15; of 1857, 25, 32, 45; of 1873, 50, 53, 66, 70–72, 93, 95, 131, 147, 156; of 1893, 149f., 156f., 160ff.; of 1907, 256, 264; of 1929, 286
Diamond Jo Line: see Hot Springs Railroad
Dodge, Grenville M.: 68, 156–57, 189
Dodge City, Kansas: 66, 90, 96, 99, 102f., 109, 113–14, 116, 150, 247, 250
Doolin gang: 179f.
Dorsey, Stephen W.: 49, 122
Douglas, Stephen A.: 19f., 22f.
Dowling, Dick: 47

Earp, Wyatt: 113f.
Eastern Oklahoma Railway: 247
Eastern Texas Railroad: 31, 47
Eastland, Wichita Falls and Gulf Railroad Company: 288
East Line and Red River Railroad Company: 71, 142ff.
Eddy, Charles B.: 235, 247
Edenborn, William: 252, 285
Eldridge, W. T.: 256, 282
El Paso, Texas: 141, 145f., 152, 175, 201, 235f., 242; and Pacific railroad, 19ff., 24, 68; outlawry, 109, 178–79, 194; growth, 195, 278
El Reno, Oklahoma: 159, 203, 252, 271

Emporia, Kansas: 42, 64f., 74, 97, 145f., 197, 215, 223
"End of track": 110–11, 175–76
Enid, Oklahoma: 204, 236, 238, 247, 286, 291
Eureka Springs Railroad: 253
Fayetteville, Arkansas: 7, 124, 136f., 196, 238
Fiske, Clinton B.: 67
Fordyce, Samuel W.: 245
Fort Scott, Kansas: 77, 97, 122, 134, 197
Fort Smith, Arkansas: 7, 21, 24, 62, 71, 123f., 135ff., 161f., 197, 203, 209, 244, 253; Indian Council, 55; origins and growth, 195–96
Fort Smith and Western Railway Company: 253
Fort Smith, Subiaco and Rock Island Railroad Company: 255
Fort Worth, Texas: 7, 85, 114, 139, 141f., 147, 149f., 154, 159, 162, 175, 184f., 208, 235, 237f., 240f., 245, 287, 291; growth and industries, 95–96, 194, 214, 278, 306, 309; aid to railroads, 156, 166
Fort Worth and Denver City Railway Company: 146, 242; construction, 156–57, 250, 286–87; population, 184, 189f.; town growth, 194, 199f.; aid to agriculture, 208, 260, 263
Fort Worth and Denver Northern Railway Company: 286
Fort Worth and Denver South Plains Railway Company: 286
Fort Worth and New Orleans Railway Company: 154
Fort Worth and Rio Grande Railway Company: 140, 142, 237f., 242, 287
Franklin, Benjamin J.: 129
Franklin (New), Missouri: 13, 26, 70, 138, 144
Frémont, John C.: 66ff.
"Frisco" Railroad: see St. Louis–San Francisco Railway Company

Gadsden, James: 18, 21
Gaines, Edmund P.: 16–17
Galveston, Texas: 45, 47, 51, 63, 149, 155, 161, 248, 297; origins and growth, 7, 15, 28ff., 91, 93–94, 193–94, 210, 213, 278; aid to railroads, 78, 147
Galveston and Red River Railway Company: 16, 28, 94
Galveston Bay Railroad and Lumber Company: 30
Galveston, Harrisburg and San Antonio Railway Company: 176; history and growth, 54, 69, 71, 94, 152, 155, 246,

Index

284; colonizing and town-building, 99, 190, 199
Galveston, Houston and Henderson Railroad Company: 29, 47, 54, 140ff., 144, 152, 194, 282, 285
Galveston, Houston and Northern Railway Company: 154f.
Garden City Western Railway Company: 256
Garland, Augustus H.: 125f.
Gates, John W.: 162, 198, 250
Geary, John W.: 45
Geyer, Henry S.: 20
Glick, George: 231
Goodnight, Charles: 205
Gorman, James E.: 292
Gould, Jay: 145f., 151–52, 158, 177, 189–90, 209, 215, 218, 282; railroad activities in Southwest, 69f., 125f., 131–44
Gowen, Franklin I.: 162
Grand Prairie of Arkansas: 4, 259–60, 313
Granger movement: 78–79, 82, 231
Great Bend, Kansas: 66, 99, 103, 134, 146
Green, E. H. R.: 284
Green, Hetty: 154
Gulf and Interstate Railway Company: 248
Gulf and Interstate Railway (proposed railroad to Gulf of Mexico): 227
Gulf Coast Lines: 235, 241–42, 282, 295f.
Gulf, Colorado and Santa Fe Railway Company: 71; local aid, 78, 166; origins and growth, 95, 147–49, 248; town development, 194, 197
Gulf of Mexico: 144, 152, 213; proposed railroads to, 45, 58, 63–64, 133, 140, 227, 240; connections with interior, 63, 68f., 136, 147–49, 161–62, 195f., 247
Gulf, Texas and Western Railway Company, 256, 284, 286
Gulf, Western Texas and Pacific Railway Company: 69, 152f., 156
Gunn, O. B.: 65, 111
Gunn City massacre: 78
Guthrie, Oklahoma: 203, 239, 247, 249, 253, 271
Hagerman, J. J.: 247
Hall, "Red": 111, 114–15
Hamlin and Northwestern Railway Company: 288
Hamon, Jake: 276, 288
Hannibal and St. Joseph Railroad Company: 26, 35ff., 59, 70
Hardin, John Wesley: 114, 179
Harlan, James: 60
Harriman, E. H.: 154, 240, 246

Harrisburg Railroad and Trading Company: 15, 27
Harvey, James M.: 81
Hawley, Joseph R.: 125
Helena, Arkansas: 6, 16, 50, 196, 253, 293
Henderson and Burkville Railroad: 31, 38
Herington, M. D.: 199
Hickok, James Butler: 112
Hicks, John D.: 220–21
Hillyer, C. J.: 120
Hogg, James S.: 143, 223, 225, 228, 233
Holden, Perry G.: 268–69
Holliday, Cyrus K.: 44, 65, 74, 97
Holman, William S.: 79
Hot Springs Railroad: 158, 239, 244
Houck, Louis: 158, 238
Houston, Texas: 9, 54, 64, 71, 85, 95, 144, 149, 152f., 155, 256, 282ff., 297; growth, 7, 15, 94, 147, 193–94; promotes railroads, 15, 28ff., 39, 240; industrial growth, 214, 278, 306f., 309
Houston and Brazos Valley Railroad Company: 250, 282, 285
Houston and Brazos Valley Railroad Company (early proposal): 15
Houston and Great Northern Railroad Company: 64
Houston and Texas Central Railroad Company: 94, 117, 153, 194, 237; origins and growth, 28, 63f., 154, 246, 284; town-building, 41, 63, 98ff.
Houston, Central Arkansas and Northern Railroad: 135
Houston East and West Texas Railway Company: 154–55
Houston Tap and Brazoria Railway: 28f., 39, 64
Houston Tap Railroad: 28, 39
Hubbard, Gardiner G.: 121–22
Hughes, Samuel A.: 260
Hunt, Alexander C.: 157
Huntington, Collis P.: 132, 146; relations with Texas and Pacific, 68, 140f., 218; activities in the Southwest, 136f., 151–56, 193
Huntsville Branch Railway: 64
Hutchinson, C. C.: 80
Hutchinson, Kansas: 66, 99, 134, 146, 159, 199, 210, 313
Hutchinson and Southern Railway Company: 159, 247
Illinois: 35, 78, 150
Illinois Central Railroad Company: 26, 35, 87, 192, 241, 278, 310
Indian leases: grazing, 104–105; coal, 168–69

Indianola Railroad: 69
Indians: *see* Indian Territory *and* specific tribal names
Indian Territory: 44, 104, 140, 144, 147; railroad construction, 45, 62, 67f., 123–27, 135ff., 149, 159, 161f., 237ff., 253; land grants, 56, 74, 119–23, 164; town growth, 98ff., 201–203, 261; industry, 106–107, 168, 209, 275f.; outlawry, 109ff., 118, 179–81; attacks on, 127–30, 169–72, 313; railroad mileage, 160, 256; population, 183ff.
Indian treaties: removal, 9–10, 44–45; Reconstruction, 55–56; effect on railroad projects, 56–57, 59, 119, 123ff.; Osage Ceded Lands, 59ff.; Cherokee Neutral Lands, 59–60; terminated, 128
Industry, development in Southwest: 107, 205, 208–15, 275–80, 300–11, 316; *see also* specific cities and states
Ingalls, John J.: 81, 224
International–Great Northern Railroad Company: 125, 139f.; history and growth, 64, 71, 132, 141f., 144, 245, 255f., 284; colonization activities, 190
International Railroad: 53, 64
Intruders on Indian lands: 60, 168, 169–71, 202–203
Iron Mountain Railroad: *see* St. Louis, Iron Mountain and Southern Railway Company
Iron ore: 3, 13, 255
Irons, Martin: 215

James–Younger gang: 115–17
Jasper and Eastern Railway Company: 248
Jefferson, Texas: 8, 30, 53, 71, 98, 144
Jennings gang: 175, 176–77
Johnson, Alexander S.: 88
Johnson, Andrew: 74, 220
Jones, Anson: 15, 29f.
Joplin, Missouri: 133, 136, 150, 161, 237, 249, 253; lead and zinc, 196, 209
Joplin and Western Railway Company: 133
Joplin Railroad Company: 136
Joy, James F.: 132, 143, 145; activities in Kansas, 59, 61; difficulties with settlers and Indian lands, 59–61, 80; collapse of network, 70
Julian, George W.: 60, 79

Kansas: 54, 250, 298; early railroad projects, 42, 45, 58; aid to railroads, 43f., 74, 76ff., 163, 165; population, 48, 84f., 183f., 258; Indian lands, 59–61; railroad construction, 61–63, 65–66, 69, 133f., 145–46, 150, 159, 161, 236, 247, 249, 251, 253, 255f., 287f.; railroad mileage, 75, 160, 257; land claims of settlers, 80–81; railroad regulation, 82, 227ff., 231, 314; colonization activities, 87–90, 188, 190, 257, 295, 313; town-building, 99, 196, 197ff.; cattle trade, 103f.; agricultural development, 105–106, 267ff., 290; industrialization, 106f., 209ff., 275ff., 306; turbulence, 109, 111–14; and Indian Territory, 124, 129, 172; antirailroad sentiment, 166, 222–25
Kansas and Arkansas Valley Railway Company: 127, 135, 202
Kansas and Gulf Short Line: 139
Kansas and Neosho Valley Railroad Company: 59, 74, 78, 93
Kansas City, Missouri: 26, 63, 71, 74, 84, 91, 124, 132ff., 150f., 161, 188f., 213, 235, 240, 251, 292; railroad promotion, 58–59, 65, 77–78, 93; growth and industrialization, 90–93, 105, 107, 193, 214f., 278, 306, 309
Kansas City and Pacific Railroad Company: 134, 144
Kansas City and Southwestern Railroad Company: 133
Kansas City, Clinton and Springfield Railway Company: 151, 236, 284
Kansas City, Emporia and Southern Railway Company: 146
Kansas City, Fort Scott and Gulf Railroad Company: 80, 150
Kansas City, Fort Scott and Memphis Railroad Company: 151, 182, 236–37, 284
Kansas City, Fort Scott and Springfield Railroad Company: 150
Kansas City, Independence and Lexington Railroad Company: 78
Kansas City, Mexico and Orient Railway Company: 251–52, 258f., 276, 287
Kansas City, Nevada and Fort Smith Railroad Company: 161
Kansas City, Osceola and Southern Railway Company: 151, 236
Kansas City, Pittsburg and Gulf Railway Company: 184, 196, 251; history, 161–62; promotional activities, 189, 213, 264; town growth, 202
Kansas City Rock Island Railway Company: 240
Kansas City Shreveport and Gulf Railway Company: 161
Kansas City Southern Railway Company: 241, 252f., 276, 283; origins and

Index

growth, 162, 250, 285; promotional activities, 259, 272, 294, 296, 300, 308
Kansas City, Watkins and Gulf Railway Company: see St. Louis, Watkins and Gulf Railway Company
Kansas, Colorado and Pacific Railway Company: 134
Kansas Midland Railway Company: 138, 237
Kansas, Oklahoma and Gulf Railway Company: 237, 288
Kansas Pacific Railroad: 63, 66, 102, 116; history, 65, 132; cattle trade, 103, 105, 111
"Katy" Railroad: see Missouri, Kansas and Texas Company
Kell, Frank: 249–50, 255, 282, 288
Kemp, J. A.: 249–50, 288
Kemper, William T.: 252
Kenedy, Miflin: 155
Kerens, R. C.: 138
King, T. B.: 29
Kiowa, Hardtner and Pacific Railroad Company: 244
Knapp, Bradford: 272
Knapp, Seaman A.: 272f.

Labor, railroad: farmers as, 207; number engaged, 214f., 278; influence, 214–15
Lake Charles, Louisiana: 6, 158, 162, 196, 245f., 306
Land grants, railroad: 217; to specific railroads, 30, 63, 95; from states, 34–35, 65; terms, 35; Texas, 38, 51, 53, 75–76; state demands, 42–44; forfeiture, 49, 78–79; Indian Territory, 56–57, 119–23, 128ff., 164; amount, 74–75; analysis, 75; termination, 79, 131, 163–64; location, 81; disposition, 87
Land League: 61
Lane, James H.: 44, 56, 58
Laredo, Texas: 9, 64, 141, 157, 194, 293
Large, Arthur W.: 292
Lead and zinc: 4, 158, 161, 196, 209–10, 255
Lease, Mary E.: 223
Leavenworth, Kansas: 42, 58, 65, 74, 92, 102
Leavenworth, Lawrence and Fort Gibson Railroad Company: 56
Leavenworth, Lawrence and Galveston Railroad Company: 80, 105; history, 58f., 62; Indian lands, 59ff., 81; aid, 74, 77, 165; Indian Territory, 171
Leavenworth, Pawnee and Western Railroad Company: 42, 65

Leeds, William B.: 236
Leedy, John W.: 225, 232
Lewelling, Lorenzo D.: 224
Lexington and St. Louis Railroad: 67
Liberal, Kansas: 150, 198f., 201, 235, 286
Little River Valley and Arkansas Railroad Company: 138–39
Little Rock, Arkansas: 6, 32, 49, 94, 98, 135, 180, 238f., 243f., 255, 277, 297, 317; early railroad interests, 16, 19; local aid, 37; growth, 96, 193, 195, 210, 278
Little Rock and Fort Smith Railroad Company: origins and growth, 32, 50, 69, 71, 134; aid, 35, 48, 74; colonization activities, 190
Little Rock and Helena Railroad: 50
Little Rock, Mississippi River and Texas Railway Company: 134f.
Little Rock, Pine Bluff and New Orleans Railroad: 49f.
Llano Estacado Railway: 248
Loree, Leonor F.: 250
Lott, Uriah: 155, 198
Louisiana: 5–6, 151, 212, 235; railroad construction, 12–13, 31, 134–35, 141, 152–53, 155, 157f., 161f., 239ff., 244ff., 248, 252ff.; railroad mileage, 32, 69, 75, 160, 256; aid, 34f., 37, 74, 166; population, 41, 48, 84, 183f.; carpetbag control, 50–51; town growth, 98, 196f.; industry, 107, 209f., 275ff., 301, 306, 309f.; agrarian unrest, 222, 225; railroad regulation, 229f., 233f.; agriculture, 263, 274, 293, 296
Louisiana and Arkansas Railway Company: 252, 285, 296
Louisiana and North West Railroad Company: 197, 252–53
Louisiana Central Stem: 51
Louisiana Midland Railway Company: 285
Louisiana Railway and Navigation Company: 252, 285
Louisiana Southern Railway Company: 277
Louisiana Western Extension Railroad: 153
Louisiana Western Railroad Company: 153
Lubbock, Texas: 248, 259, 261, 267, 286, 297, 315
Lumbering: 165, 195ff., 209, 213, 254, 310

McAlester, J. J.: 100, 107
McCluskie, Mike: 113
McCoy, Joseph G.: 103f.
McCurtain, Jackson: 124
McKee, George C.: 129

Magruder, General John B.: 47
Marion and McPherson Railroad Company: 146
Marshall, Texas: 8, 30, 51, 64, 68, 215
Maury, Matthew F.: 17, 19f.
Maxey, Sam B.: 124–25
Meat-packing industry: 104–105, 194, 210
Memphis, Tennessee: 12, 18ff., 24, 30ff., 135, 241, 306
Memphis and Little Rock Railroad Company: 158, 188, 317; history and growth, 32, 49, 134f., 238; aid, 35, 49, 71; influence on population, 84, 99
Memphis, Carthage and Northwestern Railroad Company: 68, 77, 135–36
Memphis, El Paso and Pacific Railroad Company: 29f., 38, 67f.
Mennonites: 88–89, 104, 190, 296, 313
Miami Mineral Belt Railroad: 255, 284
Michelson, C. B.: 265
Midland Valley Railroad Company: 253, 276, 288
Mileage of railroads in Southwest: 32, 69, 71ff., 131, 160, 256–57, 281–82
Mills, Roger: 139
Mississippi and Pacific Railroad Company: 30
Mississippi, Ouachita and Red River Railroad: 32, 37, 49f.
Mississippi River and Bonne Terre Railway Company: 158, 209, 255
Missouri: 3–4, 96, 103, 284; railroad construction, 13, 46, 63–64, 66–68, 132ff., 138f., 150–51, 158, 161, 236ff., 244ff., 249, 253ff., 283; early railroad agitation, 13–14, 26; railroad mileage, 32, 75, 160, 256; railroad aid, 34ff., 74, 76ff.; population, 40, 48, 84, 182, 258; railroad regulation, 40, 82, 228ff.; town growth, 41; Civil War, 46, 74; takes over railroads, 63; forfeiture of grants, 80, 163; outlawry, 103, 109; resources and industry, 106, 209f., 255, 277ff., 306, 309; and Indian territory, 129, 172; agricultural development, 269ff., 296
Missouri and North Arkansas Railroad Company: 253
Missouri-Illinois Railroad Company: 255
Missouri, Kansas and Texas Extension Railway: 142
Missouri, Kansas and Texas Railroad Company: 151, 159f., 218f., 253, 283, 288; aid, 53, 77, 166; and Indian Territory, 61–62, 104, 107, 120–21, 123, 164, 168, 170f.; origins and growth, 62–63, 70, 132, 134, 141–42, 249–50, 285–86; Kansas lands, 80; population and colonization, 87, 183f.; town-building, 93, 98f., 103, 194, 202; outlawry, 110–11, 179f.; industrial promotion, 209, 278, 308f.
Missouri, Oklahoma and Gulf Railroad Company: 253, 288
Missouri Pacific Railroad Company: 63, 146f., 151, 165, 239, 248, 252ff., 289; origins and growth, 70, 132–35, 143, 244, 282–83; town-building, 93, 199; agricultural activities, 265, 268f., 271f., 290–91, 293, 295ff.; industrial promotion, 278f., 300ff.
Missouri River, Fort Scott and Gulf Railroad Company: 59ff., 77, 81, 105, 136, 150
Missouri Southern Railroad Company: 158
Moffet, E. R.: 136
Monroe, Louisiana: 5f., 31, 47, 84, 157, 195, 197, 245
Moore brothers: 236
Morgan, Charles: 50–51, 54, 69, 94, 132, 152–53, 155, 218
Morgan's Louisiana and Texas Railroad and Steamship Company: 152
Motley County Railroad: 284
Murfreesboro and Nashville Railroad Company: 288
Murphy, Isaac: 48
Muskogee, Oklahoma: 98, 100, 123, 170, 180, 202, 253

Nevada and Minden Railway Company: 133
New Mexico: 136, 145, 236, 247
New Orleans, Louisiana: 5f., 45, 98, 141, 152f., 163, 241, 246, 252, 282, 315; early railroad interest, 12, 18f., 31; aid to railroads, 37; Civil War, 47f.; population, 91f., 192; river traffic, 92; growth, 107, 210, 213f., 278, 306
New Orleans and Lower Coast Railroad Company: 158
New Orleans and Northwestern Railroad Company: 157, 244
New Orleans, Baton Rouge and Vicksburg Railroad Company: 50, 141, 163
New Orleans, Fort Jackson and Grand Isle Railroad Company: 158
New Orleans, Mobile and Chattanooga Railroad Company: 141
New Orleans, Mobile and Texas Railroad Company: 50, 152
New Orleans, Opelousas and Great Western Railroad Company: history and growth, 31, 47, 51, 69, 152; aid, 35, 37; town growth, 41; land grant attacked, 79

Index

New Orleans Pacific Railway Company: 74–75, 141, 152, 163
New Orleans, Texas and Mexico Railroad Company: 242, 282
Newton, Kansas: 66, 96, 99, 103, 109, 113
New York, Texas and Mexican Railway Company: 153, 198, 246
Nixon, Tom: 102
Northeast Oklahoma Railroad Company: 255
North Louisiana and Texas Railroad Company: 50f.

O'Fallon, John: 25
Oglesby, T. L.: 176
Oil Fields Short Line: 254
Oklahoma: 312f.; aid to railroads, 166; industrialization, 210, 276f., 306; railroad construction, 243, 247, 249–56, 284, 286f.; railroad mileage, 256; population, 258; agriculture, 259, 267, 269, 273, 294f.; town growth, 261–62
Oklahoma Central Railway Company: 247, 288
Oklahoma City, Oklahoma: 159, 162, 237, 249, 253, 285, 288; growth, 173, 203, 261; industry, 278, 306, 309
Oklahoma City–Ada–Atoka Railway Company: 285, 288
Oklahoma City and Western Railroad Company: 237
Oklahoma City Terminal Railroad Company: 237
Oklahoma District: 147, 171–74, 202–203
Oklahoma Territory: railroad construction, 159, 236ff.; railroad mileage, 160; opening and growth, 169, 183ff., 203; outlawry, 179–80; agriculture, 207
Okmulgee Northern Railway Company: 254
Opelousas, Louisiana: 5f., 13, 24, 31, 196
Orange and Northwestern Railroad Company: 241
Orient Railroad: *see* Kansas City, Mexico and Orient Railway Company
Osage Ceded Lands controversy: 59ff.
Osage Railway: 288
Osage Valley and Southern Kansas Railroad Company: 67, 133
Outlawry, in Southwest: 103, 108–18, 175–81
Ozark and Cherokee Central Railway Company: 238

Pacific Railroad of Missouri: 102, 116; history and growth, 23–24, 46, 67f., 70; aid, 35f., 78; effect on population, 40f., 84, 92
Pacific railroad projects: 18–24, 29–32, 67, 136–37, 152, 247f., 251
Page, Daniel D.: 25
Panhandle and Gulf Railway Company: 251
Panhandle and Santa Fe Railway Company: 248
Paragould Southeastern Railroad Company: 140
Paramore, J. W.: 138
Paris, Texas: 97, 124, 136, 149, 153f., 202
Paris and Great Northern Railroad Company: 136f.
Paris and Mount Pleasant Railroad Company: 255
Patterson, John J.: 122
Payne, David L.: 169–71
Pease, E. M.: 27
Pecos River Railroad: 247
Pecos Valley Southern Railway Company: 256, 283
Peeler, Thomas Lamar: 278
Peffer, William A.: 224
Peirce, Thomas W.: 54, 69
Peter, Thomas J.: 65f., 96
Petroleum: 254, 261, 275–76, 307
Phelps, John S.: 23, 26
Pine Bluff, Arkansas: 6, 50, 134f., 196, 210, 244
Pine Bluff Arkansas River Railway Company: 140
Plainview, Texas: 248, 259, 261, 267, 286
Pleasant Hill and De Soto Railroad Company: 71, 151
Plumb, Preston B.: 170, 172
Point Comfort and Northern Railway Company: 289
Politics, railroads in: 220–21; pre–Civil War, 13–15, 27, 30, 33; Reconstruction, 48–54; Indian Territory, 55–56, 119–30; Populist period, 222–26, 231–34, 313; regulation of activities, 228, 314
Pomeroy, Samuel C.: 44
Population, effect of railroads on: 40, 84–90, 185–91; *see also* specific cities and states
Populism: 222–26
Port Arthur, Texas: 161, 198, 214, 264, 306
Port Bolivar and Iron Ore Railway: 288
Port Isabel and Rio Grande Valley Railway: 283
Poteau Valley Railroad: 250
Powderly, Terence V.: 215
Pre-emption Act: 34, 75

333

Price, Sterling: 46

Quanah, Acme and Pacific Railway Company: 242, 260, 284
Quantrill, William C.: 109, 116

Reader Railroad: 288
Reagan, John L.: 233
Reconstruction, effects of: railroads, 47–54; Indian Territory, 54–55, 119; New Orleans, 92; Little Rock, 96; outlawry, 109; southwestern economy, 212
Red River Railroad: 12–13, 141
Red River, Texas and Southern Railway Company: 237
Reed, Daniel: 236
Refrigeration: 104f., 210, 263, 277
Regional Shippers' Advisory Board: 298
Regulation, railroad: Texas, 39–40, 143; Missouri, 40; Granger states, 78–79, 83; Supreme Court attitude, 79; Southwest, 82, 222–34, 313–14
Reynolds, "Diamond Jo": 158
Reynolds, George A.: 170
Rice brothers: 49
Richardson, Asher: 256
Right of way: general act, 35; Indian Territory, 45, 119, 123–27
Ringling, John: 254, 276, 288
Rio Grande and Eagle Pass Railway Company: 157
Rio Grande City Railway: 282–83
Rio Grande Railroad: 69
Robertson, S. A.: 242, 260
Robinson, A. A.: 145
Robinson, Thomas B.: 171
Rockdale, Sandow and Southern Railroad Company: 288
Rock Island, Arkansas and Louisiana Railroad Company: 240
Rock Island Railroad: *see* Chicago, Rock Island and Pacific Railroad Company
Roscoe, Snyder and Pacific Railway Company: 256
Ross, Edmund G.: 43f.
Ross, John: 45, 54–55
Rudabaugh gang: 116
Rudolph, C. F.: 190, 200–201, 205
Rusk, Thomas J.: 21
Rusk Transportation Company: 139

Sabine and East Texas Railroad Company: 154, 246
St. Louis, Missouri: 3f., 31, 78, 132f., 135, 138, 140, 144, 151, 158, 203, 238, 240, 297, 315; early railroad projects, 13, 18ff., 25f.; river traffic, 25, 92; aid to railroads, 37; Gulf projects, 63, 68; railroad influence, 69, 92; population, 91f., 193; industry, 105, 107, 214f., 278, 306; and Indian Territory, 124, 129
St. Louis and Iron Mountain Railroad Company: origins and growth, 13–14, 26, 63–64; aid, 36, 63, 74; effect on population, 85, 97, 182
St. Louis and North Arkansas Railway Company: 253
St. Louis and Oklahoma City Railroad Company: 237
St. Louis, Arkansas and Texas Railway Company: 136, 138–40, 182, 195
St. Louis, Brownsville and Mexico Railway Company: 241f., 252, 264, 267, 274
St. Louis, El Reno and Western Railway Company: 253
St. Louis, Iron Mountain and Southern Railway Company: 125, 139, 158, 160, 163, 182, 246; history and growth, 64, 132, 134–35, 244–45, 282; promotional work, 209, 255
St. Louis, Kansas and Arizona Railway Company: 133
St. Louis, Kansas and Southwestern Railroad Company: 138, 247
St. Louis, Kansas City and Colorado Railroad Company: 151, 240
St. Louis, Memphis and Southeastern Railroad Company: 238
St. Louis, Oklahoma and Southern Railway Company: 237
St. Louis, Salem and Little Rock Railroad Company: 68
St. Louis–San Francisco Railway Company: 142, 146, 153, 183, 251, 287; origins and growth, 70, 78, 125f., 135–38, 144, 149ff., 235–38, 242f., 255, 282, 284ff.; aid, 165f.; and Indian Territory, 171; town-building, 193, 262; promotional work, 206, 260, 265, 272, 278f., 295, 308f.
St. Louis Southwestern Railway Company: 154, 252, 297, 309; origins and growth, 140, 245–46, 283, 285; aid, 166
St. Louis, Watkins and Gulf Railway Company: 158, 244
St. Louis, Wichita and Western Railway Company: 137
San Antonio, Texas: 8f., 27, 30, 69, 71, 99, 141, 152, 155f., 175f., 198, 249, 254, 256; railroad aid, 39; growth, 91, 93–94, 178, 194–95, 214, 278, 306
San Antonio and Aransas Pass Railway Company: 154–55, 166, 198, 246, 260, 283f.

Index

San Antonio and Gulf Railroad Company: 155–56
San Antonio and Mexican Gulf Railroad Company: 29f., 39, 47, 54, 69, 246
San Antonio and Rio Grande Valley Railway Company: 241
San Antonio, Uvalde and Gulf Railroad Company: 254, 282
Sand Springs Railway: 254
Santa Fe Railroad: *see* Atchison, Topeka and Santa Fe Railway Company
Schmidt, Carl B.: 89
Scott, Thomas A.: 68–69, 140
Seagraves, C. L.: 265
Sealy, George: 147, 194
Searcy and Des Arc Railroad Company: 239
Sears, T. C.: 122, 170f.
Sedalia, Missouri: 41, 63, 67, 78, 102, 133
Sedalia, Warsaw and South Western Railway Company: 133
Seligman brothers: 125, 137
Sergeant, John B.: 136
Settlers' Protective Association: 61, 80
Shannahan, Patrick: 137–38
Sherman, Sidney: 27
Sherman, Texas: 53, 68, 97, 139, 141, 144, 237
Sherman, Shreveport and Southern Railway Company: 144, 285
Shreveport, Louisiana: 5, 24, 31, 47, 51, 68, 84, 139, 141, 152, 155, 157, 197f., 245, 252, 276, 297; growth, 96, 193, 278, 309
Shreveport and Red River Valley Railway Company: 252
Simmons, C. F.: 256
Simpson, "Sockless Jerry": 220f., 223f.
Smallwood, B. F.: 124
Smith, Hoke: 173
Smith, Ralph: 12
Smith, Tom: 112
Southern Kansas Railroad Company: 99, 127, 145ff., 149, 201
Southern Pacific Lines: 136, 145, 147, 192, 240f., 252f., 276; history and growth, 140, 151–56, 246, 283ff.; outlawry, 175ff.; colonization, 189; town-building, 194f.; agricultural development, 295, 297
Southern Pacific Railroad (Texas promotional project): 29f., 47, 53, 68
Southern route to the Pacific Coast: 21, 68, 140, 152
Southern Transcontinental Railroad Company: 53, 68
South Pacific Railroad: 67f., 87, 97

Southwest Branch: 26, 35f., 40f., 45ff., 66, 84
Southwest Pacific Railroad Company: 66f.
Special School Fund (Texas) loaned to railroads: 38–39
Spindletop oil field: 254, 275f.
Splitlog Railroad: 161
Springfield, Missouri: 4, 24, 74, 138, 151, 244, 273, 278; and Atlantic and Pacific, 67; growth, 97, 182, 193
State ownership projects (Texas): 15–16, 27, 227
Stephenville North and South Texas Railway Company: 245
Stilwell, Arthur E.: railroad building, 161–62, 251–52; promotional activities, 189f., 198, 210, 213, 264
Storey, William B.: 292
Stringfellow, J. H.: 44
Strong, William B.: 145, 149
Stuttgart and Arkansas River Railroad Company: 140
Sugar Land Railroad: 256, 282
Sulphur: 250, 255, 277, 287

Taffe, John: 129
Tecumseh Railway Company: 239
Telfener, Joseph: 153–54, 190, 198, 313
Texarkana, Arkansas–Texas: 63f., 68, 85, 99, 135, 139, 141, 161, 210, 245
Texarkana and Fort Smith Railway Company: 161
Texas: 7–9, 102, 109, 124f., 131ff., 138, 144, 172, 218; early railroad agitation, 14–16, 27, 45; railroad construction, 27–31, 63f., 68–69, 139–42, 146ff., 151–57, 236, 238, 240ff., 245–56, 282ff., 286–89; railroad mileage, 32, 160, 256; aid to railroads, 38–40, 53, 75–76, 156; population, 40–41, 48, 85, 184, 189–90, 258–59; town growth, 41, 99, 198f., 260–61; Civil War and Reconstruction, 47, 51–53; agriculture, 106, 154f., 267, 269–74, 291, 293ff., 297; industry, 107, 209ff., 254f., 275ff., 301, 308f.; outlawry, 116, 175–79; antirailroad sentiment, 222f., 225; railroad regulation, 228ff., 233f.
Texas and New Orleans Railroad Company: 29f., 47, 54, 71, 94, 152ff., 218, 246, 283–84
Texas and Pacific Railway Company: 30, 132, 138, 142, 149, 151, 192, 219, 247, 250, 253; origins and growth, 64, 68–69, 95, 136, 140–41, 245, 283; land grant, 74, 163–64; lawlessness, 116, 175ff.; colonization, 183, 187, 189; town-building, 190, 194, 197; industrial develop-

335

ment, 213, 276, 293, 309; labor difficulties, 215
Texas and St. Louis Railway Company: 135, 138–39, 196ff.
Texas Central Railroad: 153f., 197, 249
Texas–Mexican Railway Company: 85, 155, 241
Texas Midland Railroad: 154, 273, 284
Texas, Mississippi and Northwestern Railroad Company: 50, 134
Texas–New Mexico Railway Company: 283
Texas Railroad, Navigation and Banking Company: 13–14
Texas Short Line: 255, 283
Texas State Railroad: 255, 283f.
Texas Transportation Company: 94
Texas Trunk Railway: 154–55, 246
Texas Western Railroad. 29f.
Thirty-fifth parallel route: see Canadian River route
Thirty-second parallel route: see southern route
Thompson, Ben: 111, 113f., 178
Three per cent fund: 33f.
Tilghman, Bill: 114, 180
Tinsley, J. D.: 265
Topeka, Kansas: 66, 74, 134, 150; growth, 42, 97, 193, 215, 278; railroad convention, 44
Touzalin, A. E.: 89
Town rivalries: 15, 18, 20, 28f., 31, 58, 94–96, 138f., 147, 153, 185, 193f., 196ff., 213, 255
Townsite speculation: 64, 97, 99–100, 198–99, 203–204, 236
Trinity and Brazos Valley Railroad Company: 240, 242
Trinity and Sabine Railway Company: 142, 285
Tulsa, Oklahoma: 138, 238, 247; growth and industrialization, 261, 276, 279–80, 306
Two per cent fund: 34
Tyler Tap Railroad: 138f.

Union Pacific Railroad Company: 110, 132, 146, 157, 159
Union Pacific, Southern Branch: 59, 61–62, 74
Uvalde and Northern Railway Company: 254

Van Horn, Robert T.: 58f., 171
Van Sweringen brothers: 283
Vest, George: 126
Vicksburg, Mississippi: 18f., 21, 24, 31, 41

Vicksburg, Shreveport and Pacific Railroad Company: 157, 197f.
Vicksburg, Shreveport and Texas Railroad Company: 31, 35, 37, 41, 51, 68f., 96, 157
Victoria, Texas: 30f., 39, 54, 69, 154, 156, 198
Vinita, Oklahoma: 67, 100, 136f., 170, 202
Voorhees, Daniel W.: 55, 122

Waco, Texas: 8, 53, 97, 138, 155, 184, 195, 245, 249
Waco and Northwestern Railroad Company: 63, 154
Waco, Beaumont, Trinity and Sabine Railway: 285
Walker, Robert J.: 29, 45
Warkentin, Bernhard: 106
Washington County Railroad: 28–29, 63
Waxahachie, Texas: 53, 98, 153f., 194, 241
Waxahachie Tap Railroad: 153
Wharton County, Texas: 39, 184, 287
White and Black River Valley Railway: 158, 239
Whitfield, J. W.: 42
Whitney, Asa: 12, 18
Wichita, Kansas: 66, 90, 134, 137f., 146, 224, 251, 253; growth, 96, 103, 193, 278, 306; lawlessness, 113
Wichita and Southwestern Railroad Company: 66, 146
Wichita and Western Railway Company: 146
Wichita Falls, Texas: 157, 199, 249–50, 278, 286
Wichita Falls and Northwestern Railway Company: 250, 260, 262
Wichita Falls and Southern Railroad Company: 250, 285, 288
Wichita Falls Railway Company: 249
Wichita Falls, Ranger and Fort Worth Railway Company: 276, 288
Wichita Northwestern Railway Company: 256
Wichita Valley Railway Company: 157, 250
Williamson, J. A.: 123
Wilson, Thomas E.: 292
Wilson, Woodrow: 281
World War I: 256, 279ff.
World War II: 307

Yoakum, B. F.: railroad activities, 155, 235–43, 246; promotional activities, 198, 260–61, 264, 271
Youth work of railroads: 272–73, 292

www.ingramcontent.com/pod-product-compliance
Lightning Source LLC
Chambersburg PA
CBHW020732160426
43192CB00006B/196